Marvelous Melba

Marvelous Melba

THE EXTRAORDINARY LIFE OF
A GREAT DIVA

Ann Blainey

Ivan R. Dee

CHICAGO 2009

www.ivanrdee.com

The photograph of the funeral procession of Dame Nellie Melba is by Archibald Longden, September 20, 1930, from the Ruth Hollick Collection, State Library of Victoria. All other photographs are reproduced with the kind permission of Lady Vestey.

Every effort has been made to contact the copyright holders of material in this book. Where an omission has occurred, the publisher will gladly include acknowledgment in any future edition.

Library of Congress Cataloging-in-Publication Data:
Blainey, Ann, 1935–
    Marvelous Melba : the extraordinary life of a great diva / Ann Blainey.
        p. cm.
    Includes bibliographical references and index.
    ISBN-13: 978-1-56663-809-8 (cloth : alk. paper)
    ISBN-10: 1-56663-809-7 (cloth : alk. paper)
    1. Melba, Nellie, Dame, 1861–1931. 2. Sopranos (Singers)—Australia—Biography. I. Title.
ML420.M35B63 2009
782.1092—dc22
[B]
                                                    2008048027

Contents

Preface

"NOBODY SINGS LIKE MELBA, and nobody ever will," proclaimed the American impresario, Oscar Hammerstein, in 1908. Like many others, he considered Nellie Melba the greatest singer in the world. The wild acclaim of her American fans led to the coining of the word "Melbamania." Year after year she toured America in the "Melba train," bringing operas and concerts to far-off cities and towns. On tour, her diamonds and her dresses were fabulous. She reigned over the operatic world in England, America, and Australia for well over a quarter of a century.

Through the magic of the new gramophone she could be heard by the remotest American and European ears. In an era in which no woman was president, prime minister, chief justice, head of a church or financial house, or universal film star, Melba became perhaps the most famous woman in the world—apart from a few queens and empresses. A valued friend of the heir to the British throne, she was also the mistress of the son of the heir to the French throne, at a time when many expected to see the French monarchy restored.

Growing up in Melbourne, Australia, I was familiar, almost from the cradle, with the name of Melba. I remember, at the age of five or six, trying to sing along with some of her records. Later, when I came to know people who had actually known Melba, I would ask, "What was she really like?" I was delighted when, about ten years ago, I met Melba's granddaughter, Lady Vestey, and visited her at Coombe Cottage. At this favorite of Melba's houses, the great diva's presence is strong, and the visit was memorable. I decided that one day I might write a life of Melba. I must pay tribute to Pamela Vestey and her book *Melba: A Family Memoir*; published in 2000, it contains many hitherto unknown letters and charming personal reminiscence. I owe Lady Vestey a deep debt.

I am by no means the first to write Melba's life. At least five others have produced biographies. I express my debt to Agnes Murphy, who in 1909 published a detailed life of Melba; to John Hetherington, a Melbourne journalist, whose *Melba: A Biography* is based on his interviews with those who knew Melba in old age; and to Dr. Thérèse Radic, whose *Melba: The Voice of Australia* casts new light on Melba's influence on Australian musical life.

I must add that large parts of this book are based on new material, which is set out in the Notes and Acknowledgments.

ANN BLAINEY

Marvelous Melba

CHAPTER ONE

The Incomparable Miss Mitchell

ON A WARM Australian evening in December 1869, a small girl stood nervously beside a stage waiting her turn to perform. A commonplace scene, there was nothing to suggest that this child would become Madame Melba, one of the great singers in the history of opera.

The stage was in the new town hall in the Melbourne suburb of Richmond, to which seven hundred spectators had come to witness the grand opening concert. The mayor presided, and the brass bandsmen of the Richmond Volunteer Rifle Corps, in splendid uniforms, played the overture. In the wings a cast of amateur singers awaited their call. All were adults, except one. Her name was Nellie Mitchell, and though very young, she was something of a veteran. Indeed, a reporter from the local newspaper sat forward eagerly as little Miss Mitchell, with her long loose hair and short dress, came out to face the audience.

Her first item was the sea shanty known as "Can't You Dance the Polk," of which she presumably sang an expurgated version, for the traditional words were risqué. She tossed it off—to quote the reporter— "in really first-rate style," accompanying herself on the piano. There followed such a storm of clapping that she swung immediately into an encore. In the reporter's estimation she was already "the gem" of the evening.

At interval it was announced that there would be no more encores, but the order was forgotten when Miss Mitchell came on stage again. This time she sang and played an Irish ballad called "Barney O'Hea," and by popular acclaim was compelled to repeat the song. "The incomparable

Miss Mitchell," enthused the reporter, "is indeed a musical prodigy," and no more than ten years old. Here he was mistaken: she was only eight.

In 1869 Melbourne was no Wild West town but a civilized city of almost 200,000 inhabitants, the largest in Australia and one of the main gold and wool ports of the world. Its fortunes had soared 18 years earlier, when gold was discovered a four days' ride from the cluster of riverside buildings that was the city. Since then, rich miners had poured money into its public works. Melbourne now had broad streets, handsome buildings, a safe water supply, and one of the most democratic parliaments in the world. Its citizens were predominantly young. Lured by the hope of gold and adventure, young Europeans had come in the thousands to this gateway to the goldfields, and many stayed on, finding steady jobs, marrying, and raising families.

Among the young immigrants were little Nellie Mitchell's parents. Her father, David Mitchell, was twenty-three when he arrived in Melbourne in 1852, a stonemason just past his apprenticeship who chose to leave his home near Forfar in eastern Scotland to make a new life on the far side of the world. Shrewd, determined, and resourceful, he sensed that in this burgeoning city his building skills could make his fortune. Although he was said to have arrived with nothing in his pocket except a single gold sovereign, he soon managed to acquire several acres of land on the Yarra River at Richmond, a mile or so from the center of the city. There, after an unsuccessful visit to the goldfields, he set up his builder's yard and built himself a cottage. A few years later, realizing Melbourne was turning from a city of wood to a city of stone and brick, he added a brickwork. By 1856 he was a rising contractor and a large employer. When, that same year, the stonemasons of Melbourne won the right to an eight-hour day—possibly the first workers in the world to do so—David Mitchell's voice was raised in their support, though not too loudly.

Mitchell's life revolved around his work and the Scots' Presbyterian Church on Collins Street. Scottish to the core, David loved his church, and when he decided to marry, he chose a bride from within its congregation. His choice was Isabella Ann Dow, the twenty-three-year-old daughter of a Scottish engineer named James Dow, who seems also to have had Spanish blood. Isabella had olive skin, dark eyes, a quick wit, and an artistic nature: she played the piano, harp, and organ, and painted china. David Mitchell was almost the opposite, being "very broad and thick set" and "very reserved, very Scotch, and, you might think, very shy." According to observers, he "did not talk so much as twinkle." Nevertheless it was said of him that he could "say more with his eyes than most men with their lips." Isabella liked the twinkle. On June 11, 1857, Isabella Dow and David Mitchell were married.

Nine months after the wedding, a child named Margaret was born. The baby died four days short of her first birthday. Four months later Isabella became pregnant again and in July 1859 gave birth to the longed-for son. They named him William after his paternal grandfather, and watched him anxiously. He died just a month short of his first birthday. Infant mortality being high in Melbourne, the deaths were not wholly unexpected, but to see two children failing to reach their first birthday was a severe trial. When Isabella became pregnant the following year, every possible precaution was taken, and this time all went well. The daughter, born on Sunday, May 19, 1861, thrived well past her first year.

The baby was named Helen Porter, after Isabella's third sister, Helen, but from the start she was known as Nellie. Dark-eyed and dark-haired like her mother, and strong-willed and sturdy like her father, she grew into a little tomboy. She loved her rocking horse, despised dolls, and liked boys' games. For more than two years Nellie had the nursery to herself; then, in November 1863, her sister Annie was born. Her sister's birth was in all probability a blow to her—later in life she did not take kindly to competitors. However, it was an experience she was forced to tolerate, because Annie was followed by Isabella, Frank, Charles, Dora, Ernest, and Vere.

David Mitchell's cottage beside his kilns and workshops was soon replaced by a large family house. Built of brick and stucco, it had bow windows and a veranda on the ground floor, and a square tower rising above the upper story. In front the house looked on to the simple graveled surface of Burnley Street; at the back its garden extended to the low cliffs that flanked the Yarra River. Although there was nothing obviously Scottish about the Yarra, David Mitchell thought it resembled the Scottish river Doon, and he called his house Doonside. His attachment to the house rather puzzled his colleagues because other businessmen, once they made money, invariably moved away from their workplaces to the fashionable suburbs east of the river. David Mitchell, however, remained obstinately at Doonside. He said he had no peace of mind unless he could wake in the morning and see his own brickyard chimneys smoking.

David Mitchell became Nellie's hero. Her infant mind was quick to grasp that within her little world of Doonside his word was law, and as she grew older she sensed that he was important in the outside world as well. Over the next twenty years his Victoria Steam Brickworks poured bricks into a market that could rarely get enough of them. Not content with brickmaking, he invested in quarrying stone and making cement, so that his building empire grew to be almost self-sufficient.

His business associates often thought David Mitchell a difficult man. Although scrupulously upright, he drove a hard bargain and demanded perfection. Within his family he was a taskmaster who exhibited "black disapproval" when his children's standards failed to meet his own. Although he was capable of sympathy, his children did not always recognize it: his softness lay under a forbidding face. Nellie seems instinctively to have understood him from babyhood. "Throughout my life," she would later write, "there has always been one man who meant more than all others, one man for whose praise I thirsted, whose character I tried to copy—my father."

From her mother, Nellie gained a passion for music. When not much more than a baby, she would crawl under the piano while her mother played and later try to reproduce the sounds of the music by dabbling her fingers across the keys. Her aunt Lizzie Dow, providing her first piano lessons, quickly recognized an unusual talent. The Dows had little doubt that the gift came from their side of the family. Although David Mitchell sang hymns in a resonant bass and picked away at the harmonium and fiddle, the Dow girls were trained musicians with voices of "rare beauty."

Nellie seems to have been six when she appeared at her first concert, a very simple affair probably connected to the local Sunday school. She later remembered that she sang a song called "Shells of the Ocean," followed by an encore of "Comin' Thro' the Rye," sung in the authentic Scottish dialect of her Dow grandmother. When she spoke about the concert later in life, she was apt to confuse the details. Sometimes she said that she stood on a chair to sing, and sometimes she said that she accompanied herself on the piano. Always she remembered the applause, and that, on returning home, she eagerly questioned a female playmate about how she had performed. In Nellie's words, the spiteful girl "inclined her face toward mine and lowering her voice to a significant pitch answered, 'Nellie Mitchell, I saw your drawers!'"

A few months after her eighth birthday, Nellie appeared in two more concerts, designed as fundraisers for the Richmond Presbyterian Church. The first, staged in the Richmond Lecture Hall on Lennox Street in October 1869, left much to be desired, droning on for more than three hours and prompting some of the spectators to jeer. A reporter from the *Richmond Australian* expected the worst when a little Miss Mitchell and a little Miss Grimwood came skipping across the stage. Within minutes he reversed his opinion. These little girls, both of whom sang and played the piano, were "the best part of the entertainment," and he described Miss Mitchell as a "perfect wonder."

Two months later, on December 6, Nellie appeared in the "grand vocal and instrumental concert" described at the opening of this chapter. The same reporter who had then mistaken her age was astonished by her performance. "She is indeed a musical prodigy," he wrote, "and will make crowded houses wherever she is announced again."

Nellie needed the praise. By the age of eight she was often receiving blame, being the ringleader in every nursery prank. Some attributed her naughtiness to her "inexhaustible energy and irrepressible spirits" while others said it came from the local lads, whose company she kept on the river flat behind Doonside. While the boys' influence may have been partly the cause, Nellie exhibited enough energy for a couple of children, and she "hated to be still herself, and hated to see other people still, particularly if they, as a consequence, exacted quietude from her." She had also learned that naughtiness gained attention, and with an ever-increasing brood of brothers and sisters, attention was a commodity she craved.

Stories of her misdeeds entered family folklore. Once while her father was playing whist, she crawled under the table and puffed a bellows up his trouser leg. Another time she woke the family in the middle of the night by playing *Moonlight Sonata* on the drawing-room piano. The worst behavior, in the eyes of her parents, came during the visit of a dour Scottish preacher. When Nellie was summoned to play him a hymn, she struck up "Can't You Dance the Polka?" The stories were embellished over time, but the theme remained the same: in childhood Nellie was an imp of mischief.

She needed discipline, and her father decided to send her to boarding school. He chose Leigh House, a school for young ladies located in a large house on Bridge Road in Richmond. Nellie hated it. Thirty years later she would remember, "I was always at the bottom of the class, and generally in disgrace." One morning she rebelled. When the pupils took their cold showers at 6 a.m., she took hers under an umbrella. The dripping umbrella was soon found, and henceforth her showers were supervised.

Leigh House was built on high ground, and from the top story Nellie could just see the tower of Doonside. Occasionally she would stand at the top windows, screaming piteously. She could sometimes glimpse her father on his daily journeys to the city, riding in his buggy or sitting on the horse-drawn omnibus. "To be in sight of my home," she would recall, "and unable to go there, to see my father and not to be noticed by him, so filled me with sorrow that I was constantly in floods of tears." She called it "perhaps the bitterest experience of my younger days."

Her pleasures were the family holidays in the freedom of the countryside. As early as 1863 her father had taken a lease on a wooden farmhouse and more than ten thousand acres of bush and pasture about forty miles east of Melbourne. Named Steel's Flats, it had tall eucalyptus trees and shaded fern gullies and fresh, running streams. The little girl would later say that she was never so happy as when staying at the "old house, shaded by immense gum trees, on the side of the steep hill."

To travel to Steel's Flats was always an adventure, and Nellie would remember the thrill of expectation as they waited at the coach stop. When the public coach pulled in, "with its four patient horses, flicking the flies with their tails," the Mitchells would clamber aboard—children, adults, servants, and carpetbags—and Nellie would crawl up to the box to sit next to the driver because "all exciting things happen there." At the pretty little township of Lilydale, the Mitchells would eat a simple lunch, then load themselves and their baggage onto a waiting wagonette, which jolted them the last fifteen miles to the rambling farmhouse.

Such journeys remained in her memory: "The flocks of sheep and herds of cattle being driven to market—the glaring heat—the burnt-up fields—the strange remoteness, as though we were alone in the world." That strange remoteness was what she prized. When she finally alighted at the house, she would race down the hill, heedless of snakes, and sit by a waterwheel beside the stream. Here she could think her own thoughts and sing her own songs while she cooled herself in the dripping water.

At Steel's Flats she rode, swam, and fished, often in company with her father. Despite her naughtiness, their relationship had deepened, for they shared many qualities. David Mitchell rejoiced that his daughter had inherited his energy and resourcefulness, though he may have been less pleased that she also had inherited his stubbornness and quick temper. He observed, too, her ability to meet a challenge. This was brought home to him when, at the age of twelve, she began twice-weekly organ lessons at St. Peter's Church on Eastern Hill with the young but talented Joseph Summers, an Oxford graduate in music.

David Mitchell approved of the organ, a godly instrument. To assist Nellie's studies, he had one installed in the drawing room at Doonside and watched his daughter's progress with silent pride. He offered her a gold watch if she learned to play twelve pieces by heart, and she rushed to learn the twelve pieces in as many days. She earned her prize, but one evening, when she was running home, she dropped her gold watch in the gutter. She searched until darkness fell. Weeks later the watch was returned to her, ruined. When her father saw the watch, he said, "You will never get another from me." And she never did. It was a lesson she never forgot.

Withdrawn by her parents from Leigh House, Nellie was now being taught at home, and while her music was flourishing, her general education was languishing. The only subject in which she thrived was literature. Devouring the novels in the library at Doonside, she fell in love with the works of Charles Dickens, laughing aloud at Mr. Pickwick and suffering with David Copperfield. When her third sister was born, almost twelve years to the day after her own birth, she was determined that the baby should be called after David Copperfield's wife. "I insisted," she later wrote, "on my young sister being called Dora."

The girl was named Dora Elizabeth Octavia, but she was always known simply as Dora.

Like true Scots, David and Isabella Mitchell believed in education, even for girls, and while they encouraged their older girls' reading, they did not believe it was enough to equip them for life. Thirteen-year-old Nellie and eleven-year-old Annie needed proper schooling, but where would they find it? Leigh House had shown that Nellie was too home-sick for a boarding school and too high-spirited for a young ladies' academy, and they suspected that Annie was the same. By a stroke of luck an answer presented itself. While David Mitchell was rebuilding Scots' Church, he learned that the Presbyterian church was planning to open a school for girls. Tenders for the building were being sought, and he applied for, and won, the contract.

The proposed school's most obvious asset, in David Mitchell's eyes, was its location, being only a mile or so from Doonside. Another was its Presbyterian ownership, for as a church institution it was bound to give a sound religious education. Its third asset—and in hindsight the most valuable—was the headmaster, Professor Charles Henry Pearson. At a time when women's brains were considered inferior to men's, and female schooling was usually a polite smattering of literature, art, needle-work, and sums, Pearson's curriculum was little short of revolutionary. Except for Greek, he was offering a course of study that was identical to that of a competent boys' school: an unheard-of proposal in Australia and rare in England and America. He was also advocating lessons in piano, singing, drawing, and painting for girls who showed promise.

The Presbyterian Ladies College opened its doors in February 1875 and within months Pearson had attracted nearly two hundred pupils. Five members of parliament enrolled their daughters, as did scores of wealthy professional men—and so too did a publican, for the school was at pains to be democratic. A few of the pupils were hoping to earn their livings as teachers, which delighted Pearson, who believed fervently in careers for women. In the following years the school would educate many of Australia's earliest female doctors, lawyers, and scientists.

Entering the school on October 1, 1875, Nellie and Annie were marked down as numbers 166 and 167 on the school roll, though an error was made with Nellie's name and she was recorded as Ellen Mitchell. Each day the two schoolgirls put on their tight, high-necked bodices and long skirts, collected their books, and boarded the horse-drawn omnibus that plodded down Victoria Street. In the impressive stone building with its arched windows and pointed turret, more like a Scottish castle than a school, they studied English, French, Latin, history, geography, mathematics, astronomy, and physics.

The teachers expected serious application, and, rather surprisingly, Nellie seems to have given it, even though she was fond of describing herself as the worst pupil in the school. In the words of one of her teachers, she was "no plaster saint," but within the classroom she was a "diligent, honourable and obedient pupil." Mathematics bored her, and she was apt to gaze into space, but she was never bored in her art classes with "dear Miss Livingstone," whom she described as "one of the best mistresses who ever held a brush," and on many evenings she stayed behind to paint until the light faded. In her English and elocution classes, too, she was a more than creditable student, indeed quite the pet of George Lupton, the dashing elocution master. He tentatively prophesied that her voice would one day bring her fame. He also fostered her love of poetry. Many years later she would tell music students that they must fill their minds with great poems like Shelley's "Ode to a Skylark" and Shakespeare's sonnets. "Let them become the delightful companions of what might otherwise be somewhat lonely hours," she told them. "Learn to speak them aloud with distinction and understanding."

Music was her chief enthusiasm. Often she would forgo lunch in order to run across the Fitzroy Gardens to practice for an hour on the organ at the new Scots' Church. Once she skipped her Latin class in order to practice and, hoping to avoid detection, crawled on all fours beneath Professor Pearson's window as she made for the school gate. To her shame, the professor spied her and sent her back to class. She was obviously recalling her love of the organ when, years later, she told pupils from her old school, "If you are fond of one thing, study and become perfect in it."

Joseph Summers remained her organ master, though she would soon change to his former pupil Otto Vogt, the well-known organist at St. Mark's Anglican Church in Fitzroy. In piano she had graduated from Aunt Lizzie's lessons to those of the school's piano master, Julius Buddee, a stern man who was quick to show his displeasure. In 1878 he withheld the piano prize from her on the grounds that another pupil, a Miss Salmon, "was more attentive." Nellie never forgot her tears of vexation, but the next year she was doubly attentive. "I think I may say without exaggeration," she would later write, "that the foundations of my musical taste were well and truly laid at PLC. I took my work so seriously that it would have been remarkable if I had not learned quickly."

In 1878 she started singing lessons with a newcomer to the school: Mary Ellen Christian, a concert contralto who had studied at the Royal Academy of Music with Manuel Garcia, the younger, and enjoyed a brief but successful career in London before illness drove her to the healthier climate of Melbourne. Madame Christian was charmed by Nellie's voice and awarded her the school's prize for singing in 1878, warming particularly to the girl's lower notes, which she said had a violinlike sweetness. Although she recognized Nellie's unusual musical gifts, it is doubtful if she trained her rigorously. It was Garcia, possibly the greatest of all singing teachers, who believed that rigorous training harmed an immature voice, and Madame Christian would have agreed with him that the voice of a sixteen-year-old was immature. Nevertheless Nellie would have learned the *bel canto* method of breath control on which the Garcia technique was based, and which would be the foundation of Nellie's career. It can be no coincidence that years later Nellie would insist that correct breathing "is the greatest technical essential" in singing, "greater than a naturally beautiful voice." She urged that girls, "even when too young to be permitted the free use of their voices, should be fully taught the principles of taking breath."

Meanwhile there were friends to be made and high spirits to be exercised. Nellie needed fun in large doses—all her life she would say, "Let's have fun." When opportunities for fun dwindled, she set about finding them and was not always careful in her choices. Once she seized the reins of a horse-drawn omnibus while the driver was absent and drove it down the street. Another time she dressed up as a nun and went canvassing for charity, almost fooling her father into making a donation. Her school friends loved her pranks and respected the kindness and honesty with which she tempered them. She was "always ready to admire and help others," wrote one affectionate classmate. "In all she did," wrote another, "we knew Nellie Mitchell would be straight; there was no meanness in her." Her friends also applauded her virtuosity at whistling and enjoyed her impromptu lunchtime concerts, and were fascinated by the trills that she tossed off with such consummate ease. "I was always humming and trilling away quite casually," she would recall, "and in the recreation hour the girls would gather round me and say: 'Nellie, what makes that funny shake in your throat?' And I would laugh and answer, 'I don't know; it just makes itself I suppose.'"

Some classmates did not like her. They feared her temper and her sharp tongue, and were not slow to gossip. They said she was able to swear like a trooper, which was probably true since she had listened from infancy to her father's workmen. But other stories, such as her bathing naked in the river with the local lads, were almost certainly fabrications, for which she herself may well have been responsible: she had learned the art of shocking her schoolmates. On the other hand, she could behave with propriety when necessary, and consequently she maintained favor with her teachers. Years later, when rumors spread that she had been expelled from school, her old mathematics teacher jumped to her defense. She was never "a naughty girl," Dr. Wilson said, "just a healthy, happy, young person, overflowing with life and energy and having, perhaps, a spice of mischievous fun in her composition." Far from being expelled, she left the college "in the full odour of scholastic sanctity, and took with her the goodwill of her teachers and the affection of her comrades."

Among her loyal school friends was sweet-natured Janet Dougal. Janet would long recall how Nellie would stop at the Dougal house on her way to school in order to borrow a handkerchief or something else she had forgotten. Another school friend recalled happy holidays at Doonside, when she and Nellie rode ponies, bathed at St. Kilda Beach, and went to the pantomime. At night, as was the custom of the time, Nellie shared her bed with her. As they snuggled into bed, Nellie said, "Tell me all my faults." Whether the faults were frankly discussed, the friend did not disclose, but she maintained that Nellie was the "most joyous and most fearless person I ever met."

At Doonside there were walks and croquet games and picnics, and much exchanging of gossip, for the three oldest Mitchell girls were one another's confidantes. Although there was teasing and bickering, it was necessary, in a household full of boys and infants, to maintain a sisterly solidarity. When Nellie was sixteen and Annie was fourteen, Belle was eleven, Frank and Charlie were eight and six, Dora was four, Ernest was two, and Vere was a newborn baby.

Although their mother's attention was focused on her babies, she did her best to foster the older girls' music. She escorted Nellie and Annie to concerts in the Melbourne Town Hall, though sometimes she must have wished she had left Nellie at home, so caustic was her opinion of some of the performers. One night in September 1875 their mother probably took the girls to hear Ilma di Murska, a Croatian soprano who had triumphed in the concert halls of Europe. She sang in Haydn's "Creation," and if Nellie did hear her she must have marveled at her dazzling voice. Already Nellie was beginning to dream of fame. "Early in my schoolday," she would later write, "long before my aspirations after an artistic career took definite shape, I pledged myself fancifully to win individual fame."

One incident, when Nellie was sixteen, reinforced those ambitions. In November 1877, after a devastating famine gripped India, relief committees sprang up in Melbourne, and Nellie's organ teachers staged a fundraising concert in the Melbourne Town Hall. Summers conducted a hastily contrived orchestra, Vogt performed on the organ, and Nellie was one of five girls from the Mendelssohn Musical Society who performed. She played two organ solos, including a rousing march, which earned her excited applause and a recall. "It is not often a young lady is heard in public on the organ," wrote the *Age* reporter, "and Miss Mitchell must be accredited with a considerable amount of execution, besides firmness of touch and commendable precision." To win applause after playing the largest organ in the grandest concert hall in Australia was an experience she could not forget. Her dream of earning fame was further aroused.

CHAPTER TWO

The Coming of Kangaroo Charlie

NELLIE LEFT SCHOOL at the end of the following year. She was seventeen years old, with dark hair and exotic looks that suggested her Spanish blood. Her skin was pale olive, darkening around the cheeks, her eyes were brown and large, and her Roman nose gave her face a particular strength. She was not tall—less than five feet, six inches—and her body was plump, but her waist was slim and her flesh was firm. Her face had the endearing roundness of youth, so that she was a very attractive girl.

Her manner was also winning, if overexuberant by the standards of the time. Restraint was then considered the hallmark of a well-bred young lady, and at school she was frequently warned against "boisterous, overbearing or unladylike conduct." Nellie was often boisterous, sometimes overbearing, and frequently unladylike, for eagerness and openness radiated from her. As one girlhood friend put it, "Being with her was like being on a mountaintop with wider vision and purer air."

Her musical studies were gathering pace, and she was now learning the piano from French-born Alice Charbonnet, a fashionable teacher and pianist in Melbourne. Under Madame Charbonnet's tutelage, Melba felt sure she could reach the top. "I knew when I was quite a young girl," she later wrote, "that I should be a success. I *knew* it." It was initially the piano, rather than her voice, that she believed would bring her fame.

Her singing teacher was Pietro Cecchi, a middle-aged tenor with an impressive black mustache and a volatile nature, who had trained as an architect in his native Italy before studying singing at the Academy

15

of Music in Rome. After five seasons of opera in Italy, he had joined troupes touring Europe and America, arriving in Australia in 1871 with a company headed by the American soprano Agatha States. While the critic in the *Sydney Bulletin* described him as a "fat, little and inflammatory tenor," his teaching skills were acknowledged, and many pupils made their way to his studio on the second floor of Allan's Music Shop on Collins Street.

Unlike Madame Christian, Cecchi was not a disciple of the great Manuel Garcia, but his studies in Rome had steeped him in the same tradition of *bel canto* singing. The literal translation of *bel canto* is "beautiful singing," and exponents of the style were renowned for their pure voices and brilliant trills and scales. From the early eighteenth century to the mid-nineteenth century, composers wrote operas to show off these qualities, and *bel canto* singing dominated the opera houses of Europe. By the 1870s, however, the style was losing favor. If Cecchi knew this, he chose to disregard it. He continued to train his pupils in the *bel canto* way.

The *bel canto* apprenticeship was neither short nor easy. When Nellie became Cecchi's pupil, she knew that her studies might last as long as seven years. The basis of the technique was control of the breath. Nellie was required to develop strong respiratory muscles to support and control her breathing, a powerful lung capacity, and a finely tuned coordination of breath, muscles, tone, and pitch. Although the training was long and hard, Nellie did not doubt its worth. Once mastered, a *bel canto* technique could extend the vocal range, produce a seamless tone up and down the scale, and provide a flexibility and technical virtuosity that other methods have seldom matched.

Madame Christian had believed that Nellie was a natural contralto, but Cecchi guessed that she was really a soprano. Now that she was old enough to be trained intensively, he coaxed her voice upward. "She was very quick and clever," he would later write, "and studied very hard." As the months passed he reached the exciting conclusion that here was "material to make a good prima donna."

Cecchi thought of Nellie as an opera singer, but she herself rejected the idea. Although she increasingly loved opera, she knew her father would never allow it. For centuries, society had decreed that any woman exhibiting herself on a public stage for money was violating feminine modesty. A concert performer might keep her reputation provided she appeared without payment, but an opera singer who painted her face and portrayed immoral characters stood not a chance of retaining respectability.

David Mitchell was so adamantly against his daughter performing in public that he once countermanded invitations to a piano recital she was proposing to give at Doonside, saying he did not wish to encourage her "professional ambitions." His plan misfired when two friends, failing to receive his message, arrived at the given time, thus giving Nellie an excuse to perform her program. Knowing his daughter was as stubborn as he was, David Mitchell seems to have deemed it best to allow her the occasional concert appearance, provided she remained a lady amateur.

In March 1881 her piano teacher, Madame Charbonnet, arranged a matinee concert for her pupils. Among the guests were the prominent music critic James Neild and Lady Normanby, the wife of Victoria's governor. Nellie both played and sang, and her singing was particularly praised by Neild and the governor's wife. Lady Normanby is reported to have said to her, "Child, one day you will give up the piano for singing." Remembering the words years later, Nellie remarked, "From that moment I knew in an irresistible way that I was to be a singer."

It was to be a significant decision, but Nellie had little time to savor it, for she had too much to worry her at home. More than a year earlier she had apologized to a family friend for missing an evening party. "Mama was not at all well," she wrote, "so of course we did not feel justified in leaving her all alone and besides we had to rush for the doctor." The doctor was often summoned in the following months. In March 1881 Isabella Mitchell was diagnosed as suffering from "chronic hepatitis."

Much of the responsibility for their mother's care fell to the two elder girls, for their father's expanding business gave him little time for home life. In 1878 he had bought Cave Hill Farm near Lilydale, attracted by its large deposits of limestone, which he began to quarry and burn into lime. The following year he began work on the Royal Exhibition Building, the biggest building to be constructed, to that time, in Australia. An antipodean version of London's Crystal Palace, it was declared open in October 1880 with the most elaborate pomp the city had seen. Today it appears on the World Heritage List.

With a household to run, a sickroom to manage, and six boisterous brothers and sisters to supervise, the two eldest Mitchell girls had their hands full. As 1881 dragged on, Isabella Mitchell faded before her family's eyes: by October she was yellow with jaundice and exhausted by pain. On Friday, October 21, from her deathbed at Doonside, she said goodbye to each of her children in turn. When Nellie's turn came, Isabella extracted the promise that Nellie would watch over the family and "always be a mother" to four-year-old Vere. Knowing that such a promise was almost a sacred pledge, Nellie solemnly gave her word.

Two days later, Isabella's funeral at the cemetery in Carlton coincided with a violent storm. Shops collapsed, ships were wrecked, and part of David Mitchell's newly built Exhibition Building blew down. Driving to the cemetery over waterlogged roads, Nellie felt as though her world had been blown apart. She had been close to her mother, closer perhaps than many daughters, for music had created a powerful bond between them. And much as she loved and admired her father, she knew that his reserved temperament precluded him from providing the warmth and nurturing that Isabella had given so freely. With their mother gone, the children found a gaping hole in their lives and "a whole host of new problems, hitherto unguessed."

Their mother's loss fell heaviest perhaps on little Vere. Nellie arranged for the girl's cot to be brought into her own room, believing that this was what their mother would have wanted. On January 19, 1882, Vere developed a sore throat and a fever. The nursemaid put her to bed, and a frightened Nellie—only too aware of the responsibility now placed on her—fussed over the little girl and longed for her mother. When darkness fell, she lit the fire in the bedroom hearth—for the summer day had turned cold—and climbed into her bed beside the child's cot. As she lay dozing in the flickering firelight, she thought she saw a figure glide out of the darkness. She believed it was her mother. The figure moved toward Vere and pointed, then vanished. Nellie, who by now was completely awake, rushed to her sister's side. The child seemed less feverish, so Nellie returned to her own bed and was able to sleep.

Next morning she hastened to tell her father about the vision, but he brushed her aside. She begged him to call a doctor, but he said he would call a doctor when he returned home that evening, if he believed a doctor was necessary. As the day wore on, Vere's swollen throat began to block her airway. One assumes a doctor was eventually called, but by then it was too late. At around four o'clock in the afternoon, Vere choked to death.

Vere's little coffin was conveyed down the same streets that Isabella's coffin had traveled three months before. The child was laid to rest beside her mother and Nellie returned home feeling "shocked and bewildered." As the numbness of shock wore off, guilt overcame her. Vere had died a horrible, gasping death; worse, the child had died while entrusted to her care, thus betraying their mother's dying wish. Worst of all, her mother—the one person who could have eased this burden of pain and guilt—was dead. Such thoughts tormented Nellie's mind during those first months of mourning. Whether she allowed herself to blame her father for not calling the doctor, one does not know, but her mere recording of his behavior may be taken as a subtle reproach.

The mixture of guilt, pain, and loss produced such distress in Nellie that David Mitchell grew anxious. Like many Melbourne men, he had recently invested in the sugar plantations near Mackay, a port on that part of the Queensland coast that was fast becoming the "sugaropolis" of Australia. Vere had been dead only a couple of months when David Mitchell announced his decision to spend the approaching winter in Queensland, supervising the building of a mill to crush the sugarcane. He proposed taking Nellie with him, but not, it would seem, her sister Annie. Although one of Nellie's biographers, John Hetherington, believed that Annie accompanied her father and sister, and subsequent biographers have followed his lead, Annie's name is absent from the ships' lists of passengers and also absent from records in the town of Mackay.

The voyage to Mackay, some fourteen hundred miles along the Australian coast, took just nine days. Father and daughter left Melbourne on the cold afternoon of Saturday, August 12, 1882, aboard the steamship *Ly-ce-Moon*, and, thanks to fine weather, sailed into Sydney Harbour two days later. Changing to a tiny steamship, the *Alexandra*, they pressed on to Brisbane and Mackay, but headwinds and rain now held them back. It was three days before the ship steamed up the Brisbane River, and three days more before they reached their destination.

For a girl who had been no farther than Steel's Flats, such a voyage was high adventure, and notwithstanding her grief, Nellie took increasing pleasure in it. As they moved toward the tropical north, where the winter sun shone hotly and the houses stood on stilts to catch the breeze, she could feel her mood lifting. She still thought of Vere and her mother, but the thoughts were less painful.

The *Alexandra* dropped anchor at Flat Top Island, near the mouth of the Pioneer River. As a boat ferried them ashore, Nellie could see a straggle of wooden buildings with broad verandas, some of which were perched on mangrove mudflats. A town of more than two thousand people, boasting three local newspapers, six schools, a hospital, two banks, a public library, and numerous hotels, it gave way to mile upon mile of green sugarcane stretching beside the river, owned by a score of planters and worked by laborers from the Pacific Islands.

The Mitchells were quickly welcomed into Mackay society. They had been escorted from Sydney by George Smith, a member of the syndicate that was about to build the Marian sugar mill, and he now introduced them to the mill's engineer, Alexander McKenzie, and to John Ewen Davidson, one of the district's richest planters. In the course of the following week they also met Charles Rawson, a well-to-do pastoralist, and his brother Edmund, an auctioneer.

Nellie was charmed by these well-mannered men, and even more by their educated wives, most of whom, she discovered, were keen amateur musicians. Sydney-born Amy Davidson, the leader of the group, was a competent singer and pianist, Louisa McKenzie and Winifred and Decima Rawson loved putting on impromptu concerts, and Jane Smith and her daughter Leila were always eager to perform. Lounging on the wide veranda of the Smiths' house—known locally as The Folly—or the McKenzies' house, Nellie was only too happy to thrust her sorrow aside. In a chatty letter to Cecchi, she reported that she was "riding, driving, or yachting every day." Even more exciting, she had been invited to play the piano and sing at two fundraising concerts.

The first concert, held in a simple wooden theatre on September 19, was designed to raise money for the Mackay Cricket Club. Nellie sang a "sweet little ditty" called "Pepita"; according to the *Mackay Mercury*, "the musical and well-trained voice of the fair songstress" was heard "with delight." At the end of the month she played and sang at Mrs. McDonald's assembly room at the nearby town of Walkerston in a concert to raise funds for the Presbyterian church. "Miss Mitchell," wrote the reviewer, "fully maintained the excellent impression she made on a previous occasion. The vocalisation was perfect and artistic." Nellie also received indirect applause when Leila Smith, whom she had been tutoring in singing, made a pleasing debut with a song called "Banbury Cross." Reporting to Cecchi with obvious excitement, she told him that she had had *great success* at both concerts. With only slight exaggeration she added, "I was encored twice for each song and they hurrahed me and threw me no end of bouquets"—so much so that "the ladies up here are very jealous of me."

Nellie also requested Cecchi to send six or seven English songs, as the inhabitants of Mackay were ignorant of Italian. By the end of October the songs had arrived and were sung at another concert. One was "Golden Love" and the other "Goodbye," composed by Paolo Tosti. Nellie adored the pathos of the Tosti song—probably it touched her own sorrow—and sang it so movingly that it was "rapturously encored."

Meanwhile a small traveling opera troupe, grandly calling itself the Royal English Opera Company, had arrived in Mackay. The season opened on October 10 with Offenbach's *Grand Duchess of Gerolstein*, and over the following week a string of popular operas was sung in English. The favorite by far was a rousing version of Weber's *Der Freischütz*, the tale of a marksman who sells his soul to the devil in return for magic bullets. The scene where the bullets were forged with skeletons, death's heads, and other "startling effects," caused a sensation among the unsophisticated audience. Nellie would long remember the crowded houses, night after night.

Nellie found those nights of opera a heady experience, and her enthusiasm colored her choice of songs and her performances. At a concert on November 25, to raise money for the Mission Church of St. Peter the Fisherman, she sang "The Angel at the Window" by Berthold Tours "in the most touching style." Her emotions in these months of mourning were volatile. She made every effort to throw off her grief with activity and excitement, yet no amount of diversion could banish the loss of Vere and her mother. Only a new and powerful love could fill that void.

Like many outback towns, Mackay had plenty of single young men who had come to seek their fortunes. At picnics, lunches, and sailing parties they flocked around a new girl, especially if she were spirited and pretty. Nellie's quickness and directness enchanted the young men. As one observer put it, her fresh and unsophisticated outlook made her "much brighter" than the reserved English girls who made up much of Mackay's society. Along with her brightness went a lively talent for flirting. In fact, as her letters betray, Nellie took the greatest pleasure in teasing and bantering any young man she fancied, and was more than happy if the young man teased and bantered back.

As the weeks passed, one admirer began to stand out from the rest. He was twenty-four years old, tall, muscular, and handsome, with sky-blue eyes, crisp fair hair, a long, thin face, and a definite sense of style. His name was Charles Frederick Nesbitt Armstrong, and his quiet charm belied his fiery and adventurous nature. There was no more daredevil rider or horsebreaker in the district than Charlie Armstrong. In the words of one onlooker: "I have seen him throw the reins on a bucking outlaw's neck and sit in the saddle with folded arms till the horse tired." He was also a competent boxer, and his fistfights earned him the nickname of Kangaroo Charlie. Being the type of young man who acted first and thought afterward, he rather pleased the impulsive Nellie. In fact she exulted in his physical prowess, his risk-taking, and his masculinity.

Charlie had the additional attraction of aristocratic birth, being the youngest of thirteen children of the late Sir Andrew Armstrong of Gallen Priory in King's County, Ireland. After his father's death he lived with his widowed mother before being shipped off as a teenager into the merchant navy. Proving no sailor, he was eventually sent away again, this time to his brother-in-law's sheep run on the Darling Downs near Brisbane. His brother-in-law's family, headed by Sir Joshua Bell, was one of the richest in Queensland, but it did not employ Charlie for long. He struck out on his own, becoming a drover of horses and cattle to Mackay and other northern towns.

By early December 1882 Charlie and Nellie were in love, and as the time for the Mitchells' departure grew closer, they began speaking of marriage. Their attachment, based on strong sexual attraction, appears to have also had a practical side. Charlie seems to have pictured his beloved as a helpmeet who would ease his lonely life in the remote settlements. Nellie seems to have seen Charlie as someone who would free her from her father's strict rules and provide the love and excitement she craved. Her ambitions for personal fame seem to have been forgotten, or maybe she believed that Charlie, being adventurous, might share them himself.

David Mitchell viewed the match with mixed feelings. On one hand he found it difficult to approve of a son-in-law who lacked a steady income, and it was all too evident that they had little intellectually in common: Charlie, though far from stupid, had had only a simple education, and his musical taste ended at popular songs and operetta. On the other hand David Mitchell knew that his daughter needed a stern hand, and maybe Kangaroo Charlie was the one to provide it. Not that it mattered what David Mitchell thought. Nellie was as stubborn as her father; if she made a decision, nothing could stop her.

In December 1882, as the heat increased and the sugar mill neared completion, David Mitchell prepared to return to Melbourne. On December 18 the Mitchells boarded the tiny steamship *Glanworth* for the journey to Brisbane, and Charlie sailed with them. On December 21 the *Glanworth* docked in the Brisbane River, and the following morning David Mitchell visited the minister of the Ann Street Presbyterian Church. His purpose was to arrange a marriage, that day, between his daughter and Charles Armstrong.

In her autobiography Nellie claimed that, being in mourning, she and Charlie were obliged to marry quietly, and consequently they decided to marry in Brisbane immediately. This does not ring entirely true because the period of mourning, according to the etiquette of the time, was twelve months for a mother and six months for a sister. Isabella had been dead for fourteen months and Vere had been dead for ten, so there was no social obstacle to a normal wedding. It would surely have been more sensible to marry in Melbourne, where the ceremony could have been in her own church, with her sisters as the bridesmaids and her friends and relatives as the congregation.

The day before the wedding, Charlie is said to have had second thoughts. Apparently he heard from a friend that Nellie had been deeply in love with a young man before going to Mackay, and was still in love with him. Charlie sought personal help and advice from a young Brisbane lawyer named Arthur Feez, who had traveled with them in the *Glanworth*. Feez advised him to marry his bride regardless.

This was remarkably unbiased counsel, because Feez is said to have disliked Nellie from their first meeting. Charlie accepted the advice, almost at the last hour.

The wedding party traveled to the church in an old-fashioned wagonette, arriving at three o'clock in the afternoon, only a few hours after David Mitchell's meeting with the clergyman. Accompanying the bride and groom and the bride's father were Charlie's best man, Arthur Feez, and Annie Mitchell, who had arrived in Brisbane in the *Ranelagh* on December 17. Since the voyage from Melbourne took about five days, Annie's presence suggests that the wedding had been planned one or two weeks in advance.

The Reverend Charles Ogg conducted the ceremony in his study in the parsonage, secretly watched by his teenage daughter who later jotted down the details. The bride wore a close-fitting white dress, buttoned to the waist with large pearl buttons, and a becoming flower-strewn bonnet, tied under her chin with a large bow. After the wedding the newly married pair spent a week's honeymoon in Brisbane, and on December 29 sailed in the *Katoomba* to Melbourne.

Doonside must have seemed sadly empty when Nellie reentered it that January 1883. It was almost the anniversary of Vere's death, and memories of her sister and mother must have confronted Nellie on every side. To return home with Charlie, however, was something of a triumph. At twenty-one she had married the son of a baronet, which in upper-class circles in Melbourne was an enviable achievement. She was already ordering writing paper bearing the Armstrong crest—an upraised arm clad in armor—and was proudly telling her friends about her husband's important Irish relatives.

Charlie was less happy than Nellie in Melbourne. A country man, he tended to feel like a fish out of water in the city; moreover he had no money. Although the Armstrongs had once been rich, Charlie's forebears had squandered their wealth, and not enough remained to give Charlie an allowance. Nellie, on the other hand, received a regular allowance from her father, and Charlie was vexed that she did not entrust it to him or even share it with him. He did not grasp that Nellie had been trained by her father from girlhood to guard her money. While she had promised obedience in the marriage service, she did not believe that obedience entailed the handing over of her purse.

Although English and Australian law had recently allowed married women to own property and money, Charlie's attitude was not unusual. Public opinion was conservative in both hemispheres, and many husbands felt that the disposal of a wife's money was morally their right, even if the law proclaimed otherwise. To be refused what he believed was rightfully his was a gnawing source of annoyance. Nellie later recalled that their quarrels in their bedroom at night were spirited, even violent, and that during one dispute about money she received a blow on the cheek.

In fairness to Charlie, one must note that many men of his time believed that physical chastisement of a wife or child was permissible, provided the husband or father had reasonable provocation. Having grown up alongside three boisterous brothers, Nellie was practiced at standing up for herself, and her refusal to part with a penny, and her habit of answering back, may well have convinced Charlie that he had reasonable provocation. His years in the harsh masculine cultures of the merchant navy and the Australian bush had encouraged him in violent ways, and when someone made him angry, he thought with his fists. This does not excuse his behavior, but it goes some way to explaining how someone who was normally kind could act so aggressively

One other word of caution should be voiced about Nellie's account of Charlie's behavior. Her accusations were made after ten years of marriage and embodied in a legal document drawn up by her lawyers. She gave extensive testimony, providing dates and places, and was prepared to be cross-examined on the details. Moreover she swore on the Bible that her evidence was true, and being a God-fearing woman she no doubt believed it to be so. But at that time she was also desperate to retain guardianship of her son and so was at pains to prove Charlie's unfitness as a parent. She would not have been human if, in such an emotion-charged dispute, she had adhered to the truth in every detail.

Nellie was dismayed by Charlie's blow in their bedroom at Doonside, but she does not seem to have been surprised by it, and she certainly was not intimidated. Like many women of her time, she seems to have accepted that this was how husbands behaved when their wishes were flouted. Unlike many women of her time, she had no hesitation in standing up to her husband. She had decided on a course of action and did not mean to be deflected from it.

The Armstrongs needed an income, and Nellie was devising a plan to earn it. She appears to have been dreaming of joining a traveling opera troupe like the one she had seen in Mackay. This would provide her with a living, allow her to continue to sing before audiences, and might even suit footloose Charlie, who relished travel and adventure. With her plan still vague and seductive, she hurried to Pietro Cecchi the moment she reached Melbourne, arranging to take lessons from him almost every day.

Toward the end of February, Nellie realized she was pregnant, and this focused the couple's minds more intently on the future. Charlie needed a steady job, and it was no doubt due to David Mitchell's influence that an offer was forthcoming. The sugar mill at Marian, fifteen miles from Mackay, needed a manager, and Charlie was deemed a suitable applicant. By mid-March he was back in Mackay, leaving his pregnant wife with her family in Melbourne.

Nellie did not sail immediately to Mackay for reasons of health. An unusually long wet season was turning the streets of the town into quagmires and spreading so much dysentery that the townsfolk feared an epidemic. Having no wish to risk her own safety or that of her unborn child, Nellie remained at Doonside until April, when she sailed for Sydney to be met, she thought, by Charlie. For some reason he was delayed. "I might have stayed a week or two longer in dear old Melbourne," she told Cecchi by letter, "for when I arrived here I found that my husband could not meet me for some time, and I have been miserable here, just thinking how many lessons I have missed."

Nellie made the most of her time in Sydney, attending performances of Italian opera and singing at musical parties. It was the end of April before she sailed to Mackay. Already queasy from pregnancy, she was seasick all the way up the coast—"A most dreadful trip." "It has been raining in torrents ever since I have been here," she wrote to Cecchi on May 11. "It is really most dreary and miserable."

The couple's house, close to the sugar mill at Marian, was still being built, so Nellie and Charlie settled at a boardinghouse in the center of Mackay. Once the rain ceased and the streets dried out, the district's social life revived, and with her queasiness gone, Nellie threw herself into the social round. "Mackay is gay just now," she wrote to a Melbourne friend, with "any amount of dances and balls." She felt, she added, "very jolly and happy."

She did not mention that one of her jolly outings had almost ended in disaster. She and Charlie and Leila Smith found themselves thrown into the ocean when the yacht in which they were sailing capsized in a squall. Fortunately a watcher at the pilot station saw them clinging to the upturned hull and summoned help. But for his prompt action, Nellie, now about five months pregnant, might well have lost the baby.

To add spice to Mackay's social season, there was also the prospect of more opera, for the Montague-Turner Opera Company arrived in town. This company was already known to Nellie, being headed by the soprano Annis Montague and her tenor husband Charles Turner, well-known American performers who had sung in the Melbourne Philharmonic Society's *Messiah* three years before. This fortunate coincidence, along with her friendship with Madame Christian, who had also sung in that *Messiah*, gave Nellie an excuse to call on the two principals. "This afternoon," she wrote to Cecchi, "Mr Armstrong and I are going to take them for a drive and show them some sugar plantations. They are having very good houses, I am happy to say, and I think will do a very good business." As the Armstrong buggy dawdled through the cane fields, Nellie must have bombarded Alice Montague with questions. She may well have elicited the fact that traveling companies were usually short of sopranos and eager for new talent. She may also have confided her dream of joining a company. Certainly she warmed to Annis Montague. "I like her very much indeed," she told Cecchi.

The Montague-Turner Company soon showed itself superior to any opera troupe that had previously visited Mackay. It brought a chorus of twelve, an orchestra, and half a dozen leading singers, all of whom were competent. Along with popular light works like *The Bohemian Girl*, it staged two serious operas, *Faust* and *Il Trovatore*, and for five nights filled the theatre in the School of Arts. Excited by the standard of the performances, Nellie longed more than ever to be part of such a troupe.

In September, Nellie and Charlie moved to their new home in the shadow of the Marian mill. Set on the rich plain dissected by the Pioneer River, walled by blue ranges and carpeted by green cane, the place was idyllic when the weather was fine and the mill was silent. When the mill was working in September and October, the thud of its engine, the smoke from its chimney, and the cloying smell of molasses from the crushed cane diminished the glamour. Nellie was used to living close to a semi-industrial site at Doonside, but this combination of smell and noise was enough to turn the stomach of any pregnant woman.

The Armstrongs' house backed onto the river, just seven miles downstream from Charles Rawson's pastoral property. This proximity to the Rawsons was a godsend to Nellie, who, with advancing pregnancy, pined for female companionship and clung to motherly Winifred Rawson. Little George Nesbitt Armstrong was born on October 16, 1883—just five days short of the second anniversary of his grandmother's death. Dr. McBurney came from Mackay to preside over what turned out to be a difficult labor, and a resident nurse, Mrs. Manfin, was engaged to care for the baby.

Nellie soon recovered her bodily health but her spirits were less elastic. For months she suffered depression and anxiety, arising partly from her postnatal hormones, partly from the conditions under which she and Charlie now lived. Their home was a one-story wooden bungalow with five cramped rooms and a veranda shading the front and sides. The Armstrongs, the baby, the nurse, and at times the nurse's husband slept, lived, and ate in those five poky rooms. It was remarkable how upsetting a baby could be in a house of that size and how frayed tempers could become. Within days Charlie had taken exception to the nurse and, even more, to the nurse's husband: the two men eventually came to blows.

If Charlie's nerves were on edge, Nellie's nerves were almost at breaking point. Her life over the past two years had been packed with disturbances and upsets. Vere's death was still so fresh in her mind that her new role, in full charge of another child, must have filled her with fear. One wonders how often the memory of Vere's choking breaths rose to her mind as she sat by George's cot.

With the start of the wet season, the warm summer rain beat "a perpetual tattoo" on the iron roof, and a steamy humidity crept through every corner of the cottage. Nellie would never forget the relentless humidity, spoiling everything it touched. "My clothes were damp," she would remember, "the furniture fell to pieces; spiders, ticks and other obnoxious creatures penetrated into our house—to say nothing of snakes, which had a habit of appearing underneath one's bed." Even her precious piano, shipped to Mackay and carted by dray to Marian, began to warp and gather mildew. The "pianos here are all so bad it is impossible to sing in tune to them," she told a friend. "There is no music, no *nothing*."

Her energy flagged, her temper worsened, and at times she felt suffocated by hot rain and boredom. At first she walked to the nearby river, hoping that a leisurely swim might cool her body and lift her spirits, but several harmless green snakes hung from the branches of the overhanging eucalyptus trees and leeches "fastened with painful precision" to her arms. Worse, a giant crocodile was said to be living in the river upstream.

"As the days passed by," she later wrote, "and the weeks, I felt I should go mad unless I escaped." There was no escape. Confined to the house, she passed her days in a chair on the veranda, gazing at the sodden landscape, listening for the baby, and worrying about money—for no matter how hard they tried, the Armstrongs found it impossible to live on Charlie's income.

In the brief intervals without rain, she and Charlie would drive along the dirt roads in the buggy. On one drive, just before Christmas, Charlie became vexed with the horse and began to whip it. When Nellie tried to wrest the whip away from him, he turned his anger on her. Recounting the incident later, she claimed that he struck her with the whip. Presumably it was only a flick, for she does not seem to have been harmed, but if it did not hurt her body, it certainly hurt her spirit. It was a grievance against Charlie that she would carry for years to come.

By the end of the year, Nellie had had enough. Taking George and a few possessions, she left Charlie at the bungalow and went to live in civilized style with the Rawsons. Here was a comfortable home with well-trained servants, a gracious drawing room, and a wide veranda for summer living. By day Nellie accompanied Winifred on her household tasks, marveling that a cultivated Englishwoman only a few years older than herself could cope so well with snakes and spiders and even the occasional crocodile. By night, as the rain drummed on the roof, she joined her hosts in sketching, playing the piano, and singing. Each day, feeling more herself, she was filled with gratitude: "Had it not been for my dear friends, Mr and Mrs Charles Rawson, I do not know what I would have done."

Here she began to shape her future. Her first step, in mid-January, was to take rooms for herself and baby George in Mackay. To faithful Cecchi in Melbourne she set out her hopes and fears in a long letter. "My husband is quite agreeable for me to adopt *music* as a profession," she told him. "I do not mind telling you that times are very bad here, and we are as *poor* as it is possible for anyone to be. . . . *I must make some money.*" She wondered if Cecchi could form a small traveling company in which she could learn the art of opera singing and at the same time earn money. "My husband will accompany me," she wrote, "and my baby will be big enough to leave in Melbourne with my sisters." She implored Cecchi to answer by return post because her health and voice were failing. "I am very unhappy," she told him; and it was a cry from the heart. Cecchi understood the message and telegraphed immediately, advising her to return at once. She must have felt weak with relief as she read his words, for she had already decided that she would fall "*dead*" if she had to spend many more weeks in the tropics.

There was no talk of Charlie accompanying her on the voyage to Melbourne, though she seems to have expected he would join her later. Whether he had really agreed to her operatic ambitions one does not know, but it seems unlikely. He may have given a guarded agreement to humor her, believing her plan to be only a fantasy, but one cannot see him acquiescing in her adopting a profession, perceived as so disreputable, no matter how hard-pressed they were for money. Probably he did agree that she should visit Melbourne, for it was clear that another three months of heat and rain would harm her health. He may also have thought that David Mitchell was the very person to knock opera out of her head.

Her departure day was fixed for early February 1884, for she had promised first to sing at a concert in aid of the Walkerston parsonage fund. On the evening of February 8 she received a heartwarming farewell from the packed hall. "If there was one more than another who contributed to the success of the entertainment," wrote the *Mackay Mercury*, "it was Mrs Armstrong. The audience was enchanted by her items and called for encores every time." In view of her imminent departure, she added "Goodbye" to her program. Its lyrics must have seemed more poignant than ever. "What are we waiting for? Oh my heart!" she sang:

Kiss me straight on my brows and part!
Again! Again! My heart! My heart!
What are we waiting for, you and I?
A pleading look—a stifled cry.
Goodbye forever! Goodbye! Goodbye!

On the morning of Tuesday, February 12, Nellie, baby George, and George's nurse were ferried to Flat Top Island, where they boarded the steamship *Wentworth*. Nellie's life was at a turning point.

A Voice in Ten Thousand

NELLIE'S RETURN to Melbourne with David Mitchell's first grandchild was a time for petting and praise. Her plans to sing in opera were never mentioned; she was simply a daughter visiting her father and enjoying a respite from the tropical heat. The illusion was strengthened by the arrival of Charlie from Mackay on March 10—but his visit produced stormy scenes.

Nellie's refusal to return to Mackay puzzled him almost as much as it hurt him, because he knew that she had been brought up, like himself, to believe that a wife's place was with her husband. To reject so fundamental a rule must have seemed incomprehensible to him, especially since he believed that she still loved him. Her refusal, however, was absolute, and in time he realized that nothing could be gained by staying. His only option was to leave her in Melbourne and hope that the passage of time might reunite them.

The city Nellie reentered was different from the city of her schooldays. Even those who lived there continually noticed how prosperity was washing away the rawness. This refining spirit was reflected in the imposing public and private buildings of European design that now dotted the broad streets, many of them built by David Mitchell. It could be seen, even more strikingly, in the manners and habits of the citizens. A social outing, a promenade known as "doing the Block," had become a ritual. On Saturday mornings, fashionable Melbournians would saunter along one block of Collins Street in order to "bow to their friends, cut their enemies, and chatter small talk." Carriages would bowl along the street with bowing and smiling passengers, businessmen would show off their pretty daughters, and fashion-conscious men and women would parade their clothes. In the words of one observer, it was the Australian equivalent of London's Regent Street or New York's Broadway, and "a very pleasant and animated scene."

With refinement came an upsurge in the arts, especially in music: concerts were more frequent, and audiences were larger and more discerning. No debutante soprano could have chosen a more appropriate year to begin her professional life. Fortune seemed to be shining on Nellie as she made her way to Cecchi's studio above Allan's Music Shop in the heart of "the Block." In Cecchi's presence, she cast secrecy aside and discussed her longing to join an opera company. He agreed that she must test her skills in public as soon as possible. A charity concert seemed ideal, for it was socially acceptable for a lady to sing for charity.

An opportunity to perform came unexpectedly. In April the composer Carl Gottlieb Elsasser, a former music master at Nellie's old school, suffered a paralytic stroke, and one of Melbourne's German-style choral societies, the Metropolitan Liedertafel, organized a benefit concert for him at the Melbourne Town Hall. Although Nellie had not been his pupil, her connection with the school was in her favor, especially as the organizers included Julius Buddee, Joseph Summers, and Otto Vogt. A crowd of performers had volunteered, but she was quickly given a place on the program, just ahead of her old teacher Mary Ellen Christian.

It remained only to persuade her father, and his objections were overcome. For one thing, it was a public-spirited event with the proceeds going to Elsasser; for another, she was appearing as an unpaid amateur. Having persuaded her father, Nellie began to feel nervous. She had enjoyed singing at Mackay because she loved a challenge, but the prospect of this concert evoked no pleasure. Too much was riding on the outcome.

The performance was advertised for the evening of Saturday, May 17, two days before her twenty-third birthday. She awoke that morning with a sore throat and a dread that grew with every hour. By five in the afternoon she was in her gold satin evening dress, sitting wretchedly in the drawing room at Doonside, wondering why had she had "ever undertaken this devastating task." At a quarter to eight she pulled herself together and joined her father in the buggy that was to take them to the

Melbourne Town Hall. As they reached the hall—almost as grand as that of any European city—her spirits rose, for she saw a distinguished crowd surging through the doors. The acting governor of Victoria was expected, and so was his guest, the governor of Fiji.

A governor was Queen Victoria's representative, and Nellie knew the honor that the presence of two governors conferred. To make one's debut in such company was as thrilling as it was daunting. For a time that thrill cast out her fear, but backstage her nervousness returned, and it was not entirely groundless. She was to sing "Ah, fors'è lui," a testing showpiece from the first act of Verdi's La Traviata, and far more difficult than anything she had so far sung in public. Moreover the town hall seated about two thousand people, and she had never sung in a space anywhere near so large. She confronted the audience with trepidation, and her first phrases were hesitant. Then her concentration returned, and her "clear and high and flexible soprano voice" soared effortlessly into the auditorium.

Early on Monday, her birthday morning, she feverishly scanned the newspapers and received the present of her dreams. The Melbourne Argus reported that she "both surprised and delighted all hearers," exhibiting the "charm that belongs only to good singing." The Melbourne Daily Telegraph said she had "a melodious ring to her voice, and a grateful intonation which fell with the utmost pleasure upon the attentive audience." Five days later she received her crowning birthday gift from Australia's leading weekly, the Australasian. It was written by the knowledgeable James Neild, the critic who had first heard her sing at Alice Charbonnet's. Describing her as a vocalist of the first rank and "a voice in ten thousand," Neild wrote that "everybody who heard her will desire to hear her again and everybody who did not hear her is at this moment consumed with regrets at not having been present."

After such a glowing review, few critics could doubt Nellie's future; nor could she herself any longer believe that her schoolgirl longing to win fame was sheer fantasy. One reviewer had expressed the hope that she would be leaving soon for further study in England; although six months earlier this idea would have seemed preposterous, it now seemed a distinct possibility. As she read the thrilling notices, her modest wish to finance Charlie and herself in a comfortable lifestyle almost vanished. Her dream was now of Australia-wide, perhaps even worldwide, success. She was brought down to earth by the recollection that neither her husband nor her father would be likely to share her dream. And while Charlie in distant Mackay could for the moment be ignored, David Mitchell, whose house she shared, could not. Once her father heard word of her ambitions, he would likely send her back to Mackay.

One crumb of comfort came from her old school. Thanks in part to the advocacy of her former headmaster, women were at last being admitted to Melbourne University, and her more academic classmates were studying to be teachers or lawyers. The operatic stage was a more dubious profession, but the principle was the same. This must have strengthened her position when she came to a showdown with her father. While she knew only too well that her husband and child complicated the question of pursuing a professional career, her strong will would not allow them, or anything else, to stand in her way. "In my own path great obstacles were placed," she would write later, "but I do not think that anything in this world could have hindered me from becoming a singer."

As expected, David Mitchell placed obstacles. He did not send her back to Mackay, because that would have meant sending his grandson back to tropical Australia, which was considered unhealthy for infants, but he did refuse to pay Cecchi's fees. This was a serious blow, because she had insufficient money to pay the fees herself and was obliged to ask for Cecchi's charity. Fortunately the reviewers' praise of his teaching had already persuaded Cecchi to continue the lessons, with or without payment. But what clinched his agreement was their friendship. As the letters from Mackay revealed, he was her ally, even her confidant. He assured her that she could pay him later, when she had earned the money.

With baby George lodged in the Doonside nursery alongside his eight-year-old uncle Ernest, Nellie dedicated her weeks almost entirely to singing. On most days she took a lesson from Cecchi, and her voice improved remarkably. She always had an aptitude for florid music, for a trill or a run, and she now made it her specialty, practicing her scales and technical exercises until they emerged with a clockwork precision. Over the next eighteen months she would come close to perfecting the superb *bel canto* technique that she would rely on throughout her career.

It now remained for her to secure engagements, and at first they were few. On July 21 she brought "infinite credit upon herself" by singing Julius Benedict's "Carnevale de Venise" at one of the Metropolitan Liedertafel's regular concerts. In August she sang at a soirée in the salon of Allan's Music Shop where Cecchi had his studio. The dearth of engagements led to a surprising change of plans. Charlie's entreaties and her lack of success seem to have persuaded her that she owed her marriage another chance. Accordingly, Nellie, a nurse, and baby George boarded the *Katoomba* for the long journey and arrived in Mackay on September 8. Joining Charlie, who seems to have been living at a local hotel, she threw herself into the musical life of the town.

The Mackay hospital was in need of funds, and Nellie enthusiastically set about organizing a benefit concert. Her newfound expertise made the work easy, and she scheduled the concert for October 20. But six days before the concert, Charlie walked into the billiard room of Wills' Hotel and engaged in a fistfight with a man named Michael Ready. When, three days later, the assailants came before the Mackay Police Court, the case was dismissed, but it left a bad aroma. The embarrassing event seems to have dashed all hope of a fresh marital start.

The concert was a runaway success, and Nellie was the acknowledged star, but she did not wait to savor the praise. The *Fitzroy* sailed from Mackay on the midnight high tide, a few hours after the concert ended. Charlie remained in Mackay while Nellie, George, and his nurse set out for the security of Doonside.

Nellie resumed her lessons with Cecchi; she also took the fateful step of turning professional. In December 1884 she was among well-known soloists at a benefit concert at the Athenaeum Hall for her old piano teacher Julius Buddee. She sang Tosti's "Goodbye" and the cavatina "Regnava nel silenzio" from Donizetti's *Lucia di Lammermoor*, and in the words of one reviewer she "took a very unsympathetic audience by surprise by the really skilful manner in which she sang the cavatina and the sensational force she infused into the song." The reviewer expressed delight that she had become a professional singer. The concert stage, he wrote, could ill afford to be without her.

At the end of the year, David Mitchell took his family on holiday to Sorrento, a fashionable resort about forty miles by paddle steamer from Melbourne. The small town offered three hotels and a sandy beach that was ideal for George. Now fifteen months old and nicknamed Jackie, the chubby, fair-haired toddler was the apple of his grandfather's eye.

Sorrento was the summer home of the impresario George Coppin, and Nellie quickly realized the value of his patronage. Hearing that he was about to organize a concert to raise money to renovate the Sorrento cemetery, she offered herself as his helper and spent part of her holiday fetching eucalyptus branches to decorate the village hall and fixing hand-lettered concert advertisements to buildings around the town. Years later she would recall these simple tasks as proof that any work was useful if it furthered a career. At the concert late in January 1885, the Melbourne reporters, summoned by Coppin, singled Nellie out for praise.

When the holiday ended she prepared to sing in Ballarat, a city known for the wealth of its gold mines. This concert proved a turning point in Nellie's career, for sitting in the audience was a young man from the Ballarat Liedertafel. He was bored to death by the performers and on the point of leaving when a "queenly beautiful woman" named Armstrong glided onto the stage and sang a brilliant "Ah, fors'è lui." Scarcely believing his luck, the young man arranged to meet Nellie in Melbourne, where he generously offered her twenty guineas to sing with the Liedertafel. She flushed with pleasure at the fee and promised to return the money if she failed to please.

That night he took a cab to Doonside and for two magical hours watched her sing and play, his heart missing a beat every time she spun "round on the music stool." He had spent far too much on the cab ride but decided it was worth every penny. Alas, when a few years later he wrote a charming account of their meeting, he did not reveal his name.

Thanks to her admirer's enthusiasm, the Ballarat Liedertafel offered her three engagements spread over the year. To celebrate she bought a concert gown of cream silk and lace, trimmed with ostrich feathers and amber beads. The expensive dress flattered her small waist and olive skin, and the flowing train drifted gracefully behind her as she walked onto the concert platform.

She wore the dress in April when, suffering from a sore throat, she sang at the Melbourne Town Hall with the Melbourne Liedertafel. She was to perform the florid and technically difficult "Ombra leggiera" or

"Shadow Song," from Meyerbeer's opera *Dinorah*; but when she came on stage her throat felt so raw she doubted whether she could cope with it. Thrusting doubt aside, she sang so brilliantly that a critic from the *World* maintained that no one since Ilma di Murska had sung the "Shadow Song" so well. This was praise indeed, for di Murska was reputedly the world's foremost performer of the song.

Four days later, with her throat even more painful, she proposed to sing the same program in a packed Alfred Hall. Anticipation ran high, and the conductor's announcement that she was singing under strain brought audible sighs from the two thousand spectators. The sighs were premature for she sang with "an ease and grace equalled by few and surpassed by none." The audience gave her riotous applause, the gentlemen clapping and shouting, the ladies waving their fans and handkerchiefs. To sing such music under such stress showed how far her skill and confidence had advanced. The following month she sang again in Ballarat and Melbourne, adding Gounod's "Ave Maria" and the waltz from his *Mireille* to her repertoire, and earning glowing reviews and armfuls of bouquets.

Toward the end of June, Nellie was engaged by the theatrical impresarios Williamson, Garner, and Musgrove to sing concerts in Melbourne and Sydney. The concerts were to feature a young violinist, Johann Kruse, who had just returned from Germany. He was to open another chapter in Nellie's life.

The meteoric rise of Kruse was well known to most Australians. The son of a German who kept a pharmacy in Richmond, he had been hailed as a child prodigy, sailing at the age of sixteen to study with Joseph Joachim, the most celebrated violinist in Europe. Now Joachim's assistant at the Berlin Hochschule für Musik and principal violinist of the Berlin Philharmonic Society, Kruse combined the authority of a performer at one of Europe's most prestigious musical institutions with the glamour of a native son returning to his hometown. In addition, he was a remarkably attractive young man with an "open countenance," a splendid physique, and "the magnetic eye of a poet."

Melbourne was agog to hear Kruse and the town hall was packed for his first concert. In the words of one excited reviewer, his playing was "so intelligent, so clearly defined, and so surcharged with poetic emotion that the audience gave themselves up entirely to him." Nellie swam on the fringes of this dream, and her singing was highly praised. As a compliment to Kruse's ancestry, she sang Schubert's "Heidenroslein," though she could sing it only in an English translation.

Kruse and his supporting artists gave several more concerts in the town hall and another performance at the gold-rush city of Bendigo. They then made the long train journey to Sydney to begin a season of eleven concerts in the Theatre Royal. The succession of performances taxed Nellie's voice and repertoire. Almost every song she had sung in past years was summoned into use, and even this was not enough. Fortunately Kruse and his accompanist Cyril de Valmency were clever teachers, and new pieces were rehearsed and performed almost daily. Kruse devised violin *obbligati* for Gounod's "Ave Maria" and Braga's "Serenade," and he would play his violin hidden behind a curtain while Nellie sang on stage. The theatrical effect delighted audiences.

Despite the pleasure they received from playing together, there were times when Kruse, Nellie, and de Valmency wished they were back in Melbourne. The Theatre Royal was too large, Sydney music lovers were too few to fill the auditorium for eleven nights, and cold, wet weather further lowered attendances. There were also mishaps on stage. Once, when Nellie swung too quickly into an encore, she failed to adjust to the change of key. Another time, an overenthusiastic spectator flung a bouquet at de Valmency's red head as he sat at the piano. As the flowers exploded across the stage, the audience exploded into laughter, and Nellie exploded with them: she was unable to finish the song. Nevertheless there were compensations. Performing together each night and staying together by day at the Metropolitan Hotel on Castlereagh Street, Nellie and Kruse and de Valmency became inseparable. With her sister Annie, who had been sent to chaperone Nellie, they formed a happy foursome, attending picnics and parties and disregarding David Mitchell's letters and his stern "sermonizing."

It was not long before the four separated into pairs. The young Frenchman Cyril de Valmency was attracted to Annie, though Annie did not really fancy him. "I think he is an awfully nice little fellow," she confided to a friend, "but as for being in love with such a child, it is too ludicrous." Kruse seems to have paired off with Nellie, but there is no reason to believe that his attentions were improper even by the standards of that era. He simply saw himself as a friend and mentor. He advised her to leave Australia at once and place herself in the hands of a first-class European teacher. He also explained that she should have made her break with Australia "four years ago." His specifying of "four years ago" reveals that she had almost certainly told him how unhappy she was with Charlie.

Kruse had become her confidant, and it seems that she viewed him with mounting affection. She was distressed about Charlie and confused about her future; and the emotional void left by her mother's death—which Charlie for a time had filled—was troubling her again. Spending every day with this magnetic young man who shared her passion for music and her dreams of fame, it is unsurprising that she fell in love.

This emotional climate was further complicated when Nellie and Annie met two new admirers. One was a young man of German descent named Arthur Hilliger, the other his Australian friend Jack Moore. Soon they too became a foursome, enjoying picnics on the wide beaches of Manly and Narrabeen. At first it was Moore who took Nellie's fancy; she invited him to her hotel after the evening concerts and dazzled him with her hopes and dreams. Her "determination and initiative," he wrote, were "as refreshing as her voice was beautiful." He was astounded by the confidence with which she predicted that one day she would be famous.

The concert party returned to Melbourne toward the end of July, for Kruse was needed urgently in Berlin. At his final concert in Melbourne he paid his supporting artist a gracious tribute. Abandoning his violin, he sat at the piano to accompany her in Schubert's famous *Lied* "Gretchen am Spinnrade," which, one suspects, she had learned especially to please him. Their visible affinity charmed all who heard them. One critic, seeing them together, observed that "Mrs Armstrong has no small share of beauty." He could have added that part of that beauty came from the joy of basking in Kruse's admiration.

The evening before Kruse sailed, he played his violin at the city Lutheran church which he had attended as a boy. Nellie went with him and sang sacred works by Haydn, Gounod, and Mendelssohn. On August 11, 1885, Kruse boarded a ship for Europe, and Nellie stood on the pier to wave him goodbye. "I miss him dreadfully," she noted privately, "more than I thought I could ever miss anyone."

She tried to banish her sadness with dreams of her blossoming career. Fortunately her reputation had grown marvelously over the past two months. The Melbourne weekly the *Federal Australian* named her "the leading exponent of concert music in this country," especially in florid music. The critic from the *Melbourne Argus* proclaimed her the "prima donna of the concert platform," prophesying that she would one day be placed "amongst soprano vocalists on a level with that occupied by Ilma di Murska." She drank in all their praise with gulps of pleasure and thirsted for more.

After singing in half a dozen concerts in Melbourne and Ballarat, she began to plan a tour of Tasmania with Cyril de Valmency. Hard work, however, was not enough to restrain her from fretting: every day now spent in Melbourne seemed like wasted time. "I would give ten years of my life to be able to get to Europe to have a trial," she wrote to a friend. "I feel certain I would have some success for I work like a trojan now, so what would I do if I had a proper trial." Only her father's disapproval held her back, for without his help she could not afford the fare. "I cannot understand my father being so pig-headed," she stormed, "especially as I have had such great success in Melbourne. O God if only I had a few hundred pounds."

Europe was on her itinerary, but not Mackay. "I never intend returning to Mackay," she informed another friend. The decision that had been pending for almost a year was at last made. It brought relief and uncertainty. Where it left her and Charlie she could not know. To make matters worse, she still—in part at least—loved him.

Ten days after Kruse's departure, she sat down to write to her new friend in Sydney, Arthur Hilliger. While her ostensible reason for writing was to convey Kruse's apologies for having failed to say goodbye to him, her real reason was to begin a regular correspondence, even though it was considered highly improper for a young married woman to correspond with a young man who was not a close relative. Nellie, however, had never worried much about convention, and in her present distress she urgently needed a confidant to take Kruse's place.

She turned to Hilliger because he was sympathetic and musical, and Kruse liked him. Indeed the two men may have seemed similar to her, both being of German descent. Moreover her younger sister Annie fancied him, and she and Annie had always been competitive. Annie had started to write to Hilliger as soon as she returned to Doonside. Her first letter, rather flirtatious, had begged him to come to Melbourne: "I am sure you would enjoy yourself very much as there is always crowds of fun on, we have been horribly dissipated since our return from Sydney, out nearly every evening; our worthy parent objects strenuously and declares he is going to put a stop to it, isn't it too bad?"

Toward the end of August influenza ran through the Mitchell household, afflicting Nellie worst. From her sickbed she began to confide in Hilliger, warning him that she had been delirious with fever and babbling about "many things which would have been better if I had kept to myself." She begged him to be reticent about their correspondence if Annie began asking questions. "Annie," she wrote, "is always wanting to know too much." She concluded: "Write soon and cheer a poor invalid."

Annie, meanwhile, continued to send her pages of artless chatter to Hilliger, offering a vivid picture of Doonside, where they were "always happy" and where there was "generally some fun on." There was indeed so much fun that Annie could scarcely afford to take a holiday, her presence being needed to keep the younger children in order. Fortunately the two elder boys had been sent to the country with their tutor, for which Annie was grateful, as they constantly teased her about de Valmency, whom they had nicknamed Baby. They kept asking when she would become Mrs. Baby. Really, she asked Hilliger, "Can you imagine anything more absurd?"

By mid-September Annie's letters simmered with plans to visit Sydney. Several dates were fixed and broken, the obstacle being her father. He refused to spare Annie from her domestic duties, and Nellie was forbidden to go alone. "Pa would not hear of my accompanying her," wrote Annie sadly. "When I asked him he got quite excited and said I am never happy unless I am on the move and that I must learn to content myself at home, so I saw it was useless arguing the point as he is very determined." It was a bitter blow for Nellie, "as she was far more anxious to go than I."

Late in September, when Nellie wrote again to Hilliger, her distress was forcing her to confide in earnest. "I have not heard anything of my husband for such a long time," she wrote. "I am rather glad for when he writes it is only to insult me." In the same letter she added, "I have nothing more to tell you except that I am awfully unhappy—if I could see you I would tell you my troubles but I dare not put it in black and white." Nellie had presumably acquainted Charlie with her decision to go to Europe, and his reaction had been angry.

Nellie's recipe for peace of mind was work. October and November were dotted with concerts, and the rooms at Doonside were filled with bouquets that had been flung or placed on stage at her feet. Her soprano voice filled the Melbourne Town Hall on October 3 in a "wonderful performance of 'Caro nome'" from *Rigoletto*, though one reviewer believed she should have shorn the aria of its final spectacular trill, the very trill that would soon captivate European audiences. Three days later she appeared with the Ballarat Liedertafel, and every song was encored. On October 17 she sang "in perfect style" at a benefit concert to farewell Ernest Hutcheson, a local teenage pianist who would later direct the Juilliard School of Music. Two days later, while carrying a huge bunch of violets, she performed Schubert's "Lo the Orb of Day" with the Metropolitan Liedertafel and "Qui la voce" from *I Puritani*. Again she was compared with Ilma di Murska.

She even agreed to be soloist at masses in St. Francis's Catholic Church, to which she was lured by the musical director, Alfred Plumpton, and his organist wife, Carlotta Tasca, and by a generous fee. Annie and Belle sometimes went with her to mass, though nineteen-year-old Belle was rather a liability in the pews where she had "the knack of making the most ludicrous remarks and looking so serious all the time," reducing Annie to helpless giggles. Nellie too made mischief. When reproved for talking in the choir and asked if she would like to be reprimanded from the altar, she replied, "Yes, very much." What her father thought of his daughters attending a Catholic church, let alone being disrespectful, one does not know, but he seems to have been surprisingly tolerant. He is reported to have dropped Nellie off from the family carriage while on his way to Scots' Church. Nor was he always averse to a little disrespect, for he enjoyed a display of spirit.

Early in November, Nellie's future was suddenly tossed this way and that. In a letter to Hilliger, Annie made the startling announcement that "Pa is going to London in February, we are not." Doonside was to be sold and "we poor mortals, transferred to a place called Camperdown, where we shall in all probability remain till Doomsday." Their father had been appointed a commissioner to represent Victoria at the Grand Indian and Colonial Exhibition, to be held in London the following year.

Knowing their mischievous natures, David Mitchell did not dare to leave his children in the city, unsupervised, for a year or more. His newly acquired sheep run, Jane Court, near the country town of Camperdown, 120 miles from Melbourne, seemed a safer choice. His children had other ideas: the words "Jane Court" sent them into a fury. "Isn't the very name enough?" Annie asked Hilliger. Why, Jane Court sounded like the name of a new cook! While Belle and Annie eventually accepted their father's decision, Nellie refused to do so. She called her sisters "spiritless," accusing them of not knowing how to assert their rights.

Nellie was incensed that her father should interrupt her career in this way. That he should be going without her to the very city she longed to reach rubbed salt into her wounds. She determined more than ever to earn sufficient money to finance her own trip, meanwhile waging war against her father's decision. So biting and indignant were some of her tirades that she was nicknamed by Annie and others "the scorpion."

Meanwhile David Mitchell had second thoughts. It seemed unwise to leave his three older girls at Camperdown, from which a train ran temptingly twice daily to Melbourne. "I am glad to tell you," Annie wrote to Hilliger on December 2, "that after much meditation Papa has made up his mind to take us to Europe with him." There were, however, strict conditions imposed on Nellie. Her father had no wish to be seen as a breaker of marriages, or to expose her to the social stigma of being perceived as an estranged wife. He decided that Charlie should come with them and also little George, and that the young Armstrongs must visit Charlie's own family in England. As these seem to have been the only conditions under which her father would take her, Nellie waited anxiously for word of Charlie's agreement. Surprisingly it came.

Earning money now became even more vital, for she would have to finance her own way when living in Europe. Eagerly she arranged engagements in Ballarat and Bendigo and accepted invitations from the Sydney Liedertafel and the Sydney Philharmonic Society. She also agreed to give concerts in country towns with the Sydney impresario Charles Heunerbein, who was to act as her piano accompanist.

In Sydney she sang successfully at two Liedertafel concerts, and on Christmas Day sang the *Messiah* in the Exhibition Hall. In later years it was said that she was unsuited to oratorio, but even the hard-to-please *Sydney Morning Herald* allowed that she received "immense applause" for her solo, "I Know That My Redeemer Liveth." When she repeated the aria a few days later in Grafton, she is said to have brought her listeners to "something akin to awe."

One of the inducements for visiting Sydney was to see Arthur Hilliger, but here a painful disappointment awaited her. "Where on earth have you been for the last three days?" she wrote to him. "You have never been near me to wish me a merry Christmas and I feel very vexed." Was it possible, she asked, that he was "huffed" because his friend, Jack Moore, escorted her to and from the concerts? "I cannot understand you," she continued. "You pretend to be my friend and you leave me alone for three days and never even send me a card."

It seemed to her that he was betraying the friendship they had built through the preceding months. To Hilliger, however, it may have been no more than discretion. It was one thing to share confidences with a married woman when six hundred miles separated them, quite another to meet her face to face. He may have judged that it was prudent to see her only in the company of others.

Jack Moore had no such inhibitions. As well as escorting her to and from her concerts, he seems to have sailed with her in the ship to Grafton, a town on the Clarence River, four hundred miles along the coast from Sydney. Here the Heunerbein's concert party of four singers and a violinist promised to give four performances, starting on New Year's Day. To Nellie's dismay, only one of the concerts drew a large audience, and in another concert she was obliged to compete with drumming rain on the tin roof of the hall. The visit, so full of promise, ended in farce. As her ship set sail for Sydney it struck a sandbank, and Nellie was thrown against an iron bulwark and drenched with water. She returned to Sydney spotted with bruises, not even carrying the generous fee she had been hoping to earn.

From Sydney the concert party set out again in January, crossing the Blue Mountains by train to perform in the rural town of Bathurst. If appearing in Grafton had carried a small risk, appearing in Bathurst carried a large one, for, according to a local journalist, the town cared only for circuses and black minstrels. The performers should not have been surprised when, at their first concert, the hall was half empty, though at least Nellie was recalled and encored. The following night, after only "about a dozen persons" appeared, Heunerbein was forced to cancel the performance. By way of compromise he allowed two instrumental items to be played before ringing down the curtain and refunding the ticket money. Not satisfied with this peace offering, the tiny audience clamored for Mrs. Armstrong and refused to budge until she appeared. A local paper reported that "she sang like a nightingale."

Fortunately a larger audience hailed her in Sydney when she sang at her own benefit concert in the Masonic Hall. A galaxy of musicians supported her, among them her old teacher Alice Charbonnet. Nellie sang the "Shadow Song": "The whole ten movements, their changes of tempo, key, and the intricacies of the very elaborate vocalisation surmounted with perfect ease—her enunciation admirable, her runs beautifully clear, the echo passages given with dainty grace, and the frequent shakes trilled to perfection." The applause was so deafening that she returned at once to sing Tosti's "Goodbye." At the end she stood on stage to receive, from a group of music lovers, a medal similar to the one Kruse had received at his Sydney farewell. Excitedly she telegraphed Cecchi: "Benefit great success. Presented with medal." In Melbourne it was observed that Cecchi was "visibly swelling with pride."

Early in February 1886, Charlie left Mackay to make his way to Melbourne. He must have felt some trepidation at facing a reunion with Nellie and no doubt perplexed at the prospect of her pursuing a career in London. His comfort was that on the concert platforms and opera houses of Europe she would surely fail. The word "fail," however, was not in the Mitchell vocabulary. To promote her prospects, Nellie began to gather letters of introduction to possible patrons. Some came from Lady Loch, the music-loving wife of the governor of Victoria, others were from Madame Pinschof, the wife of the Austrian consul. Under her maiden name of Elise Wiedermann, Madame Pinschof had sung opera in Vienna and Zurich, and was steeped in European culture. Like Lady Loch, she was convinced of Nellie's potential and wrote enthusiastically to her old singing teacher in Paris, a woman of high musical reputation named Mathilde Marchesi.

By a stroke of luck and by sheer persistence, Nellie also succeeded in gaining letters of introduction from Arthur Cellier, a London composer of operettas, who had just arrived in Melbourne to conduct the first performances of the *Mikado*. Cellier provided a sheaf of letters to musical notables, among them Wilhelm Ganz, the composer of "Sing Sweet Bird," and Sir Arthur Sullivan of Gilbert and Sullivan fame, then the most influential musician in London.

Nellie's mind was so firmly focused on preparations for departure that her reunion with Charlie in the middle of the month seemed almost a minor event. Nevertheless she found time in February to sing at a benefit concert for the victims of a forest fire, and two days later to sing farewell solos at St. Francis's Church. Her own farewell benefit was to be held on March 6, 1886, in the Melbourne Town Hall, in the presence of the governor. Two days before the concert, a touching little advertisement appeared among the regular concert notices in the *Melbourne Argus*:

In compliment to his favourite pupil
SIGNOR CECCHI
will sing the intermezzo in the operatic scena "Ah, fors'è lui"

It was testament to the depth of Cecchi's feelings that he should decide to join Nellie's farewell and sing the tenor passage that linked the soprano's wistful "Ah, fors'è lui" and her carefree "Sempre libera." Even though he was to sing from behind a curtain—in the opera the passage is sung offstage—he was exposing his voice to public scrutiny for the first time in years, and only deep affection could have induced him to attempt it. Understandably, when the night arrived, he found himself too hoarse to sing.

Some in the large audience may have regretted Cecchi's absence, but most were delighted with the soloists. Five of the city's notable performers took part, and Nellie herself sang Mattei's "Dear Heart" and Reichardt's "Image of the Rose" with a humming accompaniment from twenty-four gentlemen amateurs. Around her throat she wore a tight black-velvet band, about half an inch wide, fastened with a diamond clasp. As she sang the exuberant "Sempre libera"—which in English means "always free"—she ripped the band from her throat and cast it aside. The audience loved the gesture, but one wonders if Charlie, watching from his seat, saw her proclamation of freedom as an unhappy omen.

At the end of the concert, flowers deluged the stage: "Such beautiful bouquets, wreaths and baskets of flowers," enthused one reporter, "as have never been surpassed on any previous occasion." There was a splendid bouquet from Lady Loch and an enormous basket from Madame Pinschof, but by far the grandest came from Nellie's teacher. It was a gold laurel wreath tied with long white silk streamers, across which ran the golden inscription: "Presented to his pupil by Signor Cecchi."

In later years Nellie so downplayed her early concert career in Australia that most of her biographers have assumed that she sang in few serious concerts. She liked to believe—and several of her biographers have agreed with her—that her fellow countrymen were ignorant of her ability. Her first biographer, Agnes Murphy, drew on those feelings when she wrote that the "Australian public never allowed her to separate herself entirely from the ranks of the amateur; and when, after eighteen months experience, she decided to try her fortune in Europe, it could not be reasonably claimed that the people of her own country recognized in her the possibilities of future greatness."

Memory is selective, and Nellie chose to point to the doubters, possibly because they included her own family. In contrast, most of the critics, and the public too, hailed her as the foremost concert singer in Australia. A few days before she sailed, *Melbourne Punch* informed its readers that "the best critics have always been unanimous in her praise" and predicted a successful European career for her.

On March 11 a large crowd gathered in bright sunshine to farewell the new mail steamer *Bengal* on her voyage to England. As the small ship edged away, the pier was a colorful mass of bobbing parasols and fluttering handkerchiefs. Standing on deck with her husband and little son, and her father and two sisters, Nellie surely knew that this was a decisive moment in her life. She had a chance of achieving real fame, and she was determined that nothing would stand in her way.

CHAPTER FOUR

My First Great Moment

LIFE ABOARD the *Bengal* was very different from life at Doonside. George, who had usually been tucked away in the nursery while Nellie performed, was now often by her side. She saw afresh how engaging he had become, growing taller and chattering new words almost every day. Motherly pride in Jackie, as she called him, surged in her as never before. When she wrote to Cecchi, she rejoiced that "Little Jackie has grown so big and fat, and talks so well."

Charlie was often by her side. Shut up together for hours in the cramped cabin, their reunion was initially smoother than could have been expected, for each still attracted the other, and George was a powerful bond. Charlie may well have felt hopeful about their future, imagining—as her father seemed to do—that the likelihood of her failing in Europe would guide her dutifully back to his arms in Mackay.

As the voyage went on, the claustrophobic atmosphere began to tell, but fortunately there were diversions. Almost every night saw parties, concerts, or dances in the saloon, and by day there were games on deck. The three lively sisters with their capacity for banter could not fail to make their mark in so small a ship. As they danced and sang and threw quoits on deck, they attracted the attention of young men. What Charlie thought of them one does not know, but Nellie had already observed how easily he became jealous.

After nearly two weeks at sea, the *Bengal* reached Colombo. This was Nellie's first exposure to a foreign culture, and the sights and sounds of the tropical port fired her senses. Along with other first-class passengers, the Mitchell party was conveyed by rickshaw to the Grand

Oriental Hotel. Never had comfort and space seemed so desirable. At last, if only for one day, she was able to lie in a large bath, relax in a wide bed, and feel the solid ground beneath her feet.

At nightfall the ship sailed from Colombo, and in the following days the heat became stifling. In the close confinement of the cabin, all too reminiscent of the bungalow at Marian, nerves frayed and the slightest irritation could provoke a row. By the time they reached the coaling port of Aden on the Red Sea, Charlie and Nellie had engaged in a heated quarrel, and by the time they reached Suez they began another, in the course of which, if her recollection can be trusted, Charlie struck her a blow on the ear which made her somewhat deaf for days. Seeking comfort in her sisters' cabin, she refused to "hold intercourse" with Charlie. Although the word "intercourse" in the Victorian Era did not necessarily mean sexual intercourse—and may only have meant that she was not speaking to her husband—one wonders if some of their quarrels might not have concerned her conjugal duties. A pregnancy would have wrecked Nellie's hopes for a career. On the other hand, it may very well have suited Charlie's plans.

It was a relief to leave the sweltering Red Sea and enter the temperate Mediterranean, where tempers cooled and harmony returned. On April 17 the *Bengal* docked at the British island of Malta, and in a holiday mood the Armstrongs took little George on a tour along the steep streets of Valetta. Passing the rocky battlements they entered the Cathedral of St. John, where another row erupted. Perhaps revolving around the etiquette of whether two-year-old George should remove his cap in church, it began with a scuffle during which the cap was flung from his head and Nellie's mouth was struck by the back of Charlie's hand. It was testimony to their propensity to quarrel, for both husband and wife had received a religious upbringing and normally would not have dreamed of quarreling in a house of God.

Two weeks later they reached England, docking in the Thames at Tilbury. Now that she had reached the promised land, Nellie was filled with a sense of foreboding. After the color and sun of the voyage, the "grey skies, the dirty wharves, the millions of grimy chimney pots" chilled her. To her own depression was added Charlie's. On landing, he was handed word that his mother was ill at her home on the Sussex coast.

In the excitement and bustle of London, Nellie's spirits revived, for like all Australians of her time she felt intense pride in belonging to an empire that embraced one-fifth of the world. In Australia, the British Isles were spoken of as "home," and London, as the heart of empire, was magical even to those who had never seen it. Now, seeing the city's "hansom cabs, its vast shops, its crowds of people, and, more than anything, its tulips in Hyde Park," Nellie was carried away by "a sense of incredible adventure." Stepping inside the terrace house her father had rented in fashionable Sloane Street, she sang a little trill of joy. In her own words, it was "the first note I ever sang in London."

Next day she, Charlie, and George made a brief visit by train to the coastal town of Littlehampton to visit Charlie's mother in the nearby village of Rustington. Here, among the flint-walled cottages and tidy green fields, so unlike the wooden farmhouses and bleached, sprawling paddocks of her own Steel's Creek, Nellie became acquainted with her husband's family. She had feared that his relatives might not like her but the fear proved unjustified. That footloose Charlie had married a wife from a rich and respectable colonial family and fathered a healthy son were causes for celebration, and the family welcomed her warmly. "I like all his connections and relations very much, they are all very nice," she was able to write home to Melbourne.

Two days later, on the morning of May 4, David Mitchell and his family were among the twelve hundred ticket holders who took their seats in London's vast Albert Hall for the colorful opening of the Indian and Colonial Exhibition. Around them glowed brilliant military uniforms and rich Indian costumes while below, on the floor of the large arena, stood a burnished throne surmounted by a canopy of gold. At noon Sir Arthur Sullivan and the Canadian soprano Emma Albani took their seats beside the choir. Soon after, twenty-two splendidly dressed princes and princesses entered in procession, among them a dumpy little woman, dressed in black, with a grey feather in her bonnet. Nellie could scarcely believe that this unpretentious figure was Queen Victoria.

Later in the ceremony, Madame Albani sang, and for the first time Nellie listened intelligently to a truly great singer. To quote her own words, Albani's voice "went straight to my heart." That she herself might one day take part in a similar ceremony must surely have crossed her mind, for Albani was a colonial like herself, and Nellie possessed a letter of introduction to Sir Arthur Sullivan, who was so prominent in the same ceremony.

In the following weeks Nellie tried to secure interviews, using her letters of introduction from Cellier. She called first on the fashionable singing teacher Alberto Randegger, but he fobbed her off with the excuse that he was taking no new pupils. She called next on the composer Hubert Parry, but he also declined to see her. These responses, while discouraging, were not annihilating. She consoled herself that the letter to Arthur Sullivan was the envelope that really mattered.

When she met Sullivan at his home in Victoria Street, he was playing a tinkling tune on the piano. She sensed at once that he resented the intrusion, and was dismayed that he scarcely seemed to listen while she sang. When she had finished her song, he gave her the same advice that he regularly gave to other auditionists: she must study for a year, after which he might consider her for a small part in one of his operas. So much had been riding on his verdict that she could scarcely control her emotions, and she burst into tears the moment she left his door. It seemed almost pointless to pursue a career in England, but she had one remaining letter from Cellier, and she decided to deliver it. It was to Wilhelm Ganz on Harley Street.

It was fortunate that she decided to persevere because there was no sounder or better-connected judge of a soprano voice in London than Ganz. A professor of singing at the Guildhall School of Music, he was also the accompanist and friend of the towering singer of the age, Adelina Patti, the performer whom every aspiring soprano hoped to emulate, and the artist against whom Nellie would measure herself for the rest of her life.

The great Patti's life story ran like a fairy tale. Born in Madrid to an Italian soprano who had been singing on stage only an hour or so before the birth, Patti grew up in the United States as an infant phenomenon. Perched on a table, warbling "like a tiny thrush," she entertained audiences across America, sometimes accompanied by a nine-year-old pianist and a four-year-old drummer. In the year of Melba's birth, the young prodigy, by now eighteen, arrived in London and auditioned for Covent Garden. Her exquisite *bel canto* voice instantly secured her an engagement, and thereafter, for twenty-five consecutive years, Patti reigned supreme at Covent Garden. The diva's romantic history was widely known, and Ganz's close connection with her must have promised rare opportunities for anyone he chose to befriend.

Unlike Sullivan, Ganz listened to Nellie attentively. He needed only to hear her sing "Ah, forse'è lui" to realize that she had considerable potential: he told her that "it could not have been better sung." For her second song she chose his own composition, "Sing, Sweet Bird." He glowed with pleasure when she told him that she had sung it "a great deal in Australia and made it popular there."

Ganz was organizing three concerts for the following month, and he offered to engage her. Nellie accepted with jubilation. He "has taken a wonderful fancy to me," she wrote excitedly to Cecchi, and "declares my voice more like Patti's than any voice he has ever heard." She also admitted to being nervous. "It is rather a big undertaking," she told Cecchi, "but in for a penny in for a pound."

In retrospect Nellie took a dislike to Ganz and his concerts, and in her autobiography she compressed her three appearances under Ganz's patronage into one afternoon concert, held in an undistinguished "little hall in the city." The records of the time speak differently. Her first concert was on the evening of June 1, in the fashionable Prince's Hall in Piccadilly, and the star of the evening, a ten-year-old pianist named Pauline Ellice, played so brilliantly that even the staid reviewer from the *Musical World* praised her. Nellie, one of three supporting artists, also earned his praises. "Mrs Armstrong, from Melbourne, made her first appearance in Europe," he wrote admiringly, "and produced a very favourable impression in an aria from *La Traviata* and Ganz's song 'Sing, Sweet Bird,' the latter of which was encored." An encore was a diamond bracelet to an ambitious young singer, but Nellie chose to forget the encore when she recalled the event years later.

On the following evening Nellie sang at the forty-first dinner of the Royal General Theatrical Fund at the Freemason's Tavern. Two admirals and a bevy of knights, politicians, and actors were present, but the two significant guests were Henry Mapleson and Augustus Harris, the most powerful opera impresarios in London. Knowing that he was catering for a knowledgeable audience, Ganz had engaged nine "high-class" performers, among them the popular American contralto Antoinette Sterling. Nevertheless it was Mrs. Armstrong's "high soprano voice of fine quality" that was again singled out by the *Musical World*. Her rendition of Gounod's "Ave Maria" was applauded, and Augustus Harris, who had never heard the song before, was "charmed with it." In fact Nellie received so much praise that Antoinette Sterling, openly jealous, was "in a fearful rage," or so Nellie gleefully informed Cecchi.

Nellie was delighted to have done better than Sterling, but she was still dissatisfied. She believed that she would gain proper recognition only when she had secured a supporting engagement with a truly great artist. When she read of forthcoming concerts by Patti, she begged Ganz to try to secure her a place on the program. "I am so anxious to get on," she told him. "I hope you will put in a good word for me whenever you can."

Ganz arranged another engagement for Nellie, but it was not with Patti. It was at the Prince's Hall on the afternoon of June 21, and disappointment would color her memories of it. The concert, to raise money for a charity, featured a list of vocalists who, in Nellie's eyes, were of little importance. At the time she was right, and yet three names stand out to those reading the list today. One was Marie Tempest, soon to become a famous actress; the others were Randolph Coward and his sister Hilda, the Twickenham Nightingale, who would soon become the uncle and aunt of Noel Coward.

The concert passed unnoticed by the critics, but Ganz remained confident. He put his faith in Augustus Harris, whose Drury Lane Theatre was home to the prestigious Carl Rosa Opera Company. Convinced that, once heard, she would be "engaged there and then for a number of years" Ganz called on Carl Rosa to seek an audition for his protégée. He would long remember how Rosa took up a pencil and wrote down the time of Nellie's audition—"three o'clock, Tuesday"—on his shirt cuff.

At three o'clock on the appointed Tuesday, Nellie came to Ganz's house, nervous but determined. At four o'clock she swept out, almost heartbroken: Rosa had sent his shirt to the laundry and forgotten about the appointment. None of Ganz's apologies soothed her. When he tried to arrange another appointment, she refused to listen. Disgusted with London, she was ready now to take up the introduction written by her Melbourne patron, Madame Pinschof, to Mathilde Marchesi in Paris. One of the most famous singing teachers in Europe, Marchesi had already agreed to hear her, and it remained only to fix a time for the audition.

At the start of July, Nellie was obliged to put aside her ambitious plans for a few days and join Charlie in Ireland, where he had become a part-time lieutenant in the Prince of Wales Leinster Regiment. When his military duties ended, he and Nellie visited his brother, Sir Andrew Armstrong, at Gallen Priory. Nellie found it exciting to have an Irish baronet for a brother-in-law and to have an assured place in Anglo-Irish life. She felt surprisingly at ease with Sir Andrew and his friends, and would have stayed longer had Charlie not left abruptly for England, taking their money with him. Meanwhile her father and sisters had been traveling in Scotland, where David Mitchell had fallen ill. On medical advice he advanced the date of his return to Melbourne, booking passages for himself, Annie, and Belle on the *Tasmania*, which was due to sail in mid-September.

Nellie had no intention of returning in September. Instead she, Charlie, and George moved to lodgings on Queens Road in Bayswater. Here Charlie began to indulge in aggressive outbursts of what was ostensibly horseplay, but which Nellie believed was designed to prevent her from singing in public. Most of the outbursts occurred when she was in evening dress and ready to leave for a concert or musical party. A few weeks earlier, on Sloane Street, he had spilled a jug of water over her dress just as she was setting out for an evening engagement. At other times he would grip her bare arms so urgently that he left marks on her skin. Stubbornly refusing to allow his behavior to deflect her, she viewed it as simply another obstacle she must somehow overcome.

Charlie's anger was, in its own way, understandable. He thought that she should accept the verdict of such eminent musicians as Arthur Sullivan and Randegger. Indeed her persistence was altogether beyond his comprehension, and her iron disregard of his personal feelings made him feel powerless and angry. When Carl Rosa failed to meet her, he had at last begun to feel safe, but now he was frustrated by the news that she was committed to an audition with Marchesi and that nothing would change her mind. Even Ganz was opposed to her auditioning with Marchesi. "I thought it was hardly necessary," Ganz wrote later, "as her singing was then already so perfect."

Early in September Nellie traveled to Paris, most likely on her own. Normally the journey would have seemed an adventure, but her mind was so intent on her goal that events and scenes passed almost unnoticed. "I saw nothing of the boulevards, the gay laughing crowds, the glittering shops," she remembered. "My mind was bent on one thing and one thing only." At ten o'clock the next morning, with a thumping heart, she made her way down quiet streets to a five-story stone house north of the Arc de Triomphe. The tall front door was opened by a uniformed footman who told her that Madame Marchesi was engaged and that she must return next day. Fearing this might be another snub, Nellie bit back her tears and retraced her steps.

Early next morning, knocking again at the tall front door, she was admitted into a hallway dominated by a white marble fireplace and a high gilt mirror. After waiting, she was ushered into an even grander room with crystal chandeliers and photographs of successful students lining the walls. Here she was received by a small woman with scraped-back grey hair, "standing very upright in the middle of the room, dressed all in black." It was Mathilde Marchesi, and she radiated severity.

What followed would be the most important encounter of Nellie's life, but she so often described it that the details became blurred and no two accounts exactly coincide. It would seem that it was audition day at the École Marchesi—as the school was called—and prospective pupils were taking turns to sing from a small platform at the end of the room. As she heard their efforts, Nellie's heart beat with excitement, for she believed she was their superior.

When at last her turn came, Madame seated herself at the piano and began to take her up the scale from middle C to high F. "Why do you screech?" she barked as she heard the high notes: "Sing *pianissimo*." A few minutes later Madame's fingers were flying over the keys with the introduction to "Ah, fors'è lui." In some versions of the story, Nellie sang to the end of the aria, in others she was stopped abruptly in the middle. All versions agree that Madame Marchesi bounded from the piano stool and rushed through the door. Nellie was "flabbergasted."

Almost as quickly as she had left, Madame returned, "dragging by the hand a little man" who, Nellie later found out, was her husband. "Have the kindness to sing the song once more," she said, and somehow Nellie managed to repeat the aria. Madame then turned to her husband and exclaimed softly, "Did I not tell you she is a star?" It was some time later that Nellie learned the exact sequence of events in what was such a crucial moment in her life. Madame, after leaving the music room, had raced upstairs and shouted to her husband, "*Salvatore, j'ai enfin une étoile*"—"At last I have found a star."

A transformation took place in the teacher. From a pillar of severity, she became "a winning, gracious, kindly, motherly woman" who took Nellie's hands gently in hers and asked, "Mrs Armstrong, are you serious?" Nellie, almost too nervous to speak, whispered that indeed she was. "Then," replied Madame, "if you are serious, and can study with me for one year, I will make something extraordinary of you." She pronounced the word "extra-ordinary." "This was my first great moment," Nellie later wrote. "It was wonderful."

On returning to London, her mood was volatile. To have found someone who recognized her talent and had the skills to develop it was unbelievably elating: but to be obliged to tell her family and—worse—to tell Charlie was daunting. Her father received the news calmly and, bowing to the inevitable, promised her a small allowance for the next twelve months. Charlie took the news poorly, as a personal affront, and created a scene. As Nellie remembered it, he brandished his lieutenant's sword around her head, threatening to cut her face. She concluded he was not in earnest and that his brandishing was more for show than genuinely threatening. Even so, the sight of the blade swishing so close to her face scared her.

She had too much on her mind to permit herself to be subdued by Charlie. On September 10, 1886, with many farewells, David Mitchell and his younger daughters sailed for Australia. Soon after their departure, Nellie packed her belongings in preparation for Paris. A new chapter of her life was beginning, in which she had no alternative but to succeed.

CHAPTER FIVE

I Am Melba

MADAME MARCHESI was born in Frankfurt in 1821, the daughter of a once-wealthy merchant named Graumann. Showing early signs of vocal talent, she went to study with the celebrated Manuel Garcia, and there she fell in love with a handsome young singer called the Marchese—or Marquess—di Castrone. As his titled Sicilian family objected to his bohemian career, he abandoned his title, calling himself by the stage name of Salvatore Marchesi. Thus on her marriage Mathilde Graumann became Madame Marchesi, but never forgot for an instant that she was really the Marchesa di Castrone.

Although Madame had taught earlier in life at the Vienna and Cologne conservatories and produced at least one famous pupil in Ilma di Murska, her greatest renown did not come until she turned sixty. That year she and Salvatore opened a small singing school for girls in an obscure street in Paris. Their school prospered, and five years later they were teaching more than eighty pupils and had moved to more fashionable premises on the Rue Jouffroy. Madame made it her business to court the elite. Ambroise Thomas, Léo Delibes, and Jules Massenet, three of the foremost composers of opera in France, were frequent visitors to her soirées, and Charles Gounod, the grand old man of French music, was patron of her annual student concerts. The newspaper Le Figaro posted a reviewer to her concerts, so importantly did they figure in the Parisian musical calendar.

Although seven to ten years was the usual time required for a singer to gain a sound *bel canto* technique, Madame Marchesi's pupils normally studied with her for only three. The period of study was short because Madame seldom accepted beginners. It was said, probably truthfully, that she was bad at teaching novices, and those few who studied under her from the start often acquired faulty techniques. Her expertise lay in giving a brilliant finish to an already well-trained voice, especially if that voice was light, high, and agile.

On Madame's advice, Nellie and George took rooms in a modest apartment house at 12 Avenue Carnot, not far from the Rue Jouffroy. Nellie found life on Avenue Carnot a sobering contrast to the luxury of Doonside. Despite her father's allowance, despite her savings, and despite Madame's promise that her instruction would take only one year, she felt obliged to save every penny, for she had no real way of knowing how long her apprenticeship might last. Her rooms were at the top of five flights of stairs and poorly furnished, and she "mended and mended" her own clothes until they were visibly patched and shabby. She walked to her classes in all weather; her meals were so frugal that she became quite thin.

Little George was spared such economies. He needed clothes and good food, and since Nellie spent most of her day studying at school or at home and often spent her evenings at concerts or operas, he needed a full-time nursemaid. In fact his welfare became a pressing concern, and the burden of motherhood, easily shelved in Melbourne, was now constantly on Nellie's shoulders. George sensed his mother's insecurity, and it increased his own which, after a year of frequent change, was already high. When he felt afraid, Nellie would wrap her arms around him and tell him stories of her own childhood, which usually soothed them both. Doonside, from which she had longed to escape, became a magical haven to which mother and son mentally retreated in times of trouble.

Luckily there were neighbors who were eager to help them. Two gentle, white-haired Irish sisters, the Misses Hyland, liked to mind George, as did Madame's young accompanist, Fritzi Stradewitz, who lived downstairs. Nellie recalled how the elder Miss Hyland once offered to lend her money to pay the rent. "I know one day you are going to be famous, and that then you will repay me," said the generous Irishwoman. Nellie never forgot her kindness.

"It was only the burning desire to succeed and the absorbing interest in my work that kept me going," Nellie would remember. She also recalled what a relief it was to ease her worries by steeping herself in the various classes at the school. For Madame Marchesi gave far more than just singing lessons and was in effect running a finishing school for prima donnas. She accepted girls from all backgrounds—daughters of shopkeepers in Europe, farmers in America, missionaries in China—and completed their vocal, musical, and social education. She boasted that the best of them, when they left her care, could hold their own in any opera house in Europe, and in the highest ranks of European society.

New students at the École Marchesi began the day with a morning assembly, where they sang their vocal exercises in unison. At nine o'clock punctually, an impeccably groomed Madame would preside at the piano for the communal exercises, and thereafter would give individual lessons, each lasting fifteen minutes, until lunchtime. The afternoon was devoted to opera and musical theory classes; French and Italian language classes; acting, mime, and deportment classes; and special instruction for Madame's select pupils.

Behind her back Madame Marchesi was known as the "Prussian drill-master." The nickname was not inapt: like any capable commander, she surrounded herself with a team of able lieutenants. One was the elderly Lucien Petipa, Nellie's teacher of deportment, and once a leading dancer at the Paris Opéra. His task was to rub the rough edges off those girls who were unused to the "best society." When she came to mix in London's exclusive circles, Nellie realized just how much she owed him. Petipa taught his pupils how to sit, how to walk, how to eat, how to receive guests, and, above all, how to keep their heads whatever the situation. His rules of good taste applied even to payment of the students' fees. Once a month a special vase was placed discreetly on the piano, ready to receive the money that the students owed. Madame loftily pretended not to notice it, though, as one girl tartly remarked, Madame certainly did notice if the money failed to appear. The same disgruntled student, an American soprano called Emma Eames, found the "good taste" of the school stifling. She described the École Marchesi as "a divine school for mediocrity."

The pupils who passed through the classrooms, however, were not mediocre. Many would soon grace the foremost opera houses of Europe. So sure was Madame that Nellie would be among the successful that she removed her from the common class and gave her daily private lessons. Later she would say that she had never taught anyone more talented, intelligent, pliant, and industrious. For her part, Nellie believed she had "the best teacher in the world." She marveled at Madame's "burning spirit of enthusiasm, which made one feel, even when singing a scale, that one was singing something beautiful." She marveled, too, at the intense personal interest that Marchesi took in all aspects of her life. Madame's "pupils were all to her," wrote one observer: "She watched over them, their health, their future, everything concerning them." To some, this level of care seemed intrusive and overbearing, but to Nellie it was the answer to her prayers. After five years of grieving, she had at last found a substitute for her mother. Moreover this new mother had the capacity to make her great.

Madame, for her part, had long dreamed of molding a daughter into a fine *bel canto* soprano, and had long since accepted that none of her three daughters had a talent equal to Nellie's. So quickly did teacher and pupil recognize this powerful dovetailing of needs that within a matter of months Madame would be signing herself "your very loving old mother," and Nellie would be calling herself "your loving daughter."

During those weeks of intensive instruction, Madame gave practical advice on a variety of subjects. She forbade Nellie to wash her hair or to ride a horse. She believed that to wash the hair with water, rather than cleaning it with a fine comb and hair tonic, inclined a singer to colds in the head; and by riding a horse, a singer might injure those muscles in the chest and abdomen on which her breathing depended.

She also insisted that Nellie practice for no more than two—or at the most three—short sessions of half an hour each day. The rest of her study must be carried on inside her head, for Madame had seen too many singers wreck their voices by overuse of their vocal cords. She advised Nellie, too, on how to treat rivals, warning her to regard all rival singers as potential enemies, and to remain as aloof from them as possible. Above all, she emphasized that a prima donna should adopt the appearance and manners of a high-born European lady.

Nellie was eager to please her new mother, and she absorbed all that she was taught. The only exception was in what she wore. Appearance was of great importance to Madame, good taste in clothes being considered almost as important as good manners. When she saw her favorite pupil in the same old dress of blue-and-white-striped serge day after day, she ordered her to change it for another. When Nellie replied that this was the only decent dress she owned and that she had no money to buy another, an argument broke out, which ended with Madame offering to pay for a new dress and the poor girl running from the room in tears. The generous offer had hurt Nellie's pride. She replied that if Madame could not accept her in blue and white serge, she need not accept her at all. Realizing that her pupil could not be bullied, Madame meekly accepted the serge dress.

After a month's individual instruction, Madame declared that Nellie must now join a class, adding that the first and second grades were full. Nellie misunderstood the message, and for a horrifying moment believed she was being dismissed. Desperate to stay, she cried out, "Please, please, Madame Marchesi, do not send me away." Madame allowed herself to smile. "I am not going to send you away," she announced. "You are going into the opera class." Thus, after a bare two months, Nellie was promoted to the most advanced class in the school.

Soon after entering the opera class, Nellie attended one of Madame's musical soirées. On the evening of November 19, 1886, the distinguished actress Adelaide Ristori read the sleepwalking scene from *Macbeth*, after which Madame's two best students sang. The applause that followed was intoxicating, and Nellie longed to be in their shoes. When she heard that the next soirée was to be held after Christmas, with the director of the Paris Conservatoire, seventy-six-year-old Ambroise Thomas, as a guest of honor, she could scarcely contain her ambition.

In opera class she had been learning the "mad scene" from Thomas's opera *Hamlet*. Based on Shakespeare's play, this scene depicting Ophelia's madness was peppered with trills and runs and chromatic scales of great difficulty. Notwithstanding the amount of practice the scene would require, she believed she could perfect it in time for the next concert. Madame was of the same mind, and they resolved that this would constitute Nellie's debut.

During the following weeks of the opera class, Madame pushed Nellie to limits far beyond those she imposed on her other pupils. One day she pushed too far, causing the overwrought girl to run from the room. Madame set out in pursuit. Outside the door Madame is said to have flung her arms around her surrogate daughter and murmured, "You know I love you. If I bother you, it is because I know you will be great. Come back and sing as I wish." Nellie dutifully returned to the classroom and resumed her lesson.

One unusual decision had to be taken before Nellie could make her public debut. Madame believed that an opera singer should have a striking and easily remembered name, preferably one that sounded Italian. According to Madame, most English or American names were prosaic and far too foreign for a European to remember. As an example of a suitable name, she pointed to a former pupil from the American state of Nevada named Emma Wixom, who had changed her name to Emma Nevada and was now a prima donna in Paris and Milan.

It was essential in Madame's eyes that Nellie replace Armstrong with a surname that was distinctive and memorable. She and Nellie began examining Australian names. Richmond and Victoria yielded nothing, and then they came to Melbourne. If they chopped off the last five letters and added a final "a," they would coin a name so simple that any European could spell and pronounce it immediately. It seemed the perfect solution, especially as Nellie had long ago vowed to "win individual fame and associate it proudly with the land of my birth."

It was under this new name of Melba that Nellie faced her audience at Madame's on the afternoon of December 30. In deportment, outlook, and vocal finesse, indeed in all but basic vocal technique, she was a Marchesi creation, and Madame was filled with pride. She thanked her foresight in inviting so many newspaper reporters to the *matinée*, knowing that they would report Nellie's performance to a wider audience.

As Nellie mounted the small stage and saw the white head of Ambroise Thomas in the audience, her courage almost failed. But once in full possession of herself, her determination triumphed and she fulfilled all her teacher's expectations. Although the "mad scene" was more difficult than anything she had previously sung in public, she performed it almost like a veteran. Thomas praised her warmly. Next day *Le Figaro*, *Le Sport*, and *La Liberté* praised her too.

Fortune was smiling on Melba, the name by which she increasingly thought of herself and the name by which she was henceforth known. It is true that certain opera singers have trouble integrating or fusing their professional self with their private self. Maria Callas is said to have felt that Maria the woman was a different person from Callas the diva. Melba encountered no such problem. Thanks to her secure upbringing and robust self-image, and Marchesi's expert tutelage, she slipped effortlessly into the role of Melba and felt no confusion. "I am Melba," she would say proudly, and in her eyes and feelings the name comfortably embraced and fused all aspects of her personality.

At the *matinée musicale* there had been present an old friend of Madame's named Maurice Strakosch. Forty years before in America, Strakosch had married Adelina Patti's older sister, and managed and coached the young Adelina from her infant years until she came to Covent Garden in 1861. Since then he had managed a string of notable singers and was constantly eager to add to his stable. A few notes of Melba's voice had reached his ears by accident while he was visiting the school a few weeks earlier. "I want that voice," he is said to have exclaimed as snatches of "Caro nome" floated through the door. "I do not know whether she is short or tall, pretty or plain: I want her." When he heard the voice at the *matinée*, and saw the face and figure that matched it, he was more than ever determined to sign her.

The Marchesis had set their sights higher than Strakosch. To hear Melba at the Paris Opéra had always been Madame's goal, and forgetting that the directors were severe auditioners and that her protégée was still little more than a student, she allowed her enthusiasm to carry her away. Exerting her influence, Marchesi prematurely arranged a "special audition" at the Opéra in February 1887, and Melba found herself standing on a darkened stage while a single footlight flared in her face. Thoroughly unnerved, she felt her voice falter. She was disappointed but not surprised when her application failed.

Early in March 1887, not long after Charlie had made a quick and disturbing visit to Paris, Strakosch proffered his contract. Writing to Arthur Hilliger in Sydney—whose friendship she had resurrected—Melba detailed Strakosch's attractive terms. She was to make her debut in October and belong to Strakosch for five years. "Strakosch says I will have as great a success as Patti," she told Hilliger, "in fact he says I will take her place."

With the debacle at the Paris Opéra fresh in their minds, Melba and the Marchesis accepted Strakosch's offer, and Melba began working with redoubled effort. In the opera class she was learning a new role every month and was surpassing all other students. Unsurprisingly, her classmates were growing jealous. "I am *far* above them all," she boasted to Arthur Hilliger rather brashly. This lofty attitude did not win her friends, but even among the jealous there was recognition of her talent. One competitor who deeply resented Melba's superiority was the American soprano Emma Eames. And yet even she conceded that it "would be impossible to imagine anything lovelier, both in voice and appearance" than Melba at this time.

In the following months Melba sang in four more of Madame's concerts, which, unlike those at the Rue Jouffroy, were truly public performances and organized in aid of charities. The first, on March 21, 1887, at the Salle Erard, Melba described excitedly in a letter to Hilliger. The cries of "*brava*" when she finished had almost deafened her, she told him. The ladies, who, according to the etiquette of the time, were not allowed to call out, clapped their gloved hands and waved their lace handkerchiefs. In April, Melba sang again at the Salle Erard in aid of the Association of Musical Artists and received praise in *Figaro* for arias from *Rigoletto* and *Lucia*. Early in May she appeared at the Salle Georges Petit in aid of the Charities of Montmartre, whose patron was Charles Gounod. White-haired Gounod sat in the seat of honor and smiled benignly as the pupils sang his music. Melba had the thrill of singing that same waltz from *Mireille* that she had sung in Melbourne and Sydney. On such occasions she felt so exultant that she wanted the whole world to know of her success. "I wish you could hear me," she wrote to Hilliger. "Everyone tells me my voice is pure gold and that I vocalize perfectly. Marchesi tells me she has never had such a pupil."

In June the Marchesi pupils were to perform again at a charity *matinée* at the Salle Erard, to help the victims of a fire at the Opéra Comique. Melba was chosen to sing a part of the "mad scene" from *Lucia di Lammermoor*, with a flute accompaniment by Paul Taffanel, first flute in the Paris Opéra. In operas like *Lucia*, singers were permitted to add their own embellishments to the final cadence of an aria to show off their particular skills; and Madame and Taffanel composed one of these passages, known as a cadenza, for Melba's "mad scene." Made up of trills and runs, which were echoed by the flute, it was designed to display the birdlike quality in Melba's voice. The technical difficulties were fearsome, and Madame must have been on tenterhooks as Melba sang it.

The music critics were astounded, and the reviewer from the influential *Gil Blas* prophesied a memorable future for her. But the review most pleasing to Melba was one that called her a "delicious Australian beauty." Delighted by the compliment, she sent it to Hilliger for insertion in Australian newspapers. She added that the papers must be sure to explain that the Mrs. Armstrong praised so highly was now Madame Melba.

Thanks to Marchesi's care, all seemed to be proceeding with a wonderful smoothness. Then Madame outsmarted herself. In her zeal to place her students professionally, she had invited a group of impresarios to her recent concerts. Among them were Lapissida and Dupont, directors of Brussels's Théatre de la Monnaie, an opera house whose prestige was almost as great as that of the Paris Opéra. The two directors heard Melba sing the "mad scene" from *Hamlet* and were impressed. Ignoring Strakosch's prior contract, they called on Madame and began to discuss the possibility of engaging Melba for Brussels. Their terms were very generous and their theatre, the Monnaie—so called because it was built on the site of the old mint—was surely more desirable than anything Strakosch was likely to supply. Madame, throwing caution to the winds, gave them reassurances and told them she would speak to Melba.

Told about the new contract, Melba expressed doubt, but Madame would have none of it. Waving her long white hands, she explained that Strakosch was an old friend and could be persuaded to cancel his contract. This was wishful thinking, but it convinced Melba, whose faith in her teacher was absolute. When presented with the Brussels contract she dutifully signed it, and all parties congratulated themselves.

In the following weeks Melba concentrated on her music, and when doubts did arise, she told herself that Madame knew best. Her confidence was blown apart a few weeks later when a knock at her door disclosed Strakosch himself. He confronted her with the rumor that she had signed with the Monnaie in Brussels and asked if it were true. She explained the circumstances. At this he became indignant. For a quarter of an hour he railed against Melba, Marchesi, and "the ingratitude of the world in general." Melba wilted before his anger. She knew he had a strong argument on his side, but she continued to trust Madame. In her present plight, she could do little else.

When Madame closed the school in August for her summer holiday, Melba and George retreated to Lady Armstrong's house at Rustington on the English south coast. For Melba the following three weeks brought respite from hard work and worries over Strakosch. For lonely little George they brought entry into a magical world of dogs, horses, and Armstrong relatives. Rustington also gave the little boy a chance to visit his father, who was farming and training horses with a friend at nearby Littlehampton. Charlie now seemed more contented, though Melba's ambitions remained a sore point. He did, however, promise to visit Brussels for her forthcoming debut. Perhaps he felt obliged to see for himself what sort of life she was entering, though his imagination was already telling him it was not the life he wished for his wife and son. When next she wrote to Hilliger she confided the warning: "My husband is frightfully jealous and I have not a very easy time with him."

Ironically, in recent weeks Charlie himself was gaining notoriety in a different kind of theatre, an extravaganza that was attracting up to 25,000 spectators twice a day in London. This was Buffalo Bill's Wild West Show, featuring cowboys, Indians, sharpshooters, and scouts at the Earl's Court arena. Queen Victoria, visiting the show just before her golden jubilee, had been thrilled by Annie Oakley's shooting.

Among the audience at one performance was Charlie. When volunteers were invited to try their skills on a wild buckjumper named Misery that no stranger had ever been able to mount, Charlie accepted the challenge, and promptly produced a lightweight Australian saddle with a crupper, or strap, passing under the horse's tail to prevent the saddle from slipping. The horse had never felt a crupper, and the cowboys believed it would so enrage the animal that the rider who used it would be instantly thrown to the ground. "Stranger, we don't want to see you killed," shouted one cowboy. Charlie merely smiled and leaped on the horse. There he stayed, plunging and lurching, until he chose to dismount. "Buffalo Bill and the cowboys were paralysed with astonishment," wrote an excited reporter. Charlie, like Melba, was a star performer, and the dilemma for both was that their skills and personalities lay so far apart.

Melba and George were back in Paris at the end of August, so that she could prepare for her debut as Gilda in Verdi's opera *Rigoletto*. As usual she was a glutton for work, and her teachers could scarcely believe how fast she learned. She had been born with a capacity to trill, which she was beginning to regard as "a strange and wonderful benediction." Madame and she took pride in shaping her natural trill into an ornament of unusual regularity and length, which they planned to add to Gilda's famous aria, "Caro nome." Madame was confident that it would create a sensation.

While Melba practiced her role, Madame's husband, Salvatore, set out to cancel Strakosch's contract. Despite his efforts, Strakosch remained obdurate, and the Monnaie's directors were becoming anxious. They intended to present Melba as a "rising star" who had been hired to give guest performances in Brussels, thereby disguising the fact that she was already a contracted member of the company. Even they wondered whether this ruse would work. As she and George took the train to Brussels, she must have wondered what lay ahead.

Friends of Madame's helped Melba rent a furnished house on the Rue de Bailly, a new street on the edge of the old city, lined with three-story terrace houses set right on the pavement. (The house still stands, though its front windows on the ground floor have been turned into a shop front.) The same friends found her a nursemaid for George. The little boy's fourth birthday would fall a few days after her debut, but he was young for his age and still needed babying. "I do not know what I would do without him," Melba told a friend, "he is such a comfort."

Madame's letters, full of advice and affection, followed Melba to Brussels and told her to rest, stay calm, and forget about her voice. On October 3 Madame reversed the advice and told her to place her voice before everything. She intended to be in Brussels for the opening night. "I shall be beside you at the moment of your great battle," she told Melba tenderly. "Many kisses from your loving Mother."

It was impossible for Melba to remain calm. Charlie arrived and was thoroughly out of temper. More vexing, when she reached the Monnaie for her first rehearsal, she found the door blocked by an official waving a blue sheaf of papers. It was a legal injunction obtained by Strakosch to prevent her from working in Brussels. In "the depths of despair," Melba rushed to Monsieur Lapissida, but he was powerless to overturn the injunction. She was legally barred from setting foot inside the theatre.

Charlie's presence in the rented house did nothing to soothe her. His lack of sympathy seems to have provoked a quarrel and to have inspired a replay of the incident with the sword, except that this time, having no sword, he brandished his razor. Confronted by a volatile husband waving a blade, she retreated to George's room.

On the morning of October 10, before she had risen from her bed, Monsieur Lapissida came knocking on her door. Hearing his urgent voice, she hurried along to the top of the stairs and stared down into the hallway. "Strakosch is dead," he shouted up to her. "He died last night at a circus. I will be waiting for you at the theatre at eleven o'clock." She was at last free to make her debut.

While vocally she was ready for her role, in other respects she was unprepared. In her own words, her "dramatic experience was nil," and none of her acting lessons at the École Marchesi had prepared her for the part. At first there were hopes that she would sing in French, the normal language of singers at the Monnaie, but her French was deemed too Australian, and the directors decided to allow her to sing in Italian. There was one magic moment amidst these crises. Outside the theatre, which looked like a Greek temple, she saw banners decorating the classical façade, announcing in crimson letters the magic words, MADAME MELBA.

It was raining on that memorable morning of Thursday, October 13. The Marchesis paid an early call to the Rue de Bailly, with Madame "fluttering and excited" and Salvatore wearing a flower in his buttonhole and looking every inch the Italian aristocrat. They had reserved a box near the stage and graciously insisted on Charlie sitting with them. Brimming with quiet confidence, they had even ordered a supper after the opera in her honor, with such dishes as Côte de Chevreuil à l'Australienne, Oranges Melba, and Pudding Gilda. Melba was touched by their faith but had difficulty sharing it.

By evening she was moving like a woman in a dream. At the theatre, as the dresser placed Gilda's blonde wig on her head, she suddenly came to life. She cried out, "I hate that wig. It is not *me*. I won't have it." Fortunately the conductor was nearby and took her part. "Let her use her own hair," he ordered. "It is much prettier." And so the dresser plaited Melba's flowing brown hair into two long plaits and, contrary to custom, Gilda made her entrance wearing her own hair.

A feeling of unreality persisted as she went on stage, but the music was so embedded in her mind that she responded instinctively. There seemed to be an unearthly hush "in which I heard my voice floating out into the distance as though it were the voice of someone other than myself." Within minutes her concentration returned, and then, in the words of one observer, she sang and acted with "an easy grace, seldom shown by an artist facing the footlights for the first time." Gilda's famous aria "Caro nome" came soon after. At its conclusion Melba began her long trill. It was "like a nightingale's trill," wrote one ecstatic critic; her notes were "like a string of pearls," wrote another. The theatre became a surging sea of waving white handkerchiefs and waves of applause swept over her head. "This cannot be for me," she thought. "They are clapping and cheering for somebody else."

At the close of the second act, listeners were comparing her to great singers of the past. At the end of the opera, many members of the acclaiming, exulting audience were hailing her as a second Patti. "God! What enthusiasm!" wrote the critic from *La Réforme*. "It was a veritable triumph," wrote the critic from *Le Figaro*. Melba's own verdict was simpler. "It was a wonderful, terrible night," she wrote, "a mixture of terror and joy, such as I shall never experience again."

CHAPTER SIX

At Last a Star

ON OCTOBER 15, 1887, when Melba woke up, she found she was on the verge of fame. The main Brussels papers carried enthusiastic reviews, and two days later those in Paris described her as a "sensation" and a "revelation." Reviewers spoke of her crystalline voice, her equal scale, her wonderfully regular trill, her superb technique, her exquisite timbre, and her dramatic flair. Describing her elegant person and her beautiful, mobile face, some likened her profile to that of an empress. "You've been well feted, spoiled and pampered," wrote Madame Marchesi, "and with good reason *because you sang and acted so perfectly.*"

News of the performance traveled far, by print and by telegraph. The London *Times*, the *New York Herald*, and Milan's *Il Mondo Artistico* recorded her "splendid success," while the Australian papers—the *Mackay Mercury* among them—carried stories of the sensational debut. Sometimes there was confusion about her name. She was referred to as Melda and Melva, which must have displeased Madame since she had chosen the name as one so easily remembered. One Sydney newspaper hoped that as soon as she began to sing at Covent Garden she would drop the foreign alias and revert to her own respectable name of Armstrong. Her father and Charlie, who disapproved of opera and all its trappings, possibly agreed, though they surely felt relief that in her new profession she was not besmirching the names of Mitchell and Armstrong. Melba herself gloried in her new name and identity, for she was bringing fame to her own Australian city.

Madame was overjoyed by her protégée's success. Writing from the Rue Jouffroy, to which she had returned the day after the performance, she enthused that "the whole of Paris is talking about your happy debut." In her jubilation she even conveyed a warmhearted message to Charlie. "Tell Charlie," she wrote, "that he is my son-in-law because you are my daughter, and that I kiss him as such."

For the next three weeks Melba appeared in *Rigoletto*. At the same time she struggled to rehearse the part of Violetta in Verdi's *La Traviata*, which was to open on November 9. This role was more taxing both vocally and dramatically than Gilda, and while she was well prepared for it musically, she was not yet prepared for it as an actress.

Melba's deficiency in stagecraft derived to a large degree from a new and profound change in operatic style. As the century advanced, opera had become less like a concert and more like an integrated drama. Singers now had to act more effectively and sing louder, because orchestral scores, once merely the singers' accompaniments, were claiming a more dramatic and louder role. As singers competed with orchestras, the emphasis on agility of voice and beauty of tone declined. By the 1880s florid *bel canto* was almost out of fashion and the more dramatic style was usurping its place.

Madame Marchesi was wedded to the old *bel canto* style and believed that beautiful singing was the primary goal of an opera singer. You must spin your voice as finely and subtly as a spider draws its silky web from its body, she told her pupils. She tolerated no movement of body or mind that might jeopardize that thread of silky sound. Since Marchesi's vocal method involved a precise use of the muscles in the lower half of the torso, the act of gesturing, or even moving, while actually singing was taboo—except perhaps for the raising of an arm. Her students were also told to maintain an emotional reserve when singing, as an upsurge of emotion might sap their concentration and disturb their tone.

This restrained style was still acceptable in the older operas of Rossini or Bellini or Donizetti, where excitement was largely generated by the voice. In the operas of Verdi, however, singers were expected to arouse an audience through their acting, and in none more so than *La Traviata*. That opera revolved around the character of the courtesan Violetta, who was called upon to express a wide range of emotions. If

Melba could not portray those emotions credibly, she would probably fail.

In Brussels, during her first night in the new opera, Melba effectively projected tenderness and pathos. She was less successful in scenes where violent emotions were demanded. The technique she had been taught did not fit her for such roles, and reviewers were quick to comment on her "evident inexperience." As she read those reviews, she wept. While she knew that the criticism was accurate, there was little she could do, short of defying Madame.

Madame Marchesi missed the premiere of La Traviata, which was perhaps as well because the reviews very much displeased her. "I greatly regret not having done Traviata with you," she wrote to Melba after reading the severest criticism. Vowing she would not make the same mistake with Donizetti's Lucia di Lammermoor, which was to open early in December, she wrote to the directors of the Monnaie in Brussels demanding three days' leave for Melba, to be spent "without fail" in Paris. "It is indispensible that in Lucie you have the same success as you had in Rigoletto," she wrote sternly to Melba. "The mad scene in Lucia with all its harmonies is extremely difficult."

To return to Madame at the Rue Jouffroy was comforting for Melba, even if only for three days. It was also a relief to be singing Lucia, which was one of the older operas in which the singing mattered more than the acting, with florid music that suited her voice to perfection. Thanks to Madame's meticulous rehearsing, she regained skill and confidence, and scored a resounding success when she sang again at the Monnaie. The celebrated "mad scene," in which Lucia appears clutching the dagger with which she has killed her newly wedded husband, received cheers, shouts, and much waving of handkerchiefs.

By the time Lucia opened, the pressure of work and the nervous strain were impairing Melba's health. Gynecological symptoms that she had experienced for a year grew worse, and she was obliged to confess her illness to Madame. "I deeply regret that you didn't tell me of your indisposition a year ago," Marchesi wrote sternly. "You would have been able to undergo treatment in Paris and today you would have been already cured." She begged Melba to lie on the sofa for much of the day and to send George to a nursery school. Above all, she wrote, "Take care of yourself, take care of yourself!" She also dared to remark on the absence of Charlie, who, in Madame's opinion, should have been at his wife's side. "His native country seems to have an irresistible attraction for him," she remarked acidly. It was clear that Melba, who told Madame almost everything, had for some time deliberately disguised her troubles with Charlie.

Madame was determined that Melba, and Charlie too, should spend Christmas with her at the Rue Jouffroy. "We very much want the pleasure of seeing your *Charlie* at our house," she wrote firmly to Melba. George and his nurse, on the other hand, were requested to stay at 12 Avenue Carnot, where the Misses Hyland could look after them. While Madame's insistence that the Armstrongs visit Paris was largely inspired by concern for Melba's health, it was also dictated by her longing to see Melba again. "Dear Nellie of my heart," she wrote, "I miss you very much with all my heart. Many of the tenderest kisses from your loving Mother Mathilde."

Melba, Charlie, and George did not go to Paris for Christmas. Instead George would treasure all his life the memory of decorating a Christmas tree in Brussels and of waking on Christmas morning to streets and gardens white with snow. Charlie's weeks in Brussels, however, increased the tension under which Melba was living. He was at odds with himself, unable to reconcile his pride in his wife's achievements with his disdain for her way of life, and conscious that the marriage was steadily crumbling.

Charlie loved George, and it pained him to see the boy growing up in bohemian society and becoming more foreign and more mollycoddled every year. Altogether George was too much his mother's child; he needed the strong influence of a father. But how the boy was to receive that influence Charlie did not know, for it was foolish to imagine that they would ever again live harmoniously as a family. Helplessness over his son's future filled him with impotent anger, and he made no attempt to hide his feelings.

Melba would long remember an incident at 3 Rue de Bailly when she snatched from Charlie a book with which he was smacking George. She recalled that Charlie then turned his wrath on her, fulminating against her way of living and threatening to "maim" her for life so that she could not appear on a stage again. He often made such threats. Although they were melodramatic words devoid of real intent, they betrayed his hatred of her operatic career and his despair at being deprived of his son.

In fact time lay heavily on Charlie's hands, and boredom may have generated some of his ill humor. Fortunately he discovered an exclusive sports club at the Salle Dupont, and in no time he was the fencing and boxing champion of the club, where his "feats of strength astonished the Bruxellois." Here, only here, was he at home.

Increasingly Charlie longed to return to his uncomplicated life in tropical Australia, making a real home there. Six years earlier David Mitchell had bought about three thousand acres of swampy seaside land near the township of Sarina, about twenty-five miles south of Mackay, speculating that it might one day prove the place for a port. The drier part of the land was suitable for cattle and horses. Charlie dreamed of transforming it into his own pastoral run where he, and maybe George, could live the wholesome country life.

A pastoral property required money, and Charlie had one eye on Melba's handsome earnings. Back in 1884 his conservative ideas concerning married women's property had led him to assume that part of her allowance should also be his. He now considered part of her income from the Monnaie Opera House should go toward fulfilling his dream. Indeed, sometime before he returned to England, Melba—on her own account—gave him two hundred pounds, which would have been enough to build a small farmhouse. A garbled account of this gift would find its way into a biography of Melba by her friend Percy Colson, who also reported that Charlie had become jealous of a young Brussels artist named Wauters who was painting Melba's portrait. This episode rings true. Charlie was prone to jealousy, as Melba would often testify.

Soon after Christmas, Melba spent precious days in Paris, preparing the French operas *Lakmé* and *Hamlet* with their composers. Knowing her imperfect French, the directors of the Monnaie had been hesitant to cast her in French roles, even though she had been working busily on her accent for six hours a day. The composer of *Lakmé*, Léo Delibes, had no such reservations. Having heard her sing at Madame's the previous August, he declared she could sing his opera in French, Italian, German, or Chinese for all he cared. The language was irrelevant, just so long as she sang!

Melba opened in *Lakmé* on March 8, 1888 with "striking success." A month later she gained equal acclaim when she appeared as Ophé- lie in *Hamlet*. Ambroise Thomas, who was present on opening night, called her the "Ophélie of my dreams," and both she and Thomas were invited to the royal box to receive the congratulations of the music- loving Belgian queen.

Melba's contract at the Monnaie ran for two years, with a break of four months between May and September. She wondered where she should sing in that intervening time. She had received an invitation from Augustus Harris, who had heard her eighteen months before at the Royal Theatrical Fund dinner. He was now general manager of the Theatre Royal at Covent Garden, where, with a syndicate of five pow- erful backers, he was attempting to revive the Italian opera. Melba's name had come to him through the wife of Earl de Grey, one of those backers. An excellent judge of voices, Gladys de Grey had heard Melba sing at the Monnaie and was determined that Harris should secure her for London. Eager to please the influential de Greys, Harris had made Melba an offer.

Melba's friends in Brussels were eager for her to accept, but Madame was totally against it. Her heart was set on the prestigious Paris Opéra, which she believed was also ready to make Melba an offer. "At the mo- ment," she told Melba in February 1888, "the whole of Paris wants you. The Press is very well disposed towards you. The Opéra assures you that its doors are wide open to you." The directors of the Monnaie, how- ever, did not wish Melba to sing in Paris, and since they held her con- tract, Melba could not easily defy them. She finally rejected Paris and accepted Covent Garden, though its fee was low. When Madame heard of the decision, she made no attempt to hide her annoyance. "Look my dear Nellie," she wrote testily, "your Brussels friends are quite simply a little bit jealous!" What she minded most was Melba's disobedience. In Madame's book of rules, disobedience was not to be tolerated.

Early in May, after crossing the sea to England, George went to stay with his grandmother at Rustington while Melba took gloomy lodgings in Bayswater. Compared to small and friendly Brussels, the sprawling city seemed unwelcoming, and Melba was now all too aware of the geo- graphical and musical distance separating her from Madame and her circle. From Brussels, a three-hour journey on the train could deliver her to the Rue Jouffroy, and even in Brussels she had only to set foot in the Monnaie or the Conservatoire to be surrounded by Madame's friends. In contrast she felt isolated in London, for Paris was nearly a day away, and the name of Marchesi was scarcely known. So it was with trepidation and a sense of loneliness that she made her way past the stalls of fruit and vegetables in the Covent Garden market and entered the adjacent theatre and the office of its general manager.

Although only thirty-six years old, Augustus Harris was already well versed in evaluating singers, having grown up at Covent Garden where his father was stage manager and his mother a stage costumier. Recalling Melba's performance at the Theatrical Fund dinner, he had no hesitation in offering her the role of Lucia in his forthcoming *Lucia di Lammermoor*. To his surprise she replied that she would rather play Gilda in *Rigoletto*. This elicited from him the disheartening reply that Emma Albani, as the ruling prima donna, had already selected Gilda for herself. At that moment Melba realized just how favored she had been at the Monnaie.

Years later, when Melba described her first performance at Covent Garden, she insisted that the audience had been small and bored and that she had received no real recognition. In fact the performance took place on Queen Victoria's birthday, which, being a day of national rejoicing, ensured that the theatre wore a gala air and held a large audience. Being cast in *Lucia di Lammermoor*, however, was something of a liability. All through her career Melba would be burdened by the fact that the florid *bel canto* operas—like *Lucia*—which showed off her technique were now considered dull and out of date. Such great sopranos of the past as Malibran and Grisi had built their fame on those florid operas—and so in the future would that fine Australian soprano Joan Sutherland—but in London in 1888 many operagoers wondered why Harris included such old-fashioned, undramatic works in his repertoire.

English critics, with few exceptions, believed that drama was the essence of opera and that acting was more important than singing. Consequently those critics who reviewed *Lucia*, when it opened on May 24, were more interested in the drama Melba could convey than in her trills and roulades. The *Times*, after decrying the opera as "hackneyed and tedious" and devoting a few words to Melba's "well-trained voice," mostly praised her ability to act. Others wrote similarly, thinking well of her acting and giving cautious praise to her singing. Their verdict was that "she made a good impression"—nothing more.

Melba read the reviews with incredulity. How could it be that Brussels adored her voice but London critics scarcely noticed it? Her feelings were echoed by Harris, who considered the reviews most unfair. He had watched the audience stand and cheer her after the famous sextet and the more famous "mad scene," and he was determined that the public should know of it. On the day of the second performance of *Lucia*, he placed a paragraph in the *Times*, explaining that "the house literally rose to Madame Melba, the occupants of the boxes and stalls all joining in the spontaneous genuine ovation, and the triumphant and deafening applause."

A few days later Harris offered her the role of Gilda on a night when Albani was not singing. Melba's spirits rose, for here at last was a type of opera that might win the critics over. Rehearsals were barely under way, however, when she began to suffer from nerves. On June 12, the day of the performance, she awoke with a hoarse voice, and as she sat in her dressing room, she summoned Harris and insisted he should warn the audience before the curtain rose. On stage, however, her nerves were calmed and her self-discipline and training took over. "Caro nome" with its long trill received an encore, and by the end of the quartet the audience was shouting for more.

Once again she could scarcely believe her eyes when she read the notices. No less than fifteen newspapers praised her acting and said little about her singing, though one distinguished critic did call her "a fluent and brilliant vocalist." It was barely a drop in the ocean compared to the generous praise from the critics in Belgium. She threw down the papers in disgust.

Harris now offered her the supporting role of the page in Verdi's *Un ballo in maschera*. For a moment she was tempted. The Polish tenor Jean de Reszke, considered by some to be the finest tenor in Europe, was singing in *Un ballo*, and she longed to sing with him; but even de Reszke was not enough to induce her to stay. She asked Harris to release her, and she and George returned by train to Paris in time to sing at Madame's soirée on July 19.

During these troubled few months, both the Marchesis had been working busily on Melba's behalf. Salvatore had been in conflict with Strakosch's heirs, who were still claiming Melba as their property, and Madame had continued to promote the merits of her protégée to the directors of the Paris Opéra. Neither she nor Salvatore would rest until Melba was singing in Paris which, in their view, was the only place in the world to afford a "real artistic baptism."

Melba, certain the Monnaie would refuse permission for her to sing in Paris, turned her attention to the operas scheduled later for Brussels. She immersed herself in *Lakmé* and *Hamlet* and took lessons from their composers in Paris through the rest of the summer. She was now on the friendliest terms with charming but exacting Léo Delibes and fatherly Ambroise Thomas, two of the most distinguished composers of opera in France. To these she now added the friendship and tutelage of Charles Gounod, the finest French composer of the day, whose *Roméo et Juliette* she was also due to sing at the Monnaie. She would never forget her first time in Gounod's long music room with its astonishing table that could turn into a piano at the press of a button. The seventy-year-old composer, with his magnetic eyes and white beard, was dressed like a true bohemian in velvet skullcap and smoking jacket, with a flowing bow around his neck. She remembered that before greeting her he blotted the letter he was writing with sand instead of blotting paper. It was her first glimpse of Gounod's old-fashioned ways.

He taught her his three best-known operas: *Faust, Mireille,* and *Roméo et Juliette*. He believed that the voice was a canvas on which the emotions must be painted; and he sang portions of the roles himself, effortlessly taking on the "voice and temperament of the character he was interpreting." Thanks to his inspiring example, she began at last to understand what acting was about.

In October 1888 Melba opened in *Lakmé* at the Monnaie in Brussels, and followed in November as Ophélie in *Hamlet*. It was bliss once more to tread the boards of the Monnaie and be living again in her little terrace house at 3 Rue de Bailly. Taking brief leave to travel to Paris to hear Adelina Patti and Jean de Reszke sing *Roméo et Juliette* under Gounod's baton, she saw and heard the thrill that passed through the theatre when the great composer signaled to the waiting orchestra: she seemed to hear "the beating of heavenly wings." Although Patti was forty-five, she sang like a goddess, and Jean de Reszke strode the stage like a god and used his voice "with an artistry, which can be only called perfection." When it was whispered that he might sing at the Monnaie in February, she rushed to write to him, and was sad when he denied the report. But she was charmed by the final sentence in his letter: "I kiss your little hand," he wrote, "if that is what you wish of me."

That November in Antwerp she met another musical giant: Johann Kruse's master, Joseph Joachim, the most famous violinist in Europe. He and Melba were appearing in the same charity concert, and during the rehearsal Joachim sat in the stalls and cheerfully and mischievously played a guessing game with a nervous boy performer. When Melba sang a song by Bizet, he said to the boy, "Handel, I think," and then a few minutes later, "No, no. I was wrong; it is by Johann Sebastian Bach." The boy is said to have looked at Joachim's bearded face in puzzlement, until he realized that the great man was joking.

Like the nervous boy, many others found Joachim formidable, but Melba adored him. Their rapport was instantaneous, affection for Johann Kruse being their initial bond. She was conscious of Joachim's attraction to her, and she realized he had a partiality for female singers. He had married a contralto, whom he later divorced, but his taste for singers remained, and at fifty-seven he could still woo like a young man. With all his charm he tried to persuade her to make a concert tour with him to Germany, and when he returned to Berlin he began negotiating on her behalf.

Melba liked the idea of touring Germany, but Madame promptly opposed it. In fact she was determined that Melba's career should be controlled by no one but herself. "All those who have followed my advice," she warned severely, "have made great careers, the others have struggled and suffered without ever becoming *either famous or rich*. You understand, my dear Nellie, that your future clings to my heart; you should not blindly follow the advice of others."

Melba probably felt relief that the Monnaie withheld permission for her to spend the forthcoming Christmas in Paris. While she loved Madame and was grateful for her network of connections in the opera houses of Europe, she was growing restive under her iron rule. Nor was Madame's the only absence that caused her relief that December.

Spending Christmas peacefully with her son at the Rue de Bailly, she was profoundly thankful that Charlie had sailed to Australia.

On February 21, 1889, the Monnaie's new production of *Roméo et Juliette* opened, and Madame missed it. The reason was Salvatore's gout: he was far too ill for her to leave him alone. "Imagine my despair," Madame wrote to Melba. "I am doubly sad; for I watch him suffer and at the same time cannot come to Brussels." Salvatore added a message in his stilted English: "Your unhappy desperate friend wishes you the greatest success in the world."

In the end Melba was secretly pleased that Madame missed the opening night because she was certain to have been vexed. The English critics' insistence on dramatic power had persuaded Melba to attempt a heavier style of singing, one that was matched by her Roméo who was a well-known "bellower." The performance won a standing ovation from the audience but disappointed those who, like Madame, worshipped the light *bel canto* tone. The critic of *L'Indépendence Belge* was disappointed with the new Melba, and his review found its way to the Rue Jouffroy. "I presume, my dearest Nellie," wrote Madame after she had read it, "that being surrounded by people who scream you will have—without wishing it and without realising it yourself—*forced the medium register too hard. Watch yourself!*"

Melba obediently lightened her tone and the opera continued triumphantly through March. Such was its success that Augustus Harris heard of it at Covent Garden and, needing a Juliette for his forthcoming season, he wrote to Melba. His friendly invitation was accompanied by a letter from Lady de Grey, the powerful patron who had originally suggested Melba's name to Harris. Lady de Grey had been distressed by the London reviews of *Lucia* and *Rigoletto*, and she begged Melba to try again in that city. "One of those most anxious for your return is the Princess of Wales," she told Melba. "I know that things were badly arranged for you before, but if you come back I promise you that it will be very different. You will be under my care, and I shall see that you do not lack either friends or hospitality."

Other tempting invitations sped in from the Paris Opéra and from Berlin, requiring Melba to make difficult decisions. She postponed Berlin, accepted Harris's terms for June and July provided she could pick her own roles, and to Madame's delight also signed a contract with the

Paris Opéra. The Opéra was the first of her new engagements—the vital test had arrived. But before she could leave the Monnaie there were presents to receive and farewells to attend. The subscribers to the season gave her a diamond, the king of the Belgians presented her with the gold medal of the Belgian Conservatoire, and at her final performance more than sixty bouquets were brought to her on stage. She was so overcome that she buried her face in her hands.

There was one last hurdle to be surmounted before she could leave. The restless Charlie was back in England and thinking of visiting Brussels or Paris. Melba therefore turned for advice to Madame, who by now was conversant with all the ups and downs of the fragile marriage: "I am awfully afraid (entre nous)," she wrote, "my Husband is going to arrive very soon. I am most awfully uneasy as you know how afraid I am of him when he has one of his mad fits on." Fortunately Charlie decided to stay in England.

On the morning of May 2 Melba and George were packed and ready to leave Brussels in the train for Paris. Madame had their rooms prepared and was counting the hours till their arrival. "At midday," she wrote, "the carriage will be at the station and the apartment is all ready for my charming daughter." As a postscript she added one of those phrases Melba loved to read: "A thousand kisses from your affectionate *maman*."

CHAPTER SEVEN

It Is Applause I Live For

MELBA AND GEORGE arrived in a Paris abuzz with excitement. The Great Exhibition was about to open and its most
daring feature, the Eiffel Tower, already rose like a gigantic metal skele-
ton from the Field of Mars. Its triumphant spirit infected the populace.
Parties and balls and pageants and dinners were held everywhere, not
least at the welcoming École Marchesi. On May 4, 1889, there was a
dinner for Melba, and a week later Madame's pupils, past and present,
gave their annual concert for the Montmartre charities. Gounod and
Delibes accompanied their own songs and Melba was chief soloist. For
Madame it was a truly memorable day.

Melba herself was in a state of elation because her sisters Annie and
Belle had arrived in Paris. For three years she had been holding back
her homesickness, and now, at the sight of them, waves of nostalgia engulfed her, and she could not hear enough about her brothers and sister
and her father who remained in Melbourne. At times Melba would
have given almost anything to be back at Doonside.

Annie and Belle were overjoyed to be in Paris, and using five-year-
old George as their guide and interpreter, they set about seeing the city.
George found their antics and broken French hilarious, but there were
times when they embarrassed him painfully, especially on trams. Some
days he would run to the opposite end of the carriage to be spared the
shame of having to intervene and speak to the conductor on their behalf. When his aunts cried out beseechingly, "Tell him, Georgie!" he
would give a Gallic shrug and pretend he did not know them.

Carefully prepared for her debut in *Hamlet* at the Opéra on May 8, Melba was frustrated. The opening was postponed because the singer playing the queen was ill. Then, on the very morning of the first performance, her Hamlet awoke with no voice, and she was obliged to sing alongside a substitute baritone. She was not even certain that her own voice could fill the vast horseshoe of an auditorium, which was almost half as large again as the Monnaie. By opening night she was a bundle of nerves and, at times, almost voiceless with a form of stage fright.

Waiting in the audience were her two sisters, feeling like country cousins. They had been almost overcome by the splendor of the building as they made their way through the crowded foyer and up the ornate staircase; and sitting in their box surrounded by bejeweled ladies, they felt as if they had strayed into wonderland. Could all this pomp possibly be centered on young Nellie Mitchell of Doonside?

The audience at the Opéra was notoriously hard to please, but when Melba came on stage a flutter of murmurs welcomed her. Her "pretty appearance," observed the critic of *Ménestral*, "her natural distinction, her grace and elegance won her instant favor." At first her fears almost numbed her throat, but soon her notes were "pure and limpid."

It was the fourth act, with the "mad scene" that the audience and critics were impatiently anticipating. When Melba glided on stage in a white robe with her hair flowing down her shoulders, the atmosphere was filled with expectancy, and by the time her trills and scales and vocal leaps were flying about the theatre, the air was crackling with excitement. The audience was rocked "to its inmost fibres and quivering with emotion," wrote the critic from *Le Figaro*. Once the quivering subsided, nearly two thousand people were "yelling and applauding as only the French can." Melba was recalled three times after the curtain dropped. It was more than thirty years since a soprano at the Opéra had been accorded three curtain calls after the "mad scene." Her triumph had exceeded even Madame's dreams.

As she lay in bed at the Hotel Scribe the next morning, she read in a dozen papers that she was tall and deliciously pretty, and that her voice had exquisite purity and flexibility and precision. She was compared to the role's creator, Christine Nilsson, and to Adelina Patti, and, even more flatteringly, to the legendary *bel canto* soprano Maria Malibran. What must have pleased her most was the praise for her act-

ing. She "gave dramatic expression rare among our Ophélies," wrote
Le Figaro. She performed with "real dramatic purpose and with highly
intelligent stage movement," wrote *Ménestral.* Those months she had
spent devising ways to express emotion without impeding her voice
were at last yielding their reward.

That morning she put on a blue peignoir trimmed with lace and in
a coquettish mood received a reporter from London's *Pall Mall Gazette*
in her suite at the Hotel Scribe. As she sat amid vases of roses and li-
lacs, she told him she was "intensely happy," and she said it so girlishly
that the reporter almost expected her to clap her hands. She explained
that she was a flower that blossomed only before the footlights. "I do
not exaggerate," she said "when I say that I must be on the stage or I
must die." When the reporter asked if she owned many jewels, she exclaimed, "Handfulls!" and plunged her hands into her jewel box, pulling out chains and rings and strings of pearls. "Oh, I care nothing about
them," she told him. "It is applause I live for."

The next four weeks were sweet for Melba. She sang Ophélie and
Gilda and became the favorite star of the Parisians. Even her foreign
nationality was forgiven. "She is an Australian, but at heart a Parisi-
enne," wrote one newspaper. She also had the deep satisfaction of astonishing her sisters. "A triumph is not a triumph," she said, "until one
is able to demonstrate it to one's family"; they are "always the last to
believe that their duckling has become a swan." Her pride reached its
zenith when the directors of the Opéra decided to mount *Lucia di Lammermoor* for the first time in more than twenty years, especially to show
off her vocal expertise.

Before she could appear as Lucia, there came an unexpected opportunity. The American soprano Emma Eames had suffered miseries of
envy at Melba's supremacy ever since their time together at the École
Marchesi. It had reached unmanageable proportions during Melba's
months at the Monnaie, because for part of that time Emma also lived
in Brussels, hoping to make her debut but not achieving it. Emma had
at last been engaged by the Paris Opéra and was currently singing Juliette. On the afternoon of one of her Paris performances, she fell ill.
A substitute Juliette was rapidly sought, and Melba offered to take her
place. This was a "charming display of camaraderie," according to a Parisian journalist. The truth was that Melba seized the chance with both

hands because it gave her a chance to sing with Jean de Reszke and also a chance to annoy Emma.

The news that Melba was appearing as Juliette spread fast, and critics hurried to the theatre to see how she would perform. Melba sang superbly, making Emma seem inferior: a verdict that the reviewers were mean enough to voice. From that moment onward, Emma's jealousy of Melba turned into enmity.

In one sense, Melba must have felt satisfied at upstaging a competitor; in another, she must have regretted it, for it unleashed an ill feeling that she had so far been at pains to avoid. Knowing that opera companies were breeding grounds for resentment and that one must always be on guard, she had tried to show goodwill to almost everyone at the Opéra. She was so sweet-tempered and good-natured to all, gushed one columnist, that she was called "Sweet Melba." An English journalist named Robert Sherard, who interviewed her at the Hotel Scribe, was amazed by her generous praise for her colleagues. Melba "spoke so nicely of everybody," he wrote, "it was a pleasure to listen to her."

Meanwhile Melba prepared to sing *Lucia*, which despite its much-lamented outdatedness, drew a large and glamorous crowd to its opening night. The evening proved memorable. Scarcely had the tenor, Emile Cossira, come on stage than his voice grew hoarse and he clutched his throat. Melba tried to help him by singing his part as well as her own, but it soon became clear that they could not continue, and the curtain was rung down. No understudy had been provided, and confusion ensued until Melba remembered that she had given a ticket that night to Pierre Engel, her former tenor in Brussels—the singer whom Marchesi had unkindly dubbed "the bellower." A messenger was sent to summon the bellower from his seat, and he was bundled into Cossira's costume. Half an hour later *Lucia* recommenced, gaining strength with every minute. The first two acts received ovations, but they were nothing to the demonstration after the "mad scene." Melba "fairly electrified the whole house." Next day the critics, beside themselves with superlatives, called her exquisite, delicious, the total mistress of her voice: she had touched the summit of the singer's art.

Among those who came to see *Lucia* was Lady de Grey, Melba's English patron. Her ladyship was also staying at the Hotel Scribe, and on a brilliant spring morning, she invited Melba to her suite. Melba would remember how the sunshine fell on the brilliant green of Lady de Grey's dress. "She was sitting at her writing table," Melba recalled, "and as she turned around the sun illuminated her lovely profile, making me catch my breath with the beauty of it."

Melba was well aware that in prestige the Countess de Grey out-ranked Madame Marchesi's aristocratic patrons. She also knew that Gladys—pronounced "Glay-dis"—was one of the "professional beau-ties," a select group of a half-dozen society ladies who, like today's su-permodels, were constantly talked about and whose portraits were on sale to the public. Melba had probably seen her picture in shop win-dows, but to see her in the flesh was a rare treat. Everything about her seemed impressive. She was six feet tall—an unusual height then for a woman—and "her dark eyes and brilliant colouring made any woman near her look pale."

Her looks were not entirely English, having been inherited from the Russian countess who married Gladys's grandfather, the Earl of Pem-broke. Russian style, good looks, and immense wealth had descended to Gladys's father, Sidney Herbert, who earned fame as secretary for war and as collaborator with Florence Nightingale. With such a back-ground Gladys could not fail to make a mark, but whereas her father's talents went into philanthropy and politics, hers went mainly into the pursuit of pleasure. Some of her pleasures were impeccably respectable. She ran a glittering salon at her house in Bruton Street—"A Mecca," it was said, "for all the gifted artists and foreign intellectuals that come to London." She harmoniously mixed guests from various backgrounds, rendering her invitations "amongst the most prized in England." She was also capable of loyalty and friendship, and remained a lifelong con-fidante of Queen Victoria's daughter-in-law, the Princess of Wales.

Some of Gladys's interests were on the louche side. From childhood she had shown a restless desire for excitement; one of her governesses had predicted she would "go to the devil in a coach and four." In adult-hood she fed her cravings with bizarre friends and bizarre activities. Once, in Paris, the police are said to have cordoned off part of the red-light district so that she could inspect the brothels and prostitutes. "She had one fault," wrote her closest female friend, "and that was an overwhelming curiosity to know everything and experience every sen-sation, and this inquisitiveness led her into dark places and amongst undesirable people, but fortunately it neither altered or debased her mind."

At the time of her first meeting with Melba, Gladys was in her second marriage. Her first husband, the young Earl of Lonsdale, had been a drunkard and a womanizer who conducted his liaisons in a rented house in Bryanston Street where he died in 1882, leaving Gladys with a baby daughter. Although no moral comparison was possible between Charlie and Lord Lonsdale, Melba's position as an unattached wife may well have called forth Gladys's empathy and established an early affinity between them.

Gladys's second husband, Frederick de Grey, was far tamer, but he had money and position, a kind heart, and remarkable skill with a gun—he was reputedly one of the five best shots in England. Lady Randolph Churchill remembered him shooting fifty-two birds out of fifty-four, using only one hand to hold his gun and pull the trigger. At Gladys's urging, Frederick joined the syndicate of five prominent men who in 1888 took over the reorganization of the Covent Garden Opera, and it was common knowledge that she was the power behind the scenes. Although in no sense a trained musician, she had a shrewd ear for a singer and a natural affinity for opera: in the words of one observer, its "pageantry and artifice suited her sophistication." In the regeneration of London's opera she found a mission worthy of her talents. "She wanted it," wrote another friend, "she intended to have it, and hers was a personality that usually got what it wanted."

Her unusual interest in Melba may have been partly self-serving. During her unhappy first marriage and widowhood, Gladys and the Jersey beauty Lillie Langtry became friends, each taking the other into a different social world. Lillie, of the alabaster skin and Grecian profile, was the model and muse of painters and poets, and introduced Gladys into artistic circles. Gladys in turn introduced Lillie into the select group that surrounded the Prince of Wales, and basked in reflected glory as her protégée ensnared the prince. Gladys was now looking for entry into the bohemian world of opera singers, and she may have chosen Melba as her guide. As with Lillie, she was prepared, in return, to promote her protégée's career both socially and professionally.

At that first meeting in Paris, Melba must have been heartened by her patroness's kindness. When she confided her fears that Albani would again have first choice of roles, Gladys swept the fears away in a moment. She would interview Harris personally and make sure that Melba received her choice. When Melba apologized for being almost a bore, Gladys replied reassuringly, "How can you talk of 'boring' me? I am only too happy to be of any use to you."

At the start of June Melba arrived in England. What a difference to her arrival of twelve months before! Gone were the gloomy lodgings at Bayswater. Instead, probably on Gladys's advice, she installed herself, prima-donna style, at the Grand Hotel in Trafalgar Square in the heart of London. The social season was in full cry, and Gladys and her friends were devoting fourteen hours a day to pleasure. Engagements began at noon, with walks or horse rides, followed by luncheons, drives in the park, teas, dinners, suppers, and balls. Melba knew the importance of that social round and the worth of the invitations that came to her from Gladys and her friends. They constituted the magic key to a privileged world, and many singers and artists and patrons would have given anything to receive them.

On June 6 Melba sang the role of Gilda at Covent Garden along with Jean Lassalle, the voiceless Hamlet from Paris. Maybe Gladys's influence extended to the press, or maybe London critics did not want to seem less discerning than their Parisian counterparts, but whatever the reason Melba's voice was enthusiastically praised. The *Standard* expressed the general opinion: "Madame Melba seems absolutely incapable of false intonation, and is almost unsurpassed in the purity and sweetness of her tones . . . none but the warmest terms of admiration can do justice to the performance."

Departing from the rule that all performances should be in Italian, Harris prepared to mount a French-language version of *Roméo et Juliette*, with Melba and Jean de Reszke as the star-crossed lovers. At last she was to have a season with the magnetic de Reszke; she was almost aflame with excitement. The chemistry generated between the two produced a soaring performance, which audiences and critics were quick to recognize. "Madame Melba's beautiful voice and excellent method are heard at their very best," enthused the hard-to-please *Times*. As the public flocked to the opera, Harris quickly advertised more performances.

Partly through the personal influence of Lady de Grey but mostly because of the opera's merits, the Prince and Princess of Wales became fans of *Roméo et Juliette*. Queen Victoria also heard the favorable reports, and Melba was among those commanded to sing at a state concert at Buckingham Palace on June 28. Thrilled at the thought of appearing before that little black figure whom she had seen at the Colonial and Indian Exhibition, she chose the "Bell Song" from *Lakmé* and anxiously awaited the day. Alas, on the morning of the performance she awoke with a cold, and a doctor delivered the miserable verdict that she must not sing. Four days later and in good voice, she made up for part of her disappointment by singing at a gala concert at Covent Garden held especially for the Shah of Persia. In a theatre decked with flowers and packed with princes and dukes, Melba sang the "mad scene" from *Lucia* and Juliette's waltz, the last by special request of the Prince of Wales. Next day *Punch* delivered its verdict: "Madame Melba continues to be the star of the day."

The invitations from high places multiplied. One of the first was from the chairman of the Covent Garden Opera Syndicate, Lord Charles Beresford, a future admiral and close friend of the Prince of Wales. His wife, Lady Charles Beresford, was one of the most fashionable hostesses in London. Born without eyebrows, she slapped false eyebrows haphazardly across her forehead. As one friend put it, "a firm eyebrow drawn of charcoal and steeply arched might be the decoration on one side," while she might have "forgotten to draw the eyebrow on the other side, or had put on an eyebrow of another species made of an adhesive strip of a sort of fur."

At Lady Charles's, and at a party given especially for her by Lady de Grey, Melba met high life at its highest. A succession of stunning, aristocratic women drifted into the de Greys' drawing room: the Duchess of Leinster in white satin and sapphires, Lady Dudley almost covered in turquoises, the lovely Lady Warwick, and the equally lovely Lady Helen Vincent. In past years at Doonside, Melba and her sisters had pored over their portraits in the social pages of magazines. To meet these goddesses in the flesh, at a party given in her honor, was almost more than she could believe.

Melba soon realized that this small and select group which centered on the Prince and Princess of Wales contained a few who would normally have been considered too vulgar for aristocratic society. These were rich bankers and industrialists, and also actresses, for whom the prince had a special partiality. The prince craved pleasure and favored those who had the wit and money to indulge him. Denied a share in ruling the country by his dominating mother, he drowned his frustration in eating, shooting, and gambling, and in sleeping with pretty women.

Melba met the Prince of Wales several times that season and they took to one another immediately. He said that he liked American women because they were livelier, better educated, and less hampered by etiquette, and he may well have liked Melba for those same reasons. She was well educated and, thanks to her Australian upbringing, unusually outspoken. Melba in turn found the prince intelligent, courteous and tactful, and at ease relaxing in the company of his friends. In Gladys's drawing room, where he seemed so like "a happy schoolboy," she had to keep reminding herself that he was her future king.

The opera season closed at the end of July, after which fashionable London took a holiday. On the final night, Melba sang Juliette at a gala performance to celebrate the marriage of the Prince of Wales's daughter to the Duke of Fife. The boxes were filled by the prince and his family and wedding guests from the great royal families of Europe. The brilliance of the scene inspired the singers, and Melba and de Reszke sang with unusual fire.

Two empty months now lay ahead. Melba was relieved, for she needed the rest. She had made plans for George, Annie, Belle, and herself to share a holiday in Europe through the month of August. Meanwhile she traveled to Rustington to collect George and to see Charlie, who was living on his farm. George loved the country life and was learning to ride a pony, and Charlie was seizing the chance to turn his boy into a proper English gentleman. Hoping for more time with the lad, he proposed that he accompany the holidaymakers to Europe. Although Melba's heart must have fallen, she felt obliged to agree.

Before they could set out, there was a ceremony to be performed: Lady Armstrong was grieved to discover that her grandson had not been baptized. The ceremony was carried out immediately, and George's godmother was none other than Winifred Rawson, who had known him as a baby in the sugar town of Marian, and was now living with her husband in England. As the baptismal water drained noisily out of the font, solemn little George called out in French, "There, that's the Devil leaving."

With George christened, Melba and her son and sisters traveled with Charlie to Paris. There, in a bedroom at the Hotel Buckingham, all hell broke loose. The initial cause was a misplaced pearl tiepin, for which Charlie blamed his wife; but this trivial dispute so escalated that Charlie seized his razor and slashed his hat. Having destroyed his hat with this implusive, aggressive gesture, he reputedly turned to Melba, saying, "It would have been your head if you had been there." Whether she exaggerated one cannot know, but three years later she swore on a Bible that her memory was accurate. She claimed that she was so distressed that she ran to her sisters' room for safety.

After such a troubled start, it was a wonder that the trip continued, but the end of August found the travelers on the shores of Lake Geneva. There they lodged at the Beau Rivage Palace, one of the most luxurious hotels in Europe, built beside the lakeside port of Ouchy, close to Lausanne. The hotel still stands, and its charming gardens still run down to the tranquil waters of the Swiss lake.

Surrounded by breathtaking views of majestic mountains and blue water, the couple resumed their warfare. Realizing the futility of trying to halt Melba's career, Charlie made an attempt to reshape George in his own masculine image. Remembering his own free-roaming childhood, and the way George had blossomed in the carefree life at Rustington, Charlie believed that Melba's restrictive discipline was thwarting the child's natural initiative. Wanting a spirited, adventurous son, not a pampered mother's boy, he kept urging George to defy his mother. Once, beside the lake, he persuaded the boy to throw stones at his mother and aunts. Perturbing as Melba found this attack on her authority, it was nothing to the growing fear that she might lose her son. In Queensland during the past eighteen months, Charlie had transformed the marshy land at Sarina into a working pastoral property and had built a house overlooking the sea. She was increasingly afraid that he planned to take his son to live with him there. She did not doubt his power to do so, because in the eyes of the law a father's rights outranked a mother's.

To improve the land at Sarina, Charlie needed money, and once again he asserted his right to part of Melba's earnings. Tempers flared and, according to Melba's testimony, Charlie let fly with a heavy candlestick that struck her in the back. Whether she retaliated by hurling the candlestick back at him one does not know—rumor says she threw things at Charlie—but she eased the tension by giving him two hundred pounds. In September, to her great relief, he sailed for Australia.

Melba knew it would strengthen her claim to custody of George if she and her son had an established home. After a few weeks she took a lease on a fashionable apartment at 97 Avenue des Champs Élysées. To her delight, George welcomed the idea of living again in Paris, for he loved its parks, especially the Bois de Boulogne with its merry-go-round and goat carts. A reporter, discovering him there just after his sixth birthday, recorded an interview; in a melodious little voice that sounded like the song of a tiny bird, the child intimated that he loved Switzerland, London, and Paris, but if he had to choose he loved Australia best. Melba may have taught him to love Australia best, but she had no intention of allowing him to live there.

During the following six months in Paris, Melba was also to sing *Hamlet, Roméo et Juliette,* and *Faust,* and while she felt competent in the first two roles, the third was another matter. She had sung the role of Marguerite in *Faust* only once, at an unscheduled performance at Covent Garden, and knew that she had struggled with it. Seeking an answer to her problem, she persuaded Madame to arrange a visit to Sarah Bernhardt, the finest actress in France.

Never would Melba forget the room in which Bernhardt received them. Rather like a bazaar, it was strewn with stuffed animals, busts portraying the actress, tapestries, antiquities, and dying plants. The divine Sarah declared her intention of teaching Melba "to act like an angel," and began at once with Marguerite's part. Her instruction was an amalgam of subtle detail and common sense. She vividly explained, with dramatic gestures, that when the dying Valentine curses Marguerite for yielding to Faust and tells her that her white hands will never again spin with the virgins, Marguerite must whip her hands behind her back in shame. "See," she told Melba, suiting her actions to her words. All the while she stared at Melba with an expression of such torture in her eyes that thereafter, whenever Melba heard Valentine's curse, she "called up the vision of Sarah Bernhardt."

While Bernhardt's lessons were inspiring, it was Gounod's lessons that counted. He was delighted to have Melba as his pupil again, believing her to be the very embodiment of all his heroines. At rehearsals of *Faust* and *Roméo et Juliette* and even at performances, he sat in the director's box and studied every move and listened to every note. Afterward he gave his "*chère* enfant," as he called her, lengthy criticism and sometimes, if she pleased him, a kiss.

Gounod's teaching paid dividends. When she sang Juliette and Marguerite at the Opéra, she received long ovations. An Australian visitor heard her in *Faust* that season and was astounded to hear the storms of applause that rewarded the "Jewel Song." The whole of the vast Parisian audience stood and waved handkerchiefs and programs, and cheered itself hoarse. Of all singers at the Opéra, wrote one critic, "she is the priestess, she is the most feted."

In February 1890, with permission from the Paris Opéra, Melba set out for Monte Carlo, the capital of the tiny principality of Monaco, set high on a promontory above the Mediterranean. Over the past twenty years Monte Carlo had become a rich man's playground, with a splendid casino and scores of villas and grand hotels. On balmy nights, when the lamps glowed in the terraced gardens and the sea gleamed silver beneath the city, it was the most beautiful resort on the coast. But a town dependent on gambling had drawbacks. Although kings and millionaires patronized its tables, so did the riffraff, and, since fortunes were lost as well as won, the town had its share of suicides. Monte Carlo needed culture to lend it respectability. Charles Garnier, the architect of the Paris Opéra House, was commissioned to design an opera house in Monte Carlo, and in 1879 a smaller version of his Paris masterpiece was built next to the casino overlooking the sea.

Shortly before Melba's arrival, Monaco gained a new princess, the glamorous, American-born Alice Heine, heiress to a banking fortune. Before her marriage to Monaco's ruler, Alice had run a salon in Paris, so it was she who fostered the city's culture. Fired by her patronage, Raoul Gunsbourg, the flamboyant new director of the Opéra de Monte Carlo, planned a brilliant season. On the advice of Léon Jehin, a former conductor at the Monnaie, he recruited Melba.

When Melba played Juliette on February 5, the ornate little theatre was crammed. By the final curtain nearly everyone was praising Melba and bewailing the leading man, who became Melba's leading man again a few days later when she sang Ophélie. His name was Etienne Dereims, and he sang the tenor role of Roméo and the baritone role of Hamlet with equal incompetence. Melba, however, profited by the comparison. Princess Alice, sitting in the royal box, let it be known that those who missed her performances had missed the great event of the season. Melba, she announced, was undoubtedly the new Adelina Patti.

CHAPTER EIGHT

Melba's Duke

MELBA ARRIVED BACK in London at the end of May 1890 in a mood of elation. In a mere four years she had stormed Europe's operatic heights and turned the London critics' apathy or lukewarm response into acclaim. So popular was she that Harris was proposing to place her in seven operas in the forthcoming season. Following her reentry in *Roméo et Juliette*, she was to sing three Gildas, three Lucias, four Juliettes, one Ophélie, and one Marguerite. She was also to sing Elsa in an Italian-language version of Wagner's *Lohengrin*. Neither she nor Madame cared for German operas, nor did Wagner's heavy music and dramatic style suit her voice or temperament. But Richard Wagner was now increasingly seen as the greatest of all composers of opera, and if she wished her career to prosper it was almost mandatory to sing his work.

Melba's opening night on June 3 proved one of the most brilliant of the season. In the presence of the Prince and Princess of Wales, high society crowded the boxes. Critics were almost united in declaring that Melba "sang with even more *aplomb* and brilliancy than last season." The *Daily Chronicle* argued that she was the closest to the Juliet of Shakespeare the operatic public was ever likely to see. A week later, feeling rather jittery—for she had had no chance to rehearse with the orchestra—she attempted the role of Elsa. To her surprise, the audience and critics loved her. There was "never a better Elsa," wrote the *Era*; and the *Pall Mall Gazette* went even further in declaring that "she plays the part, sings the music, and looks the character to perfection."

Embarked on the busiest season she had so far encountered, Melba had little time for the persistent problem of Charlie. At the start of their marriage she had convinced herself that, being cleverer than he, she would be able to manage him; but when she later realized that he was not so easily managed, she focused her energies on her career and her child and elbowed her husband to the margin of her life. In Switzerland she was forced to recognize that Charlie, by refusing to stay on the margin, was threatening the welfare of her son. Having once balked at the idea of legal separation, she was arriving at the view that it was the only solution.

Out of the blue, someone else was about to have a dramatic effect on her marital life. Philippe, the Duke of Orléans, was the eldest son of the Comte de Paris, heir to the abolished French throne. Although France had been a republic for two decades, there were many who agitated for the return of the Orléanist monarchy, and it was by no means impossible that the comte, and then his son, would one day be king of France. Young Philippe had been brought up to expect that the mantle of kingship would fall upon his shoulders, and he often found it an uncomfortable burden.

Although destined perhaps for the French throne, the Duke of Orléans had been born in England. He was the great grandson of Louis Philippe, the most democratic of French kings until the mob forced him from his throne in 1848. King Louis Philippe took refuge in England, and Philippe was born during his family's exile. Between the ages of three and seventeen he was permitted to live in France, but in May 1886, just when Melba landed in England, a nervous republic banned Philippe and his father from French soil for life. Accordingly, for the next three years the young duke trained at the Royal Military College at Sandhurst and saw service as a British officer in India. Early in 1888 he left the army and returned to England to prepare for his twenty-first birthday. Under French law, all male citizens of twenty-one were required to report for compulsory military service and, as Philippe counted himself a citizen of France, he planned to defy the edict of exile and report for military duty. On February 7, 1890, while Melba was singing in Monte Carlo, he presented himself at a recruiting office in Paris and requested that he be enlisted as a humble private. When the bewildered sergeant asked his name, he replied emphatically, "Louis Philippe Robert, duc d'Orléans."

Nervous at the prospect of enrolling the banished heir of an abolished throne in the army of the republic, the poor sergeant summoned his superiors. The duke was arrested, convicted, and sentenced to two years in prison—but not before he had made a declaration that moved every patriotic Frenchman. In a vibrant voice he cried out in court, "Prison will be less cruel than exile, for this prison will be on the soil of France."

So magnificent a gesture could not fail to melt hearts. Monarchists, some republicans, even socialists gathered beneath his window at the Conciergerie prison and doffed their caps, and cheered and waved. They called him *"le premier conscrit de France"*—the first conscript of France—or more affectionately and less respectfully, *"Prince Gamelle,"* a *gamelle* being a pannikin or tin mug that the common soldiers drank from in the mess.

Embarrassed by Prince Pannikin's popularity, the French president signed an order for his release, and on June 4 he was escorted by train across the Swiss border. He traveled by a roundabout route to Belgium, where he was feted, and in England he was met by a large band of supporters. Later that week the young hero held court at his father's house at East Sheen, near London.

Among those who welcomed him back were several members of the British royal family, which was not surprising, for the two families were linked. Queen Victoria's favorite uncle, the king of the Belgians, had married a sister of King Louis Philippe, and the queen regarded the Orléans exiles as part of her extended family. The relationship became particularly close because the Prince of Wales's eldest son, Eddy, had fallen in love with Philippe's sister, Princess Hélène of Orléans. Eddy's sisters and mother adored the girl and approved the romance, notwithstanding the fact that Hélène was a Roman Catholic and thus forbidden by law to marry the direct heir to the British throne.

When Philippe returned so gloriously from France, the royal family could not wait to congratulate him. Four days after his arrival, he lunched with the Prince and Princess of Wales, and on June 12 he sat with the princess and her daughters in the royal box at Covent Garden and watched a performance of *Roméo et Juliette*. Melba sang the role of Juliette, but whether she was called to the royal box is not known. A fortnight later, Melba and other celebrated singers and elocutionists,

Bernhardt among them, appeared at a morning concert at St. James's Hall in support of a pianist named Zoe Caryll. Melba sang "Caro nome" with her usual flair, and the duke heard her. Afterward he congratulated her in the performers' room. A newspaper report of their meeting is preserved in her cutting book, with a cross in ink beside it. It may have been the first time they spoke to one another.

When she and Philippe met in the performers' room, Melba had barely finished her singing, so the aura of the artist still clung to her. That aura, and her vitality and beauty and perfect command of French, created an overwhelming impression on the romantic duke. Melba, in turn, saw a charming boy: lithe and handsome with the same fair hair and sky-blue eyes that had so attracted her to Charlie. Indeed, as people would later point out, he strikingly resembled Charlie.

Like all of fashionable London, Melba was well aware that her admirer was probably the most glamorous royal duke in Europe. To be singled out for his attention must have been intoxicating. As he made no attempt to hide his admiration, she responded. She could not really have been surprised when Philippe began calling at her hotel, nor could she have had much doubt that he was proposing a love affair.

It was a serious step, but she did not hesitate. She may have had qualms when she realized he was engaged to his cousin Marguerite of Orléans; but thanks to quarrels between the prospective fathers-in-law, the engagement was virtually over, and the duke seems to have considered himself a free man. Melba certainly considered herself a free woman. Her marriage was dead, she longed for the delights of sex without the accompaniment of quarrels, and an affair with so coveted and charming a prize must have seemed irresistible. Through her friendship with Lady de Grey, she had entered a world where lovers were normal for married women. The Prince of Wales set the example by sleeping with a variety of ladies, most of them married to his friends and acquaintances.

Since Melba was contemplating a step into what, for her, was uncharted territory, one imagines she turned to Gladys for advice on the appropriate etiquette. She would have learned that it was mandatory in the prince's circle for adultery to be discreet and for lovers to preserve a veneer of respectability. Once an affair became public or threatened a marriage, the relationship as a rule had to be smartly extinguished, and jealousy and revenge were outlawed. Emotions, however, were not so easily governed. Thus Lord Charles Beresford and his wife would be banished from the prince's favor the following year when Lady Charles sought revenge on her husband's former lover. And Gladys—usually so discreet—came close to disgrace when she found she was sharing her lover, the journalist and parliamentarian Harry Cust, with Lady Londonderry, a hated rival. She is said to have broken into Cust's apartment and stolen Lady Londonderry's love letters, reading them aloud to friends before posting them to the deceived husband.

Although an affair was necessarily kept secret from the outside world, it was not kept secret from one's friends. Their support was needed to maintain discretion, and an up-to-date knowledge of the frequently changing pairs was essential to a hostess. At country houses care was taken to arrange guests' bedrooms so that lovers could visit secretly during the night. Even so, mistakes sometimes happened. The story goes that Lord Charles Beresford once blundered into the wrong bedroom and shouted "Cock-a doodle-doo" as he leaped into bed with a bishop.

In both town and country it was safer to dally by daylight, and the favorite time was from five to seven in the afternoon. Corsetless, and dressed in a flowing tea gown, a lady would receive her admirer in her boudoir, and no servant would dare enter until it was time to dress for dinner. Lovers reportedly left their hats and sticks on display in an outer room so that a husband, returning too early, could discreetly withdraw until the coast was clear.

Fortunately, with Charlie in Australia and George at Rustington, Melba was relatively safe from detection. Thus reassured, she could confidently welcome Philippe to her suite at the Metropole Hotel on Northumberland Avenue and rediscover what it was to be desired, admired, and courted. Philippe was everything she could have wished. In addition to his exalted rank and sexual magnetism, he proved to be intelligent and considerate, with a sense of fun and a genuine understanding of singing. Within weeks they were waiting feverishly for their next meeting. Between these, Melba resolutely devoted herself to her work. Her new opera, *Esmeralda*, by the English composer Arthur Goring Thomas, was to open July 12 and was taking an inordinate time to prepare. One rehearsal ran for five hours, leaving her so exhausted that she was obliged to cancel her next performance of *Lohengrin*.

In addition to her heavy operatic load, she appeared in numerous concerts. She sang in the annual state concert at Buckingham Palace on June 26 and, even more importantly, in a private concert for Queen Victoria at Windsor Castle on July 4. On the afternoon of that day, Melba, Jean de Reszke, his basso brother Edouard, and the baritone Jean Lassalle boarded a train for Windsor station, where a rickety cab conveyed them to the castle. The concert was scheduled for four o'clock, and since Melba was performing in London that night, she was anxious she should sing on time. She was dismayed when at a quarter to five they were still waiting for the queen's daughter, the Empress Frederick of Prussia. At five they began—in the absence of the empress—and worked their way through nine vocal items, including the last act of *Faust* sung by Melba and the de Reszkes. They had just concluded the concert when the empress returned from her drive and to Melba's dismay, Queen Victoria insisted that the whole program be given again. Melba was never sure how she managed to reach Covent Garden only fifteen minutes after curtain time, but she long remembered her pangs of hunger as she sang Gilda's music.

Melba eagerly accepted invitations to private recitals that season. In mid-July she sang for an old admirer of Gladys's, the colossally rich and musically sophisticated Alfred Rothschild, at his exquisite house at Seamore Place. A few days later Gladys invited her to sing for the Prince and Princess of Wales. "My dear friend," wrote Gladys to Melba, "the Princess has asked me to bring you to tea at Marlborough House at 5 tomorrow, after rehearsal, and she wld think it so nice if you wld sing a song for her and the Prince." The princess also wanted Jean and Edouard de Reszke to be in the party and asked if Jean could play the piano to accompany Melba. Her reason was that a professional accompanist would "make it stiff at once—and she wants it only to be a little tea party." The "little tea party" was described in the *Times* as one of the social events of the season.

At an impromptu musical evening at Gladys's house at Bruton Street, Edouard de Reszke, six feet tall and with a powerful bass voice, did his comical party piece from *Faust*. Parodying himself, he sang Méphistophélès's aria "Le veau d'or" with "melodramatic gestures and at full volume," so that "the windows rattled, and the crystal festoons of the chandelier quivered." His elder brother Jean, not to be outdone, perched himself on a pile of footstools and sang a parody of himself singing the "Prize Song" from *Die Meistersinger von Nürnberg*. The guests fell about laughing, especially as neither song managed to wake the Duke of Cambridge, who snoozed in a corner. Such fun could only have happened at Gladys's, wrote the novelist E. F. Benson, who was among the guests. It was "Bohemia in excelsis: Bohemia in tiaras."

Despite her social training at the École Marchesi and the advice of Gladys and the duke, Melba felt slightly nervous and unduly alert in grand society. Normally she loved a challenge, but here she was aware of her colonial middle-class origins and of the high penalty that might attend a social gaffe. It was only as the season ended that she relaxed sufficiently to accept herself—to quote her own words—as "part of this great procession and not merely a spectator of it." Her newfound ease emboldened her even to bend some of the principles Madame had enforced. While attending a luncheon where the Prince of Wales was also a guest, she received an unexpected request from Harris to sing that night in *Faust*. As it was already 2 p.m., and as she was not following the disciplined routine she had been taught to observe on the day of a performance, her first instinct was to refuse. The prince, however, begged her to sing, and she found herself agreeing. Happily, the performance "passed off very well." The Prince of Wales, now her devoted admirer, told her that her Juliette had given him more pleasure than any operatic performance he had seen for years. She met him many times that season: at Mrs. Henry Oppenheim's, at the Duchess of Manchester's, at Lady Mandeville's, and of course at Lady de Grey's.

Toward the end of July, in the middle of that happiest of summers, Melba's voice began to sound strained. Jean de Reszke, who had transformed himself from a baritone into one of the greatest tenors in operatic history, was skilled at diagnosing vocal ailments and he was the first to detect it. He had formed an affection for "Melbie," as he called her, and had begun to worry about her voice. Before a performance he would ask her, *"Comment va l'attaque impertinente ce soir?"*—how was her "impertinent attack" this evening? He was referring to a "ping" that was audible in her voice when it leaped to a high note. Given the French name *coup de glotte*, it came from hitting the note hard in the first few seconds, and was almost a fashionable practice at this time.

Melba liked the effect—it had a touch of bravado—and her public seemed to like it too.

Jean de Reszke, hating the sound, warned her that the habit could ruin her voice. She laughed away his kindly advice, but as the season progressed she realized she could no longer sing a high note "as safely as usual." She also noticed that on the mornings after a performance, her speaking voice was husky for several hours. Not wanting to face the truth, she ignored the symptoms, so it was almost the end of the season before she consulted Felix Semon, the eminent Prussian laryngologist who attended most of Covent Garden's singers. His verdict was one that all vocalists dread. A small nodule sat on her left vocal cord, almost certainly caused by that fatal pinging. If not cured, the nodule could ruin her voice. In a state of shock, she pondered her predicament. Today a surgical operation would be prescribed, but in 1890 no such operation existed. Although Dr. Semon was a celebrated surgeon of the larynx, he could suggest no treatment other than complete rest for the voice. Even then a cure could not be guaranteed.

The critics were now noticing her strained tone, particularly in *Esmeralda*. On the final night of the season she was supposed to take the small, cameo role of Micaela in *Carmen*. At the last minute she canceled the part and went instead to the Armstrongs' home at Rustington, announcing to the press that on medical advice she was spending a few days in the country. It was a sad visit because Lady Armstrong had died the previous March and, notwithstanding Melba's problems with Charlie, the two women had been fond of each other. The Armstrong house seemed empty without its mistress, but the quiet eased Melba's mind. Returning to London, she decided to abandon all engagements for the autumn and settle in a secluded spot, not singing, or even speaking, for as many weeks as Semon deemed necessary.

Philippe shared her concern and may even have felt relieved, because several months of separation fitted in well with his plans. For part of August he had agreed to visit his mother in the Hapsburg spa town of Marienbad; and at the end of September he had promised to join his father in the United States, where the comte was planning to introduce his son to his old comrades of the Army of the Potomac, with whom he had fought on the Union side in the American Civil War. Between those engagements Philippe planned to be with Melba, for this was not simply a lustful liaison. What had started as a summer diversion had developed into a serious attachment. The two knew it could not last—he was a prince and she a married commoner—but they deliberately did not look that far ahead.

Seeking the best place in which to effect the prescribed cure, Melba decided to return to Switzerland. Casting her mind back to her previous visit, she recalled quiet little health resorts dotting the slopes above Lake Geneva with agreeable hotels and spectacular views. Les Avants, high above the town of Vevey, met her requirements. One reached it by a mountain train that climbed through vine-clad slopes and flowery meadows. Here for two months she could gaze across the lake to the snowcapped peaks of France, and use her voice as little as possible.

Melba took refuge in Les Avants and after six weeks was ready to travel to nearby Geneva to consult a doctor recommended by Semon. He found the nodule was still visible but shrinking. On September 20, throwing caution to the winds, she took the train round the lake to Ouchy and joined Philippe at the Beau Rivage Hotel. Given the quarrels she had had there with Charlie the previous year, the hotel was a curious choice. One can only imagine that Melba hoped that Philippe's love would drive out the bitter memories.

The lovers, during their three days together, ran a fearful risk of detection, but this lent spice to their meeting. Indeed Philippe, or Tipon as she now affectionately called him, was enchanted by Melba's cheeky attitude to authority and her willingness to take risks. He had grown up in the claustrophobic climate of exile, where life was dominated by pride in royal blood and by intrigues to regain the throne. As the eldest son, he was expected to continue down this constricted path for the rest of his days, no matter how fruitless it might prove. Kicking against his fate, he longed for freedom and adventure. Melba sympathized with those feelings, for she herself was no stranger to rebellion. With three wild brothers and a rebellious streak in her own nature, she found his frustration easy to understand. Although she valued him as a lover, she treated him as a friend and tried to give him courage. Years later he would say to her, "You know me and understand me!"

On leaving Melba, Philippe was to sail to New York to join his father, and, on returning from America, he was to stay at the royal palace near Lisbon with his brother-in-law, King Carlos of Portugal. It would be months before the lovers could meet again. They had both known there would be long separations, and they accepted them as inevitable. Lonely but stoical, Melba completed her cure of silence in Switzerland.

In Paris a string of engagements awaited her, and there was even the prospect of performances in Russia, for Tsar Alexander had heard of her triumphs and had summoned her and the de Reszke brothers to St. Petersburg in four months' time. But first she needed Felix Semon's approval, which caused her much anxiety. Deep was her relief when she finally learned that the nodule had gone. Semon gave her his blessing, provided that she completely eliminated the "ping" from her singing. This she did at once with excellent results. The American critic W. J. Henderson would later write that the gentleness of Melba's attack when she sang a note was "little short of marvellous." She simply opened her mouth and "a tone was in existence."

Buoyantly, Melba resettled herself and George into their apartment at 97 Les Champs Élysées and took up the threads of her Parisian life. In November, Gladys de Grey came to Paris, and together they indulged in *le High Life*. A succession of French princes, princesses, dukes, and duchesses crammed Gladys's drawing room, along with visitors such as Oscar Wilde, holding forth imperiously and sprouting a bunch of violets from his buttonhole. He greeted Melba dramatically with "I am the Lord of Language and you are the Queen of Song, and so I suppose I shall have to write a sonnet to you." He did not write a sonnet, but he called on her in London. "We did not seem to breed that type in Australia," Melba would later say.

Thanks to her operatic renown, to Gladys's aristocratic connections, and to the liaison with Philippe, which had become an open secret in select French circles, Melba's social stocks were high that season. Her opening night at the Paris Opéra was attended by the cream of the royalist nobility, and in the following weeks the impeccable Prince de Sagan, who sported a perfectly waxed mustache and an ever-fresh flower in his buttonhole, sent her boxes of orchids and took her driving in the Bois de Boulogne. When she sang at a party at the house of the American hostess Kate Moore, she was applauded by the Duchess d'Uzes and the Duchess de Luynes, two of the haughtiest royalist matriarchs in Paris. Melba's spirits soared. "Everything," she wrote happily, "seemed *couleur de rose*."

Melba sang *Rigoletto*, *Hamlet*, and *Lohengrin* that season with success. Her performances were sold out days ahead, with eighteen-franc tickets selling for as much as fifty francs. She caused a sensation when she sang the part of Micaela in the Opéra Comique's *Carmen*, for onlookers were amazed that an acknowledged prima donna would take so small a role, even though it was one that perfectly suited her voice. Micaela's costume also caused a sensation, coming from the inspired hands of Jean Worth at his celebrated salon in the Rue de la Paix. Jean Worth, "with his little beard and polished French manners," now designed most of Melba's stage and street clothes, first studying his client carefully before calling for cloth and a drawing board. "This is the outline," he would murmur as his pencil moved across the paper, "this—and this." His costume for Micaela, purporting to be the dress of a peasant girl from Aragon, was a fabulous creation. It consisted of a maroon and blue velvet bodice, white gauze sleeves embroidered in black and gold, a blue skirt ending in a red ruffle, and a black mantilla to be worn over the head. The clothes-loving Parisians gasped in admiration, but a few months later the same costume received sharp criticism from English critics. They considered it most unlikely that a peasant girl would wear such an elaborate dress, particularly in so warm a climate.

Responding to the tsar's summons, Melba and Edouard and Jean de Reszke embarked by train for St. Petersburg. The winter in January 1891 was exceptionally cold, and Melba was convalescing from influenza, so she sat encased in furs in her heated carriage, refusing invitations from Edouard and Jean to alight at the stops to stretch her legs. It was therefore with dismay that, awaking from a doze at the Russian frontier, she saw customs officials dragging the cloak she wore in *Lohengrin* out of her trunk and flinging it onto the ground. Like the *Carmen* costume, it was an exquisite Worth creation, made of cloth of gold, hand-painted, and sewn with jewels. As she watched it fall, glittering, onto a drift of snow, she erupted. Oblivious of the cold, she leaped from her carriage, shouting in four languages until the cloak was safely restored to its trunk.

St. Petersburg seemed "a city of ineffable sadness" when Melba first saw it, "given over to strange silence, broken only by the cold, monotonous jingle of sleigh bells." The "universal mantle of snow gave to the fine buildings a look of shadowed brightness," she remembered, "as though they were clothed in a light that never shone on land or sea. I felt melancholy, and very very far away from all my friends."

Her mood did not last. Warmth awaited her at the Hôtel de France, and later that day at the palace of the tsar's brother, the Grand Duke Alexis. Escorted on a tour of the palace by the grand duke himself, she was filled with awe at the magnificence of the display, marveling at the glowing tapestries, pictures, and porcelain on show in every room. When she and her host finally reached the dining room, she ate too freely of the *hors d'oeuvres*—thinking they were the entire meal—and was astonished when double doors swung open to reveal a handsome table, set with gold plate, at which the guests were to dine formally.

Melba and the de Reszke brothers were happy to sing at the grand duke's dinner, and next morning an exquisite diamond and sapphire bracelet came to Melba from their host. Throughout the weeks in Russia, gifts continued to arrive from aristocratic admirers: Melba could scarcely believe such generosity. The Grand Duchess Paul sent her a turquoise and diamond bracelet, Count Tolstoy sent her a tortoiseshell writing set with her name spelled out in gold, and Tsar Alexander gave her a bracelet of engraved diamond cubes strung on a platinum chain with large baroque pearls. It looked so exotic that she chose it as her lucky piece and often wore it.

Roméo et Juliette opened at the Imperial Theatre on January 11, 1891, in the Russian calendar, or January 24 in the European tabulation. As it was the first performance of that opera in St. Petersburg, the theatre was packed. The response from the spectators was tepid, though they happily applauded the duets between Melba and Jean de Reszke. When *Faust* followed two days later, the reception was also muted, though there was long applause at the final curtain. Of the three operas, only *Lohengrin* was instantly acclaimed. When Melba appeared on stage in her Worth cloak to sing Elsa's wedding scene, a gasp went around the house. Later, when Melba was summoned to the royal box, the tsarina—who was the Princess of Wales's sister—took the fabric between her hands and sighed: "How perfectly lovely this is."

When *Lohengrin* ended, the applause was so prolonged that a chair was brought to the wings for Melba to sit and rest between the recalls. On the first night she had twenty recalls, on the second night thirty-three, and on the last she took so many it was impossible to keep count.

As she took her final bow, she was startled to see what seemed like a vast white sheet being lowered from the balcony. "It was only a chain," she later remembered, "of scores of handkerchiefs which the students had tied together, and were waving frenziedly to and fro." As she left the theatre, the students swarmed around her, "their breath showing white and misty in the cold northern air." Coats were flung on the snow to make a path for her feet, and a hundred programs were thrust forward to receive her autograph. When she finished with her pencil, a young man seized it from her hand and crunched it in his strong white teeth, distributing the pieces to his friends. It crossed her mind that this was how medieval peasants might have apportioned holy relics.

Over the following weeks the Russian critics sang the praises of Melba's Elsa. "As an artist," raved one reviewer, "she is without competition." The sweetness and clearness of her tones "combined with her classical and spiritual declamation" had provided him with "heavenly pleasure." Some Russian critics found it hard to believe that she was from the uncultured antipodes. One columnist had been informed that "Australian women have feathers on their heads, and wear beads and short skirts," and yet here was a soprano from a land of feathers and beads who could outperform a million European singers. He said she was like "a young canary who has taken singing lessons from the best nightingale."

Amidst the cheering operagoers at *Lohengrin* had been Philippe, Duke of Orléans. He had newly arrived from Lisbon, and when questioned by reporters, gave the reason for his visit as a desire to join the Russian army. Noticeable in his box, he made himself the more conspicuous by applauding Melba louder, longer, and earlier than almost anyone else. His exhibitionism perturbed the tsar, who according to Russian etiquette was the only one permitted to lead the applause. When questions were asked about this presumptuous young man, the answers proved embarrassing. The story goes that Philippe was ordered to leave Russia, though this has never been confirmed.

Certainly Philippe had already departed for Austria when, in mid-February, Melba traveled back to Paris. Here a shadow fell across her rose-tinted life. Charlie was waiting for her. The opulent apartment, the fashionable friends, and his son's French governess aroused his deep resentment. In Charlie's opinion, Melba could well afford to share her wealth with him. Moreover she should regard it as her duty to raise their son as an upper-class English boy. Repeating his behavior of eighteen months earlier, he began to encourage George to disobey his mother and teacher, and even tried to sack the governess. The quarrels became so fiery that Melba left Paris hurriedly, leaving Charlie and George behind. By February 25, 1891, she was in Vienna, with Philippe at her side.

CHAPTER NINE

What Say They? Let Them Say

MELBA'S DECISION to join Philippe seems to have been a reckless gesture. There was good reason for them to expect that the affair would be discovered. As a cousin of the Austrian imperial family, Philippe was likely to be recognized by a few upper-class Viennese, and as a celebrated prima donna, Melba was likely to be identified by a few Viennese opera-lovers. That they stayed together in the fashionable Sacher Hotel, opposite the opera house, and sat together in a box in the opera, made their presence more public.

Melba was taking a particular risk. The recent quarrels with Charlie must have shown her that there was a strong likelihood that he would demand custody of George. She must have known that to be publicly discovered with a lover would deliver a devastating weapon into Charlie's hands.

Melba and Philippe spent a week together at the Sacher Hotel, and they might well have spent longer but for an incident that publicized their tryst. One evening a tenor named Ernest Van Dyk, who knew Melba from Brussels, looked out through the spy hole in the opera house curtain and saw Melba and the duke together in a box. He passed the news to a friend who was a reporter at a local newspaper. The journalist is said to have sought confirmation that it was Melba by interviewing Madame Marchesi's youngest daughter, Blanche, who was living in Vienna.

Blanche had long felt antagonism toward Melba. Not unnaturally, she resented the intense relationship that had developed between Melba and her mother, and being an aspiring soprano herself, she was envious of Melba's superior talent. On the other hand, Blanche acknowledged Melba's loyalty to her parents, and loved her mother too dearly to burden her with the pain of seeing her favorite pupil pilloried in the press. Accordingly, Blanche did her best to persuade the journalist not to print the story and to persuade Melba to leave Vienna. She failed in the first, but succeeded in the second. Melba returned to Paris and to the presence of Charlie.

Luckily Charlie was preoccupied with his departure for Australia and did not read the gossip columns. Melba, however, was on tenterhooks. So deep was her anxiety that when Charlie insisted that six-year-old George should be sent to an English boys' boarding school, she lacked the courage to fight him. She agreed that the child should go to a school at Worthing near Rustington, where her sixteen-year-old brother, Ernest, was already a pupil. The decision caused her heartbreak, but by this concession she hoped to avert a storm.

Her apprehension was well founded. When she publicly waved goodbye to Charlie as he set out for London, a French reporter was taking notes. Confused by Charlie's likeness to Philippe, he reported that the duke was secretly and illegally visiting Paris, disguised as one of Melba's servants. The Orléans family was indignant at this demeaning imputation, to say nothing of the implication that Philippe was seriously flouting French law for the purpose of a love affair. Philippe felt obliged to write to the French press denying he had set foot in France. By the end of April, Australian papers were carrying the story, even the *Mackay Mercury*, which described the duke as a "hare brained young scapegrace." Loyal to Charlie and Melba, the paper dismissed the story as "absurd."

Charlie seems to have heard for the first time the gossip about Melba's affair while he was still onboard the *Massilia*. His anger and perhaps incredulity can be imagined; and at the first Australian port, on April 29, he responded with a letter to Melba, couched in violent language. Notwithstanding his distress, he did not attempt to return to England, for he was absorbed in another dispute. Shearers were on strike in central Queensland, and fights between strikers and nonunion workers had flared across the colony. The leading trade unionists had been arrested and sent to face trial in Rockhampton, along the coast from Mackay. Charlie arrived home to learn that his friends who served as volunteers in the Mackay Mounted Infantry had left for Rockhampton to maintain order at the trial. By mid–May, Charlie was in the courtroom at Rockhampton, ostensibly supporting his friends in the infantry yet showing sympathy for the strikers as well. The defendants would later recall that "Kangaroo Charlie" Armstrong called out "cheery greetings to us across the crowded courtroom, unawed by the men in blue who tried to silence him." As usual, Charlie was fearlessly his own man.

In Paris, Melba resumed her own life as best she could, but she was jinxed and accident-prone. Her apartment building caught fire, and she fled, clutching her jewel box and clad only in her nightdress. She claimed a fireman plucked her from her bed with the words, "Apologies, Madame, but my business is pressing!" He then flung her into a canvas chute which deposited her outside the building. After the fire, she took refuge with Madame and devoted her energies to the Opéra, whose directors—angry at her absences—demanded her undivided attention. Her brilliant reentry in *Rigoletto* in March to some extent restored good relations. She found that the events of past months had sharpened her mind and quickened her emotions. The critic of *Le Sport* had never seen her "in better voice or beauty." In his opinion her Gilda was unsurpassed.

Melba made her first appearance for the season at Covent Garden early in June 1891 in *Roméo et Juliette*. As she made her first entrance in the ball scene, sweeping down a flight of stairs and "looking even brighter and prettier than she did a year ago," applause resounded throughout the house. Instead of the chaste white dress of the previous year, Melba wore a stunning gown—from Jean Worth—of violet velvet embroidered with gold and pearls and a small embroidered skullcap. Her appearance drew forth sighs or silences of envy or admiration from almost every woman in the audience.

Remembering Melba's strained singing at the end of the previous season, the critics had come half-expecting to hear a "reedy and tremulous" Juliette. Their fears were silenced, for Melba sang with the same incandescence she had shown in Paris. By the end of the performance almost every reviewer was enthusing over the change in her voice and the warmth of her acting. Intermittently for two months, she sang in *Lucia* and *Rigoletto* as well as in *Roméo et Juliette*; and excitement, success, and, above all, love again liberated her emotions. The *Observer* pointed out that so far "she has not been conspicuous as an emotional actress," but *Lucia* proved her to be "the possessor of dramatic powers hitherto unsuspected."

Her trills and roulades earned bravos from a galaxy of royal dukes and duchesses when she sang Lucia's "mad scene" at an operatic concert at the Albert Hall and at a state concert at Buckingham Palace. These were mere curtain-raisers, however, to the gala of the season on July 8, when the German emperor visited Covent Garden. Although the French singers, remembering the Franco-Prussian War of two decades earlier, refused to appear before the emperor, Covent Garden's arrangement could not have been faulted. Six boxes facing the stage were opened into one silk-lined salon, with thrones in the center for the emperor and empress. Lilies and orchids spilled over every corner, and a massive German flag, suspended from the parapet, completed the decorations. The massed flowers, the bright military uniforms, the gorgeous dresses, and the jewels that twinkled on female breasts and heads transformed the theatre into a fairy-tale spectacle. *Melbourne Punch* informed its readers that Madame Melba had sung with "fire, passion and extraordinary tenderness, and aroused the house to uproarious enthusiasm."

Melba chose to rent an apartment for her stay in London, believing it safer for assignations than a hotel. The red-brick apartment block in Ashley Gardens, overlooking Westminster Cathedral, was one of the newest and most fashionable in the city, possessing bathrooms with hot and cold running water and that latest of innovations, electric light. Near Melba's apartment was a congenial neighbor named Maude Valérie White, a well-known composer of songs, whose nephew Jack sometimes played with George. The story goes that one day Jack came to his aunt with the news that "young Armstrong" had volunteered to unstring his mother's pearls to provide counters for a game they were playing. "What do *you* think?" Jack is supposed to have asked. Miss White quickly vetoed the idea.

Philippe often visited Melba at 19 Ashley Gardens, and she also visited his house at 94 Mount Street. Their liaison was now openly acknowledged by their friends; as love affairs were deemed acceptable in their circle provided they did not become public knowledge, neither she nor Philippe felt concern. Melba continued to be invited to fashionable parties, continued to sing at soirées held by fashionable hostesses, and was even received by the Princess of Wales at Marlborough House. When Melba lost her hairpiece on stage during one of Juliette's duets, the Princess of Wales teased her about the incident afterward. Such intimacy from a member of the royal family almost took Melba's breath away. With Philippe by her side, and with her social and professional life succeeding beyond her dreams, her happiness seemed almost unclouded. The one dark cloud was Charlie. Her happiness was only safe as long as he stayed far away.

While Melba believed it was unlikely that Charlie would dare to return to London with the aim of openly confronting the heir to the French throne, it was all too possible that he might return in order to exercise his paternal right to take George back to Australia. Her fears multiplied when news came in August that Charlie was about to embark for England. Determined to foil him in advance, Melba consulted Gladys's husband and also Charles Rawson, her old friend from Mackay, before seeking legal advice. The lawyers Wadeson and Malleson advised Melba to set in motion a legal procedure whereby George might become the responsibility of the Court of Chancery. On September 4, Rawson and Lord de Grey became trustees of an indenture for one hundred pounds, bought by Melba to provide for George's maintenance. Rawson and de Grey were then, in turn, sued by a Frederick Cheesewright on George's behalf, simply in order to have the execution of the indenture overseen by the Court of Chancery, whose presiding judge initiated an inquiry into the arrangements for George's maintenance. Through this involved legal procedure, Melba managed to attain her object. George, though not officially a ward, was now under the court's eye. Charlie would be obliged to weigh the legal consequences before he attempted to whisk the boy out of the country.

The prospect of Charlie's arrival also goaded Melba into legal action on her own behalf. A judicial separation had long been in her mind as an acceptable means of terminating her marriage and gaining custody of George, for in the social climate of the day, a wronged wife who sued for separation was usually regarded more sympathetically than a divorced wife by both a court and society. On the advice of Wadeson and Malleson, she petitioned the High Court of Justice for a legal separation and for the custody of her son, informing the court that she was too alarmed to cohabit with her husband. She submitted, as evidence, a sworn statement reciting Charlie's acts of cruelty toward her. She signed the petition for a legal separation on September 12 at the office of the British consul in Paris, for she and Philippe deemed it prudent to be outside England when Charlie arrived. Thus Charlie returned from Australia to find the battle lines drawn up against him.

Melba gravely misjudged her husband in believing that he would not dare openly to oppose the duke. In his own way "Kangaroo Charlie" was a heroic figure and felt no more fear at taking on a prince of the royal blood than he did a bucking bronco. He decided to fight. He consulted lawyers and hired private detectives to investigate the activities of Melba and her lover. On October 27 he petitioned for a divorce and custody of his son, citing his wife's adultery and naming the duke as corespondent. Never one to fight with gloved fists, Charlie submitted a claim for damages against the duke for 200,000 pounds, then the equivalent of almost one million dollars. There was little hope of gaining such a high sum, but it showed the world that he meant business.

As the implications of the chain of legal events sank in, Melba realized what a punishment she had brought on Philippe and herself. She might even be bidding goodbye to her hard-won social ascendancy, for society was often pitiless toward a divorced woman. As for Philippe, his Royalist supporters would most likely turn against him, to say nothing of his father's anger. Charlie was in a position to do immeasurable harm to both of them.

On their lawyers' advice, Melba and the duke denied the specific charges. Melba produced an affidavit from her father in Melbourne, corroborating her evidence, but Charlie's lawyers devised other means to support his case. It was possible in Vienna to engage a civil tribunal to examine witnesses and supply sworn evidence; and since the waiters and chambermaids from the Sacher Hotel refused to come to London, Charlie employed the tribunal to obtain their sworn statements. Evidence from this civilian tribunal began to appear in the press with varying degrees of accuracy, and reports of Melba's life with Philippe were spread across European newspapers.

Melba affected indifference. She repeated the maxim of the Prince of Wales: "They say—What say they? Let them say." At heart she suffered. It was one of the few times in her life when she felt her social standing and her career to be in peril, and herself at the mercy of events whose outcome she could not control.

By the end of December 1891 the respective cases were complete, and all parties put on a show of confidence. Charlie assured his friends that his pedigree was almost as long as that of a royal prince and that he was ready for a duel whenever he should succeed in finding the duke. He is said to have asked his former fencing partners at the Salle Dupont in Brussels to act as his seconds. Meanwhile Melba received a deputation from Lady de Grey "and other prominent ladies," who declared their belief in Melba's innocence. This pledge of loyalty somewhat revived Melba's spirits, and *Melbourne Punch* referred to the "universal expressions of sympathy which have been extended to her" in England.

Agnes Murphy, the aspiring young novelist who edited the social pages of *Melbourne Punch,* became Melba's champion in her homeland. She described Charlie's action as "a measure of retaliation" and reported with relish that he would be opposed by two of the most brilliant lawyers in England: George Lewis, a solicitor renowned for his astute handling of society scandals, and Sir Charles Russell, a former attorney general. As Melba's champion, Agnes Murphy resolved to pin the blame on Philippe, who she believed had irresponsibly embroiled Melba in a scandal. She denounced him as an "utterly selfish, headstrong, theatrical youth," repeating a description that had appeared in an overseas newspaper: "At a distance he looked like a German, but nearer he looked like a fool."

Of the three participants, it was the Duke of Orléans who initially fared the worst, for he spent months dodging Charlie, the would-be duelist, and those solicitors' clerks who were intent on serving him with divorce papers. In September he had quit London for his brother-in-law's palace in Portugal; but a month later, thinking the danger was over, he returned to England, only to be faced with the publicity arising from Melba's divorce action. On the advice of his lawyers, he retreated to the castle of St. Johann in Austria, owned by the Jewish financier and philanthropist Baron Hirsch. The visit could have been no hardship because the millionaire's shooting parties were celebrated, and the de Greys and the Prince of Wales were among his regular guests. Lady Randolph Churchill recalled that six hundred beaters roused the pheasants, partridges, and blue hares, and a battalion of grandly uniformed servants carried gargantuan meals to the shooters.

The duke had been warned to receive no suspicious strangers at St. Johann; so when a solicitor's clerk carrying divorce papers and a writ arrived at the castle early in November, he was refused admittance. The clerk caught up with Philippe, however, at a railway station in Vienna. As the duke stood on the platform, he was accosted and handed the writ and the divorce petition. Looking puzzled, the duke passed the documents to his secretary, who, realizing their nature, tried to hand them back. When this proved unsuccessful, the secretary dropped the papers on the platform, where a servant eventually picked them up. "As this way of serving writs is unknown in Austria," wrote the London *Times*, "the novelty of the scene attracted some attention among the passengers who happened to witness the proceeding."

Newspapers on both sides of the Channel reported the incident, along with rumors that the Comte de Paris was "frantically indignant" at Philippe's rash behavior, and that the French Royalist party had respectfully requested the comte to censure his son. Melba must have felt for her young lover as he tried to fend off the combined censures of his father and the French Royalists, and the insatiable curiosity of the newspapers. It was impossible for her to comfort him in person. She was to sing at the Paris Opéra in the first week in November, and Philippe was prohibited by law from visiting France.

Melba's home in Paris was now an apartment on the mezzanine floor of an old mansion at 9 Rue de Prony. It was a fashionable address, only a few blocks from the Parc Monceau, which George particularly loved. She had chosen the apartment with her son in mind, hoping it would cheer him up when he came home on holidays. George was unhappy at his English boarding school, for he was accustomed to the French language and French ways. He had difficulty adapting to the school's strict Englishness, and he hated his nickname of Froggy. George's unhappiness sometimes filled Melba with sadness, but at the same time she was proud of his transformation into an upper-class English schoolboy. A photograph of him in the schoolboy's outfit of long trousers, cropped jacket, and top hat was displayed in her bedroom. When she looked at it, she saw a vulnerable child in man's clothing, and the image tugged at her heart.

Melba did not altogether look forward to her forthcoming appearance at the Opéra, for she knew that Adelina Patti, in the course of her divorce six years earlier, had been greeted by hisses as she came on stage. But Patti's lover had been a third-rate tenor, in no way comparable to Philippe. On opening night, as Melba warily entered the stage, she was met by "a tremendous ovation," instantly suggesting that Parisian operagoers—who loved a love affair when it involved a French prince—had taken her to their hearts. This spontaneous swell of sympathy was too much for her nerves, and she broke down. At once, according to one observer, "there was a renewed outburst of kindly feeling, the cheers of the audience increasing to deafening pitch." Touched almost beyond words, Melba began to throw kisses toward the audience, which responded with more cheers. The "greater jury of the Paris public has entered an emphatic verdict in the *diva's* favour," proclaimed one Melbourne periodical.

Although Melba welcomed this public approval, she was obliged to leave Paris in the New Year, for she was contracted to sing at opera houses in Palermo, Marseilles, Nice, and Rome. Palermo in far-off Sicily may have seemed an odd choice, but it was currently hosting an international exhibition, and in honor of the occasion its opera house, the Politeama Garibaldi, was employing a first-class singer. Melba was rumored to be receiving four thousand francs for a single performance of *La Traviata*. It was also a city to which Philippe had ties. His great-grandmother had been a Sicilian princess, and his family owned a palazzo in Palermo; when Melba's engagement was originally contracted there, he may have intended to accompany her.

The Marchesis were delighted that at last Melba was singing in Italy. Salvatore sent letters introducing her to notable Italian journalists. He wrote also to the elderly Guiseppe Verdi, one of the most revered figures in Italy, asking the great composer to teach Melba his opera *Otello*, which the Paris Opéra was hoping to stage the following year. This was not an unreasonable request, for Melba and Salvatore knew that Verdi had taught Patti his later operas. Nevertheless Verdi refused. A few years earlier he had declared that he would not have singers foisted on him. "Not even," he added, if Malibran herself "were to return from her grave."

Sailing for Sicily in January 1892, Melba and her maid endured a rough passage, arriving ill and sleepless at Palermo just before dawn.

In the course of that morning, as she tried to sleep in her hotel bed, a cellist in the next room persisted in repeating over and over a well-known serenade written by the composer Gaetano Braga—a serenade she had sung at Australian concerts with Kruse. Since sleep was now impossible, she joined in with her voice. "Who are you?" came the cry from beyond the wall. "I am Melba," she replied. "Who are *you*?" It was Braga himself.

Although over sixty years of age, Braga still burned with romantic ardor, and he proposed visiting her room immediately. Amused but firm, Melba told him to wait until two, and promptly at that hour he appeared with a beaming smile and a large bunch of flowers. For the rest of the day he played and she sang, and they talked incessantly. He had been a singer before becoming a concert cellist and composer, and he had written nine operas and coached well-known singers. "Your singing is an incomparable caress," he told her poetically. His admiration warmed her heart, which was as well, for she was entering an operatic city more volatile, and yet more reserved in its opinion, than London and Paris.

Melba's reputation had preceded her to Palermo, but in every Italian audience, whatever the city, Melba was to encounter a wall of reserve. Regarding themselves as the most discerning listeners in the world, Italians demanded that divas prove themselves. Discovering that wall for the first time, Melba was chastened. She had long known that a cold audience could drain color from a performance, and that even experienced singers "could fall incredibly below their normal standard for no other reason than of irresponsiveness on the part of the audience." Worse, the boxes in an Italian theatre tended to be buzzing drawing rooms that ceased their chatter only when a stirring singer was on stage, and it was often necessary to fight for attention. On this occasion, however, she held Palermo in the palm of her hand—and she triumphed.

From Palermo she sailed to Marseilles, where she performed *Rigoletto*, *Hamlet*, and *Lucia* at the Grand Theatre. Its French audiences needed no convincing, being only too thrilled to hear a star of the Paris Opéra. Reviewers heaped her with praise: she was a poetic Ophélie, a moving Gilda, a tragic Lucia. "The public," wrote one critic, "was hanging on her lips." When she sang in Nice a week later, she drew "frenetic applause." The Carnival was in progress, and the city was packed with merrymakers who poured into the streets to dance and shout, and to pelt each other with petals in the famous Battle of the Flowers. Melba, joining in the fun, decorated one of the colorful open carriages that paraded through the streets. Covered with roses and carnations, and with a *papier mâché* swan attached to each side, her carriage was considered so novel that it won first prize.

From Nice, Melba traveled by train to Rome, arriving at the Quirinale Hotel on March 3. Preparing to sing *Lucia* at the Argentina Theatre, the main opera house of the city, she was already anxious. She had always been nervous before a performance, and experience and fame had increased her fears. "It's when you are a diva that you become nervous," she once commented. "When you are a diva you have to be the best always." The cream of Rome society was coming to her opening night: a veritable Almanach de Gotha, as one reporter put it, "translated into flesh and diamonds." She guessed those proud and knowledgeable Italian opera-lovers would judge her sternly.

From her first step on stage she knew she could not succeed. Her voice was as clear as ever, but anxiety deprived it of color. Nerves were robbing her of the joy she normally felt as she surmounted difficult passages, and the communication of that joy was an essential part of her performance: without it, her singing seemed mechanical and "dead." In the foyers at intermission the spectators voiced their disappointment. Melba had been advertised as a second Patti, but her vocal and thespian skills did not meet that expectation. The more disgruntled summoned their carriages and went home.

In her dressing room, Melba used every particle of will to pull herself together. The next act contained her "mad scene," so it was imperative to calm her nerves and harness her strength. As the scene commenced she could feel the audience thawing, and with that welcome knowledge her voice began to soar. As the closing notes fell from her lips, the audience burst into what one spectator called "that unstoppable applause that makes one forget the long tedium of waiting and the bitterness of disappointment."

"What a battle and what applause," wrote one of the kinder critics next day. "Signora Melba can inscribe yesterday evening's performance among the more glorious of her career." Other reviewers were less kind.

While the "mad scene" was admitted to be brilliant, the rest of her performance was accounted a failure. Newspapers across Italy did not mince matters. They called it *"un fiasco strepitoso"*—a resounding failure. Melba's fortunes had seldom seemed lower as she traveled from Rome to Paris.

Fear Nothing, Melba

THE DIVORCE lay in her lawyers' hands, the loss of her son was probable, and the parting with Philippe seemed inevitable. Melba faced these facts with as much courage as she could muster. Even though she and Philippe had known that his royal obligations prevented a long-term relationship, they had hoped for more time. The divorce case destroyed those hopes, and at the insistence of his family, he was avoiding Melba this summer.

Gladys's brother, the Earl of Pembroke, once told an actress friend that the best emotional safeguard a woman could possess was "passion for her art and career, which absorbs her to the exclusion of most other things, and makes her look on men as mere dummies or useful adjuncts in her busy life." These were sentiments that his sister undoubtedly repeated when she attempted to console Melba at the Rue de Prony. Her advice was readily received. Melba had been brought up to face ill fortune with Scottish stoicism, and now in Paris she refused to dwell on sorrow. And whereas Gladys's recommended remedy—taking another lover—might have shocked her a few years earlier, she had now grown used to the aristocratic approach to affairs.

News from the divorce court gave her some hope. The flow of embarrassing snippets about Philippe and herself that had been leaked from the Viennese tribunal to the European newspapers now ceased. The judge ruled the tribunal's evidence inadmissible in an English court and granted an injunction to prevent Charlie from using it. Since the servants from the Sacher Hotel were Charlie's chief witnesses, this Viennese ruling seriously impaired his case. He immediately appealed against the ruling, only to lose the appeal. As legal costs were awarded against him, he was very much out of pocket.

Melba gained heart from a point of law that Philippe's lawyer, George Lewis, raised. An action for divorce could be brought in England only by someone deemed to be permanently domiciled there. Lewis astutely argued that Charlie's fifteen-year sojourn in Australia and his house near Mackay had established his domicile not in England but in Australia. If Charlie were judged ineligible to bring an action, the case would be dismissed. Calling for more evidence on Charlie's domicile, the judge adjourned the case. Reporting the news, *Melbourne Punch* added that "the *diva* is still hopeful and fearless as ever."

With the burden of the divorce temporarily lifted from her shoulders, Melba was free to plan her singing engagements. Despite Augustus Harris's pleas, she had not yet renewed her contract for the forthcoming season at Covent Garden. With high legal costs looming, she was adamant that her salary must be raised. She had been negotiating meanwhile with the Metropolitan Opera in New York for a season at the end of the year, and this in turn sparked rumors that afterward she might travel on to Australia. The speculation reached a peak in June when Australian newspapers announced that a contract had been signed, but the rumors proved false.

Gladys de Grey, worried about her friend's reluctance to resume at Covent Garden, once again offered herself as a go-between with Harris. Realizing that some of Melba's hesitancy was based on fear of social ostracism, she began organizing a series of brilliant musical parties in her apartment in the Champs Élysées, at which Melba was to be the star. All the great ladies of Paris came, including the wife of the French president. Melba found herself feted, and her spirits rose noticeably.

Her spirits rose even more in the presence of a young French composer named Herman Bemberg. Their relationship had started the previous year when he paid her a morning call, shuffling into the room on his knees to present her with a huge bunch of orchids. She had been so enraptured by his act of homage that she begged him to stay, and he stayed all day. A few weeks later he wooed her with an elaborate practical joke. On April Fools' Day of 1891, he and his friend, the Comte Charles de Mornay, sent her twenty proposals of marriage from invented noblemen, plus a large turkey, a live rabbit, mounds of cakes, and a pile of oranges, which they scattered on the floor of her box at the Opéra. Practical jokes were then the rage in fashionable circles in London and Paris, and Melba was enchanted by the young men's inventiveness. The following April Fools' Day—less than a month after she returned from Rome—she turned the tables on Bemberg by ordering a bath-hire agency to deliver a bath to him every quarter-hour until noon.

Fortunately Bemberg also had a serious side. He had composed an opera for Melba called *Elaine*, based on a poem by Alfred Tennyson, and she loved its music. Hearing that Harris was planning to include *Elaine* in his next season's schedule, Melba forgot her reluctance and renewed her contract. She longed for rehearsals to begin because she was becoming addicted to Bemberg's brand of humor. "He was like some faun dancing mischievously down the Champs Élysées, piping cheerfully to those who would follow his folly," she wrote years later. "And I was perfectly prepared to follow it."

By June 4, 1892, Melba was installed in the Grand Hotel in Trafalgar Square and performing with the de Reszke brothers in *Roméo et Juliette*. Over the following two months she also appeared as Gilda, Marguerite, Elsa, and Micaela, and earned great praise. The emotional alchemy that had fired her stage portrayals in London the previous year was still at work, and one imagines she had Bemberg to thank for it. While it was not likely that their relationship was sexual—he was known to be homosexual—it was close and affectionate. Bemberg called her his "little adopted sister," and she called him her "old brother," even though they were in fact almost the same age.

By mid-June *Elaine* was in rehearsal, with plenty of fun to raise Melba's spirits. Bemberg was in and out of her dressing room as though it was his own, strewing his belongings in inconvenient places and interrupting her orderly preparations to such a degree that she decided to teach him a lesson. Finding his hat, coat, and umbrella lying across her chair, she "cut his hat completely round the brim, covered the inside with black greasepaint, cut his umbrella so that it would fall to pieces when it was opened, and put two eggs in his overcoat pockets." Dashing back to the dressing room, Bemberg only had time to grab his hat and coat and make for Gladys's box where he was to meet an assemblage of dignitaries. Gladys duly reported, with much merriment, that he arrived with a blackened face, and that when he removed his hat, it fell at his feet.

Elaine premiered on July 5 with one of the most splendid casts Covent Garden had mustered. Melba, the de Reszke brothers, the superb French bass Pol Plançon, and the contralto Blanche Deschamps produced what the *Times* described as a "perfection of vocalization." After the curtain fell, there were scenes of "wild enthusiasm" and the bashful composer was dragged on stage by Melba to take his bows. Bemberg's Argentinean mother—a close friend of Madame's and a former opera singer—was so elated that she presented Melba with a diamond and sapphire tiara and a brooch of turquoises and diamonds. The critics, however, were more impressed by the singers than by the opera. *Elaine* ran for only four more performances.

One who panned *Elaine* but praised Melba was the celebrated music critic and playwright, George Bernard Shaw, who hitherto had been lukewarm toward Melba's talent. Since he ordained that acting in opera was no less important than singing, he had found her musically excellent but "hard, shallow, self-sufficient and altogether unsympathetic" as an actress. In *Elaine*, however, he perceived a warmth in her acting that he had not seen before. He wrote that from being "merely a brilliant singer," she had suddenly become "a dramatic soprano of whom the best class of work can be expected."

Grateful to Shaw for his generous review, Melba was even more grateful to Gladys for her loyalty at a time when, thanks to the case before the courts, her reputation could have been in jeopardy. Through Gladys's influence, Melba continued to be invited to the best houses and engaged to sing at the best parties and at fashionable concerts. In June she sang at a memorial concert for *Esmeralda*'s composer, Goring Thomas, who had committed suicide at the West Hampstead railway station. On July 1 she sang in the state concert in honor of the king of Romania at Buckingham Palace. "As the divorce proceedings against Madame Melba are still pending this latter circumstance is altogether unprecedented," wrote *Melbourne Punch* triumphantly, "and must be set down as a distinct expression of sympathy and confidence from Her Majesty."

The divorce action was still alive, but not for long. Charlie was unable to prove that he was a resident of Great Britain, and rumor had it—probably correctly—that his lawyers were advising him to abandon the case. The uncertainty was ended on August 8, 1892, when the court dismissed his case for a divorce and hers for a judicial separation. "I am so happy," Melba told Madame Marchesi, and her words were charged with feeling.

Three weeks earlier Philippe had returned to England, landing at Folkestone with his father, brother, and sisters. Now that the action was almost resolved, it must have seemed safe for him to return to his home. Two months later his social rehabilitation was completed after he was commanded to dine with Queen Victoria at Balmoral Castle.

Whether Philippe saw Melba on his arrival one does not know. If he did, it marked the parting of their ways. A few days later, giving a newspaper interview at the Grand Hotel, Melba displayed jewelry bestowed on her by admirers. Along with a handsome diamond and sapphire brooch from Queen Victoria, she showed a gold chain studded with pearls from the Duchess de Chartres, and a diamond bracelet from the Duke de Nemours. The duchess and duke were Philippe's close relatives, and the jewels may have been a parting gift and a reward for her discretion. One imagines that she displayed them to insinuate that she was still in high favor with the Orléans family. It is fair to observe that Melba's increasing flair for handling the press was not quite matched by her capacity to handle her personal life.

With the deadlock of the divorce resolved, an invitation to sing at the French health resort of Aix-les-Bains was more than welcome and, enticed by thoughts of relaxing steam baths and massages, she set out with Gladys for the mountains of Savoy. Aix-les-Bains had been a spa since Roman times, its hot and sulfurous springs being a reputed cure for a multitude of illnesses. By day its patients took care of their health; by night they gambled in the casino and attended the theatre. A fortnight after the dismissal of the divorce case, Melba sang *Lucia* in the Cercle d'Aix theatre, before what a reviewer described as "one of the most fashionable and critical audiences of Europe." The spectators, rising in a body at the end of the "mad scene," applauded until she sang the scene again. The performance was so memorable that a report of it appeared in the far-off *New York Herald*.

Her success at Aix was welcome, and her fee even more so. Short of money after she paid her lawyers, she was relying on new engagements to restore her credit. She was contracted to sing in New York at the Metropolitan Opera in December, and it was therefore a serious blow to learn, on arriving at her apartment in the Rue de Prony, that the Metropolitan Opera House had been gutted by fire the week before. According to her contract, she was still legally entitled to her salary, and the two directors of the Metropolitan Opera, Henry Abbey and Maurice Grau, came to Paris to discuss it. They hoped of course that she would be willing to forgo payment, which placed her in a quandary. On the one hand, she needed the money; on the other, her Presbyterian conscience—of which several strong elements remained—forbade her to take money she had not earned. In the end her conscience won.

Realizing that if she was to stay at the top she would have to perform the increasingly popular dramatic repertoire, she had decided to take the title role in Verdi's masterwork *Aida*, even though she knew it presented problems for her. This was not a role that she could expect Madame to teach her. Madame remained focused on the *bel canto* and lyrical repertoires, and she had little time for operas like *Aida*. In her opinion, Melba was foolish to attempt them.

There seems little doubt that Melba's decision to sing in *Aida* at Covent Garden led to tension in her relationship with Madame. For several months Melba did not write to her, but in Aix les Bains she had a change of heart and sent a contrite note. "Darling Madame," she wrote, "Please don't think that because I have not written I have not thought of you—not a day passes that I don't think of you 50 times and long to be with you to have a nice talk about everything." She promised to visit the Rue Jouffroy as soon as possible, bringing George with her.

Although she knew it was fruitless to ask Madame's advice, she wished she could receive Madame's reassurances, for to sing in *Aida* was a gamble. For one thing, the opera featured a heavier orchestral accompaniment than she was used to and would consequently demand a more powerful style of singing. While it was true that her voice had force—a "clarion quality," one critic called it—that could fill vast auditoriums, she wondered if she could summon sufficient volume to hold her own against her fellow singers and the orchestra.

The style of acting required by the role also presented difficulties. The enslaved Ethiopian princess whom she was about to portray was a heroic character torn by conflicting passions, far removed from the la-dylike roles to which Melba was accustomed. Was she capable of creat-ing such a character? Even she did not know. While critics agreed that her acting had greatly improved, some still joked about it. One story in circulation insisted that an audience always knew when Melba wanted to exhibit emotion because she raised one arm. When she wanted to exhibit intense emotion she raised two arms. Another story pretended that she dare not show any passion when singing with Jean de Reszke, because Gladys and he were lovers, and Gladys's opera glasses followed them jealously throughout the performance.

Melba must have heard these tales, and they could not have given her confidence. Nor could she have taken heart from the arrival at Covent Garden that summer of a French farmer's daughter who was as much an actress as a she was a singer. Her name was Emma Calvé and she had studied briefly with Madame, though they had not always seen eye to eye. At Covent Garden she had sung Santuzza in *Cavalleria rus-ticana*, a fiery drama about jealousy and revenge among Sicilian peas-ants, and her performance had electrified the audience. Melba sensed that this type of opera, which blended earthy realism with operatic melodrama and was sometimes called by the Italian name *verismo*, was the coming fashion, and that actress-singers like Calvé were the ris-ing stars. It is doubtful whether Melba believed she could ever act as persuasively as Calvé, yet she had to embrace the fashionable dramatic repertoire, and *Aida* was her stepping-stone.

Adelina Patti had sung *Aida* in 1876, preparing for the role by tak-ing lessons from Verdi himself: her subsequent success was said to have owed much to his teaching. Having been angrily refused by Verdi the previous year, Melba did not dare approach him again, so she went in-stead to the composer Paolo Tosti. He was an inspired choice, because though a pillar of the English musical scene—having taught music to the royal family—he remained a robust Italian with a deep understand-ing of Verdi's later music and a shrewd approach to teaching. Madame had taught Melba that she must always maintain complete control of her emotions, otherwise her singing would suffer. Tosti, on the other hand, taught her to sacrifice some of that control in order to become the character she was portraying. So enthusiastically did Melba imbibe Tosti's teaching that she told an interviewer, "An artist must lose herself in her part and forget everything. . . . It is this glorious absorption of oneself in one's role that enables one to succeed."

Melba was now determined to turn herself into an actress, no matter the cost, but in fact she found the lessons easier than anticipated. The key was laughter. Tosti had an endless fund of funny stories, some of them decidedly improper, and he kept her laughing. This lighthearted approach built her confidence, and he assured her that she would make "an *incomparable* Aida!"

When the opera opened at Covent Garden at the beginning of November, Melba felt apprehensive. The weather was bleak, the audience was small, and she hated blackening her skin to look like an Ethiopian. In fact she hated her costume altogether, for her wig resembled black rope more than hair, her apple-green robe ended halfway down her legs, and her black feet protruded monstrously. She wondered what the critics would make of her.

The critics, more interested in her acting and the power of her voice than in her black wig, were mostly delighted. Her Aida was "superb," cried the *Sportsman*; she was a "dramatic vocalist of the first rank," proclaimed *Era*; she showed "greater energy as an actress than ever before," wrote the *Sporting and Dramatic News*. The reviewer in the *London Stage* noted that her lighter passages were exquisitely sung and that her heavier ones gave promise of a time when her acting and singing would achieve "full tragic expression." More thoughtful critics, however, warned her that the clarion quality of her voice was not forceful enough to penetrate the density of *Aida's* big vocal ensembles and orchestration. In attempting such a role, she was running the risk of harming her voice.

At the final curtain of *Aida*, a gigantic basket of chrysanthemums, orchids, and lilies was hauled on stage. When it was placed in front of both the female stars, a power struggle ensued. Melba's costar, the mezzo Guilia Ravogli, claimed the flowers were hers, and Melba said that they were sent to her. To the public's delight, the dispute lasted several minutes and ended in Melba's victory. Ravogli left the stage vowing never to sing with Melba again—though needless to say, she quickly forgot the vow. Next day there were hints in the newspapers that the flowers had come from the Duke of Orléans.

On the afternoon of Melba's second performance, Harris suggested that in four days' time she should take over the role of Desdemona in

Verdi's most recent opera, *Otello*. Allowing her heart to rule her head, she found herself agreeing. Again she was accepting a challenge because, like its predecessor, *Otello* was a heavily orchestrated and highly dramatic opera. At least she was partially acquainted with the score, this being the opera she had been hoping to sing in Paris, and which Salvatore had hoped that Verdi might teach her.

The role also had a significant advantage. Otello's wronged wife, Desdemona, was a gentle patrician, and her arias were more lyrical than dramatic. Such qualities suited Melba's voice and temperament, and under Tosti's tutelage she was able to make much of them. The effort, however, was more than she could sustain. On the scheduled day she fell ill and the opera was canceled. Three days later the opera was staged, and Melba made an exquisite Desdemona, the pathos of her last scene leaving few reviewers unmoved. The *St. James's Gazette* exclaimed that it seemed as though the part had been written for her. But Melba herself remained unsatisfied.

The strains of the divorce, and these two taxing roles, sapped her strength. In the second performance of *Otello* she faltered at a crucial point, and Gladys de Grey watched with alarm. Next day she wrote to Melba: "I was so frightened last night. I was afraid you were going to faint at the beginning of the love duet." Melba did not faint, but there was little doubt that the two roles in quick succession were fraying her nerves. The type of singing she was now attempting was pushing her voice to its limits. The memory of the nodule on her vocal cord was never far from her mind, and by the second performance of *Otello* she felt afraid.

Deciding that retreat was wise, she canceled her forthcoming performances and retired to rest at her hotel. Soon after she confided to a reporter that a "light soprano should sing light soprano music and not try to excel in heavy dramatic parts."

Fortunately she was staying at the Savoy, the most luxurious hotel in Europe, where every comfort was instantly procurable. Opened in 1889, the novel structure was the brainchild of the impresario Richard D'Oyly Carte and built with his proceeds from Gilbert and Sullivan's operas. Seven stories high, it boasted its own electricity, water supplies, and central heating, and each room had a speaking tube by which one could order instant room service. At a time when even the best hotels had only half a dozen bathrooms to serve several hundred bedrooms, suites at the Savoy had their own bathrooms and lavatories. Melba's suite, overlooking the River Thames, was virtually an apartment, with a sitting room large enough for her grand piano and space enough for her maid and her newly engaged secretary.

Her new secretary was pretty, fresh-faced Louise Bennett, a niece of the Melbourne surgeon and baritone Henry O'Hara and a relative of Joseph Bennett, music critic for the *Daily Telegraph*. Competent and tactful, an excellent linguist, and an accomplished musician, soft-spoken Louie more than fulfilled Melba's needs. Indeed, with each week Melba found herself relying on her secretary more. Lonely little George loved Louie too, and he liked to stay with her and Melba at the Savoy. There the staff became his friends; sometimes the elevator driver let him push the buttons, and the hall porter let him cloak the guests' top hats.

The luxury, the service, and especially the cooking at the Savoy enchanted Melba. When the hotel first opened its doors, respectable women were still forbidden by custom to eat in public restaurants, but D'Oyly Carte was determined to overturn this rule. He shrewdly enlisted Gladys and Lillie Langtry to eat at the Savoy and thus make dining out more respectable for women. When the Prince of Wales and Lillie ate together at the hotel, the battle was almost won, with dinner parties in the restaurant becoming a popular London pastime. At the first supper party that Melba gave, after a performance of *Aida*, she received her guests while still dressed in her stage costume because it would have taken too long for her to remove her black makeup. Late in October she gave a party one Sunday in her suite at which Cheiro, the celebrated palm reader, entertained the guests by telling their fortunes. The Duke of Newcastle's hair was said to have "stood on end" when he heard Cheiro's predictions.

Melba, fully recovered, spent Christmas Day of 1892 in Paris with George. Two days later Madame transformed the ground floor of 88 Rue Jouffroy into a theatre, with chairs in the classrooms, hall, and parlor. Melba and Pol Plançon performed the fourth act of *Elaine*, with Bemberg himself accompanying them on the piano. It was one of the school's grandest days.

After the performance, Melba laid before Madame a surprising invitation that she had just received. Although her fiasco in Rome had been widely reported in the Italian press, La Scala Opera House in Milan had invited her to sing a brief season the coming March. To fail at La Scala would be a blow, but to succeed would put the seal on her reputation—she believed it was a risk worth taking. Madame agreed, and knowing that Melba would need careful preparation, was eager to discuss the choice of repertoire. Melba had been advised by friends to discard *bel canto* and sing a modern-style opera—perhaps *Rigoletto* or *La Traviata*—otherwise she would be considered hopelessly old-fashioned. Her common sense nevertheless told her that she must choose an opera like *Lucia di Lammermoor* that showed her technique to best effect. It was a decision with which Madame agreed.

In those intervals when she was not perfecting her Lucia with Madame, she redecorated her apartment in the Rue de Prony. An American journalist who came to report on her Parisian lifestyle was admitted into a stunning drawing room furnished in green, pink, and gold, with an Aubusson carpet, silk curtains and cushions, antique gilt furniture, and intricate lampshades made of feathers and lace and green silk. Through draped, folding doors lay her boudoir, and beyond that her music room. Glancing at the top of her Erard piano, the journalist made a list of the signed photographs: the Prince and Princess of Wales, the Prince and Princess of Monaco, Lord and Lady de Grey, Massenet, Gounod, Bemberg, and Augustus Harris. In her bedroom were other photographs bearing affectionate inscriptions. Jean de Reszke had inscribed his photograph to his "dear little Juliette from her most devoted Roméo"; the Prince de Sagan had dedicated his to the "touching Ophélie, enchantress Gilda, and sphinx Elaine"; and Tosti had presented her with a sketch of himself with his head ringed by musical notes. In pride of place were the photographs of George and Madame. As Melba reclined on a soft velvet sofa with her feet on a white bearskin rug, she explained that she could never repay even half of what she owed to her beloved Madame.

That winter Melba faced a concert tour of the British Isles, undertaken to fill those months left vacant by the burning of the Metropolitan Opera House. Normally she did her own negotiating with employers, but being ignorant of the concert circuit, she engaged Daniel Mayer, a London concert agent of whom it was said he "had only to whisper to be obeyed." He secured her a party of eight supporting singers and instrumentalists, and concerts in Liverpool, Manchester, Birmingham, Hull, Bradford, Edinburgh, Glasgow, Dublin, and Cork, to run through January and February of 1893.

Having made no concert tour since leaving Australia, the prospect rather daunted her. Concert audiences, as she was well aware, were of a different breed from opera audiences. Whereas Covent Garden was largely filled with the affluent upper classes who went as much to be seen as to hear, provincial halls were filled with humbler music lovers intent on improving their minds. Not knowing how to please them, she chose her showiest arias—such as "Caro nome" from *Rigoletto* and the "mad scene" from *Lucia*—and favorite songs such as Tosti's "Good-bye."

In Ireland, Melba and her concert party were feted. The king's representative, the lord lieutenant, came to both concerts in Dublin, and the critics declared that Patti herself could not have sung better. In England audiences were less enthusiastic, many halls being sparsely filled and reviewers diffident. At the end of the tour she was three hundred guineas in debt and obliged to pay the sum out of her own pocket. Depressed by the result, Melba decided she preferred operas to concerts. "All the sparkle seems to have gone out of life," she told an interviewer, "when you stand motionless before an audience, dressed in evening costume and holding a sheet of music in your hand."

Now nothing stood between her and Milan, where she was sure she would face her severest test. The most celebrated of Italian opera houses, it was also the most critical, and her Lucia in Rome was sure to be remembered. Moreover Patti was to precede her at La Scala, and though the diva was almost fifty she was still a superb singer. Inevitably Melba would be judged against her. On the other hand, Melba had confidence in her own powers, and being a fighter she was prepared to believe that she had a good chance of winning. She told an interviewer that the more demanding the audience she was about to face, "the more stimulated and braced I feel." Moreover it would be stupid to refuse a challenge, as she believed that "the artist has always new worlds to conquer. There is no standing still for us."

As the time approached, she could feel her courage draining, and she turned to her adopted mother for reassurance. On March 3 Madame Marchesi responded generously. "Fear nothing," she wrote, "from the people of Milan! With *your beautiful voice* and some added *emotion* (that's what the Italians demand), you will have *boundless success.*" Offering letters from Papa Salvatore to Italian journalists, she ended with the message: "I kiss you as tenderly as I love you."

In the first week of March 1893, Melba arrived by train in Milan with the indispensable Louie by her side. Around her was one of the most exciting cities in Europe, but she noticed none of it. She had expected a cautious reception but not the animosity that she now encountered. At first it was mostly expressed through neglect, for conspicuously few members of the musical establishment bothered to pay her a call. Then anonymous letters began to arrive, about thirty in all. They told her to go home, they threatened to poison her food and tamper with the elevator in her hotel, and they warned her to "beware of trapdoors on the stage." Rumors abounded that she was certain to fail, and recollections of her failure in Rome were bandied about. In a weak moment Melba even contemplated leaving. "You can't go, Nellie," Louie is supposed to have said to her. "It would not be you. You have got to stay and face the music." Melba acknowledged the wisdom of Louie's words, but she freely admitted that she felt a twinge of fear every time she raised food or drink to her lips or entered an elevator.

On March 15, clad in Lucia's braided and ruffled dress, she waited in the wings of La Scala, holding Louie's hand to give herself courage. As the harp solo signaled her entrance onstage, she could feel her heart throbbing and prayed it would not be Rome all over again. Her first sight of the audience unnerved her. The spectators in the boxes appeared to have their backs to her. Redoubling her concentration, she somehow managed to finish the recitative, though, in her own words, it was "a terrible ordeal." Then she realized that the chairs in the boxes were arranged in such a way that it only seemed that the spectators were looking away; in fact their eyes were upon her.

At the end of her first aria there was applause. Her voice had managed the difficulties with ease, and she knew that she was singing well. The delight she always felt when her voice answered her commands began to communicate itself to the audience. There were murmurs of approval and more applause. At the end of the first act she was recalled twice. By the second act she was singing freely, and the celebrated sextet at the end of that act was received with "frantic clapping." The "mad scene" consolidated her triumph. Listeners held their breaths as her voice soared to higher and higher levels of technical virtuosity without apparent effort. Toward the end of the scene, wrote one observer, the audience could "hardly contain its enthusiasm, and broke out after the cadenza into a noisy roar, and into deafening ovations which lasted for several minutes." He added that few artists could "lay claim to having such an uncontested and triumphal success on the stage of La Scala."

After "an infinity of recalls," Melba's excitement gave way to signs of tears: she wept in her dressing room. Taking up her pen, she dashed off an urgent letter to her "dear, much loved little Mother." "Mon Dieu," she told her, "I will never forget it—it was absolutely the greatest triumph of my career." The enthusiasm of the audience reminded her of her debut in Paris but was a hundred times greater. "I know I could never have made the career I am having without you dear dear Madame. With heaps of love to you all from your ever loving daughter." And she added as postscript: "I am so happy."

Next day her voice was described as the most brilliant to be heard in Milan for years. "Its ease of production, firmness of utterance, ductility of timbre, sureness and confidence in vocal means, finish in modulation and coloratura" left the critic from *La Perseveranza* overwhelmed. *L'Italia del Popolo* put it more succinctly: "Her voice is truly marvelous for spontaneity, equality and liquidness of tone." Melba's voice "conquered everybody."

At the beginning of April, Melba gave one performance as Gilda to an equally rapturous reception. Meanwhile the Pagliano Theatre in Florence and the San Felice Opera House in Genoa clamored to employ her, and composers in Milan hastened to her side. Ruggiero Leoncavallo, handsome, thirty-six, and a celebrity since the recent success of his opera *Pagliacci*, met her at dinner at the house of the French baritone Victor Maurel. Next day he played the score of *Pagliacci* to her, exacting a promise that she would be his leading lady when the opera went to stage at Covent Garden in a few months' time.

In Marseilles and Lyons, on her way back to Paris, Melba sang to overflowing houses. Although it has been suggested that her popularity waned after the divorce case, the opposite seems to have been true.

French audiences, in particular, were eager to set eyes on the woman who had snared their royal duke. One reviewer reported, after seeing and hearing her, that he could well "understand the magic that emanates from her and the success that follows her persistently on all the opera stages of the world."

CHAPTER ELEVEN

Across the Atlantic

MELBA WAS as good as her word, singing the role of Nedda in *Pagliacci* when the opera premiered at Covent Garden on her thirty-second birthday. A clever *verismo* tale of jealousy and murder among Italian strolling players, it held the first-night audience "spellbound." Melba was singled out for praise, especially in the second act, in which she performed a mime scene alone on stage. The part "requires a considerable degree of pantomimic skill," wrote the *Times*, "and the singer's recent improvement as an actress stood her in good stead." As she led Leoncavallo forward to acknowledge the applause, she must have reflected that she could not have had a happier birthday.

Far less successful was Pietro Mascagni's *I Rantzau*, in which Melba took the leading soprano role. Ponderously rehearsed and conducted by its composer, it was "wanting," as one bored reviewer put it, "in every element of melody." While *Pagliacci* ran for nine performances, *I Rantzau* closed after one. Melba concurred with the critics' verdict, but she could not help warming to the boyishly handsome Mascagni. She also had faith in his talent, for she was an admirer of his *Cavalleria rusticana*, which had been thrilling audiences for the past three years.

London was awash with parties to honor Leoncavallo and Mascagni. Alfred Rothschild—the financial genius who managed Patti's money and now also managed Melba's—gave a splendid dinner where thirty-three guests ate off gold plates and the Livornese baritone, Mario Ancona, sang Mascagni's music. On a less grand scale, Melba gave a dinner for twenty-two at the Savoy, where the composers rubbed shoulders with the de Greys, the Earl of Hardwicke, and the Portuguese

ambassador. The most exciting event that season, however, was undoubtedly the marriage on July 4 of the Prince of Wales's son George to
pretty Princess May of Teck. The night before the wedding, the Covent
Garden theatre was transformed into a flowery bower, with garlands
adorning every pillar and a huge marriage bell of white roses hanging
over the staircase. The royal box, festooned with rainbow silk and or-
ange blossom, was lit by electric lights which flashed across the auditorium as the royal couple took their seats.

Mascagni sat with Gladys de Grey during the opera, which was *Roméo et Juliette* shorn of its last act, considered too tragic for so happy an
occasion. In a nearby box sat Philippe, watching Melba and Jean de
Reszke play the star-crossed lovers. Biographies of Melba sometimes
say that Philippe set out on an African safari as soon as he parted from
Melba, but the safari was made by his explorer cousin, Prince Henri
of Orléans, who set out for East Africa in 1892. Philippe remained in
England, with occasional trips to Europe, and was present at dinners
and receptions for foreign royalty all that week in London.

Did he meet Melba? It is likely that they sometimes met in public.
It is less likely that they met in private, for Philippe could not risk
offending his royalist supporters. Despite physical separation, Melba's
attachment to him continued. More than twenty years later she would
tell a friend that she believed Philippe was as true to her as when they
first met, and that she continued to love him with "all the passion and
intensity of their first love."

Melba seems to have believed that Charlie was in a phase of with-
drawal or retreat. In fact he was rather busy. Following his triumph at
Buffalo Bill's circus, his prowess as a rough rider had become public
knowledge in English equestrian circles. The previous year a Mr. Harry
Bentinck Budd, the owner of a large estate near East Grinstead, invited
Charlie to tame shiploads of South American broncos he was import-
ing into England to sell as hunters. Charlie was now in charge of Budd's
horsebreaking and riding school known as the Barbican, near the village
of Lingfield, and so well known that a journalist from the *New York Herald* came to interview him. The journalist vowed that eighty minutes of
Charlie in the saddle rendered the wildest bronco as docile as a lamb.

Charlie was visiting George regularly at his boarding school at
Worthing, and on an idyllic summer's day he took the boy to the Good-

wood races. George would never forget the bright colors of the jockeys' silks, the thundering hoofs, and the excitement of the crowd. There could be no doubt that ten-year-old George loved his father and that Charlie loved his son. The recent troubles in Charlie's life had turned that love into a fierce possessiveness.

During the summer of 1893 Charlie decided to take custody of his son. Charlie and his older brother Montague arrived at George's school and took the boy to the Liverpool docks. There, father and son embarked on a transatlantic steamer. The removal of the boy, accomplished swiftly and presumably with his cheerful agreement, was the easy work of a few hours. In the Armstrong family's version of events, Charlie took George with Melba's full consent. Melba—so it was said—wished to avoid scandal; believing that Charlie was bound to gain legal custody of George anyway, she decided to give in, thereby avoiding further disputes. The Armstrongs appear to have been unaware that Charlie effectively lost his case when the court refused to accept his English or Irish domicile. Therefore Melba did not have to make further concessions. Moreover she was unlikely to give up George without a fight. It seems almost certain that George was taken without her knowledge.

Once the child was gone, there was little she could do. The Court of Chancery, once Charlie had escorted George safely to America, was powerless to act. Moreover a father's right, in law, possibly outranked that of the court. It certainly outranked a mother's right. Melba could only hope that the Armstrongs spoke the truth when they declared that this sudden visit to the Armstrong cousins in the American South would last only a year or so. One year, even one week, was too long for Melba. She had always accepted that she would lose Philippe, but she had never been able to accept that one day she might lose George. Now that it had happened, it was almost like a death. In months to come, friends would notice an expression of sadness in Melba's unguarded face: they called it the "evidence of sorrow's discipline."

Melba was a resolute fighter. When her mother and then Vere died in quick succession and depression engulfed her, she had fought back by throwing herself into activity. She acted similarly now. She took the train to Livorno on the Italian west coast to visit Pietro Mascagni. Their friendship, based on mutual admiration, had taken hold despite the failure of *I Rantzau*. He was "very nice and simple," she told her friends, adding that she considered him "at the head of all Italian composers of the present generation." He in turn considered her the "perfect interpreter" of his music and had written an opera for her called *Romana*, which he now began to teach her. Despite the Italian heat, she tackled the score with enthusiasm. "It is beautiful and I think it will be the greatest thing he has done yet," she wrote proudly. Sadly, the opera seems to have vanished into oblivion.

At the beginning of September, Melba left Mascagni to prepare for her trip to the United States. She was to sing with the Metropolitan Opera at the World's Fair in Chicago, then join the Metropolitan's season in New York. "I loathe and hate the idea of going," she wrote from Livorno, "but I *must* I suppose." At the last moment, however, the engagement was postponed. Thereupon she temporarily offered her services to the impresario Karl Strakosch, a nephew of that same Strakosch who had so fortuitously died on the eve of her Brussels debut.

Karl, in the words of an observer, was "a pleasant-looking young man with a black hat and burgundy gloves, the tone of a world citizen and the sharp gaze of a businessman." It was a meeting of two sharp gazes, for Melba drove as hard a bargain as any member of the Strakosch family, and the young impresario was intrigued to discover that she would not sing unless she received her money by noon on the day of the performance. Knowing that she would make money for him, he engaged her for *Faust* and *Roméo et Juliette* in the French provincial town of Lille. Even better, he booked her for a gala to honor a Russian admiral at the Paris Opéra House, the first time she had sung there for almost two years. To crown his endeavors, Strakosch then secured her half a dozen appearances in Scandinavia.

At eight on the morning of October 25, Melba, Louie, and a maid boarded a ship for Stockholm along with Strakosch and sixteen trunks of clothes and costumes. Scandinavian newspapers were filled with advance publicity, most of it inaccurate. Melba was described as Minnie Armstrong Mitchell, married at eighteen to the son of an Irish baron, widowed at twenty-one, and now aged twenty-eight. For some of these mistakes Melba had only herself to blame. She had decided to subtract four years from her age and now claimed she was born in 1865.

In the space of two weeks, Melba sang *Lohengrin*, *Faust*, and the "mad scenes" from *Hamlet* and *Lucia* to audiences in Stockholm and

Copenhagen who could not hear enough of her. Journalists were so desperate for interviews that one disguised himself as a quarantine officer
and bluffed his way into her suite in Stockholm's Grand Hotel. Those
who did manage to interview her called her an "adorable beauty" with
a tall and stately figure, shining brown eyes, an aristocratic profile, and
"precious lips"—a real lady "of the first class."

Amid the hubbub, there was a sole dissenting voice, a Swedish critic calling himself Black Domino, who thought her singing was cold and
her acting was inept. He likened her movements in the "mad scene"
from *Lucia* to those of "a little lap dog that has fallen into the water
and runs around the beach in an attempt to shake itself dry." Strakosch
was furious and told reporters, "No matter where she has performed, be
it France, England, Russia or Belgium, she has never experienced such
treatment."

King Oscar of Sweden offered consolation in a practical form.
An amateur singer and lover of opera, he requested a personal performance, and chose "four of the most strenuous acts of four different
operas." The day after the performance the king invested Melba with
the order of Literature and Art. As he pinned the order to her breast,
he remembered with dismay the ancient superstition that said a sharp-
edged gift could cut a friendship. Fortunately he also remembered that
a kiss could break the spell. With kisses on both cheeks duly bestowed,
he declared happily, "Now we shall always be friends."

Three years later, back at Rue de Prony, Melba's agitated butler
explained that a giant of a man was at her door, claiming to be the king
of Sweden. A few moments later the king burst in, jovially requested
tea, and, after tea, demanded music. Flinging open her opera scores, he
proclaimed, "You will be Melba and I shall be Jean de Reszke." Soon his
fresh tenor voice was partnering Melba's in operatic duets.

At midnight on November 17, Melba, Louie, and a maid traveled
by train to the French port of Le Havre, from where they embarked for
America. The seas were rough and Melba was seasick, so it was with
relief that she sighted the Statue of Liberty and prepared to disembark
in New York. Once ashore she was astonished by what she saw. As she
rode in a cab over cobblestone streets—much rougher than those of
London—she gazed at a railway raised on iron pillars, at buildings more
than twenty stories high, the world's tallest, and at a mass of telegraph

wires that seemed to block out the sun. Near the green expanse of Central Park she alighted at the impressive portal of New York's Savoy Hotel. Here she found the latest comforts, including central heating that raised the temperatures of the rooms to near tropical levels. That first night, feeling almost suffocated, she went about the suite, opening the windows. Next day she felt too exhausted to rise from her bed.

When finally she reached the lavishly restored Metropolitan Opera House on Broadway, she saw, firsthand, the power of American energy and American money. Formed in 1883 at the whim of a few rich New Yorkers, the Metropolitan Opera Company had suffered mixed fortunes until Austrian-born Maurice Grau joined Henry Abbey as its joint director and, for practical purposes, its general manager. Believing that success depended primarily on the skill of its singers, Grau made it his business to secure the very best. Canvassing the foremost opera houses of Europe, he engaged the de Reszke brothers, Pol Plançon, Mario Ancona, Jean Lassalle, Victor Maurel, Lillian Nordica, Emma Eames, and Emma Calvé. Melba was delighted to see so many old friends.

To be part of so glittering an array was reassuring, but the prospect of competing—at a disadvantage—against three rival sopranos did not please her. Nordica, Eames, and Calvé had been performing since the season's opening and had already established their roles and reputations. Moreover Nordica and Eames were Americans, which naturally increased their popularity. If she were to obtain the parts and the partners she wanted, she realized, she would have a contest on her hands.

Fortunately she and Lillian Nordica already got on well, even though they sometimes competed for roles. Born Lillian Norton, a farmer's daughter from Maine, Nordica came, like Melba, from down-to-earth immigrant stock. She valued common sense and spoke her mind, and somehow that forged a bond. Fortunately, too, Melba was on reasonable terms with Emma Calvé, since the dissimilarity of their voices meant that they seldom aspired to the same part. A shared dislike of Emma Eames also contributed to their amity. Moreover Calvé spoke affectionately of Madame, which was always a sure passport to Melba's favor.

The envious Emma Eames produced no such passport. Since the incident over Juliette at the Paris Opéra, Eames's resentment of Melba had reached monstrous proportions. Any setbacks she encountered in Paris or London, she now tended to attribute partly or solely to Melba's malign influence. Eames's accusations, however, had little basis in fact. As her husband later admitted, it was Emma and not Melba who nursed the deep-rooted jealousy. Melba—possibly on Madame's advice—tried to maintain an attitude of indifference and had little to do with her rival. When their paths met, Melba would call out civilly, "Good day to you, Eames" and go on her way.

It was not easy to ignore Eames. According to many in the company, she was invincible in the eyes of the public. Melba would do well, they said, if she managed to stay in the second rank. Melba, fuming privately at these comments, kept her composure. With a shrug and a laugh, she replied that though Eames and Calvé and Nordica were favorites at the moment, she herself would be favorite by the season's end.

Her brave words concealed anxiety. In Brussels and Paris her position was cushioned by Madame's formidable influence, and in London by the de Greys' patronage. Here in New York she had no such allies. She would have to rely on herself and be careful how she did so, for no one knew better than she the malice and intrigue that ripened inside an opera company. She had tried to be seen—not always successfully—as "sweet Melba," but now she would have to be prepared to abandon the sweetness.

Even the choice of *Lucia* for her debut seemed ill-starred. While it was pleasing to have secured a role that would display her virtuosity—most of her usual parts having been captured by Eames—she soon discovered that *Lucia* had its drawbacks. Adelina Patti had performed the role twenty months earlier on the Metropolitan stage. Since Patti was generally considered the greatest Lucia of the age, the comparisons would probably be to Melba's detriment.

On the morning of her debut, December 4, 1893, came more disturbing news. Eugene Dufriche, a baritone who had sung with her at Covent Garden, fell ill. The opera would have been canceled had not Jean de Reszke met the baritone Victor de Gromzeski strolling down Broadway. Although the opera went ahead with de Gromzeski as substitute, the cast was unnerved, the chorus missed its cues, and poor de Gromzeski sang off-key. A voice in Melba's head kept warning her that this could be another fiasco like Rome.

The first act gained scant applause. In the second act the audience seemed sunk in apathy until suddenly, during the famous sextet, Melba's voice seemed to dance over the theatre, sweeping away the cobwebs of the earlier scenes. The matriarchs of New York society, who occupied the first-floor boxes known as the Diamond Horseshoe, had just arrived; so had forty romantic young gentlemen from the opera-loving Vaudeville Club, who were seated in the "omnibus box." Having heard tales of Melba's tragic love affair with the duke, they were already half in love with her; when they saw her face and figure and heard her voice, they fell totally in love. In the words of one observer, their hearts could be seen heaving heavily under their "immaculate shirt bosoms." When the act was over, they thundered their applause.

The next act contained the "mad scene" for which her audience was waiting avidly. Sensing the anticipation, Melba soared to the occasion. Trill after trill ascended to the galleries, setting "thousands of ears quivering with delight and expectation." In the "mad scene," wrote one critic, "you could feel the note of passion in her voice that may have been missed before, and it thrilled everyone with its intensity and warmth." At the final curtain, few in the theatre were not cheering.

In the following weeks Melba scored success after success, appearing in *Hamlet* and *Rigoletto* and *Faust*, and in Rossini's *Semiramide*. This last, most difficult *bel canto* opera, learned in record time even though she had contracted influenza, earned her the title from one critic of "the most gifted lyric soprano of our time." She also played Nedda in the Metropolitan premiere of *Pagliacci* and confounded those critics who claimed she could not act. From her first entrance in a very becoming hat, she was adored by the audience, and what she lacked in passion she made up in charm. There was just one actor in *Pagliacci*, however, whom she could not outshine. It was the pretty little donkey that pulled the cart for the strolling players. A born exhibitionist, it jumped about so friskily that it almost threw Melba out of the cart.

Although her successes came quickly and surely, they were slow to convince the directors of the company. To her great annoyance, it was not until January 14, 1894, that she found herself officially elevated to the first rank. On that night she was permitted to sing with the stars of the Metropolitan at one of their Sunday night concerts. Coming on stage, she received such a thunderous welcome that the tears trickled down her cheeks. Hastily composing herself, she sang an exquisitely florid song by Handel called "Sweet Bird," in which the voice and the flute mimicked the song of the nightingale. The acclaim when she finished was astonishing: "Women wept hysterically, and men shouted themselves hoarse." The entire audience, including the orchestra, wrote one jubilant reporter, "joined in a paean of applause."

Five days later, as proof of her elevation, she was cast with Jean de Reszke in *Roméo et Juliette*. She should have been delighted, but she was not. It was insufficient to be acknowledged as a leading singer in the *bel canto* and lyrical repertoires: too many Americans despised the old-fashioned operas. She wanted to sing modern works, being only too aware that Calvé's portrayal of Carmen was taking New York by storm.

Although she could not hope to equal Calvé as a dramatic actress, she was determined to show that at least she could sing Wagner. On January 29, forgetting her fears about singing heavier music and with only a few days preparation, she took over the role of Elisabeth in Wagner's *Tannhäuser*. The critic for the *New York Sun*, the well-known W. J. Henderson, wrote that her emotional scene in the second act was so beautiful that it "amazed the soprano's friends, and put her enemies, if she had any, to confusion." A week later she sang the part of Elsa in *Lohengrin*. The *New York Herald* called it "incomparably the most attractive thing she has done."

Melba's fame was now such that she was increasingly sought out by reporters. In interviews she was described as "tall and very stately of carriage"; to accentuate her stateliness she liked to greet interviewers in an austere black velvet gown, with long gold chains studded with turquoises and pearls hanging to her waist. Gone was the flirtatiousness with which she had often greeted reporters in France. In New York she was cordial and straightforward, like an American, and conveyed a simple friendliness.

In answer to requests, she described her typical day. She was awakened by her maid with an early morning cup of tea at eight o'clock, before taking a brisk walk in nearby Central Park. After breakfast she and Louie answered her correspondence. She received many begging letters, the latest from a criminal in prison who asked her for a banjo and promised never to forget her. She told reporters that she considered all these requests and responded to those she believed to be worthy. In the morning she also worked silently on her roles—she knew seventeen by heart and was keen to extend the number. After lunch she attended rehearsals at the theatre, and in the late afternoon she either rested or saw her friends. On the days when she sang, she ate a small meal at five in the afternoon; otherwise she had her main meal just before eight in the evening. She told reporters that she ate sparingly, took plenty of exercise, and preserved her voice by practicing for no more than ten minutes a day.

When answering questions, she declined to reveal the number of performances she was giving, possibly because she did not want to admit it to herself. In the Marchesi rule book, a singer who sang more than three operas a week risked damaging her vocal cords; ideally, according to Madame, one should sing no more than two long roles in a week. By the end of February, Melba was on tour with the company, singing in Philadelphia, Boston, Chicago, and St. Louis, and obliged some weeks to sing more than three roles, some of them undeniably long. More-over the train journeys and intense cold of the North American winter, coupled with the oppressive heat of the buildings, sapped her energy and troubled her throat. She dreaded passing from an overheated hotel or train into the freezing air outside.

While Melba often worried about her throat, by far her greatest worry was George. Predictably Charlie and he had stayed only a brief time with the Armstrong cousins; his last known address was a post office box in Cherokee, North Carolina. Where Charlie and his son were now his relatives did not know, for father and son were moving westward, prompted by Charlie's roving spirit and probably also by his desire to avoid detection. Meanwhile George, bewildered by constant change and the strange, wild life of the American frontier, pined for his mother, clung to his father, and retreated into himself.

To be in the same country as her son and not know where he was became a torture to Melba. As she reached each new city she hoped she might see him, even though she knew that America was vast and her hopes were unreasonable. Her spirits plummeted when she left a city no wiser than when she came. Almost every little boy she saw seemed to remind her of George. In Chicago, as she stepped from her train, she confronted a tiny newsboy, shivering in the cold. In answer to her question of how long must he stand there, she received the reply, "Until I sell these fifty papers." "Well, I'll buy fifty," returned Melba. Whereupon the astonished child asked in surprise, "But have you got enough money?" It was not just the newsboy she saw: in her mind's eye it was George.

Her anxiety over George was exacerbated by her loneliness. She missed Madame and Gladys de Grey and felt alone and unprotected. She did not even have a succession of parties to take her mind off her troubles. Most leaders of New York society regarded her as no more than an opera singer, and it would be years before they welcomed her to their dinner parties.

That year, apart from her secretary Louie, she had no confidante, no diverting friends, indeed little social life at all. She was consequently overjoyed when Comte Boniface de Castellane, the nephew of her Parisian admirer the Prince de Sagan, called at her hotel. One of the most preposterous dandies in France, Boni entered her suite "like a breath of the Boulevards on Broadway." His "exquisite clothes, his glistening cane, his elaborate buttonholes, and the air he always had of holding all the riches of the East in fee, even when he was hard put to pay his hotel bill," made him an extraordinarily exotic creature in workaday America.

Boni saw himself as an eighteenth-century courtier. "Faced with an uncomprehending middle-class society," he wrote, "I put myself back in the past, and there I composed for myself an existence of curious pageantry, beautiful women and rare spectacles." To live thus he needed vast sums of money, so he had come to America to marry an heiress. He began by proposing to Anne Morgan, daughter of the multi-millionaire Pierpont Morgan. When she turned him down he proposed to equally wealthy Anna Gould and was accepted. At the time of his call on Melba, he was awaiting their marriage. Melba respected his honesty in openly courting heiresses, but she also knew that spendthrift and unfaithful Boni was likely to make any wife miserable. She was in no mood to lecture him, however; nor was he in any mood to listen. He was bent on frivolity down to his painted pink toenails, and Melba embraced his mood thankfully.

Another who brought her the welcome flavor of Europe was the popular novelist Francis Marion Crawford. Although an American citizen, Crawford had grown up in Italy and later made his home in Rome, where he spent part of each year with his wife and four children. The rest of his time was spent courting adventure, which he subsequently shaped into the pages of his novels. When Melba met him in New York early in 1894, he was convalescing from surgery and behaving like one of his dying heroes.

Knowing he had written a series of best-sellers, Melba was flattered by his interest. She was also attracted by his muscular body, dark mustache, and the "sad and far away" expression in his pale blue eyes, which were prone to weeping. Sometimes the tears ran down his face while she was singing. As a young man he had taken singing lessons in Boston, and Melba sometimes partnered him in duets. She praised his voice, which proved that she saw him through rose-colored glasses, because neither his aunt, Julia Ward Howe, nor his singing teacher in Boston believed he could sing in tune.

Crawford played on Melba's wish for romance, and she happily accepted him. He would "throw absolutely all restraint to the winds and bring out the deepest secrets of his heart." One day he confided the story of his faithless first love. Since then, he explained, he had grown cold and had "lost faith in all women," but Melba's singing had made him alive again. Taking up her autograph book he scrawled across the page, *Credo in resurrectum mortuorum*—"I believe in the resurrection of the dead." Later he would work the incident into a trilogy of novels—*Fair Margaret*, *Prima Donna*, and *The Diva's Ruby*, the heroine of which was loosely based on Melba.

"I don't think I have been more thankful for my gift of song than on that occasion," Melba later wrote, recalling his inscription in her autograph book. Whether more was involved than song one cannot know, but it seems likely. He was a practiced seducer, and she was in the mood to be seduced.

Much has been rumored about Melba's sexual activities. It is said that she had an insatiable appetite for virile young men, an assertion impossible to confirm, as most of those who might have testified were bound by a social code of silence. All one can say is that in Melba's social set lovers were readily accepted, and Melba was a young, vigorous, and attractive woman. It would be surprising if she did not have an active sex life. Against this one must remember that to stay at the top as a singer, she was required to exercise unremitting self-discipline. Her diversions, such as they might have been, had to be carefully regulated, and, after Philippe, were seldom allowed to touch her too deeply. Crawford may have been among the exceptions. She called him "one of the greatest friends whom I have ever had."

On April 26, 1894, Melba sang her final *Lucia* for the season. So insistent were the calls for her at the end that, though she had taken off her costume, she was obliged to don a dressing gown and come in front of the curtain to acknowledge the applause. Even then the fans would not let her go. In response, a piano was wheeled onstage, and Melba played and sang "Home Sweet Home." The gesture had a touch of effrontery because Patti was renowned for concluding her concerts by playing and singing that song. By performing it, Melba was, in a sense, proclaiming herself the new Patti.

The audience did not resent the gesture. On the contrary, it appeared to agree with her. For a moment "the house was completely hushed." Then it burst into prolonged applause. Those sitting near the stage saw that Melba was in tears.

I Won't Sing "Home Sweet Home"

MELBA SAILED from America with mixed emotions. On one hand, she exulted in the warmth of the audience's fare-well to her at the Metropolitan. On the other, she was glad to escape from the painful search for George and was "dying for a breath of European air." To Madame Marchesi she wrote: "Oh! won't I be glad to get back." Nevertheless on arriving in Paris in the first week of May 1894 she barely had time to visit her old teacher before scurrying to Milan for a second season at La Scala. "You can imagine how happy I am at the idea of singing at my beloved *Scala*," she told Madame ecstatically.

Her season in Milan opened with *Lucia* on May 13. The opera house was packed, and it was packed again a week later when she sang the role of Gilda. Dressed in a simple white dress, with her "gold brown hair beautifully styled," she looked charming and sounded superb. Her "interminable trill" at the end of "Caro nome" elicited such shouts that she was obliged to repeat the whole of the aria. "Madame Melba has achieved another brilliant victory," wrote *La Perseveranza*, "even more significant if we consider that not everyone believed that her artistic talents were suited to an adequate interpretation of the sweet and passionate character of Gilda." Not all Milanese critics concurred, and at least one believed that a successful Gilda required more passion than Melba could deliver. The belief that an opera singer should embody the skills of a dramatic actress as well as the voice of a nightingale had permeated even that stronghold of *bel canto* singing, La Scala.

It was probably on this visit to La Scala that Melba met Giuseppe Verdi. In her autobiography she claimed they met in Milan in 1893, but she was obviously confusing the dates, as in that year he left the city one week before her arrival. He was certainly in Milan late in May 1894, and a meeting could have taken place, though one of Verdi's distinguished biographers denies it. He believes that Melba was so stung by the composer's refusal to teach her in 1892 that she invented the meeting to soothe her wounded feelings, and that she broadcast it after Verdi's death when there was no fear of contradiction.

According to Melba, the eighty-year-old Verdi visited her in her dressing room after a performance of *Rigoletto*. Being told he was waiting, she hurried to the door crying, "Maestro! What an honour!" and found herself greeted by an austere old man who bowed slowly, putting her in mind of "a gnarled, wonderful old tree" bending in the wind. "There was an impenetrable reserve about him," she remembered, "which made one's conversation with him slightly stilted. And yet, he had bright eyes, like a boy's, and eager, restless hands."

Gathering her courage, she begged the favor of singing him *Otello*. He replied gravely that it was "not a favour" and arranged for her to visit him the next day. They met in a long, cool room with the sun streaming through the windows and he played and played on the piano until they had finished the whole opera. She recalled that he was an inspiring master. "He made one feel his phrases as he himself felt them," she wrote, "and gave to each phrase an added loveliness." As she finished, his face lit up in a rare smile. "Tell me—" he asked, "with whom have you studied this role?" She answered, "With Tosti." At that he nodded and added, "He is the only man who would have taught you to sing my opera like that."

Melba's account is so vivid that one suspects it is true. Moreover there is a snippet of corroborating evidence. "We parted firm friends," Melba wrote, "I hugging a precious photograph." Melba's granddaughter, Pamela Vestey, now owns that photograph, and across one corner in almost illegible French runs the message: "To my celebrated"—the next word is unreadable—"Nellie Melba." It is signed with a straggling "G Verdi." Their relationship was therefore not confined to Salvatore

Marchesi's request for lessons and Verdi's curt refusal. At the very least, Verdi thought enough of Melba to give her a photograph of himself and to address her as a "celebrated" singer.

After leaving Milan, Melba seems to have stayed briefly with Tosti in Venice. Maybe it was on this trip that they hired a gondola and a harmonium and ventured onto the moonlit lagoon, where Melba sang Tosti's songs. Soon a "chain of gondolas followed, like a black serpent with a hundred eyes" and the air quivered with cries of "Brava Melba, Bravo Tosti." Remembering the scene, she wrote nostalgically: "Never shall I forget the marvellous feeling that I had as my voice echoed over the water in that city of dreams. I can see at this moment, the little gondolas drifting in on us from all sides, out of the dark canals, curving round corners with lanterns gleaming faintly."

At the start of June 1894 Melba was in London and ready to open the Covent Garden season with a performance of *Faust*. She followed it in quick succession with *Lucia*, *Rigoletto*, and *Roméo et Juliette*, and on July 7 with a revised version of *Elaine*. According to the *Times*, her voice had increased in volume and her acting had "gained remarkably in intensity." George Bernard Shaw, reviewing *Faust*, marveled at the constant accuracy of her intonation: "You never realise," he wrote, "how wide a gap there is between the ordinary singer who simply avoids the fault of singing obviously out of tune and the singer who sings really and truly in tune, except when Melba is singing." Of *Elaine* the audiences and critics spoke less glowingly. The singers were praised—and Melba received five curtain calls—but the opera was nonetheless considered dull.

On June 15 Melba sang the last performance of *Lohengrin* she would ever sing in London and it gave rise to an event that earned her more enduring fame than any one of her stage appearances. Many versions of the episode exist, including Melba's own, which seems to be among the least accurate. The most likely version comes from Auguste Escoffier, the great French chef who made the Savoy Hotel dining room the gastronomic envy of Europe.

To thank Escoffier for his superb dishes, Melba presented him with tickets to *Lohengrin* and the shy little man repaid his patroness with a splendid dessert when next she entertained guests at the Savoy. He peeled and poached ripe white peaches in vanilla syrup, covered them

Above: Nellie Mitchell—the future Melba—was the eldest of eight children, and is seen here at left with her sisters Annie and Belle. Her first public performance was in childhood, at a Sunday school concert. Afterward one of her playmates told her, "Nellie Mitchell, I saw your drawers."

Left: Melba met Charles Armstrong in Mackay in 1882. Nicknamed Kangaroo Charlie, he was a fearless rider and boxer and appealed strongly to Melba's sense of adventure. After a brief courtship, she insisted on marrying him.

Dressed in a white dress and flowered bonnet, Melba wed Charles Armstrong in the parsonage of Ann Street Presbyterian Church in Brisbane. Arrangements for the marriage were made by her father only a few hours before the ceremony.

In 1886 Melba entered the École Marchesi in Paris, a kind of finishing school for divas. The principal, Mathilde Marchesi, became Melba's singing teacher, mentor, second mother, and one of the strongest influences on her life.

Philippe, Duke of Orléans, was the great love of Melba's life. When they met, he was the most glamorous royal duke in Europe and second in line to the French throne if the monarchy were to succeed in being restored. He so much resembled Charlie that observers sometimes confused them.

Their time together in Paris in 1887 forged strong bonds between Melba and her only child, George.

Ophelia, in Thomas's opera *Hamlet*, was one of Melba's finest roles. Her brilliant performances of the fearsomely difficult "mad scene" earned wild applause from audiences and the fervent admiration of the composer.

Melba as Mimi in *La Bohème*, one of the few modern roles well suited to Melba's *bel canto* voice. She would be identified with the role for more than twenty years.

When Melba toured Australia in 1902, her fame, voice, clothes, and jewels dazzled audiences. She is seen here in one of her concert gowns, with her father and her niece Nellie Patterson.

Melba here poses at her Thames-side house with Australian playwright Haddon Chambers (holding his hat) and the Australian sculptor Bertram Mackennal. Chambers was Melba's long-term lover and, like the duke, looked not unlike Charlie.

Above: Melba made numerous rail tours of North America, sometimes with her concert party, sometimes with her opera company. She traveled in luxury, in a residential railcar, dubbed by the press her "palace on wheels."

Right: On June 15, 1920, at the Marconi Studio at Chelmsford, England, Melba sang in the first concert ever to be broadcast on radio. She opened the concert with her characteristic trill, then sang "Home Sweet Home." Listeners as far away as Madrid heard her.

Above: Melba's son and daughter-in-law, George and Evie Armstrong, pose with Melba's pet parrot and bulldog. George's happiness was paramount to Melba. She was overjoyed when, after a disastrous first marriage, he wed her protégée Evelyn Doyle and gave her a granddaughter, Pamela.

Right: Melba fought old age, ill health, and declining vocal powers to the last. She told her accompanist, "I must sing or I will die."

Melba in Paris, September 20, 1930, shortly after she is rumored to have had a face-lift.

Melbourne, February 26, 1931: Melba's funeral was stupendous. Flags flew at half-mast, and thousands lined the streets to bid her farewell.

with a puree of strawberries, and laid them on a bed of vanilla ice cream. This in turn he dramatically presented on the back of Lohengrin's swan, carved from a single block of ice. The result so enchanted Melba that Escoffier gave his *Pêches au Cygne* the new name of *Pêches Melba*, and as such it became a staple of the Savoy cuisine. About ten years later Escoffier improved the dish by substituting raspberries for strawberries. It is the revised recipe that has been passed on to us.

From Escoffier's inventive hand there also came another dish named after Melba, though its first recipient was Marie Ritz, the wife of the Savoy's manager. By placing thin slices of bread in a cool oven to dry, Escoffier made a type of toast which he presented to Madame Ritz when she was trying to lose weight. Melba, who after the age of thirty was always longing to be thinner, took a fancy to the bread and eventually gave it her name. As Melba toast it can be found today on many menus.

"I am very busy and very tired," Melba wrote to Madame in mid-July. After a dearth of social life in America, she was experiencing the other extreme in London, being rushed off her feet with parties. She was also receiving Australian visitors, among them a contralto named Ada Crossley who came bearing letters from Annie and Belle Mitchell. Almost always ready to help aspiring Australians, Melba auditioned her and urged her to enroll at the École Marchesi. To Madame she wrote that Ada had "a most *glorious* voice and I predict a great future for her if she has your tuition."

Another Australian seeking her help was a flautist of Greek parentage named John Lemmoné. The moment she saw his name, Melba remembered the dapper, dark-haired young man who had played a flute solo at her Elsasser concert in Melbourne in 1884. She recalled that he had told her that he had bought his first flute with gold he had extracted from a stream at Ballarat. Inviting him to call at her suite at the Savoy, she peppered him with questions. "Her tongue never stopped," he later remembered. "Australia was more to Melba than the rest of the world put together." Next day he played his flute for her, Melba herself providing the piano accompaniment. She was so admiring of his skill that she gave him a letter to Tosti and another to her own agent, Daniel Mayer.

Lemmoné's concert career was launched by Mayer, but Melba had her own plans for him. She had not lost sight of her girlhood dream "to win individual fame and associate it proudly with the land of my birth." Having accepted a second season at the Metropolitan, she had thoughts of sailing across the Pacific at the end of the season and performing in operas or concerts across Australia, accompanied by a team of expatriate Australian musicians. In June, full of enthusiasm, she may even have signed a contract with the Melbourne impresario J. C. Williamson; but by August the tour was shelved.

At the end of September 1894 Melba and Louie Bennett sailed for America. Melba left with a certain reluctance, anticipating more loneliness and more anxiety over George. She also feared possible wrangles with Maurice Grau over roles and singing partners; but to sing at the Metropolitan now conferred such prestige that singers refused its invitation at their peril. Fortunately her concern over her ranking quickly proved unfounded. Grau now rated her as one of his finest singers. No sooner had she arrived than she was on the company train, performing a preseason concert tour with the other stars.

The previous year touring had depressed her, but now, in a more relaxed mood, she enjoyed it. Traveling with her fellow performers to Philadelphia, Albany, Buffalo, New Haven, and Boston through October and early November, she found little time to be lonely or sad. In the confinement of the railcars the de Reszke brothers, Plançon, Maurel, Ancona, and Nordica became her operatic family, and their gossip—and even their squabbles—took her back to days at Doonside. A superlative mimic, Jean de Reszke used to give "marvellous imitations of the various artists of the company coming into his dressing room to offer their congratulations after his first appearance." He would be in turn a patronizing Frenchman, an overcorrect German, a wildly emotional Italian, and a "real Yankee." As the Yankee he would exclaim in a broad American accent, "Jean, you done fine!"

That year the Italian tenor Francesco Tamagno joined the company. His astounding voice was said to have "the metallic penetrativeness of an eight-inch shell," but at heart he remained a simple peasant, and his peasantlike parsimony was a source of amusement. One night Melba and Jean de Reszke watched openmouthed as he pocketed the after-dinner candies and souvenired a bunch of orchids from the table. Soon after, at a lunch, Melba saw him gather up his neighbor's uneaten cutlets and wrap them in a newspaper. He said they were for his dog, but Melba guessed they were for his own dinner.

The touring musicians made fun of Tamagno, but none dared to joke about Jean de Reszke. The highest-paid singer and a favorite of royalty, Jean was always treated with deference, not least by Melba. He was her ideal singer and her mentor. After one of their early performances together she wrote to him: "Is it possible for you to know how great you are? You gave me an emotion last night such as I have never experienced in my life. What art, what perfection, in short, what everything!" He returned the compliment by thanking her for "her smile, her style, her games of fancy," and for the faithful affection she gave to her friends.

To be in such company gave her increasing pleasure, but three weeks into the tour she caught a cold. Her hoarseness became so pronounced that she canceled her engagements, striving to be ready for the opening opera in New York on November 19. Fortunately she was to appear that night as Juliette, a role she had sung so often that it gave her no uneasiness. In fact all but one of her operatic roles that season were well known to her. The one exception was the queen in Meyerbeer's *Les Huguenots*. An historic production featuring seven of the company's finest singers, it would pass into operatic history. "There was without doubt never before or since such a star cast," wrote W. J. Henderson half a century later, citing *Les Huguenots* as proof that the 1890s were indeed "the golden age of opera."

In mid-December, Bemberg arrived at the Metropolitan for the American premiere of his opera *Elaine*. Whatever loneliness Melba might still have felt was banished by the excitement of his visit. His impish ways quickly reappeared. Not content with making free use of Melba's dressing room, he began to take over the dressing room belonging to the bass, Pol Plançon; indeed he was reputedly surprised there in the act of having sex with Plançon. Although audiences found his operas boring, no one could say the same of Bemberg the man.

Nor could anyone accuse Melba, that season, of being bored or boring. In the New Year of 1895, she celebrated her budding relationship with the Boston Symphony Orchestra by singing at a matinee concert, the like of which Boston's staid music lovers had never seen. With a flirtatious charm that had earlier captivated the members of the orchestra, she "dragged" a shy young composer out of the green room and onto the stage and proceeded to sing "I Love and the World Is Mine" to his piano accompaniment. When it was over she even persuaded him take a bow with her. The incident was considered so unusual that the writer Thomas Sullivan related it by letter to the grande dame of Boston culture, Isabella Gardner, who was traveling in Italy. He also reported that Clayton Johns, the young composer, was completely under Melba's spell, and Tymoteusz Adamowski, the Polish conductor of the Boston Symphony Pops concerts, "had hitched his wagon to a star" and was now "Melba's slave." "I have met the lady," he added, "and understand the fascination, which isn't Bostonian in the least."

Melba's popularity was now so high that the phenomenon was discussed in the newspapers. The *New York Globe* called it the "Melba rage" and doubted "whether demonstrations of equal intensity have ever before been witnessed in the metropolis." Melba, aware of her drawing power, claimed that the company lost money on those nights when she did not appear. "The other night," she wrote privately, "Eames sang Faust and there were not 500 people in the hall which holds 900, and it was a good lesson to her and she is in her own country here, HA! HA! God is punishing her." Melba herself, on the other hand, sang "always to crowded houses." In the face of such evidence it seemed extraordinary to her that the directors of the Metropolitan would not acknowledge her worth by paying her more.

Melba knew that in America opera was regarded as virtually synonymous with culture. She knew too that almost every American town of reasonable size aspired to have its own opera house, be it a simple wooden hall built above commercial offices holding about five hundred spectators or a free-standing Greek temple holding more than a thousand. Traveling troupes, like those Melba had known in Mackay, provided the operas. Costumes, lighting, and scenery were sketchy, mishaps were frequent, and standards of performance were mediocre at best. Nevertheless these troupes gained audiences. As one observer put it, ordinary people craved enchantment and longed for a connection with the great world beyond the plains or mountains. Opera satisfied those yearnings.

Having lived in Mackay, Melba understood these cravings. And being her father's daughter, she was alert to the opportunity to make money. She was convinced that she could profit by taking a first-class company to remote towns. In the past ten years Adelina Patti had made three successful opera tours of the United States, traveling with her own company in her own train—almost a royal tour. If Patti could do it, so could Melba. Losing patience with the Metropolitan's directors, she decided to form her own troupe. While her obvious aim was to spite Henry Abbey and Maurice Grau and earn fame and fortune on her own, she may well have had a further motive. The tour would take her westward, where Charlie and George were most likely to be found.

She confided her idea to Charles Ellis, the manager of the Boston Symphony Orchestra, a young man whose equable temperament and business acumen so impressed her that within twenty minutes of their meeting she had appointed him as her American business manager. In no time the *New York Times* had wind of her plans. "Madame Melba Affected with Starring Fever" ran the headline of an article in April 1895; the reporter went on to accuse Melba of harboring "fond delusions." There was no singer alive, he argued, "who can carry the burden of an opera season in the United States unaided." He also warned that if she shunned the Metropolitan the next season, Abbey and Grau might well engage the Polish soprano Marcella Sembrich and not invite her again.

Melba's determination wavered. Possibly the reporter was right. Patti's tours had been financially backed by an impresario, but Melba would be risking her own money. On April 30 she sang the "mad scene" from *Lucia* at the Metropolitan's final concert. At the end she stood "glowing with triumph, radiant in the glory of the moment, while the crowd yelled itself hoarse." Should she be content with scenes like this, or should she risk money and reputation by creating her own company? She was not yet sure of the answer.

Sailing back to England, Melba opened at Covent Garden on May 25. Two weeks later, during a performance of *Faust*, she found herself on the brink of disaster. As she stood in the wings watching Méphistophélès enter in a carefully contrived burst of flame, something went wrong. Within seconds the scenery was alight. Plançon, with his back to the blaze, continued to sing, but the audience realized the danger. The curtain descended abruptly, leaving the spectators close to panic. Of all those standing on or near the stage, only Melba had the presence of mind to go before the curtain and calm the audience. She was greeted with "ringing cheers."

Melba sang the role of Marguerite again on June 12, following it with Lucia, Juliette, and Gilda. In addition she played Micaela to Emma Calvé's Carmen, audiences flocking to hear the greatest dramatic soprano of the time perform alongside the singer who was already being nominated as Patti's successor. For at the age of fifty-two, Patti had just given notice of her retirement. That season, as part of her farewell, she returned to Covent Garden for six final performances, her voice still beguiling but clearly aging. Melba, on the other hand, was singing in a manner that "would be difficult to surpass" and acting in a way that "left little to be desired." Few doubted that Melba was the new Patti.

To lighten the burden of performing, Melba rented a house for the summer called Fernley, overlooking the River Thames and near the picturesque towns of Marlow and Maidenhead. Here the river was wide and its banks were lush and broad, and Melba's tree-shaded garden ran down to the water. In a way it was a little like the landscape at Doonside, and to lie in bed and listen to the river revived memories of her childhood. Moreover the house proved an ideal launching place for excursions and adventures. At the regatta town of Henley, she and Tosti, imitating their impromptu concert in Venice, boarded a boat with a harmonium and made music on the river. But at Henley there was "not a cheer, not even a clap from the assembled punts." Their attempts to collect money for a charity raised only a trifling sum.

Melba entertained a succession of guests at her house, including some of the Irish Armstrongs, whose friendship had withstood the warfare with Charlie. She also entertained visiting Australians, one of whom was lively, brown-haired Agnes Murphy, who had championed her from the pages of *Melbourne Punch*. It was a thrill for Agnes to meet her idol and to report the event to her readers. Melba was "so natural, wholly unaffected and entirely fascinating in her debonair bearing," wrote Agnes, and—she added kindly—more slender than she appeared in her photographs.

Agnes was at Melba's matinee concert at the Queen's Hall on June 15, 1895, when Melba sang with the renowned Hungarian conductor Arthur Nikisch. She described Melba as wearing a gown of pink silk shot with bronze and a black hat trimmed with plumes, and reported that she sang the "mad scene" from *Hamlet* and Handel's "Sweet Bird." Melba had chosen the pieces for their flute *obbligati* in the hope that her Australian flautist friend, John Lemmoné, could enhance his career by playing them for her. But in fact her plan had the opposite effect. The *Times* spoke disparagingly of the "coarseness of his style," which was made all the more noticeable when juxtaposed with Melba's re-fined singing.

At the conclusion of Melba's songs, a congratulatory arch of or-chids—taller than she was, with a canary suspended from its apex—was hauled onstage. Melba herself considered the canary an amusing gift, but the *Times* called it vulgar. George Bernard Shaw had already written sarcastically about Melba's floral tributes. He called them those "large baskets which English ladies and gentlemen invariably carry with them to the theatre, and which they present to singers in moments of uncon-trollable admiration."

The arch may have come from Madame Marchesi, because she was known to favor lavish floral tributes. Madame had enjoyed an emo-tional reunion with Melba after their long separation, and had been persuaded to join her beloved Nellie at the Savoy for June and July. She was certainly present at Covent Garden on July 8 when the house literally rose to Melba after the "mad scene" in *Lucia*. Agnes Murphy, also present, reported that a "lusty Australian" bellowed from the up-per stalls a coo-ee, which was easily heard above the shouts and storms of clapping. A few days later Melba and Madame sat in a box to hear Emma Eames sing the part of the countess in *The Marriage of Figaro*. As Madame's dislike of Emma was equal to Melba's, they no doubt had a lively and loquacious evening.

At the Savoy there was another guest with a claim on Melba's af-fections. It was Philippe in a wheelchair, having broken his leg while attending the ninth birthday of the king of Spain. On June 25 his sister Helene was to marry the Duke of Aosta at a church near London, and as head of the family—for the Comte de Paris had died the previous September—Philippe was to preside over the celebrations. Like many a rebellious son who has vainly tried to escape his responsibilities, he embraced his new duties with overbearing correctness. He was angry to find that the Savoy's manager, César Ritz, had double-booked the banquet room: a dinner to be attended by the Prince of Wales was being given precedence over the dinner Philippe was holding for his royal relatives. Conscious that the hotel had behaved disgracefully, Ritz spared no expense and ordered that the basement be transformed into a second banquet room.

Melba must have read the descriptions of the wedding and dinner, which filled long columns of the newspapers. One imagines she may also have met Philippe, if only by chance, as both were living at the hotel. It cannot have been easy for either of them, for his role as head of the royal house demanded Melba's exclusion from his life. This phase of her life seemed to be a series of losses and there seemed no remedy but to bear them patiently.

Patience, however, was not one of Melba's virtues, so she threw herself into her work. She needed a new accompanist, and one night, while waiting in the wings, she noticed an intense, dark-haired young man in his early twenties, gazing at her with "big brown eyes that shone out of his pale face like stars." "And who on earth are you?" she asked bluntly, whereupon the youth went hot and cold and red and white. He stammered that he was Landon Ronald, one of the company's accompanists. Melba liked his looks—after satisfying herself as to his musicianship, she invited him to the Savoy to coach her in the score of *Manon* by Jules Massenet. The poor boy had never set eyes on that opera, but he bought a copy and spent a sleepless night learning the music. Next morning they worked together on the opera score and also on songs, the music of which she sent her maid to fetch. Eventually she was so pleased that she told him: "Remember, that for the future, you are Melba's sole accompanist."

A few months earlier in America, Melba had set her sights on the role of Manon. It was one of the few parts written in the previous ten years that suited her voice. At the Metropolitan it had been sung exclusively by a red-haired American from the École Marchesi named Sybil Sanderson, but Melba intended to capture it for herself. She even ordered the appropriate costumes from the celebrated French couturier Jacques Doucet and arranged lessons with the opera's composer.

At the end of the season Melba traveled to Paris to study with Massenet, who, since Gounod's death in 1893, was France's foremost operatic composer. Melba found him "a charming oldish man with a passion for flowers, and a habit of coining very pretty phrases." She also found him a devil for work: "He never let anything pass, however slight; and if he did not like my singing of a phrase, he would go over it a hundred times." Fascinated by her ability to pitch her voice to whatever the size of the auditorium, he told her that she was like a Stradivarius violin, renowned for accommodating its tone to the space required of it. He began calling her Madame Stradivarius, a name that may have signified more than just the coining of a pretty phrase. Massenet had been infatuated by Sybil Sanderson, but the infatuation was ending. He may have hoped to make Melba her successor. If so, he hoped in vain.

By September it was almost time for Melba to return to America. This time she was eager to sail, and it was her secretary, Louie Bennett, who went reluctantly. Louie had promised to marry a stockbroker named Kenyon Mason and hated leaving him. On the other hand, she lacked the heart to desert Melba when seven months of taxing work awaited her. In the end they both sailed aboard the *St. Louis* in mid-September.

Melba was returning triumphantly to the Metropolitan because Abbey and Grau had raised her salary almost to the level of Jean de Reszke's. This triumph, however, had not dissuaded her from forming her own touring troupe. Arriving in New York on September 21, Melba told reporters that she and Charles Ellis had formed the Melba Operatic Concert Company to give fifty opera concerts in Canada and the United States over the following three months. The concerts would feature arias from opera in the first half of the program, and scenes from opera in the second, to be performed in costume but with a minimum of scenery. She and Charles Ellis had engaged an experienced team of singers, all former colleagues from the Metropolitan Company: the mezzo Sofia Scalchi, the baritone Guiseppe Campanari, the tenor Lloyd D'Aubigné, and the soprano Mathilde Bauermeister. In a burst of inspiration, Melba was bringing Landon Ronald to conduct the thirty-five-piece orchestra, misleadingly describing him to the press as the musical director of Covent Garden.

Energy, determination, and ingenuity were needed to run a touring company. Trains were often late, baggage went astray, theatres and hotels tended to be primitive, and fire from the theatres' gaslights was a constant hazard. Ellis, although a veteran of orchestral tours, had no experience with theatrical troupes and found himself having to learn fast. Melba, however, already knew something of opera touring and had a flair for solving practical problems. By the end of the tour there were few details of management that she had not examined. Years later, when she had her own company in Australia, onlookers would be surprised by her almost obsessive concern with costumes, lighting, and stage props.

Many prophesied failure for the fledgling company, but it scored remarkable success following its opening night in Montreal. Towns that rarely saw grand opera provided overflowing houses. Reassuring Madame from St. Paul that her voice was in beautiful condition and that the opera concerts had been "extraordinarily successful," she boasted that in the space of three months she hoped to clear 400,000 francs, and "no one has done this except Patti." "I am blowing my own trumpet," she added disarmingly, "which is a thing I particularly object to: but I know this will interest you."

In Landon Ronald's recollection, Melba on tour was a magical companion. He remembered her "laughing incessantly, telling one joke after another, recounting all sorts of experiences with much humour." She had "a rare gift of mimicry" and could convulse her companions with "imitations of some of her colleagues." He remembered how a crowd would be waiting outside her hotel as she set out for a performance. There would be shouts of acclaim, old ladies would thrust flowers into her hand, and children would be held up to catch a glimpse of her. It was all part of what the press called "Melbamania."

Among the plain-speaking Americans, Melba abandoned the image of sweet, ladylike Melba and reverted to the uninhibited tomboy of her Australian youth. These days, wrote Landon, "bluntness" was one of "her most marked characteristics," and when she vented her displeasure she was not above using the colorful swear words she had learned from her father's workmen. Always punctual and well turned out herself, she would not countenance slovenliness or tardiness in her employees. In St. Louis she used the bluntest of words when her musicians appeared in the pit in ordinary clothes. They claimed that the train had arrived so late that there had been no time to change, but Melba refused to accept their excuses. They were instructed to return to the hotel and reappear in their evening clothes.

Melba was a magnet for adventures, which were sometimes dramatic and even frightening. In Chicago she preferred to stay at the four-hundred-room Auditorium Hotel, in the same massive edifice as the four-thousand-seat theatre known as the Auditorium. Opened five years earlier by Patti, it was by far the largest and grandest of those American opera houses that shared their buildings with commercial premises.

When Melba arrived at the Auditorium Hotel, she was vexed to find her favorite suite occupied and was displeased that she had to take another. But the mix-up proved a blessing. On the evening of her concert, two armed men broke into her usual suite, unaware that Melba was not in residence. Holding the unfortunate occupant at gun point, they searched for the jewels they believed Melba had brought with her.

Charles Ellis regarded the incident as a warning that Melba's most valuable pieces should be left behind in London, but it was a warning she refused to heed. Ever since Adelina Patti had made a point of parading her jewelry, Melba was aware that, in the public mind, divas and jewels were inseparable. She meant to build up a collection of fabulous gems and to parade her collection, regardless of risk.

Now that she was in charge of a company, Melba took enthusiastically to the peripatetic life. Long train journeys passed quickly in lively games of whist, and her card skills increased enormously. Nevertheless as the weeks passed she sometimes grew tired and sometimes discouraged, for her longing for George traveled with her. Nowhere could she find news of him—with every mile he seemed more lost to her. In one of her letters to Madame she confessed that she had "never felt so lonely" in her entire life. It was with a degree of relief that she returned to the Savoy Hotel in New York to prepare for Christmas.

Her first public engagement in New York was on Christmas morning, when she sang "Ave Maria" at a solemn pontifical mass at St. Patrick's Cathedral at the invitation of Archbishop Corrigan. "I am sure no sweeter voice in the whole world invoked the Virgin Mary on this anniversary of her great glory," proclaimed the archbishop, and he hoped that "the prayer, so sweetly made" would bring Melba many blessings. She was certainly conscious of her blessings when she sat down for Christmas dinner. At the festive table sat Louie and her English fiancé Kenyon Mason—invited by Melba as a Christmas surprise—and, joy of joys, her sister Annie and brother Ernest, who had just arrived from Australia. To Melba, who never ceased to miss her family, no Christmas gift could have been more welcome. And they all drank to the health of her sister Belle, now Mrs. Thomas Patterson, who had given birth to a son only a week before.

Three weeks later, at Melba's insistence, Louie married Kenyon Mason in Archbishop Corrigan's own house adjoining the cathedral. Afterward Melba gave a reception at the Savoy Hotel, where her Australian family joined her opera family. Landon Ronald, the de Reszkes, Plançon, Maurel, Ancona, Nordica, and Calvé were present, and also blond and suave Tim Adamowski from the Boston Symphony Orchestra, whose devotion to Melba was beginning to cause comment. Melba herself made a grand entrance, almost upstaging the bride. Finding a soulmate in Archbishop Corrigan, she entered on his arm, dressed in a pale mauve gown that harmonized with his episcopal purple. The archbishop, admiring the toning colors, quipped that he had never seen Heaven and Earth so charmingly blended.

Melba enjoyed contriving every detail of the festivities, right down to the lettering on the menus, but it was a great blow to lose Louie, and a measure of her unselfishness that she insisted on the pair marrying now rather than later. She loved Louie like a sister—maybe more than a sister, because she and her sisters were prone to bickering, and she seldom bickered with tactful Louie. When the bride and groom sailed for England, Melba wrote that she felt "very sad."

Turning to her brother and sister for comfort, Melba embarked on a program of familiar operas at the Metropolitan. She also appeared for the first time in *Manon*. To the eyes and ears of her many fans her performance was a triumph, but as always there were contrary voices who lamented the poverty of her acting. Preferring to believe her fans, Melba wrote to Madame that she was having "the most extraordinary success"; the "papers are unanimous." She also sent the more favorable reviews to Massenet, who wrote in reply, "I can't adequately explain all that I owe you."

That season, in all, she gave forty-six performances at the Metropolitan, which brought her grand total—when one counted the fifty nights in the preceding concert tour and some additional concerts of her own—to about a hundred performances in seven months. This was a far greater number than Madame would have considered safe for her voice. To these was added the strain of extensive travel, for as well as accompanying her troupe though Canada and the Midwest she sang with the Metropolitan Company in Chicago, Detroit, Boston, Philadelphia, Buffalo, and Baltimore, and met with upsets along the way.

At the Auditorium in Chicago, an intruder "with staring eyes and the face of a lunatic" managed to climb onstage while she and Jean de Reszke were singing. Jean repelled him with his costume sword—or so Melba remembered. The critic William Armstrong, who was in the audience, recounted it more dramatically. While the stagehands chased the madman around the stage, Melba and de Reszke maintained their poses without turning a hair, and sang, once the music recommenced, without a waver.

A gala concert on April 24 marked the last night of the season. Melba had caught a cold, but otherwise her spirits were high. In fact they were possibly too high, the prospect of returning to Europe having expanded them beyond the bounds of propriety. Her manner must have astounded Landon Ronald, for she once told him that she despised the exhibitionism of other prima donnas and would "never in her life degrade herself as an artist by imitating them." On this last evening she "cantered" out in front of the audience like a hoyden and shook her fist at the young men in the boxes who were calling her name. "Oh! Go home. I have a cold and I won't sing 'Home Sweet Home,'" she shouted at them in mock anger. "Go home! Go home!"

A critic who described the scene was mortified by her vulgarity. Melba, he said, comported herself in far too "free and untrammelled" a manner. But he was forced to admit that her singing more than compensated for her impropriety, and would have caused him to forgive even greater sins. "She sings," he wrote, "like a bird, with a beautiful bird-like voice that fills the whole atmosphere of the opera house with the vibrancy of its silvery tone. It is a pleasure to hear such lovely tones projected with such consummate ease and certainty." For that, he said, he could forgive her almost anything.

CHAPTER THIRTEEN

Brünnhilde

ALTHOUGH MELBA could not wait to return to Europe, sadness enveloped her almost as soon as she set foot in her Paris apartment. Madame and her daughter Blanche were in deepest mourning, for Blanche's infant daughter, Mathilde, had just died. Writing a letter of condolence to Blanche, Melba felt memories of Vere flooding back. "Poor little angel," wrote Melba, "she will be happier where she is, but alas that is no consolation to a mother." And she added, with a pain that surely sprang as much from George as from Vere, "It is too horrible to lose a child."

Melba and Madame were also in mourning for Ambroise Thomas, who had died the previous February. Of those great French composers who had fostered Melba's early career—Delibes, Gounod, and Thomas—none now remained. Melba grieved for her dead mentors, and some of that feeling went into the seven memorial performances of *Hamlet* that she gave at the Paris Opéra during that May and June.

Melba's return to England was also marred by sadness. On June 22, four days after she returned to Covent Garden, Augustus Harris died. His tact, judgment, and theatrical expertise had steered his performers to success, and the knighthood he received in 1891, bestowed because he was sheriff of London, conferred prestige on the entire company. The appointment of Maurice Grau—who was to retain his directorship of the Metropolitan—as the future manager partly calmed the singers' unease. Grau had a flair for gauging public taste but was artistically less expert than Harris. One associate described him sitting "in his office like a spider from morning until night, working out repertoires, quarrel-

ling with singers or placating them, and having no interests in life beyond that—except perhaps the national game of poker." Melba, while
mourning the loss of Harris, was grateful that she retained Lady de
Grey's patronage and thereby could still largely dictate her own terms.

During that London season of 1896, Melba performed the roles she
had sung during the preceding Metropolitan season, beginning with
Roméo et Juliette, to which her Australian friends Ada Crossley and
Agnes Murphy sent a basket of red roses on opening night. At her own
insistence she included two performances of *Manon*. "I am crazy about
the part," she told Madame. She also had the pleasure of seeing Landon
Ronald emerge as a Covent Garden conductor. He had been invited to
conduct before Harris's death, and almost lost his chance when Gladys
de Grey's brother-in-law, Henry Higgins—now chairman of the governing syndicate—canceled the engagement, but Melba intervened.

Melba was delighted to help this shy young man who, despite his
inexperience, had conducted so sympathetically for her in America.
Never would she forget the disastrous night in the Midwest when the
orchestra fell out of step with the baritone Campanari, and Landon was
forced to halt the music and reconduct the aria. She had bitten back
her blunt words and quickly forgiven him, for she knew that it was "far
better to own up frankly and to start again, than to blunder on from
bad to worse."

At Covent Garden in July 1896, at the end of a scene from *Faust*,
which Landon was conducting, she tried "to inaugurate what was an
unheard-of thing in those days." Traditionally conductors did not
emerge from the orchestra pit, and so the audience could not applaud
them in person. On this memorable evening Melba sent a messenger
into the pit to summon Landon on stage so that he could take a bow
with her. He was so surprised that he thought the summons was a joke
and disappeared backstage, thereby missing his moment of glory.

Landon and Ronald were in fact the young conductor's given names.
His family name was Russell, but he never used the name professionally, being anxious to avoid confusion with his older brother Henry
Russell, a well-known teacher of speech and singing. The previous year
Landon had introduced Henry to Melba, and Henry had subsequently
visited her in Paris. From such a chance beginning, Melba's friendship
with Henry Russell had grown.

At a dinner at Henry Russell's house, Melba met a young Sydney playwright who quickly caught her fancy. His name was Charles Haddon Chambers, and at thirty-six he was just a year older than Melba. Fifteen years before, as an ambitious newcomer in London, he had been so determined to see his plays performed that he had pursued the actor-manager Beerbohm Tree into a Turkish bath; he read aloud from one of his scripts as Tree sat captive in the steam room. The play, *Captain Swift*, was successfully staged by Tree a few months later. By the time Melba met Haddon in the summer of 1896, he had plays running in London, Melbourne, and New York.

Haddon Chambers had long admired Melba, not only for her voice but for the skill with which she had bridged the cultural gap between Australia and Europe. He also sympathized with her difficulty in combining *bel canto* technique with displays of emotion. "What a pity she is so cold," he remarked to Russell. "Her voice is the most divine thing in the world, and if someone would only teach her to act, she would be perfect." Being knowledgeable about opera and even more so about acting, he believed he could help her. At Russell's dinner party—which included Tosti, the aristocratic music critic Robin Grey, and Lady Charles Beresford—he offered his services as a drama coach. Melba accepted, inviting him to the house beside the Thames which she was renting for a second season.

Haddon reminded Melba of Charlie in happier days. He had the same long face, sloping blue eyes, and fair hair, and like Charlie he was an expert horseman, having trained in his teenage years as a stockrider. Like Charlie, too, he had a devil-may-care attitude toward life. One could see it in his writing, which had a freshness and boldness that immediately attracted playgoers. George Bernard Shaw called him a "rough and ready playwright with the imagination of a bushranger," but he added that it was a true imagination and "it sufficed."

With Haddon's help as a drama coach, Melba could feel herself improving as an actress—and she could also feel herself responding to him as a woman. The news had just broken that Philippe was to marry the Archduchess Maria Dorothea of Austria on October 5 in Vienna. Although she had long since accepted that Philippe would find a royal wife, Melba would not have been human if she had not felt a pang. The meeting with Haddon had come at the right moment. Henceforth he would play an important role in her life.

It was opportune that she was improving as an actress because she had daring plans to increase her versatility. Itching to be free of her constricted repertoire, and knowing that Richard Wagner was still widely considered to be the greatest composer of operas, she was determined to sing one of his later works, such as *Siegfried*, even though its orchestration was far heavier than that of Verdi's *Aida*. Nordica and Jean de Reszke provided her with the precedent. From being light-voiced singers like herself, they had transformed themselves into leading Wagnerians. Shrugging aside her unsatisfactory performance in *Aida*, Melba felt confident that she could equal their achievement.

It so happened that Jean de Reszke was to perform the name part in *Siegfried* at the Metropolitan the following December and was looking for a soprano who could partner him as Brünnhilde. The obvious choice was Nordica, the Metropolitan's chief Wagnerian soprano, and many, including Nordica herself, believed the part was hers. De Reszke, however, did not want her. His reluctance centered on the fact that Brünnhilde does not enter until almost the end of the opera, when the tenor playing Siegfried is nearing exhaustion. He knew that Nordica's robust voice would drown his own voice in the final duet. In searching for a less dominating partner, his thoughts turned to Melba. He knew that she had been learning German so as to be able to attempt an opera like *Siegfried*. He believed that, given the chance, she would accept the role.

Although some of this is surmise, it seems the most likely explanation of events at the Metropolitan Opera in mid-1896. Another version, given by Jean de Reszke's biographer Clara Leiser, maintained that Jean wanted Melba for the tiny role of the Forest Bird and was dismayed when she insisted on singing Brünnhilde; but this version does not explain the known facts. Although Melba may well have rejected the insignificant role of the Forest Bird, Leiser's account ignores rumors circulating from May onward that de Reszke was encouraging Melba to learn Brünnhilde's music. It also fails to explain why de Reszke urged Grau to engage Melba for the part.

When Grau made his offer of Brünnhilde, Melba was overjoyed. Madame, as might have been expected, was horrified. In Madame's view,

Melba's voice and temperament were totally unsuited to Brünnhilde, and it would be dangerous to her voice to attempt it. She looked, said Melba, "as though I had threatened to cut my throat." For the only time in her life, Melba openly defied her teacher. Knowing she would receive no help from Madame, she summoned the Bayreuth répétiteur Professor Kniese to help her learn the part.

At the beginning of November, Melba arrived in America, accompanied by her sister Annie and by the younger Bennett daughter, Marnie, who had taken Louie's place as her secretary. A week later the news that Melba was to play Brünnhilde broke in the American press. Melba had probably expected criticism but could not have expected the storm that burst forth. The press sympathized wholeheartedly with native-born Nordica who, deprived of a role that she longed to sing, poured out her feelings to reporters. "I learned to my amazement that Mme Melba got the role through the interference of M. Jean de Reszke," she told them angrily. "I was as much wounded at heart as though I had been struck a blow in the face."

Melba was about to catch a train to Philadelphia when the newsmen caught up with her. She denied any mischief, declaring truthfully that she and Nordica had always been friends. She also proclaimed Jean de Reszke's innocence, laughing, according to one reporter, "at the idea that M. Jean de Reszke was the director of the opera and could arrange parts to suit himself." But Nordica remained unconvinced. She had made careful inquiries and knew the extent of de Reszke's double-dealing. At first, not unnaturally, she also blamed Melba. In the end she came to see de Reszke and Grau as the villains and herself and Melba as their dupes. Somewhat miraculously, her friendship with Melba not only survived but grew closer.

Melba, meanwhile, had other problems to occupy her mind. With Grau's blessing she had agreed to occasional performances with the Damrosch Opera Company in Philadelphia before and during the Metropolitan season, and she was discovering she had bitten off more than she could chew. Her exhausting study of *Siegfried*, the public controversy over Nordica, the Philadelphia appearances, and a respiratory infection all took their toll. She sounded tired when she opened at the Metropolitan Opera House on November 16 in *Faust*; one week later, when she sang Juliette, she was so hoarse that she felt obliged to apologize to the audience. There followed three weeks of indifferent or canceled performances.

On December 16, 1896, fully recovered, she sang what was described by the *New York Times* as one of the most brilliant Lucias ever given at the Metropolitan: her trill was "simply dazzling," and her scales were "showers of spring raindrops." She followed it with *Les Huguenots* and her first American performances of *La Traviata* on December 18, 21, and 26. All gained splendid reviews. Although Agnes Murphy would later claim that Melba was recovering from "a severe attack of blood poisoning" and singing poorly at the end of December, these reviews testify that she had fully recovered her health and was in excellent voice.

Siegfried was to open December 30. As the night drew closer, Melba grew increasingly agitated. Madame had been correct when she said that Brünnhilde was alien to Melba's temperament. The warrior-maiden who falls asleep as a goddess and awakens as a mortal woman required a heroic style quite foreign to Melba. She doubted whether she could achieve it, even though some would have claimed that there was more than a touch of the warrior goddess in her nature.

Madame's warning about the difficulties of singing over a huge Wagnerian orchestra were also proving correct. The clarion quality in Melba's voice that had served her so well in Wagner's earlier and lighter operas had met its match in the orchestration of *Siegfried*. She was thankful that Brünnhilde's role was confined to only one scene, but it lasted forty minutes and contained a climax so difficult that everything she had sung before seemed simple by comparison. She had every reason for her increasing fear.

Brünnhilde does not appear until the last act of the opera, when she is discovered asleep on a rock in the midst of a ring of fire. On the opening night Melba was obliged to wait two and a half hours before appearing on her rock, and the waiting eroded her composure. Always nervous before a performance—and trebly so before this one—her anxiety soared. When at last she took her place, she was consumed by dread.

Years later Melba would write in her autobiography that from the moment she started to sing, she knew Madame had been right. "The music was too much for me," she remembered. "I felt I was struggling beyond my strength. I had a sensation almost of suffocation, of battling some immense monster." The monster was the orchestra, and the suffocation came from panic. In desperation she moved to the footlights and vainly tried to project her voice across the tide of sound, while Siegfried abandoned his carefully rehearsed moves and ran after her. The American Quaker baritone David Bispham watched them from a box with growing dismay. "Jean de Reszke," he wrote, "in the heavy fur coat of Siegfried, was kept busy patrolling the forward part of the stage to keep the white-clad Melba from rushing into the footlights."

When the curtain fell, Melba went straight to her dressing room, and summoned Charles Ellis. "Tell the critics," she is said to have told him, "that I am never going to do that again. It is beyond me, I have been a fool." Her decisive honesty, shrewdly delivered, seems to have deflected the worst of the criticism. The reviews were kinder than she could have dared hope.

"Madame Melba's Brünnhilde, all things considered, was surprisingly good," wrote the New York Herald. The Evening Post believed that her voice had "an unusual touch of fervor and a beauty all its own," even though its strength was unequal to its task. "The sincerity of her effort was admirable," declared the New York Tribune. Nevertheless "it is much to be feared there will soon be an end to the charm which her voice discloses when employed in its legitimate sphere. The world can ill afford to lose a Melba, even if it should gain a Brünnhilde." Melba was pleased when a distinguished and benign critic took the trouble to say to her in person, "Your voice is like a piece of Dresden china. Please, don't smash it."

Melba could only agree. Never far from her thoughts was the time when the misuse of her voice had caused the nodule on her vocal cord. The Metropolitan's doctor, Holbrook Curtis, confirmed that she was suffering from vocal strain, but he did not diagnose a nodule. Nor did he forbid her to sing, though he advised her not to attempt Brünnhilde. Like Grau, he continued to believe that Melba could safely appear as Lucia, Juliette, and Violetta, the roles she was contracted to sing in the forthcoming months.

Melba, for her part, was no longer confident. On the mornings of her advertised appearances she would wake in a panic, decide that her voice was hoarse, and send for Dr. Curtis. Unable to calm her, he would be obliged to sign a certificate stating she was unfit to appear. Grau, in turn, would be obliged to summon an understudy or substitute another opera.

Gossip claimed that Melba's voice was in sound health: pique, wrote the *Chicago Post*, "is the real trouble with Madame Melba"—pique and "nerves and blues." In a sense the paper was correct, for her troubles were as much emotional as physical. They did not originate in bad temper and self-indulgence, however, but in a very natural fear of wrecking her voice and in the unremitting pressure of too many performances over too short a time.

While Melba agonized over her vocal cords, Grau worked overtime, shuffling operas, hiring replacements, and cursing her indecision. On January 18, 1897, when she canceled at short notice for the seventh time that season, the *New York Times* dubbed her "Melba, the Great Indisposed."

The following day Dr. Curtis brought a medical specialist to examine Melba in her suite at the Manhattan Hotel. Later the doctors issued their bulletin. After they certified that the patient was suffering from "severe constitutional depression" and that her vocal cords showed signs of strain, they advised two months of "absolute rest." Melba submitted her own apology to the *New York Times* the next day. Desperately sorry to disappoint Grau and her public, she believed that only convalescence in England or Paris could effect a cure. She hoped that, with care, she might be able to return in two months' time and sing in the last weeks of the season. "Thanking you all for your kindness and courtesy," she concluded, "Your sincere and very sad friend, Nellie Melba."

At midnight on January 24, 1897, Melba boarded the steamship *Bourgogne*. Kind messages and flowers awaited her from many friends, among them Calvé, Bispham, and even her rival Emma Eames; but no bouquet or message was reported from Jean de Reszke. It seems likely that Melba blamed him, at least in part, for her predicament. At that moment, however, she was more intent on saving her voice than on placing blame. Her one thought was to cross the Atlantic and consult Dr. Felix Semon, who had cured her voice seven years before.

CHAPTER FOURTEEN

With the Americans
Heart and Soul

FELIX SEMON, the doctor who had diagnosed Melba's nodule seven years earlier, took a serious view of Melba's condition. Agreeing with Holbrook Curtis that she needed rest in mind as well as body, he packed her off for three months to Paris. This proved a mixed blessing, for while Madame was certainly ready with comfort, she was equally ready with scoldings.

For years Madame had worried about Melba's "Voice" which she tended to regard as a separate entity, to be spelled with a capital letter. All along Madame had feared that the American tours would overtax the Voice, and she anxiously and frequently inquired about its welfare. Melba invariably reassured her, carefully omitting evidence to the contrary. "Please don't worry," she would write, scoring the words with heavy underlining. Now Melba had been proved wrong, and she had only herself to blame.

Throughout these months of recuperation, Melba's spirits were low. In the past, activity and success had been her antidotes to depression. She had told herself that disappointment, and even bereavement, could be borne with relative equanimity, provided that hard work and willpower brought about the success she craved. With her failure as Brünnhilde she had abruptly discovered a success she could never achieve, no matter how strongly she willed it. Her defenses tumbled, and the grief she had so long suppressed at last found its mark.

As well as worrying about her voice, she was haunted by the fear that she may have wrecked her operatic reputation. But in a perverse way she may have enhanced it. Opera audiences crave excitement and admire singers who take risks. Until now Melba's singing had seemed to some to be almost mechanical: in Madame Marchesi's words, it was more like the song of a bird than that of a woman. By attempting Brünnhilde, Melba had shown herself a risk-taker, and by failing she had proved herself human. The episode may well have enlarged her fame.

She seems also to have felt pain over the part that Jean de Reszke played in her failure. Madame Marchesi reputedly told William Armstrong, music critic for the *Chicago Tribune*, that Melba suspected "the *Siegfried* affair" to be part of a plot devised by Grau—presumably with de Reszke's connivance—to rid the Metropolitan of Nordica and herself, both of whom could be seen as troublemakers. As Melba had long viewed "darling Jean" as her dear friend and mentor, the suspicion that he had betrayed her trust must have been a bitter burden.

Possibly it was too bitter to bear for long, and too harmful to her career, for a serious quarrel with de Reszke might well have prevented her from singing at Covent Garden. The breach between them—if indeed there was an open breach—was quickly mended.

Melba's brother Ernest and sister Annie were still with her. Their company brought solace, and Melba mothered them in her own generous and idiosyncratic way. Months before, at Tiffany's in New York, she had bought Annie a gold bag decorated with diamonds; and when Annie lost the bag and fretted about its loss, Melba marched straight back to the famous jeweler and bought a replica, pretending that the original had been found. Now, in Paris, she took Annie to her favorite couturiers, and bought her hats and shoes and gowns. Believing Ernest had the makings of an operatic tenor, she arranged lessons for him with the well-known teacher Trabadello. Although Melba made plans with the best intentions, they were not always appreciated. The Mitchell boys and girls had minds of their own, but this did not stop Melba from continuing to believe that she knew what was best for them.

Felix Semon, who had just received a knighthood from the queen, gave Melba permission to sing again in May. In a flurry of gratitude she thrust a photograph into his hand bearing the inscription, "To Sir Felix Semon, my guardian angel, from his sincere friend and grateful patient, Nellie Melba." The description of "guardian angel" was merited, Sir Felix proclaimed: "For I had actually saved her voice!"

The cure had been achieved just in time. Queen Victoria was about to mark the sixtieth year of her reign, and London was preparing a feast of celebrations. Melba, whose zest for life was fast returning, gave a "Grand Morning Concert" at the Queen's Hall, choosing as supporting artists a young contralto named Clara Butt and the baritone Kennerley Rumford. The *Times* reviewer complained that Melba sang no Wagner, but the fans who packed the hall made no complaints. They wished only to be reassured that Melba's voice had not been harmed. When she sang the "mad scene" from *Lucia* as exquisitely as ever, they cheered with relief.

On June 22, 1897, Queen Victoria drove along six miles of London streets through huge crowds. The people's pride in their empire and personal affection for their sovereign astonished foreign onlookers. Outside Buckingham Palace a lone voice from the crowd proclaimed the common feeling. As the queen was wheeled onto the balcony in a wheelchair, the voice cried out, "Go it, old girl!"

On the following night Covent Garden was to host a gala performance in which Melba, being unsure of her voice, had initially refused to sing. But a royal gala without Melba seemed no gala at all, and the Prince and Princess of Wales were said to be counting on her. In the face of such pressure she surrendered, and with no apparent qualms joined Jean de Reszke to sing the third act of *Roméo et Juliette*, performing it with "all her wonted sweetness and skill." Emboldened by success, she then agreed to sing the entire opera on June 28 and two performances of *Faust* in the following month.

Her voice graced at least one private party that summer. The wife of Alfred Harmsworth, later the newspaper baron Lord Northcliffe, hosting a party for the premiers of British colonies, paid handsomely for Melba and Ada Crossley to sing and for Tim Adamowski to play the violin. Mrs. Harmsworth also engaged the brilliant Polish pianist Ignacy Paderewski, whom Melba had first met in Brussels when both were fledgling artists. He was one of her favorites. She admired his "magnificent head, his flowing hair, and above all the radiant personality which flowed from him like a light." Adhering to what was now her rule, Melba insisted on attending Mrs. Harmsworth's party as an invited guest as well as appearing as a hired performer. To appear only as a performer lowered one's social status, and Melba had no intention of being perceived as socially inferior.

Melba herself gave a celebratory party at the Savoy. The guests were greeted in her suite before moving to the hotel dining room, where the menus were decorated with Australian and British symbols and flags, and the top table bore an iceboat bearing Melba's name. After dinner she and Ada Crossley sang and everyone joined in a jolly game called American Post, in which Melba took the part of postal director. Melba was feeling particularly buoyant. Delivered from the nightmare of a ruined voice, she had many reasons to feel thankful.

There was also lavish entertainment at her house beside the Thames, where Haddon Chambers was her favored guest. He fitted easily into her life, was welcomed by her friends and family, and yet still managed to maintain a charming unpredictability. As one observer put it, "Haddon is one of those men who never wears out; he's always new and never repeats himself." Melba owed him much, not least the noticeable improvement in her acting. The previous winter in New York, the critic W. J. Henderson had written that her Juliette "would have done credit to some of the historic Juliets of the dramatic stage."

Although Haddon was often by her side, Melba felt lonely when her sister Annie sailed home. Fortunately her loneliness was not prolonged because Annie was quickly replaced by the youngest Mitchell girl, Dora. Staying at the Rue de Prony, Dora was enchanted by all she saw and especially by Melba; after more than ten years of absence, she could scarcely remember her eldest sister. Wishing to give her a taste of Europe, Melba took her to Ostend and Brussels and bought her an opal and diamond ring and a diamond brooch shaped like a swallow. Melba also bought her shoes, boots, and gloves, because David Mitchell had severely limited Dora's dress allowance and was behaving—in Dora's estimation—like a wealthy miser. Reporting by letter to her sister Belle in Melbourne on August 25, Dora related that Melba was managing to lose weight despite consuming a whole tin of biscuits in one sitting, and that she continually asked for news of Belle's children. "She is awfully simple and loves home life," wrote

Dora. "She is so awfully funny, does and says such funny things, everybody loves her."

Early in September, Melba prepared to travel to picturesque Bergamo, set in the foothills of the Alps, not far from Italy's Lake Como. The city was celebrating the centenary of the birth of its most famous son, the composer Donizetti, and Melba had been invited to perform. Another guest performer was the violinist Joachim, who was overjoyed at the prospect of seeing Melba again. Over the years he had applauded her success from afar, occasionally meeting her in London, more often gleaning news of her from their joint friend Johann Kruse. In Bergamo, with boyish ardor, he fell in love with her.

Melba had brought Dora and Joachim had brought his niece and a party of friends. Chaperoned by their retinues, the two celebrities saw the sights together, traveling by funicular to the hilltop churches and cobbled lanes of the old city. They also viewed manuscripts of Donizetti's music copied by a young and impoverished Richard Wagner. That Wagner had been forced to earn his bread by copying the work of "a composer so infinitely below him in genius" moved Melba more than she could say. "I sat there looking at those copies with Joachim," Melba later wrote, "wishing I had known Wagner in those days."

It was an emotional moment, probably the only time the two enjoyed a true reciprocity of feeling. Charmed and intrigued as she was by Joachim's attentions, there was no disguising the thirty-year age difference and the fact that his bulky body and bearded face reflected every month of his sixty-six years. Although she liked him, flirted with him, and smiled when he called her his Nelmel, there is no evidence that her feelings matched his.

Joachim proved valuable to Melba that autumn, for she needed help with her brother Ernest. Having quickly tired of his singing lessons, Ernest declared he would sooner be a composer, and Joachim obligingly found him a teacher of composition in Berlin. As Melba attended to Ernest's impetuous requests and listened to Dora's chatter, a wave of nostalgia for her family swept over her. Feeling "very miserable and blue," she confessed to Belle by letter how keenly she missed Doonside, and, by implication, how sorely she missed George. She wrote that she longed to see Belle's three children, if only Belle could lend her one of them. She also longed to see her father, begging Belle to persuade him to have his photograph taken, so at least she might have a recent likeness of him. Her main comfort was a little Japanese pug dog that Alfred Rothschild had given her. The pug was "such a darling," she told Belle, "I love him."

Melba's spirits revived in the following weeks when she successfully toured the British provinces. Douglas Powell, one of her supporting artists, reported that the warmth of her reception was unprecedented, with the "cold, phlegmatic, English audiences rising *en masse*, cheering and waving handkerchiefs." A week later she and Dora were crossing to the United States. Like a migratory bird, Melba was on her way to her winter sojourn.

Melba was not to sing this year with the Metropolitan Company. Disturbed by the death of his partner Henry Abbey and burdened by his duties at Covent Garden, Grau had canceled the Metropolitan season for 1897–1898, renting the theatre instead to Walter Damrosch, the young German-American musician for whose company Melba had sung briefly the year before. By temperament more a conductor than an impresario, Damrosch regarded opera singers as irresponsible children and, as a devoted Wagnerian, he regarded those singing the French and Italian repertoire as the most irresponsible of all. This did not stop him, however, from listening to Melba when she offered her services. Her terms were fifteen hundred dollars a night, with ten performances a month guaranteed: a steep price, but he had no doubt she was worth it. Disregarding accusations from the Metropolitan board that he was stealing its property, Damrosch immediately engaged her. He also appointed Charles Ellis as his business partner, placing him in charge of the French and Italian operas. Since Ellis put Melba's interests first, this virtually made Melba a partner as well.

Welcoming Melba and Dora to America, Charles Ellis carried them off to his house in Boston for Thanksgiving. It was a kind thought but his plan misfired, because Dora hated the overheated houses and intense cold, and Melba was depressed, admitting that she had seldom felt "so blue." Needing activity to drive away her melancholy, she went early to Philadelphia, where Damrosch had rented the Academy of Music, a pretty opera house holding about three thousand people and renowned for its excellent acoustics. It was here that Melba scored her success of the season. On December 27, 1897, for the first time on any stage, she played Rosina in *The Barber of Seville*. Playful, coquettish Rosina was the perfect role for Melba, and Rossini's florid music was a gift to her technique. Her runs and trills reminded one admiring critic of diamonds poured "from a cornucopia."

The scene in which Rosina takes a singing lesson proved the high point of the opera, for here Melba was allowed by the composer to sing a song of her own choosing. On Madame's advice she selected Massenet's showy "Sevilliana" and followed it with Tosti's "Mattinata," for both of which she played her own piano accompaniment. At the end of the opera she reputedly received twenty curtain calls. Melba confided to Madame that it was "*perhaps* the biggest triumph of my career."

What she did not tell Madame was that in two weeks' time she was intending to sing Verdi's *Aida*. To choose *Aida* was an act of defiance. It was as though she was saying, "Well, maybe I harmed my voice by attempting Brünnhilde, but I am perfectly capable of coping with the dense orchestration of Verdi." Madame probably would have disputed this opinion, so Madame was not told.

Melba was nervous on the night of January 13, 1898, but she sailed through *Aida* with surprising ease. Her "clear and liquid notes," wrote the *Philadelphia Inquirer*, "pierced the volume of the sound like a shaft of light flashing from a thunder cloud." Such praise did much to relieve her mind and soothe the pain she still endured at the thought of her failure as Brünnhilde.

The company moved on to the Metropolitan Opera House in New York, where Melba opened in *La Traviata*. Since the popular de Reszkes were not in the company, there were doubts that high society would bother to attend; but on opening night the Goulds and Astors and Vanderbilts turned out in force. Despite Melba's triumphs in Philadelphia, doubts had been expressed about the state of her voice, so there was obvious relief when her notes came forth with "consummate ease." The moment her first aria ended, the stage was almost deluged with flowers.

Melba sang in *Faust* on January 22 and two days later gave her first New York *Aida*. Once again she was nervous, but it was a nervousness tinged with confidence—having conquered Philadelphia, she fully expected to conquer New York. When she read the papers next day, she was astonished. The New York critics could scarcely summon a word of praise. Why, begged W. J. Henderson, did she insist on singing a role "so utterly unsuited to her voice, her style and her temperament?" Surely she realized that heavy roles could "wreck one of the most precious gifts that heaven ever put in a human throat." His sentiments were echoed by the majority of reviewers. Such was their condemnation that Melba canceled her next *Aida* and sang in the role of Juliette instead. That she was angered by the reviewers' judgment goes without saying. It must have seemed as though she was forever to be confined to an out-of-date repertoire. Nevertheless four days later she picked herself up, sang *The Barber of Seville*, and heard the critics change their tune. Rossini's comic masterpiece might seem outdated, wrote the *New York Times*, but Melba's Rosina was brilliant.

When the New York season ended, the company moved first to Boston, then to Chicago. Here Melba's costumes in *La Traviata* were particularly praised, especially her black feather fan nearly a yard long and her chain of turquoises, as "blue as the eggs of nesting robins and big as walnuts." After Chicago the company split in two, Damrosch's half to perform Wagner in the eastern states and Ellis's to take French and Italian opera westward.

For the western venture, publicity and style were all-important. When Adelina Patti had toured America a decade earlier, she had traveled in a private railcar with her name emblazoned in huge letters on the side. Her car contained a saloon hung in embossed leather and cloth of gold, and a bedroom, and bathroom lined with satinwood and mirrors. Not to be outshone, Ellis rented a larger and even more luxurious car from the Pullman Company, with Melba's name emblazoned on the side. Inside were a piano and organ, bedrooms, bathrooms and a sitting room for six people, and a kitchen, and servants' quarters. In addition to Melba's two personal maids there were a porter, chef, and waiter. The chef and waiter were quickly dubbed Jean and Edouard because they reminded Melba of the de Reszke brothers. Writing to Madame from Denver on April 1, she enclosed a newspaper cutting that described the car as "a private palace on wheels," in every way ideal for "the reigning queen of song."

Melba was not alone in the luxurious railcar. Although Dora had found the American winter unendurable and returned to England, Marnie Bennett accompanied Melba, along with a soprano named

Florence Toronta, a former pupil of Madame's who now sang minor roles in the company. While Melba missed Dora, she sympathized with her sister's departure, for she too hated the cold. As the train sped toward sunny California, she anticipated warm days. One morning she awoke to hear her maid calling "Madame—look! look! We're in Paradise." "We had left behind," Melba remembered, "the dreary clouds and snows of the eastern states, and here, like a dream, lay orchards of peach blossom, glittering in the sunshine, and green fields and the full beauty of spring."

California reminded her of home. San Francisco and Melbourne were both former gold-rush towns, far from the great centers of culture and craving refinement. Melba's tour was consequently a gala event, and wardrobes were raided for evening clothes. A sharp-nosed young reporter, passing through the foyer of the California Theatre on opening night, was almost overcome by the smell of mothballs emanating from the faded opera cloaks and outdated evening dresses.

It was a sign of the city's isolation that Melba's first entrance on stage as Violetta went virtually unnoticed. "They didn't know me," she told an interviewer, "and the silence frightened me at first. It has happened in other Western cities but just for a moment the silence seemed of the grave." Accustomed to "the wild, florid, explosive" school of opera singing, they were also puzzled by Melba's restrained performance. Luckily, confusion gave way to reverence as they concluded that this was the "simple, unaffected expression" of the truly great artist; being simple and unaffected people themselves, they welcomed her warmly.

In her private railcar, Melba must have read the reviews thankfully, but the heavy black headlines across the front page relayed a more sober message. For months the United States had disputed Spanish claims to the sovereignty of Cuba, and on April 19, 1898, it had issued an ultimatum to Spain to withdraw. War was imminent, and in the former Spanish territory of California, anti-Spanish feeling ran high. With *The Barber of Seville* scheduled for the following night, Melba began to have doubts. Might there be an attempt to disrupt an opera set in the Spanish city of Seville? Should another opera be substituted? These were questions that Melba and Ellis had to decide quickly, for every seat was sold.

Ellis and Melba decided to go ahead, but just before curtain time Melba deemed it wise to make a statement to the press. "Oh, I'm sorry we chose this Spanish opera, and just for tonight, too," she confided candidly to an interviewer. "I know they'll hiss me when I go out in the Spanish costume. I shan't blame them a bit if they do, but I'll die, I'll surely die if they do." If they did hiss her, she added with a decisive click of her Spanish heels, she would "make a little speech and tell them that, though the opera's Spanish, I am an English woman, and I am with the Americans heart and soul in this."

As it happened, Melba was not hissed, though the baritone play-ing Figaro was booed when he entered. Otherwise the opera proceeded normally, but Melba was taking no chances. In the lesson scene, sitting at the piano, she sang Stephen Foster's "Old Folks at Home." This most popular of American songs was greeted with delight. Then, judging the moment to be right, she swung into the opening bars of "The Star-Spangled Banner." The emotional audience responded. "People rose in their seats and cheered themselves hoarse, and the handkerchiefs that waved made the house as white as a fruit orchard after a March breeze," wrote one reporter. Melba, contemplating "the packed house as it burst into white, was moved beyond the powers of expression. She could not have sung another stanza then to have saved her life." She was speech-less and songless; tears were coursing down her cheeks, and many in the audience were weeping with her.

It was one of the most momentous nights of Melba's life, and there-after the tour felt tame. In Los Angeles on April 25 she repeated "The Star-Spangled Banner" but this time her public was forewarned. Al-though the audience stood and cheered, the demonstration did not overwhelm her. It seemed that only San Francisco could provide real drama; and when she returned for a farewell concert on the last day of April, it lived up to its reputation. During a scene from *Rigoletto* in the California Theatre, a boiler pipe burst beneath the stage, enveloping Melba in a mist of steam. A short while later, as she was about to give the "mad scene" from *Lucia*, a fire broke out on the theatre roof. Melba remained calm, though when Ellis reached her, Marnie Bennett was fanning her face. "Madame did not faint," Ellis told the press proudly. "She is very brave in the hour of danger." The audience, however, fled in panic, abandoning thirty sealskin capes, eleven pocketbooks, and twelve lace fichus. Miraculously no one was hurt and the theatre was saved.

Melba left California with mixed feelings. On the one hand she rejoiced at her success, on the other she experienced the emptiness that she always felt in America when she heard no news of George. A recent encounter with a young candy seller on the train had done nothing to lessen her longing for him. She had offered the boy tickets to her concert. In return he had asked her who she was. "I am Melba," she told him. "Go on!" he answered, "I've seen Madame Melba, and she's real pretty." She laughed and applauded his honesty, and later recounted the story against herself. But there was pain in her amusement. In her mind's eye she saw George.

Fortunately in New York there was much to occupy her. Grau was offering her a contract for the next winter, but she was reluctant to accept it for her own plans were expanding. Damrosch was selling his half-share in the company, and she and Ellis were determined to buy it; they had already made a bid for the costumes and scenery. Rarely out of her thoughts, too, was the problem of her repertoire. "Just what place is open to her in the field of lyric art?" W. J. Henderson had asked when he reviewed *Aida*, and the question haunted her. She needed a modern opera that suited her voice.

It so happened that the Royal Italian Grand Opera of Milan was performing at New York's Wallack's Theatre. As Melba waited at the Manhattan Hotel for her passage to Europe, she could scarcely fail to notice the favorable reviews. On May 16 the company performed a new opera by Giacomo Puccini called *La Bohème*. Its plot was drab—a series of scenes from the lives of poor students—but the audience liked it and the critics acknowledged its "abundance of melody." If Melba saw the opera—and it seems fairly certain she did—her search for a contemporary opera to suit her voice was at last over.

By the end of June 1898 Melba was in London and ready to recommence at Covent Garden. She was to sing one performance each of *La Traviata*, *Roméo et Juliette*, and *The Barber of Seville*. Alfred Rothschild brought Patti to hear her Violetta, but it was her Rosina that made the deepest impression. It seemed as if she had been born to sing Rossini. At the end of the month she made her only concert appearance of the season, singing the aria "L'Amero" from Mozart's *Il Re Pastore*. The occasion was a charity concert at the Duke of Sutherland's, where her co-performer was Joachim.

Joachim had composed a cadenza to the aria with a violin *obbligato* for the Swedish soprano Jenny Lind, blending the voices of the singer and the violin into an exquisite duet. Since visiting Bergamo he had reworked the cadenza, the better to exhibit Melba's talents. It was a love gift, and Melba recognized the devotion behind it.

Although Joachim told the press that he had come to London to help charity, his primary aim was undoubtedly to see Melba. He stayed at her house beside the Thames and Landon Ronald has left a colorful account of the visit. The excitement began on the train, just before Melba and her guests set out. A "regular dude, with an eyeglass in his eye and a drawl, sauntered up to their carriage and addressing Madame Melba, who was nearest the window, said in a very affected voice, 'Is there any room he-ar?'" Melba replied that the only room was on the floor. "The young man stared at her for a second and drawled, 'Oh, no! I should prefer to sit on your lap.'" His words were met by silence until the train began to move. Then one of Melba's companions leaped to his feet—Landon described him as the "the foreign fiddler," but it was obviously Joachim. From the safety of the moving carriage, the fiddler shouted out the window: "You blackguard! You scoundrel! If you come here, I gif you one ponch in ze nose."

Melba and Joachim met often during this period. "I must admit they made a funny couple together," wrote Landon, this time singling out Joachim by name. "The heavy, ponderous, learned Hungarian fiddler, used to being listened to with awe and bated breath; the vivacious, chaffing, light-hearted prima donna, throwing all seriousness to the wind, heartily disliking hero-worship in her own home. They were in very truth the two extremes meeting." After dinner there was informal music, with Landon playing the accompaniments. He remembered Melba singing "L'Amero" and Joachim collaborating in the brilliant cadenza. He remembered how, halfway through the evening, he and a fellow guest realized they had missed the last train back to London. As the fellow guest was a "stock-exchange magnate," a special train was hired in which he and Landon steamed back in style.

Melba's other cavalier, Haddon Chambers, was also a guest that summer. Whereas Joachim may or may not have been her lover in the physical sense, Haddon seems to have been her lover in every sense of the word. Over the past year their affair had grown into an emotional partnership. At her Thames-side house they were often together, strolling in the garden, taking tea under the cedars, or boating on the river. In London he was present at fashionable luncheons she gave at the Savoy and at a select little dinner she gave at the Hotel Cecil for Alfred Rothschild and the young Duke of Manchester.

Knowing the Prince of Wales's strict ideas about the need for outward respectability, Melba hesitated to parade Haddon openly, but she seems to have sought ways to publicize their relationship indirectly. One day when Haddon was drafting a business letter to an Australian impresario, she playfully snatched the letter from his hand and finished it herself, adding at the end that it was written, at Haddon's dictation, by "an Australian of whom you may have heard, Nellie Melba." The letter and her signature were duly quoted in the Australian press, as Melba had no doubt hoped they would be. She wished her public to know that she had admirers.

Haddon himself was more circumspect. While in private he called her Nellie, in company he referred to her as Madame Melba. His admiration, however, was openly expressed. Madame Melba "is the most efficient woman I ever met," he told a friend. "Had she taken it into her head to set up a bonnet shop she would have been the first milliner in Europe." Not that he believed she had great talent for making or selling bonnets. Rather he knew that she would have surrounded herself with experts, paid close attention to detail, and managed her finances with meticulous care.

Comforting and diverting as Haddon's presence was, she tore herself away at the end of August, for she was due to visit the Italian city of Lucca where she was to meet Puccini. A closer study of *La Bohème* had convinced her of its suitability, for the role of the consumptive heroine, Mimi, called for pathos, at which she excelled; and though the vocal score contained no trills or scales or roulades, she was delighted to find that it offered "so many exquisite opportunities for *bel canto*" singing of an unembellished type. On the other hand, being a "music drama" of the modern school, its style was alien to her. She required a teacher, and who better than Puccini himself? She recalled him from previous meetings in London as a "peasant of genius" with a bushy black mustache, a shy manner, and an abrupt mode of speech. He was spending that autumn at Monsagrati in the hills near Lucca, seeking seclusion to compose his new opera *Tosca*. She was overjoyed when he agreed to teach her Mimi's music.

Melba has left three conflicting accounts of her visit to Lucca. Six years after her visit she told Agnes Murphy that Puccini coached her "for two hours daily during the ten days of my study, and I was thoroughly well pleased with the work I did. He thoroughly explained his ideas of the music; we rehearsed it bit by bit; and my score is full of his pencil markings and annotations." Twenty-six years after her visit, in the pages of her autobiography, she claimed that the lessons lasted for six weeks, Puccini appearing "almost every day" at her hotel, "very often lunching, and marking my copy of the score in his neat little handwriting."

Her earliest account, written soon after leaving Lucca and mailed to Madame Marchesi from Florence on September 9, 1898, was different again. She told Madame that the heat and the mosquitoes were trying, and that she had studied with Puccini for "nearly a week." She added that his lessons were "*most interesting* and he is very enthusiastic at my interpretation." Of the three versions, this is almost certainly the truest. Although she did not always tell Madame everything, she is unlikely, in the circumstances, to have told her teacher a deliberate lie. Her mastery of *La Bohème* was too important for the future of her career.

CHAPTER FIFTEEN

There Is No Melba But Melba

THANKS TO HER lengthy tours, Melba was as well known now in America as in England or Europe. "There is no fame on earth so intoxicating, so universal as the fame of a great singer," wrote the popular novelist Ouida. In the American cities of the East and Midwest, Melba received the kind of worship that is today reserved for pop stars. Newspapers called it "Melba rage" or "Melbamania" and it was fueled by thousands of loyal fans, eager to read about her, catch a glimpse of her, and, above all, hear her voice. In the American West her fame was even greater, for here she was seen as the bearer of high culture. In Los Angeles, Denver, and Salt Lake City, people dreamed of hearing singers from the great auditoriums of Europe, and it was Melba who made those dreams come true.

The tour she was arranging for the winter of 1898–1899 was among her most extensive. This time she would again lead her own opera company and would go where she pleased. Ellis, her manager, had spent five months recruiting singers, including the Wagnerian sopranos Johanna Gadski and Milka Ternina, the German tenor Ernest Kraus, and the American soprano Zelie de Lussan. True, the company was to be called the Ellis Opera Company, but everyone knew that Melba was the driving force. They also knew that hers was the controlling voice, and that pleased her even more, because she always desired to be in control.

Meanwhile Melba had been rehired by Maurice Grau to sing two Juliettes and two Marguerites with the Metropolitan Company. He engaged her reluctantly, and to keep her in her place he imported a formidable rival: Marcella Sembrich, a Polish soprano with a splendid *bel canto* technique and a repertoire close to Melba's own. When Melba opened on December 2, Sembrich had already sung Violetta, Lucia, even Rosina, all to great acclaim and at only half of Melba's salary. Fortunately the tour occupied Melba's energies; otherwise she might have challenged the decision to enthrone such a powerful rival.

Foremost in her mind was *La Bohème*, which she intended to introduce during her own tour. At New York's American Theatre on November 28 she heard an English-language version of the work put on by a local company. Sitting in a neighboring box, Grau had doubts as to its viability, but Melba had none. She believed *La Bohème* was an answer to her repeated prayers. Over the following weeks her abundant energy was focused on making sure that this was so.

When her own tour opened in Philadelphia on December 17, 1898, Melba's Rosina received an enormous welcome. There "are no words to describe Melba's beautiful voice," proclaimed the critic of the *Philadelphia Inquirer*. Puzzled that in New York Sembrich was being classed as the equal of Melba, he responded emphatically: "There is no Melba but Melba." But even as his review was being read, an epidemic of influenza hit the city. Melba was among the casualties, being too ill to sing for more than a week, and nursing her voice even when she felt better. She knew that nothing must be allowed to spoil her debut in *La Bohème* on December 30.

Philadelphian opera-lovers, while ready to welcome Puccini's new music drama, were puzzled by its modernity. As the critic from the *Inquirer* noted, there were no brilliant stage sets or costumes, "no gorgeous concerted movements," and "practically no chorus and no arias." Its style was conversational, its plot was episodic, but with a stroke of genius Puccini told his story by means of "an unbroken thread of melody—sweet and suave and penetrating." It was this unbroken thread that Melba exploited.

It is often claimed that on this tour *La Bohème* failed to please either audiences or critics. The claim conceals the truth. After the initial shock wore off, Americans took to it eagerly. In Philadelphia Melba and her fellow principals took more than twenty curtain calls and earned splendid reviews. "There is no voice on the stage today so wonderfully suited to the music written for Mimi," wrote the critic of the *Inquirer*. He found Melba's portrayal, both musically and dramatically, "a victory of the very highest kind." Relieved more than she could say, Melba wrote to her sister Belle in Melbourne, "How I wish you could have been present. I think you would have been proud of me."

The opera's success continued to snowball as the Melba train swept through the eastern states and across the Midwest, but it was among the less sophisticated Californians that both she and Puccini's music found their highest approval. In California they could not wait for the opera to begin. Dressmakers in San Francisco had been sewing evening dresses for weeks; ushers at the Grand Opera House were fitted out in new uniforms of red jackets and Turkish turbans; and florists were preparing, especially for Melba, bouquets that were "as big as haystacks." For the first night of *Faust* on March 13, 1899, streetcars came to a stop as three hundred carriages converged on the theatre. In defiance of fire regulations, standing room was sold for every corner of the house, and "outside the foyer, women and men who hunger after music pressed their faces against the brass rail and drank in the music that trickled through the swinging doors." In the words of one reporter, it was "the most brilliant of all the houses San Francisco has ever seen."

If the previous year's audience had failed to recognize Melba upon her first entry, this year's audience was alert and expectant. In her dressing room after the opera, Melba exclaimed excitedly to reporters, "Hooray, hooray. Isn't it fine, how nice they are to me? There was no coldness tonight. They responded from the very first." Two days later, when Melba gave them *La Bohème*, they again responded from the very first. The opera's naturalness enchanted the audience. "Simple to the last degree, without trill or *cadenza*," wrote one reviewer approvingly: Mimi's death was "one of the most beautiful things" he had ever seen.

Would Melba's Mimi be equally successful when played before a critical London audience? At Covent Garden on July 1, 1899, having dutifully sung Juliettes, Gildas, Lucias, and Marguerites, Melba at last had the chance to find out. "The delicious duet in the dark," wrote the London *Times*, was "one of the prettiest duets ever invented." After three more performances before crowded houses, *London Punch* pronounced *La Bohème* the "hit of the season."

That summer of 1899 Melba hired a house again beside the Thames and there she entertained many guests. Haddon Chambers was naturally among them, as was a young Australian sculptor named Bertram

Mackennal, who was sculpting a bust of Melba and another of Queen Victoria. Melba also plunged into parties, one of which celebrated Arthur Sullivan's fifty-seventh birthday at his apartment on Victoria Street. The Prince of Wales was to be among the guests, so Sullivan begged "dear Nellie" to "be the angel" and sing for the prince. "You know I never worry you to sing at my home," he continued, "but this is an exceptional occasion, and a song from you would be the best birthday present you could give me." His hesitancy possibly arose from the memory of a previous party at which the prince had chatted through Melba's song.

In the autumn Melba embarked on a string of grand country visits to the Duchess of Portland, the Duchess of Sutherland, Lady Saville, and Lady Hardwicke. She also visited Alfred Rothschild at his exotic chateau at Halton in Buckinghamshire. Slim, blond Alfred lived in a style so flamboyant that one observer called it an "exaggerated nightmare of gorgeousness." He kept a private zoo, drove four zebras in a carriage, and maintained a private orchestra and circus. He liked to conduct his orchestra with a diamond-studded baton and to dress up as a circus ringmaster in a frock coat, a whip, and lavender gloves.

Melba found him a splendid host: he "does everything royally," she told her sister Belle by letter. When she walked in the park, a pony carriage followed, ready to scoop her up the moment she felt tired. Pageboys stood on the lawn all day in case anyone wished to play tennis or croquet. She found it "all very jolly," by which she meant that to stay among rich and powerful people, and to be courted and deferred to and admired, gave her immense satisfaction.

Her visit was necessarily curtailed, for winter plans required her attention. Although the American tours had been both lucrative and exciting, she decided to bypass the United States in favor of Europe, where Joachim had for so long been urging her to sing. But she had barely arranged her opening performances in Holland when an unforeseen event caused her to hesitate. In South Africa a dispute between the British and the Boers turned into war, and in the Boers' ancestral homeland of Holland, anti-British feeling was rife. Melba, a loyalist to the core, began to wonder if the tour was an act of disloyalty. Nevertheless, after a concert at the Albert Hall on November 4, she set forth to sing *Faust*, *La Traviata*, *Rigoletto*, *Lucia*, and *Manon* in Amsterdam and Rotterdam. The tour met only muted success, young Queen Wilhelmina being noticeably absent from the performances.

The war continued to disturb Melba. British losses in South Africa were multiplying, and since many of her friends were army officers or the families of officers, she saw familiar names in almost every casualty list. "All my friends are in mourning or dreading to be," she told Belle in a letter. She was uncomfortably aware that Britain's expansionist policy was evoking hostility in Germany, and since her next concert was in Berlin, she felt anxious about her reception. Even her finances were affected by the war because the stock market—in which Alfred Rothschild had carefully invested her money—was falling. Watching her assets decline, she confided to Belle that she felt "rather miserable."

She was still in this low mood when she received a severe shock. It was a communication from Charlie. He was living near Galveston, Texas, and was filing for divorce on the grounds of his wife's desertion. According to his petition, he had been a bona fide resident of Texas for almost five years and had invited Melba to live with him. He maintained that she had refused to come. He added, rather to her astonishment, that he "always supported her in good style and conducted himself lovingly towards her."

Quickly consulting her lawyers, Melba framed a response. She denied Charlie's allegations, but she did not choose—possibly on her lawyers' advice—to offer a defense. Above all else, she desired her freedom: to contest the case would also have attracted unwelcome publicity. But the mental picture of George, living with Charlie at the Buena Vista Ranch near Galveston, greatly distressed her. What kind of life did he live on this remote cattle ranch? How much education had he received? She had little doubt that the Texas court would award the boy to Charlie, and he would probably be lost to her—maybe forever.

"It does not agree with me to be idle," she told Belle. "I get so blue." Knowing she must shake off depression with activity, she set out at once on her tour of Germany. In Berlin she was greeted by Joachim, who immediately raised her spirits. At her first concert in Berlin's Philharmonic Hall, Joachim played his violin while she sang his cadenza to "L'Amero." The sight of the two taking their bows to-

gether roused the audience to such a fervor that Melba was obliged to
sit at the piano and play and sing several English songs by way of an
encore. She might have been there a whole hour, but her hair became
loose, and she left the platform pushing back her curls and laughing at
her own disarray.

Eight more times she sang in Berlin, giving a final *Lucia* at the opera
house in the presence of Kaiser Wilhelm II, who summoned her to the
royal box even though she was still dressed in mad Lucia's nightgown.
In January 1900 she traveled to Austria and sang in Vienna's Musikv-
ereinsaal, and despite her initial nervousness, she quickly thawed her
audience with Lucia's "mad scene." The ringing power of her high
notes, the length of her trill, the inaudibility of her breathing, and the
perfection of her intonation captivated even the sternest of Viennese
critics. Why, wrote Ludwig Speidel of the *Fremdenblatt*, her trill filled
every corner of the large hall, "causing all ears and all hearts to vibrate
in an uncanny manner!"

Writing to Madame, who had taught singing when young in Vienna, she described the night as "*truly wonderful.*" "*I shall never forget
it,*" she continued. "I wish you had been there, I think you would have
been proud of me." To Belle she wrote at length a few days later:

> I must tell you of my wonderful success in Vienna. I am only now
> beginning to realize it. *What enthusiasm.* After I finished my last
> song, I was called out perhaps 40 times, I sang several songs and
> played my own accompaniments—they screamed and shouted for
> more, then when they realised I would not sing any more hundreds
> of people came on the platform and shook my hands and nearly tore
> me to pieces—all the flowers on my dress were *torn* off, it really was
> *wonderful.*

A few days later she moved to Budapest where her appearances
were brief, for she was obliged to return, at the command of Emperor
Franz Joseph to sing *La Traviata* in Vienna on January 19, 1900. To cap-
italize on her drawing power, tickets for the performance were doubled
in price, the money going to the opera pension fund, to which Melba
also generously donated her fee.

Delayed in Budapest, she had no time for a rehearsal before her performance in front of the emperor, but she assured the conductor Hans

Richter that she invariably sang a score precisely as it was written. The opera therefore went forward without a hitch, as did her afterpiece of the "mad scene" from *Lucia*. This was not so unusual a juxtaposition as some have imagined, since she was already used to singing the "mad scene" after *Rigoletto* and had even interpolated it in the lesson scene during *The Barber of Seville*.

No sooner had Melba's trill vibrated through the Vienna opera house than there broke out a storm of excitement that continued almost until she drove off in her carriage. "When I left the opera house last night," she wrote to Madame next day, "there were hundreds of people in the streets all trying to kiss my hands; one woman asked for a flower and I gave her a bouquet whereupon the crowd fell on her, and nearly tore her to death. I was obliged to get out of my carriage and throw all my bouquets to the crowds. . . . Otherwise I believe she would have been killed."

Not everyone admired Melba's singing. Among those who thought it was "mechanical" was the young director of the opera house, Gustav Mahler, already a composer of symphonies and admirer of the loud and forceful operas of Richard Strauss and Richard Wagner. He had little time for Melba's style of performance, but he was obliged, as director of the opera, to crown her with a laurel wreath at intermission. The crowning must have gone against the grain. He is reputed to have said in private, "I'd rather listen to a clarinet."

Next morning Melba was summoned to the Hofburg Palace to be awarded the title of "Chamber Singer to the Imperial Court." Here, in a small back room, "an old man in a black coat standing very erect" pinned a medal to her breast. It was Franz Joseph, emperor of Austria, and he told her that her singing had brought him out of retirement. For the past fifteen months he had been mourning his wife, who had been killed by an anarchist's knife as she stood in a street in Geneva.

Back in Berlin after concerts in Leipzig and Dresden, Melba was feeling tense and tired, and troubled by a cough. It was "very anxious work," she wrote to Belle, "singing in different towns 2 or 3 times a week. I hate it." And much as she loved praise, she was finding that lionization also had a negative side. "One of the drawbacks of Fame," she wrote a little wearily, "is that one can never escape from it." Fortunately in Berlin she had someone to divert her. This was young Fritz Muller, a promising piano student whose father had been German tutor to Madame Weiderman Pinschoff's children in Melbourne. Finding him lonely and overworked, Melba interviewed his teachers at the Hochschule and was appalled to find that they regarded him "not so much as an Australian boy with blood in his veins as a sort of automaton." Filled with concern, she decided to become his "loving Aunt" and bought him a Kodak camera for his thirteenth birthday. Fritz's company raised her spirits, but she was also aware of an underlying pain. Fritz reminded her of George, who was sixteen at his last birthday.

Her pending divorce was by now public knowledge and was provoking embarrassing gossip. American newspapers carried reports that Melba and Joachim were to wed. The reports were immediately denied; for one thing, her divorce from Charlie was not yet granted. But tongues were always wagging in an opera house. She anticipated many more rumors before the year was out.

The previous year Melba had agreed to sing *La Traviata* and *The Barber of Seville* at the opera house in Monte Carlo, beginning on February 22, 1900, but now that the time had come she did not look forward to it. She was exhausted, depressed, the weather was cold, and she caught influenza almost as soon as she arrived in Monaco. Struggling to fulfill her contract, she missed five performances, but her spirits rose when the de Greys arrived with a party of friends. These included Joachim, whose presence added fuel to the papers' speculations. Nevertheless she was delighted to see him, for he always managed to lift her spirits.

As soon as her health recovered, Melba gave a luncheon for the new arrivals in rooms decorated with bowls of Australia's national flower, the yellow mimosa—or "what we call wattle blossom in Australia," as she explained to the uninitiated. A brief holiday in Cannes after the operas were over restored her a little before she set out for more concerts in Leipzig, Prague, Cologne, and Berlin. "I still feel *very weak*," she told friends. Dora was to rejoin Melba, and the prospect of sisterly company and visits to dressmakers raised her vitality. "I am all excitement about Dora's arrival," she told Belle by letter. "I suppose she won't have a rag to her back."

From Berlin she returned briefly to France, where she was pounced on by reporters, agog over her divorce. "My divorce from Mr Armstrong delights me," she is reported to have said to them:

> It is what I have longed for. I have never had any desire to live in those awful Dakota and Texas places. Now all is done. As for me, I will soon marry Haddon Chambers. I never thought of marrying Herr Joachim. Why, he is eighty. I have already bought a house in Great Cumberland Place, London, where I expect to be very happy as Mr Chambers' wife.

Whether Melba actually uttered this frank statement one cannot know. Some reporters were adept at spoon-feeding their words into her mouth, but the sentences do carry the cheeky, devil-may-care ring of Nellie Melba.

Melba may have wanted to show the reporters that, even if Charlie did not want her, there were those who did. But for her to announce that she would soon be "Mr Chambers' wife"—*if* she did say it—was unfair to Haddon. He was in no position to marry her. Some years before meeting Melba, he had married the mother of his illegitimate daughter, and though the couple soom parted, neither sought a divorce. Haddon was still a married man. After the rumors ebbed, Melba wrote to her sister Belle, "I could annihilate the American press, it is *too shocking*—I shall *never* marry again, I could never put up with a man bossing me—*I should kill him.*"

Certainly the reported interview was correct in one particular: she was moving from Paris to London. Having spent no more than a few months in France during the last three years, a change of home seemed sensible. Moreover she was disenchanted with some of her Parisian friends over their attitude toward Alfred Dreyfus, a French army captain of Jewish ancestry, falsely convicted of espionage six years previously and recently granted a retrial. Philippe and his Orléanist supporters were militantly anti-Dreyfus and saw the divisive case as a golden opportunity to bring down the republic and restore the monarchy. Melba, on the other hand, proclaimed her sympathy by writing an impassioned letter to Madame Dreyfus, saying that she had "hoped and despaired" and "wept and prayed" during the captain's long ordeal.

The house that Melba rented in London was at 30 Great Cumberland Place, within sight of the majestic Marble Arch. Although not as fashionable as nearby Mayfair, this corner of London held such friends as Lady Charles Beresford and Lady Randolph Churchill, and its former owner, Mrs Hwfa Williams, was a great favorite of the Prince of Wales. Of elegant Georgian design, the house boasted eleven bedrooms, three bathrooms, and six reception rooms.

An army of workmen now renovated the interior under Melba's orders—"along Versailles lines," in the words of her friends. Melba chose the furnishings personally, many on the advice of Boni de Castellane who, thanks to his wife's money, was now, according to Melba, "one of the finest connoisseurs in Europe." The gilded chairs, sofas, and tables came from the time of Louis XV and Louis XVI, and the blue and white Aubusson carpets wreathed with pink roses were the finest Boni could find. The wall decorations of cupids and garlands took French craftsmen two years to carve. In the stables Melba installed fine carriage horses, including a new colt to which she sometimes gave sugar in her cupped hand. She also bought the latest automobile in order "to save the dear animals from night work."

Once again Melba also rented a house beside the Thames for the summer and bought a motor launch, which she christened the *Mimi*. To be able to sit in an easy chair and steer up and down the river seemed wonderfully luxurious, and when she was not singing at Covent Garden it became her favorite occupation. Among the friends who visited that year was Herman Bemberg, who arrived in clothes he jokingly maintained were those that an English gentleman would wear on the river. He wore a garishly striped blazer and flannel trousers so tight they split at the seat, forcing him to mend his trousers with safety pins. Dressed more soberly, he was captured for posterity in a photograph taking tea with Dora, Haddon Chambers, and Bertram Mackennal in Melba's garden.

London's mood was gloomy in the face of adverse news from the Boer War, and not even Dora's lively presence could quite lift Melba's spirits. "You meet nothing but people in mourning with long faces," she wrote to Belle, "and you hear nothing but the most awful stories of suffering of all one's best friends. I am afraid it is going to last a long time."

The relief of the besieged South African town of Mafeking on May 18, the day before Melba's thirty-ninth birthday, temporarily brightened faces in the streets. London was still rejoicing three days later when Melba returned to Covent Garden in the role of Mimi. The Prince of Wales was in his box, and for an hour or so it seemed like old times.

Over the next three months Melba sang at Covent Garden and traveled to Ireland to perform a charity concert at the Royal University Hall in Dublin. She had scarcely recrossed the Irish Sea when newspaper headlines filled her with alarm. They described how a hurricane at the Texas port of Galveston had killed five thousand people and flooded vast low-lying areas. Charlie's ranch was near Galveston and, in her mind's eye, Melba pictured George's body among the flood waters. Desperate to learn the truth, she contacted the newspaper magnate Alfred Harmsworth, at whose parties she had sometimes sung. His reassurances that neither George nor Charlie was among the fatalities eased some of her tension and she was able to breathe easily again.

The hurricane came early in September, not long before Melba, accompanied by Dora, sailed for America to join the Metropolitan Company. Thanks to the success of her Californian tours, Grau had decided to take his troupe to the West Coast and they opened in Los Angeles November 10. "Grand Opera in the Angel City" ran the headline in the *Los Angeles Daily Times*, as it described the crush at Hazard's Pavilion, a venue normally used for prizefights. Well-dressed opera-lovers arrived from as far off as San Diego, and few who came were disappointed, for *La Bohème*, followed by the "mad scene" from *Lucia*, measured up to everyone's expectations. In San Francisco, Kansas City, Denver, Lincoln, Minneapolis, Philadelphia, Cincinnati, Pittsburgh, Chicago, Boston, and of course New York, Melba repeated her success, singing *La Bohème, Lucia, Faust, Roméo et Juliette, La Traviata, Rigoletto, Les Huguenots*, and two performances of a new role in Massenet's *Le Cid*. She sometimes felt tired but never displeased, for her reception was almost all she could have desired. The *Chicago Tribune* critic summed up the public feeling: "For charm and purity of voice the great Australian soprano stands easily alone."

When Melba returned to England in May 1901, Queen Victoria had been dead for nearly four months, and the former Prince of Wales ruled as King Edward VII. Melba had every reason to welcome the change, for her friendship with the new king and queen placed her in the highest circles of society. But while it was the hopeful beginning of a new era, there was much to sadden Melba that spring. The war in South Africa was still raging, with victory not yet in sight. And there was mourning too, of a sort, at Covent Garden, for Maurice Grau had resigned, giving way to the French conductor André Messager, who seldom bothered to visit England. For a time Melba doubted whether she would rejoin the company, but in the end she sang *La Bohème*, *Faust*, and *Roméo et Juliette*.

With Dora's return to Australia, Melba again felt lonely. Fortunately her sister Belle agreed to come to England and arrived in June with her two youngest children. Thanks to their presence, the summer of 1901, which had begun so unpromisingly, turned into an idyll. Melba again rented an ivy-clad house beside the Thames, this time called Quarrywood Cottage, though the name belied its size and grandeur. There she set up a nursery for the children, and life revolved around their sayings and doings. Melba adored little David; he had "quite captured my heart with his beautiful eyes," she told Belle. But her love was tinged with melancholy, for he reminded her of George. Her small niece and namesake, Nellie, brought no sad memories: "I am her slave," wrote Melba.

A charming photograph still exists of Melba and Belle taking tea on the lawn. Three-year-old Nellie, dressed in an enormous white bonnet, sits beside them in a high chair, with a cake on the tray in front of her. Behind the child stands Haddon Chambers, holding a cup and saucer and looking proprietorial. He was by now widely regarded as Melba's unofficial consort.

Australia was much in Melba's thoughts that summer, and uppermost was the possibility of a homeland tour. Each year she received offers from Australian impresarios, and each year she toyed with the offers, but when it came to the signing of contracts she always resisted. Paragraphs appeared in Australian newspapers proclaiming she was coming, only to be followed by denials. Indeed Melba's canceled tours of her homeland were becoming a national joke, and she knew that further procrastination would harm her reputation. Moreover the gloom of London winters and the personal warmth of Belle—these days her favorite sister—were providing strong incentives to revisit Australia.

Foremost among the offers was one from James Cassius Williamson, whom she remembered from Melbourne days. An American comedian before he became a manager, Williamson was the most successful of Australian impresarios. He had brought Sarah Bernhardt to Australia and for years had been keen to arrange a tour for Melba. He wanted, however, a larger share of the profits than she thought fair. He argued that to give her the terms she sought, he would have to charge "high English prices" which he did not believe the Australian market could sustain. Melba was not persuaded. In listening to propositions involving money she was her father's daughter: she weighed each financial argument down to the last shilling. She confided her feelings to Belle by letter after her sister and children sailed home in September. "I have done everything I can to bring him to reason," she wrote impatiently, "but he really is *too ridiculous*."

Realizing she needed an agent in Australia, she begged Belle's auctioneer husband, Tom Patterson, to act for her. A month later she rejected the offer from Williamson with elaborate politeness. "My feelings of friendship for you are unaltered," she told him, "and my best wishes are always yours." Instead she approached his erstwhile partner George Musgrove, whom she remembered from the time in her youth when she had toured with Johann Kruse. Musgrove offered her more generous financial terms. By late October she was able to write to Belle and other friends that she had "arranged all with Musgrove who is really splendid." This time she was "really and truly coming to Australia," leaving London in ten months' time and sailing across the Pacific to escape the heat of the Red Sea.

In the meantime she was preparing for a tour of the British Isles. In Ireland in October she sang to the largest audience ever gathered in Belfast's Ulster Hall. Later she visited the Irish Armstrongs near Dublin, who, despite the divorce, welcomed her with open arms. Indeed she was the life and soul of their party, producing her jewels after dinner so that everyone could try them on. In Scotland, with Haddon Chambers in attendance, she sang in Edinburgh and Glasgow. Afterward she and Haddon were fellow guests at picturesque Duart Castle on the Isle of Mull in Scotland's windswept Hebrides Islands. Staying also at the castle was "a little Eton Boy, David by name, who has captured my heart," she told her friends. "He reminds me of my own beautiful Boy, he even calls his mother Mummy. . . . I can't bear to think of it."

The Eton boy, after returning to his school, wrote a polite note to Melba. She replied maternally but sternly, commenting on his spelling. "Dear Eton Boy," she wrote to him, "I wonder if Mr Broadbent teaches you to spell awful with two ls—do ask him for me. Yours truly, Nellie Melba." Her communications were not always so pithy. When writing to those she loved, she let her thoughts and feelings tumble out: her letters were usually four pages long and were often scored with heavy underlining. Her sister Belle received many such letters during the winter of 1901–1902.

Belle, rather unwisely, had sent Melba an Australian news clipping frowning on the proposed tour. Although Melba argued that "nothing can take away from the glory of my visit to Australia," the negative article was obviously a blow. That egalitarian trait in the Australian character which leads some of its citizens to defame those who achieve eminence in anything but sports was noticeable even in 1901. It was one reason why Melba had been reluctant to return until her supremacy in opera was indisputable. This did not make the condemnation easier to bear. Even more disappointing was the pain she felt at her family's lack of welcome. Although hundreds of strangers had written enthusiastically about her projected tour, she had so far received "not *one* line" from Annie, Dora, Frank, or Charlie. "I have strange brothers and sisters. You don't know how I *feel* it," she confided to Belle.

Relations with Annie had been strained ever since her last visit to Europe. Melba guessed that sisterly rivalry was at the root of their differences. "Do you know I think Annie is jealous of me and my position this is *entre nous*," she confided again to Belle. She had consoled herself that at least Dora was her ally. Now she began to suspect Dora of mischief, and Belle seemed to agree with her. "I am so hurt by Dora's behaviour after all I have done for her," she told Belle. Although Melba could not see it, her brothers' and sisters' lack of enthusiasm over her return was in a way understandable. Melba was about to arrive like a whirlwind, demanding and receiving the public spotlight, and expecting innumerable services and sacrifices from members of her family.

Their settled lives would be turned upside down, and they viewed the prospect with mixed feelings.

Pertinent to these considerations was the question of where she should stay in Melbourne. Her father had invited her to stay at Doonside, but her instincts were against it. For one thing she would have her maids, companion, and secretary with her, and even that rambling family house could not accommodate so large an entourage. For another, she suspected that her siblings would not welcome it. Having no notion of how dislocating her visit was likely to be, she could feel only resentment at their attitude. "If my family are not going to be nice I prefer to stay away," she told Belle firmly. "I simply *couldn't* stand it." From all points of view it was essential she have a house of her own. "I *must* have one," she told her sister emphatically.

Differences with her independently minded brothers and sisters were not, of course, new to Melba. Disputes were engaged with excitement but were usually short-lived: one could always count on family affection prevailing. Her real anxieties centered on George. After the hurricane Charlie had left Galveston, and his whereabouts had been traced to Oregon. Father and son were living near the remote township of Klamath Falls, close to the California border, where Charlie had set up a ranch beside the fir forests. Seventeen-year-old George was working as his ranch hand. This news, probably supplied by a private detective, greatly distressed her, especially when she remembered the eager and articulate child her son had been. She believed that George was on the way to becoming a rolling stone like his father—but while Charlie had chosen this life, George had not. "I have had frightful accounts of the way Georgie is being brought up," she wrote to Belle. "I am broken hearted about it; the solicitors say there is nothing to be done. I can only hope that God will one day punish that bad man—surely he must be punished some day."

Uneasy at leaving her money to George while he remained in Charlie's custody, she altered her will. "Under the circumstances it would never do," she wrote to Belle, "for my Boy to have too much money so I am taking care of every detail." Part of what had previously been intended for George she decided to divert to Belle's small daughter, Nellie. "You can imagine how sad it is for me to write this," she informed Belle and her husband, "but my heart is breaking and I must talk to someone and I know I can trust you and Tom."

Fortunately there was little time for her to dwell on her worries: she was engaged to sing in Monte Carlo on February 1, 1902. The visit proved a tonic, for she found much to divert her, and the weather was so mild that she could sunbathe every day. Spending some days at the Hôtel L'Ermitage and some days with a new friend, Lady Wilton, she sang, gambled, went to parties, lost a purse studded with diamonds and turquoises, which caused her some heartburn, and visited poor Haddon Chambers, who had fallen ill while staying at nearby Cap Martin.

Another diversion was a prizewinning Brazilian aviator who had just won an air race around the Eiffel Tower. His name was Alberto Santos-Dumont, and to her delight he sailed his gas filled airship close to her window. She found him "such a nice little modest man" when she and her hostess inspected his machine next afternoon. The noise of the engine, however, was shattering: "How his nerves can stand it," wrote Melba, "is beyond my comprehension." Despite the noise, Melba decided to ride in his airship, and it was agreed that he would fly her back when next she visited Cap Martin. After waiting in vain for the promised ride, she was making her own way home when she saw what looked like "a huge tent with a little man struggling in it" way out in the middle of the Bay of Monaco. It was Santos-Dumont salvaging his waterlogged machine.

Giacomo Puccini was also in Monte Carlo, overseeing rehearsals of *La Bohème*. On opening night he was too nervous to watch the opera, finally appearing with notable self-effacement to take his bow. He had no need for nervousness, for the opera went off marvelously: Melba's Mimi was described as "impeccable" and her tenor, though short and stocky, was considered a remarkable find. Named Enrico Caruso, he partnered her again in *Rigoletto* eleven days later with exquisite singing and passionate acting. Melba could not wait to tell Nordica about him when they lunched together, soon after, at a restaurant in Paris. Another of Nordica's guests was Jean de Reszke, toward whom neither woman now seems to have felt even a shadow of animosity. A reporter, catching sight of the supposedly rival divas, drew his own mistaken conclusion. To Nordica's and Melba's amusement, a headline in a New York paper proclaimed: "Melba and Nordica Bury the Hatchet."

Melba spent part of her time in Paris that spring calling on artists' studios, for her interest in painting had blossomed beyond youthful enthusiasm into an intelligent knowledge of artistic technique. She was particularly excited by a new movement in her homeland in which young artists, influenced by French impressionism, painted outdoor scenes—many located a half-day's walk upriver from Doonside—where they caught the harsh blue skies and bleached grassland of the Australian summer. Melba found the pictures produced by these Australian impressionists enchanting, and over the years would become an avid collector of their work.

Meanwhile she supported several promising Australians who were studying art in Paris. One was Ambrose Patterson, a relative of Belle's husband; another was Hugh Ramsay, who was engaged to Fritz Muller's sister in Melbourne. Exquisitely dressed and chauffeured in a resplendent automobile, Melba and Haddon Chambers descended on Ramsay's humble studio late in March, looking and feeling a little like visitors from another planet; but once they viewed his canvases, it was they who felt humbled. His paintings proclaimed his talent, his portraits being particularly impressive. Melba, "intensely sympathetic," showed signs of commissioning a portrait from him. "Think of it," Ramsay wrote home. "If I could make a successful portrait of her, I'm a made man." Describing Melba, he wrote that she was "a charming lady, so natural, sincere and unaffected. Although she's a great lady, you feel at home with her from the first, she doesn't put fears into your heart, as many in her position would, but makes you feel quite at your ease." Haddon too was, in Ramsay's words, "an awfully nice fellow, and he has also promised to do all he can for me. He knows heaps of people whom it'll do one good to know. He's quite a celebrity himself."

Melba dared not dally in Paris, for she was to sing in Germany and Switzerland. She could not even wait for Madame's forthcoming golden wedding concert, of which she was the chief organizer. "I think it will be very chic," Melba told a friend, "as all the artists I have asked have promised to come and do something. Poor old thing she is 83 years of age and still goes on working all day." In fact Melba should have had more sympathy for Madame's desire to keep working. Like Melba, Madame looked on work as the tonic that cured all ills.

Before leaving her beloved Madame, Melba had an important proposal to discuss with her. The manager of the Paris Opéra had offered her the role of Wagner's Isolde opposite Jean de Reszke's Tristan. There seems little doubt that she longed to do it, for to perform the heavier Wagnerian operas was now her greatest challenge. And there seems little doubt that at times she believed she was capable of succeeding. At other times she recognized that Isolde was more taxing vocally than *Siegfried*'s Brünnhilde and required a force and spirit of which she was not capable. "I will be guided entirely by your judgement," she told Madame. Needless to say, her teacher said no.

Melba's visit to Germany diverted her from this disappointment, for there she received praise aplenty. To Madame she wrote, "The Germans are crazy about me, I am overwhelmed with congratulations—I don't think I have ever had *such a triumph*. Are you glad?" And she added, "In all my interviews you will find your name, I have told them you were my *only* teacher and that I owe everything to you."

It was noteworthy that Cecchi's claims as Melba's vital teacher were now forgotten, for Madame demanded that no teacher other than herself be acknowledged as the teacher of Melba. And since Melba loved Madame and had come to believe that she owed her "everything," her response was to bury the memory of Cecchi and to omit all mention of his name. Melba certainly owed much to Madame Marchesi, for Madame's contacts, knowledge of repertoire, and skills in providing polish and deportment had helped Melba to gain her exalted place in European opera. On the other hand, Madame could have achieved little in so short a time if Melba had not already possessed the first-class technique imparted by Cecchi.

For years there had been muted complaints in Australia that Cecchi's name and influence were not acknowledged. These mutterings became louder after his death in 1897 when obituarists remembered how the old man would waylay friends and acquaintances on Collins Street to remind them—though few needed reminding—that he was Melba's teacher. "His pardonable pride in Melba's success," wrote one obituarist, "came to be a well-worn joke with musical people." In 1898 Cecchi's claims were championed by the Melbourne magazine *Table Talk*, which usually took Melba's side. Three years later the widely read and sensationalist *Sydney Truth* carried a scarifying denunciation of Melba's treatment of Cecchi written by its editor John Norton. The attack included a letter purportedly written by Cecchi, lamenting that Melba was disowning him. "But for me she would not be where she is now," wrote Cecchi, "and I have many letters from her, written here and in London, which prove the truth of all I say." Although Norton was not above fabricating evidence, the letter would seem to be genuine.

In May 1902 Melba returned to a London that was eagerly anticipating King Edward's coronation, already hailed as likely to be one of the greatest pageants of the new century. Concerts and parties abounded, and Melba sang at some of the grandest, including two at Alfred Rothschild's, where she chatted to the soldier Lord Kitchener and to Cecil Rhodes, the South African politician and mining magnate. At the home of Mrs. George Cooper in Grosvenor Square, she gave a dramatic rendering of Bemberg's "La ballade du désespéré," with Sarah Bernhardt reciting the words, Melba singing the vocal score, Bemberg playing the piano, a teenage protégée of Melba's named Ada Sassoli playing the harp, and Melba's future biographer Percy Colson playing the violin. She also held a party for her forty-first birthday at which her cook produced a cake in the shape of a book propped up against a lyre. Across its pages was written in sugar the name *Rigoletto*, the opera with which she and Caruso had opened the Covent Garden season five days earlier.

The hospitality Melba herself provided at Great Cumberland Place during that coronation summer was almost as grand as the hospitality she received in the great houses of England. It astonished young Hugh Ramsay when he dined with her early in June. The guests ate off gold and silver plates, and a footman stood behind each chair. After dinner Melba announced that she was commissioning several portraits from him, and soon after took him to the Royal Academy to inspect a full-length portrait of herself by another Australian artist named Rupert Bunny. "No one likes my portrait by Bunny except the *painter*," Melba told close friends. John Singer Sargent's work was another matter. "What a genius he is," she sighed, and vowed to be painted one day by Sargent.

Melba threw herself into the coronation celebrations. On June 11, 1902, she opened the Grand Coronation Concert at the Albert Hall, her "golden voice" ringing "through the vast building in the opening verse of the national anthem." At Covent Garden on "Melba nights," when the price of tickets leaped to unusual heights, she sang Mimi, Juliette, Gilda, Violetta, and Marguerite to glamorous audiences, swelled by groups of Australian soldiers who had recently been fighting the Boer War. "She was a pretty woman," wrote one of those operagoers:

> Pretty in the comely sense rather than handsome, as she stood there, her bouquet of roses over her heart, her hair done in a crown upon her shapely head, and coming up to a queenly twist. I can still see her dress of white silk, *décolleté*, but with its slip drawn modestly to hide the bosom. One always felt that here was a woman capable of deep affectionate love . . . if any man could be found to awaken her—for she was the "The Sleeping Beauty" of life as of opera, with a certain proud modesty about her poise and smile.

Then suddenly London was plunged into gloom. On the morning of June 25 the newspapers made the startling announcement that the next day's coronation had been canceled. The king lay gravely ill, stricken with near-fatal appendicitis. Writing to Belle that very morning, Melba poured out her consternation: "*It is appalling*," she told her sister, heavily underlining each word. Three days later she finished the letter with hope, for a note from a member of the royal family reassured her that the king was recovering. The coronation was now delayed until October, by which time she would be in Australia.

Disappointment at missing the coronation heightened her misgivings about her Australian tour, and her anxiety was communicated by letter to Belle. Had Belle found a house for her in Melbourne? Could Belle advise her on what clothes to pack and what jewels to bring? She had just bought a collar of perfect pear-shaped diamonds that the renowned jeweler Cartier had taken six years to match and mount. "He says no Queen or Empress has anything finer," she wrote to Belle. "I am sure you will like it."

There was fussing too over her accommodations at sea. She was to sail to Australia by way of North America, boarding the steamship *Miowera* in Vancouver. Four cabins aboard the *Miowera* were to be made into one large stateroom for Melba, and other cabins were to be reserved for her secretary, Miss Gill, and for her Melbourne friend, May

Donaldson, a woman of "exceptional intellectuality and charm of manner" who had already acted as her companion on the German tour.

Cabins also had to be booked for her concert party: for Louis Arens, a dashing tenor from Riga with whom she had sung in Europe; for young Ada Sassoli, her Italian harpist protégée; for Federic Griffith, whose flute accompaniments were essential for her "mad scenes"; and for Mauricio Bensaude, a Portuguese baritone with whom she had toured in America. With them came Griffith's and Bensaude's wives, Ada Sassoli's mother, and Melba's accompanist, Llewella Davies.

On July 31, in a flurry of activity, Melba left by train from Euston Station to board her ship in Liverpool. An "immense crowd" thronged the platform, and flowers and presents soon swamped her railway carriage. Among the gifts were eleven gold pencils set with jewels, a diamond ring, long-stemmed pink roses from Ada Crossley, and a diamond and turquoise necklet from generous Alfred Rothschild. The king sent good wishes through the Prince of Wales, and Haddon Chambers was at the carriage door to take a tender farewell. Although part of her was apprehensive, part of her was buoyant. If "by the exercise of my art I am able to add some joy to the lives of my countrywomen and countrymen," she told her public, "my happiness will be complete."

CHAPTER SIXTEEN

My Native Land

WHEN MELBA first saw the Australian coast from the deck of the *Miowera* on the afternoon of September 17, 1902, she bowed three times toward it for luck. "My native land!" she told a reporter who had come aboard with the ship's pilot near the entrance to Moreton Bay: "Yes, that is my country." Then she added, "Oh, I do hope the people will like me in Australia." The reporter sensed her tension and noticed that she interspersed her comments with short bursts of uneasy laughter. He also noticed that when she spoke of her father, her eyes held tears. As they leaned over the steamship's rail and gazed at the smoke rising from a string of wildfires burning along the coast, their talk turned to music. She spoke lovingly of Madame Marchesi, "with whom," she added firmly, "I studied first." She spoke also of Puccini. He "touches one here," she said, and placed her hand on her heart.

Night was by now beginning to close and sleepy seagulls were flying overhead; soon they would be docking at the wharf in the Brisbane River. Melba offered the reporter tea or perhaps a whisky and soda, and begged him to wish her luck, especially for her concert in the Melbourne Town Hall where her "dear old father," now aged seventy-three, would be in the audience. "It will be a very emotional occasion," she predicted. Just then the mayor and mayoress of Brisbane appeared at the side of the ship, ready to present her with a bouquet of Australian wattle blossom. Suddenly every inch a diva, Melba left the reporter and graciously advanced to greet them.

Although outwardly self-assured, Melba was filled with uncertainty. Now aged forty-one, she was conscious how much she had changed— and how Australia had changed—in the sixteen years since she had last set foot on its shores. The country's population had swelled by more than a million, its cultural life had blossomed, and its six colonies had joined together in a federation known as the Commonwealth of Australia. The first parliament of the new Commonwealth had been opened just a year before in Melbourne's Exhibition Building, the very building that her father had built not long before her mother's death. It was about to pass a law making Australia the first country in the world to give all women not only the right to vote in federal elections but the right to stand for parliament. From a colonial backwater, Australia had become a progressive nation.

Would Australians like her? As she crossed the Pacific in the slow *Miowera*, she had had ample time to ponder this question. That strain of egalitarianism in Australian society, largely the legacy of the country's convict past, was sure to predispose some to dislike her, even before they saw and heard her. Those who enjoyed cutting down the "tall poppy" would reject and possibly defame her. Such a response would be grossly unfair, because she had been raised with a strong sense of duty and had long ago vowed to use her fame in the service of her country. She could only hope that the rest of her countrymen would take pride in her success and accept her as an example of what Australians could achieve.

It was now almost time to disembark, and as they approached the wharf in Brisbane, she could see a bevy of admirers fighting for a glimpse of her. Unable to face a crowd, she slipped away as quietly as possible, and few saw more than a retreating figure in a navy suit and a wide black hat with a curling ostrich feather. That night she slept at the Gresham Hotel, her body still tossing with the movement of the ship and her mind preoccupied with what lay ahead. But next morning she was up soon after dawn—"fresh as a rose" according to the newspapers—and off to the railway station with May Donaldson and Miss Gill to begin the long journey south to Sydney and Melbourne.

At the station she saw, with relief, just how groundless her fears of rejection had been. A throng of well-wishers waited to cheer her as she boarded the train, while more stood ready to cheer her along the way.

Looking out of her carriage window, she saw lone spectators standing beside the line and clumps of people at the primitive sidings where the train did not stop. At the larger stations, mayors were ready with addresses of welcome, and hundreds more people waited just to see her face. She shook their hands and waved and smiled, conscious of tears pricking at her eyes.

Close to Sydney, her brother Charlie boarded the train, to be followed soon after by her sister Belle. It was an emotional reunion, for she had not seen Charlie for sixteen years and they had much to say to each other. Belle she welcomed with relief, for her sister was the rock to which she intended to cling if the tour became too much for her. By now she had been traveling for nearly thirty hours, and she felt faint from emotion and fatigue.

When at last the train steamed into Sydney, Melba faced a surging multitude of about two thousand people who shouted and even scrambled for flowers from her bouquet. After two policemen cleared a path to her waiting carriage, she decided that she needed a respite. As she rested at the Australia Hotel before boarding the evening train for Melbourne, she summoned her concert manager, George Musgrove, and they postponed her first Melbourne concert by three days. The postponement was not without good reason: the *Miowera* had been two days late in docking, so she was already two days behind, and her unstrung nerves cried out for rest. While in some ways it was a wise decision, in other ways it was not. Many of her fans were coming long distances to hear her. At worst they would be obliged to miss the concerts, at best their plans would be upset.

All over the country, newspaper readers were following Melba's triumphant progress, and while editorials in major papers hailed her as "one of the greatest artists whom the world has known" and spoke seriously of her talent, the weekly journals filled their columns with those personal snippets they believed their readers would relish. Outside Sydney reporters came aboard her railcar and began to badger her with questions. Mostly she answered cheerfully, but sometimes she grew impatient. When one reporter asked what roles she had studied but never sung, she snapped: "Elvira, Zerlina, Leila, Martha, Amina— how can I remember them all in this frightful railway train?" When another asked her about the Duke of Orléans, she refused to answer.

Shaking her finger at the intrusive reporter, she fixed her gaze on the passing bushland, and called his attention to the white cockatoos.

As she sped toward Melbourne, she anticipated the reunion with her father. He was to meet her in a few hours in the inland town of Albury, from which he would escort her the last 190 miles in style. Throughout the journey her thoughts had been turning to him. She knew he was bound to ask her questions. On some subjects she doubted she would be able to give him satisfactory answers, and since she longed for his approval, this troubled her.

She knew that her marital troubles and her affair with Philippe had distressed his stern Presbyterian soul. Perhaps it would be better not to discuss them, though she knew her father understood her need to leave Charlie, for he had contributed an affidavit to her petition for separation. Her industry, however, would be sure to please him. He detested idleness, and the Covent Garden seasons, the Metropolitan seasons, the tours of America, Germany, Austria, and Scandinavia had scarcely given her time to draw breath. When she did draw breath, she ached for George. Would her father understand this? She prayed that he would, because she had craved his understanding since babyhood, and never more so than now.

While the warm spring day was breaking, Melba began a careful toilette. She chose a favorite tan and navy dress and navy hat and asked her maid to arrange her hair in a fringe of curls "from ear to ear." It was an old-fashioned coiffure, resembling the style she had worn when last she saw her father. Perhaps she chose it to calm herself. She knew she must keep a tight rein on her feelings because David Mitchell hated an emotional display.

About an hour out of Albury she was handed a telegram. Its content is not known, but it would seem to have been designed to prepare her for a shock that was about to follow. If this was the intention, its wording was too timid for it failed in its effect. As the train steamed into Albury station, Melba hung her head out the window looking for her father. When she could not see him, she forced her way through the crowded doorway and searched the platform. "Where is my father?" she kept crying out, but the only answer was "an inarticulate murmur." When a strange man approached her with a nurse by his side, she suspected the worst; and when she heard the word "stroke" she swayed backward. If Belle and her husband Tom Patterson had not been with her, she might have fallen onto the platform. Their arms supported her as she stumbled to the house nearby where David Mitchell lay. Years later she described her first steps into the sickroom:

> There in the corner was my Daddy, lying in bed, very still. The nurse put her finger to her lips as we tiptoed towards him. I knelt down by his bed, and kissed his hand. And then very slowly, and with an air of infinite weariness, he opened his eyes; and as soon as he saw me the tired mouth twitched itself into a smile. What I said to him, how long I stayed there, I do not know.

Melba's first instinct was to abandon her concerts and official engagements and stay with her father. She told him so, and at once the speechless man found speech. He spoke "with infinite effort" the words: "You must go on. You must go on." They were not wishes but commands, spoken with that "air of unbreakable will" she remembered from her childhood. Even now he would not tolerate what he saw as a dereliction of duty. Reluctantly she kissed him goodbye and reboarded the train.

Meanwhile her journey grew every moment more royal as the train steamed closer to Melbourne. At each station where it briefly halted, Melba was expected to step outside and greet mayoral deputations and presenters of bouquets. Even when the train did not stop, she was obliged to acknowledge those who threw up their hats, waved handkerchiefs and Australian flags, and held up placards saying "WELCOME."

The enthusiam was understandable. As the papers were quick to point out, Melba was the first celebrated performer to visit Australia in the prime of her career. She was also the best known in overseas countries of all living Australians. More important, she was the famous hometown girl, whose adopted name echoed the place in which she was born and raised. She was Melbourne's own Nellie Melba, and her people were enormously proud of her.

The train arrived in Melbourne soon after noon. It was a Saturday, and even though the platform was shut to the general public, half of the city seemed to be outside Melbourne's Spencer Street station. As Melba stepped onto the platform, little boys on a neighboring roof shouted out, "Three cheers for Nellie." Their "hip, hip hoorays" brought forth such a roar that it drowned the welcoming words of the governor-general's emissary, Lord Richard Nevill. Minutes later relatives and friends were clamoring to shake her hand, among them a child in a fluffy blue and white dress. It was little Nellie Patterson, and Melba swooped on her with hugs and kisses. Meanwhile Tom Patterson and burly George Musgrove clasped Melba by the arms and attempted to edge her toward the gate.

Outside the station, even with the help of police, it was a struggle for Melba to reach her horse-drawn carriage. As she entered it, she passed a bunch of violets she had just received into the waiting hands of her companion, May Donaldson. "Give us all some," shouted a voice from the crowd. Delighted by the idea, Melba began tearing apart the bouquets piled high in her carriage and throwing the blooms into the throng. Little boys fought one another for violets and daffodils and soon were plying a brisk trade in "Melba momentos."

As her carriage sped through the city streets, trams were halted as eager well-wishers spilled onto the roadways. Outside the stock exchange, the staid members waved and cheered as they saw her drive by. Outside Allan's Music Shop, a band played "Home Sweet Home" and "Auld Lang Syne," and bystanders joined in the choruses. So many of the places coming into view held memories for Melba. Allan's Music Shop, though it had been rebuilt, still occupied the site where she had studied with Cecchi. The "quaint little rambling house" she passed a few moments later had belonged to her Dow grandmother. The town hall where she had sung her first adult concert almost matched the splendor with which she had enshrined it in her memory.

Elsewhere she noted changes. New city buildings had sprung up, higher than any she had seen in London or Paris. Cable trams, like those in San Francisco, could be seen running to a dozen suburbs. There was even the occasional automobile, chugging among the horse-drawn cabs and carts. To be witnessing these sights, old and new, seemed just short of miraculous. Her anxiety and fatigue gave way to wonder. In the words of one observer, Melba seemed to radiate happiness.

As she neared the suburb of Toorak, she had a curious encounter. A cable tram had stopped for her carriage to pass, and eager passengers craned out the windows. Among them was a blind man who turned his face toward her, though he could not see her. He called out, "Welcome back to Melbourne, Nellie." It was old Armes Beaumont, the well-known Melbourne tenor, who had sung with her in her girlhood. He imagined she would not recognize him, but she did and she greeted him excitedly.

In fashionable Toorak, Belle had rented a large house for her called Myoora. Built years before by a Scottish merchant, it lacked modern amenities but had plenty of grandeur, set amid spacious lawns, terraces, and gardens. Here her own family awaited her. Tea was served and differences were forgotten as she and her brothers and sisters affectionately embraced.

With the last visitor gone, Melba was at last able to retire to her bedroom to shed the tears that had been threatening all day. Tears, however, could not be indulged for long, because there was work to be done. Her clothes were waiting to be unpacked and sorted and matched, under her eye, to the forthcoming engagements. She had brought twenty-seven trunks, many of them containing exquisite outfits from Paris, the most glamorous being her filmy concert dresses, worn over shimmering satin linings and decorated with spangles and sequins and silk flowers. Almost all were cut in a clinging princess style to show off her tightly laced, hourglass figure.

She must also interview her housekeeper, for she could not hope to succeed without a well-run household. In England, where first-class cooks, butlers, and parlor maids were commonplace, it was easy to maintain an efficient establishment. In democratic Australia, where servants were fewer and notoriously independent, it was difficult, especially as Melba had adopted the English attitude of the time toward servants and did not hesitate to reprove them when they did not measure up. "After having known all the luxuries and all the amenities of Europe," she would remember, "I was soon to discover that this country of my birth had a very great deal to learn about the things which go to make life comfortable."

Melba's cooks proved particularly troublesome. Her first cook at Myoora refused to work on Sundays. Efforts to find a replacement failed—"Melbourne seemed to be absolutely devoid of cooks," she wrote incredulously—until her father offered her the services of his cook from Doonside. Even then another obstacle arose: the cook would not come unless her tram-driver fiancé was transferred to work on the tramlines near Myoora. Melba, who, when not reproving the servants, was often kind and generous, went in person to the head of the tramways and successfully arranged for the young man to have his wish. The girl proved an excellent plain cook, but she could not cope with big parties. Melba resorted to hiring the cook and waiters from the fashionable Vienna Café for her large dinners and suppers.

Security was not easily arranged at Myoora. Fabulous jewels were now part of Melba's public presence, worn like a diva's badge of office. Taking her cue from Adelina Patti, who was the first prima donna to wear real gems on stage, Melba draped as many on herself as she could comfortably fit when she sang at concerts or played roles like Violetta, and wore as many as etiquette would allow when she attended social functions. To a reception given for her by the lord mayor of Melbourne, she wore the diamond collar made by Cartier, a diamond and turquoise necklet, a diamond stomacher with a swaying pendant, and elegant brooches of diamonds and turquoises. The *Argus* newspaper assessed the value of her jewels at 100,000 pounds, which may well have been an exaggeration but brought her welcome publicity. It also increased the likelihood of robbery. Patti was guarded by a brace of detectives who masqueraded as members of the chorus when she wore her jewels on stage in operas. Melba did not go that far, but she did hire a pair of constables from a nearby police station to patrol Myoora's walls and grounds.

King Edward VII had taken the unprecedented step of writing to the Australian governor-general—ceremonially the highest official in the land—with a request that Madame Melba have every attention. Henceforth the doors of high society stood wide open to her. That first week she dined with the governor-general and the state governor. She also attended the Princess Theatre to see the Australian star Nellie Stewart perform in *Sweet Nell of Old Drury*; Melba entered her box to such applause that she almost upstaged the other Nellie. In fact her box was like a personal stage, for it was festooned with bizarre emblems proclaiming her Australian birth. Yellow wattle blossoms adorned its walls, among which was placed an Australian magpie, "the most typical of Australian songbirds"; while across its front the Southern Cross was simulated in electric lights. That first week Melba's name was never out of the newspapers. "Melba here, Melba there, Melba everywhere," wrote the social magazine *Table Talk*. "Melbamania has come to Melbourne."

Foremost among the gatherings where Melba felt most at home was the afternoon reception hosted by schoolmates at her old school, the Presbyterian Ladies College. Arriving with her sisters Annie and Belle and Melbourne-born May Donaldson, she entered the school hall beside her elocution teacher, Mr. Lupton, and when the band played "See the Conquering Hero Comes," she blushed and laughed and put her hands over her face. Despite her embarrassment, her delight was obvious. One of the ever-present reporters noted that she exuded an "air of lingering, jolly girlishness." Speaking from the dais, Mr. Lupton read an address in his fine elocutionary style. "When you left us to go to Europe," he told Melba, "our hearts and hopes went with you." The words moved her, and she seemed "quite overcome for a moment." Then she said what was expected, and said it genuinely: "This is the happiest day of my life."

After the speeches came tea and gossip. She mingled happily with her old school friends, remembering most faces and many names. A common exclamation was "You haven't altered a bit!" and amazingly this seemed true of Melba. She seemed "the same, bright Nellie, a little plumper, and generally improved, apparently unspoiled by success." Suddenly a guest inquired if Melba would autograph a school photo. This set in motion a stampede. Cards and photographs were pulled out of handbags and one by one signed. Those who could find no suitable paper turned to the empty sandwich plates and snatched the white labels reading "ham" and "chicken," on which Melba obligingly wrote her name. She "has great charms," declared one admirer; and everyone agreed, though not all approved of her dress and hat, brown in color and matronly in style. Petite May Donaldson, on the other hand, looked straight from Paris, in a hat with a bird perching on the brim.

Melba had blushed when the band played "See the Conquering Hero Comes," but she undoubtedly was a hero to her countrymen and the knowledge was sweet. It buoyed her up through those first days when her thoughts were so often with her stricken father. In England she had pictured him at her first concert, happily imagining his pleasure and pride. Now, though back at Doonside, he was too ill to leave his bed.

No cultural event had been so awaited in Melbourne as that first concert. Additional chairs were packed into the town hall, and tickets changed hands at vastly inflated prices. On the night of the performance Melba's name glowed in colored lights above the stone portal, and more than forty policemen on foot and on horses were needed to control the traffic. Of her supporting artists the public already knew Louis Arens, who had toured the previous year in Musgrove's Opera Company, but Bensaude and Ada Sassoli were unknown in Australia. Fifteen-year-old Ada, from the Italian city of Bologna, was especially welcomed. A reporter said that her lissome fingers plucked the harp strings like cavorting kittens, while another vowed that she looked as "innocent as a fleecy black puppy."

Melba was advertised to sing only in the second half of the program. When she came on stage, the audience jumped to its feet and cheered "frantically." The volume of sound, the affection in which she was visibly held, and the public pride that she belonged to this city hit her like a wave. She later confided that she almost fainted; those near to her could see the tears in her eyes. As the noise subsided, she placed her hand on her heart and launched into Lucia's "mad scene." When she ended there was such shouting and clapping, wrote one reporter, as "Melbourne has never before witnessed." Overcome, she rushed from the stage with her hands pressed to her eyes. When she returned, she motioned for silence and tugged off her long white gloves, breaking the buttons in her agitation. Sitting at the piano, she played and sang "Home Sweet Home." It was a touch for which her audience had been longing, and their excitement knew no bounds.

It was natural that Melba would conclude with "Ah, fors'è lui." She had sung the aria at her first adult concert in the town hall and at her last concert before leaving Australia. To sing it there again fulfilled a long-standing dream. When the song ended, her hearers would not let her go. Standing, applauding, shouting, they demanded an encore and would not leave until she sang. Hurrying backstage, Melba returned with a sheet of music, and while the audience still stood she sang Bemberg's "Chant Venetien." It was not what her fans would have chosen, but it was Melba's choice, and she could do no wrong.

Melba sang four more concerts in her home city, but none could match the ordeal and the excitement of the first. Thereafter, wrote

one critic, she was less Melba the woman and more Melba the artist, switching with ease between Handel and Rossini and Verdi and
Gounod. While most critics went into raptures over the smoothness
and brilliance of her voice, a few were disappointed. In Australia as
in Europe, the fashion for heavy, dramatic singing had lessened the
popularity of the light soprano, and to a few modern ears she sounded
thin and bland.

At the second concert David Mitchell, defying his doctors, sat in
the front row. Years before, when news of her triumphs began reaching Australia, he had called on George Musgrove to ask if the reports
of his daughter's fame could really be true. Now, at last, he was able to
judge for himself. His daughter sang "Comin' thro' the Rye" especially
for him, and smiled and even winked at him from across the high stage.
Those sitting close to the white-haired old gentleman saw that he was
"greatly moved."

In mid-October Melba and Belle and the concert party traveled
to Sydney, where they settled into the Australia Hotel. Within hours
Melba had a sore throat, prompting the cancellation of her first Sydney
concert. It was an unfortunate cancellation, for scores of countrypeople
had come to town to hear her and were now obliged to return home,
dissatisfied.

When she finally did sing, spectators in the town hall stood on their
chairs and shouted and waved their programs. At the end of the "mad
scene" from *Hamlet*, one woman kept shouting "Core, Core"—meaning
encore—in a voice that boomed like that of "a bookmaker." Every Syd-
neysider seemed to want to hear Melba, and her fourth and final concert
drew the largest musical audience seen to that time in the city. About
four thousand sat on seats in the hall, and another five hundred stood in
doorways and aisles. So tight was the crush, and so indignant and excitable were those who were turned away, that an official guarding the door
had his hand smashed in trying to hold back the crowd.

Four days later Melba gave her first concert in the northern city
of Brisbane, where she encountered an audience that seemed to have
little idea of what it was hearing or how it should respond. Her listeners applauded dutifully, as if they were in church but plainly they were
not enjoying themselves. Melba had come across this wall of incom-
prehension in the American West but never before in Australia. Being

a seasoned campaigner, she knew that only perseverance could wear it down.

Present in the hall was a friend from her old town of Mackay, to whom Melba had thoughtfully sent a ticket. He has left an intriguing account of audience's reactions. Even the "mad scene" from *Hamlet* failed in its effect, though, in the words of the man from Mackay, it was "certainly the most dramatic piece of singing," containing "wild shrieks and insane laughter changing to a melodious sort of croon." Rather than excite the listeners, it seemed to unsettle them, and when it concluded their faces were "the picture of misery."

Fortunately Melba had an antidote. It was a ballad called "Three Green Bonnets," recounting in English the death of a child. Its pathos invariably moved its hearers: the man from Mackay thought it "the sweetest of ditties . . . so pretty and so sad." The vast audience suddenly felt at home, and the evening was redeemed.

It was during this concert that a small boy of eight was found under one of the seats. He had crept there early and had fallen asleep: so "I didn't hear Madame Mulbry," he reproachfully told an official. When Melba heard the story she said, " Gracious me! You don't mean to tell me that's true?" Having been assured that it was true, she called for the child's name and address, and at the next concert "a severe-looking parent" and a triumphant small boy sat in the best seats. Again it was her own lost boy that she saw in her imagination. Even in Australia, surrounded by her father and sisters and brothers, she was beset by longings for George.

Melba now decided to offer her country a glimpse of herself in opera, announcing that she would present operatic excerpts in costume, similar to those given by her own company in America six years earlier. Reserving three nights at the Princess Theatre in Melbourne and three at the Theatre Royal in Sydney, she engaged Gustave Slapoffski, late of England's Carl Rosa Opera Company, to conduct an orchestra of fifty players. She also persuaded Slapoffski's soprano wife, Lillie, and Lempriere Pringle, an Australian bass who had sung at the Metropolitan, to join Bensaude and Arens in supporting roles.

Reports lamenting Melba's deficiency in acting had traveled to Australia, and the local critics, having seen her, were divided in opinion. Some thought her acting was colorless, others thought that she was an excellent actress who had learned how to act "without apparent effort." They found her charmingly vivacious in the three acts she performed from *La Traviata*, touchingly innocent in the second act of *Rigoletto*, and "almost uncanny" in the "mad scene" from *Lucia*. But it was as Marguerite in *Faust* that she most pleased. As she entered the garden scene she removed her cape, folded it carefully and placed it on the bench beside her. This seemingly spontaneous gesture charmed those critics who believed that she acted well. She lacks abandon, responded their opponents. "Bunkum," retorted loyal *Melbourne Punch*: "Europe and America have proclaimed her the greatest singer of the day. Which sounds right to us. We ought to be glad to claim Melba as one of ourselves."

The magazine certainly claimed Melba for its own. Accounts of her doings filled long columns of its weekly pages and its social editor attended most of her parties. At one party Melba turned the garden at Myoora into a fairground, with a brass band, a fortune-teller, and games where the prizes were solid gold trinkets. At another party she turned the music room at Myoora into an art gallery, the better to sell poor Hugh Ramsay's paintings, for the young artist, fatally ill, had returned home to die. Guests overflowed the music room, but the social editor was forced to admit that they looked less at Ramsay's canvases than at Melba's collection of gold-framed photographs. Madame Marchesi had pride of place on top of the piano, next to Joachim, not far from Gounod, Verdi, and Tosti. On the mantelpiece, the German kaiser looked out from a frame surmounted by a coronet, as did the king and queen of England and a selection of lesser royals.

The omnipresent social editor also described Melba's visit to her father's new winery in the Yarra Valley, where Melba spoke French and Italian to her father's winemakers. Later her brother Charlie, who lived at nearby Cave Hill, joined them in a pony cart, and Melba seized the reins and raced along the carriage drive. "Gairlie, ye ha' no' improved," cried David Mitchell, "ye're still the larrikin." To which Melba replied in what was described as "a laughable caricature" of her father's Scots accent, "N' na'; larrikiness, ye mean, dad."

Next day the journalist was on duty again as Melba visited the small town of Lillydale, where she was received with civic pomp before traveling in a triumphal convoy to her father's limestone quarries at

Cave Hill. Here his employees entertained her and her followers with a tea party on the top of the hill while the lime kilns belched smoke on the slope below.

At many of these events, Melba was accompanied by Lord Richard Plantagenet Nevill, son of the Marquess of Abergavenny and private secretary to the governor-general. Tall and handsome, with bright blue eyes, a bushy black mustache, and an engaging way of saying funny things in a serious way, he and Melba knew each other from London and made no attempt to hide their mutual liking. Tongues soon began to wag, and there was even speculation that they might marry. Maybe they were lovers, as some commentators hinted, though the openness of the association tends to suggest otherwise.

Lady Tennyson, the prim and proper wife of the governor-general, was one who took exception to their relationship. Melba had Lord Richard "under her thumb," she wrote acidly, and had turned him into one of her "many mad adorers." She had to admit, however, that his lordship was a man of the world and knew "how far to go and no further," and she hoped he would soon put the diva in her place. She thoroughly disapproved of Melba, whom she labeled "not good form"—in other words, vulgar.

Melbamania had now reigned along Australia's eastern seaboard for three months, in some forms so extreme that it did little service to Melba. "It isn't particularly edifying to see one's fellow creatures make fawning fools of themselves," wrote one witness to a particularly fulsome speech made in Melba's honor. Melba herself took little pleasure in the fulsomeness: during one exaggerated speech she found herself giggling "like a schoolgirl" with amusement and embarrassment. She was experienced enough to know that excessive flattery was bound to provoke a reaction. By the end of 1902 there were signs that the reaction was coming.

Her detractors began to speak out. They complained largely about the cost of her tickets, which by Australian standards was unusually high. A seat for her opera performances cost between one and three guineas, at a time when one guinea equaled three days' wages for an unskilled man. Not since the gold rush of fifty years before had prices been so high. Moreover this was a time when the worst drought in the history of white settlement in Australia was parching the island continent. Australia's prosperity rode, as it was said, "on the sheep's back," but nearly half the flocks had succumbed to the drought. To sell expensive tickets when money was so scarce was impractical; worse, it appeared greedy and uncaring. Melba ought to have listened to J. C. Williamson when he told her a year earlier that the market could not sustain such prices.

Melba was well aware of the rural distress. On her way down from Brisbane she had been saddened by "the skeletons of cattle and sheep dotting the paddocks, and the signs of desolation and starvation everywhere." Rather than drop her prices, however, she proposed setting up a "Melba fund" for drought relief, to be financed by donations from her overseas millionaire friends. She herself was ready to launch the fund with a check for two hundred pounds. To her chagrin the offer was refused, first by the Melbourne chamber of commerce, then by the Australian government. Both bodies agreed that it would harm the country's overseas reputation, making Australia seem like a poor nation, unable to help itself.

In Melba's private life too, clouds were gathering. It began with the death from peritonitis of her personal maid who, after serving Melba for twelve years, had become her friend and confidante. It seemed impossible to find a suitable maid to replace her because Australian girls were wary of submitting to Melba's demands, to say nothing of taking responsibility for her jewel boxes. To increase her discontent, Melba was losing May Donaldson, who was joining her sister in Delhi for the military review known as the Durbar. She was also losing Arens and Bensaude, who were returning to engagements in Europe, and her flautist Frederic Griffith, who was lying ill in Dr. Hooper's hospital in Melbourne. To add to her gloom, in far-off New York, Haddon Chambers had been accidentally cut in the face while fencing with a saber and was lucky not to have lost his eye. The edifice of support that she so relied on suddenly seemed to be toppling down.

A prima donna of less courage might have given up her tour. Instead she arranged concerts in other states and in major Victorian country towns. She also contracted to tour the neighboring country of New Zealand. To fill the gaps left by Arens and Bessaude, she hired a student contralto named Elva Rogers and a fashionable young Melbourne tenor, Walter Kirby, who had once been a student of Cecchi.

In January 1903 Melba and the Pattersons and her new concert party sailed in the mail steamer *Ormuz* to Perth on Australia's west coast. Bad luck continued to pursue her, for they arrived in the middle of a heat wave where temperatures exceeded one hundred degrees for four successive days, turning the halls in which she sang into hotboxes. A month later she and Tom Patterson and the concert party took ship again. This time they sailed for New Zealand, with a one-night engagement on the way in the small city of Launceston on Tasmania's north coast, where a wealthy promoter had deposited one thousand guineas in a local bank to guarantee Melba's earnings. They set out for Tasmania in a little iron bucket of a ship called the *Coogee* and began to cross Bass Strait, which can even nauseate passengers on huge ocean liners. Within a few hours Melba's throat was bleeding from vomiting.

In Launceston preparations for her coming were gaining speed. Special excursion trains were about to leave from the capital city of Hobart, bringing the governor of Tasmania and other dignitaries to her concert. Down at the main Launceston wharf reporters were ready with their pencils and notebooks. "And did the Queen of Song have a pleasant trip across the Strait?" inquired one reporter as Melba came shakily ashore. "Horrible," replied Melba in a husky voice. Barely able to endure the mayoral welcome, and just able to smile when a bouquet was presented to her by Ada Crossley's infant niece, she hurried away to her hotel. She was still in bed at eight that evening while a band played a welcome beneath her hotel window and a crowd gathered to greet her. When Melba sent word that she was too ill to speak to them, some of the crowd marched off in disgust.

That night, with fears of a nodule not far from her mind, she called for a doctor to examine her throat. Since there had been bleeding from her right vocal cord, the doctor instructed her to rest her voice. Next morning, still hoarse, she summoned him again. Deciding it would be dangerous for her to sing, he wrote out a bulletin: "Madame Melba is suffering from strain as a result of sea-sickness, and will be unable to sing tonight." The concert arrangements were hastily undone and a message was telegraphed to railway stations across the state to forestall those now on their way to Launceston or about to depart. As news of the cancellation spread through the city, the mood became excitable and indignant.

Since Melba's timetable in New Zealand would admit no delay, she could not possibly wait in Launceston for her throat to recover. The best recompense she could make was to promise to sing on her way back from New Zealand. Her promise was met with scorn. "She had her chance of singing to us," reported one paper angrily, "and she threw it away, and with it the largest concert fee for one concert that has ever come her way." They emphatically "had no desire to see Melba in Launceston again."

Melba boarded the train from Launceston next morning in sickness and distress, but there was no opportunity to hide her feelings or rest her throat. At almost every station along the hundred miles to Hobart, she glimpsed the same waiting crowds and mayoral deputations. There was even a painful stop at the halfway station in the tiny rural town of Parattah, where the governor of Tasmania and his wife had been halted while on their way to her abandoned concert. Welcoming Melba at the station, they escorted her to tea; but sandwiches and conversation were the last things she wanted. She was profoundly relieved to reach Hobart.

Next morning, Friday, February 13, she and all but one of her concert party boarded the SS *Moeraki* for the South Island of New Zealand. The exception was her tenor, Walter Kirby, who missed the boat and thereby missed the first concert in Dunedin. When he finally appeared for her next concert, he received such a scorching from Melba's tongue that he never forgave her. As she watched the rotund, pop-eyed tenor walk onstage, she is said to have remarked beneath her breath: "Lovely voice! Pity he's such a fool. He looks like a pregnant frog!"

In all her New Zealand concerts Melba sang the same vocal items: the two "mad scenes" from *Hamlet* and *Lucia*, encores of "Three Green Bonnets" and "Comin' Thro' the Rye," and a final encore of Tosti's "Goodbye." When, on the evening of February 20, she sang this program in the city of Christchurch, critics from two rival newspapers were present in the hall. One came from the *Christchurch Press*, the other from the neighboring *Lyttleton Times*. Next day these newspapers contained opposing reviews; the *Press* gave her columns of praise, the *Times* insisted that her voice was cold and her tickets were overpriced.

It is often said that, on reading the negative review, Melba was driven to a fury. She is supposed to have shouted that the reviewer deserved to be horsewhipped, then stormed to the newspaper offices to give the editor a verbal lashing. It should be explained that Melba was staying at Warner's Hotel in the central square, in which a knot of reporters stood all day, recording her every movement. It should also be explained that the return train journey from Christchurch to Port Lyttleton, where the offending paper had its office, would have taken well over an hour. So long an absence could not have escaped detection.

No journey by Melba or absence from Christchurch was mentioned in any paper in Christchurch or Port Lyttleton either that day or succeeding days. In the evening she certainly boarded the train for Port Lyttleton, where she was to catch her steamship to Wellington, but she allowed no time to visit the newspaper offices. She went straight from the train to the SS *Rotomahama*. Like so many anecdotes about Melba, the incident does not survive close scrutiny, and is largely a figment of a storyteller's imagination.

In the capital city of Wellington Melba was billed as the "World's Greatest Singer," and not one critic took exception. The prime minister came to her concert in the opera house and the box office sales set a record. The towns of Wanganui and New Plymouth were equally enthusiastic. In Wanganui the police were forced to turn firehoses on feverish fans to prevent them from storming the stage door. In distant Auckland men doffed their caps as her carriage passed while women clapped their hands and cheered. Nor were white New Zealanders the only ones to pay her homage: Maori chiefs presented her with gifts and young Maori men performed their "weird, impressive measure known as the *haka*."

It was as well that she was feted in New Zealand, because when she returned to Sydney in mid-March she found a different atmosphere. By yet another stroke of bad luck, the Sydney journalist John Norton, who had already denounced her ingratitude to Cecchi, had been in Tasmania at the time of her canceled concert, traveling to Launceston in the hope of hearing her. He refused to believe the excuse about her bleeding throat. In his sensationalist paper *Truth* on February 28 he informed his readers that Melba had abandoned the concert out of sheer bad temper. She was "just a plain, cross woman with—throat or no throat—the popular disease of megalomania in an acute form." Melba was indignant, but knowing how resentful many in Launceston were, she was half expecting some form of attack.

Meanwhile she prepared for her farewell concert in the Sydney Town Hall. She and Musgrove had decided to drop the price of tickets to five shillings, and to donate the proceeds to the Sydney lord mayor's fund for drought relief, which gladly accepted this offer. The concert, held six months to the day after her arrival in Australia, netted seven hundred pounds for its cause. Back in Melbourne she engaged in more good deeds, presiding over the vegetable stall at a charity fete for the blind. Dressed in Irish lace and a floral hat, she stood with a vegetable marrow draped over her shoulders and disposed of bundles of carrots and parsnips at what a cheeky reporter described as "high concert prices."

On March 28 a new edition of *Truth* appeared on newsstands, and it made Norton's previous outburst seem like a harmless pinprick. As usual Norton crafted a provocative headline. "Open Letter," he wrote, "to Madame Melba concerning her Champagne Capers, Breach of Public Faith, Outrages against Good Manners, and Insults to Australian Citizens." Norton publicly called Melba a drunkard who canceled concerts, abused hotel owners, tyrannized servants, bullied colleagues, and overcharged audiences: "You are a constant infliction to maddened managers, a harrowing handful to harassed hotel keepers, a terrorism termagant to trembling time servers." He then proceeded to rake over her divorce, her "intrigue with the French royal rotter, the Duke of Orléans" and other unspecified lovers, and by implication her relationship with Lord Richard Nevill. His ramblings took up almost an entire page. At the end he challenged Melba to a lawsuit. "Your scandalous breaches of public faith and private propriety are no longer to be borne without protest," he told her. "I invite you to vindicate yourself by civil or criminal process."

Like many alcoholics, Norton found solace in blaming others. A binge drinker, he was only a couple of weeks away from being admitted to Dr. O'Hara's hospital for inebriates in Melbourne for one of his periodic detoxifications. Nor was Melba the only famous person he savaged. A hater of authority figures, Norton had already tackled and dragged to the ground Queen Victoria, King Edward VII, several archbishops, the Australian governor-general, and the Australian prime minister.

Norton had a noisy following who accepted his pose as a champion of propriety. His hatred of authority found special favor with those extremists who enjoyed cutting down the "tall poppy." So when he set out to accuse Melba of intemperance, many believed he was revealing the truth. As several of the specific criticisms in his long manifesto were true and a matter of public record, he naturally gained credence for his other accusations.

Booked to sail away on the mail steamer *Orontes* on April 14, Melba spent her final days at Government House in Melbourne. She and Violet Clarke, the governor's daughter, had become close friends, and she was taking the young girl back to Europe to enroll her in the École Marchesi. And when would she return to Australia? asked the reporters at her last press interview. Although she did not mention Norton by name, his venom obviously provoked her reply. She announced that it was improbable she would ever come back to her native land.

The day before sailing Melba had a harrowing farewell with her father at Doonside, and that night she slept at the Menzies Hotel. The following morning the governor conveyed Melba and his daughter to the ship in his carriage. At the pier they joined Ada Sassoli and her mother, who were also sailing to Europe, and Melba's sisters and brothers who had come to bid her farewell. The assembled group then boarded the *Orontes* where Melba held an informal reception on deck for her family and the many friends who had come to say goodbye.

She appeared, wrote one observer, to be "quite broken down under the ordeal of leave taking." Once the last visitors had gone ashore, she stood dejectedly by the rail, looking down into the crowd. As the ship's mooring ropes were loosening, a voice on the pier led the crowd in three cheers. Melba, rousing herself at the applause, gave her formal bows of acknowledgment. She then dropped her head to her arms on the steamer rail and hid her face from view. The *Orontes* was carrying away the Queen of Song, in her own words, "never to return."

CHAPTER SEVENTEEN

Patience, Dear Madame, Patience

"I HAVE HAD TO FACE hostility, to hear lies and not answer them, to be the victim of scandals which tortured me, more because they were so utterly undeserved, and force a smile when it was a woman's privilege to weep." Thus wrote Melba in old age, and she must surely have been remembering her departure from Melbourne in the *Orontes*. In front of her fellow passengers she put on a brave face, but in the privacy of her cabin she shed tears of pain and wondered how anyone could hate her as implacably as Norton. It would be fruitless to sue him because the publicity of a trial was what he craved. There he could play the part of a fearless crusader and win more publicity for his newspaper. while she might suffer a humiliating cross-examination. Heaven knew what embarrassing facts about her past might be elicited. She welcomed the sight of England, and tried to slip back into her secure and satisfying way of life.

Although Melba tried to slip back, she did not entirely succeed. In the first weeks there were signs that she felt insecure, and there came two episodes which have darkened her reputation down the years. Both happened at Covent Garden, both are said to have been motivated by her jealousy of younger singers, and since they are often quoted against her, both are worth examining closely.

The first episode took place on June 12, 1903, when she was preparing to sing *Rigoletto* with a newcomer named Titta Ruffo. In that opera Melba had become accustomed to singing with the experienced

229

baritone Antonio Scotti, and one imagines that in her present mood she did not relish having to exchange him for an excitable twenty-six-year-old with a big voice, an undisciplined technique, and too much self-confidence. At the orchestral rehearsal she remained in a box, refusing to come on stage, presumably the better to observe Ruffo. He sang the third act in full voice, not a usual procedure, but one supposes he hoped to impress the orchestra. He certainly succeeded: the orchestra applauded vigorously. Melba, who had the right to choose her singing partners, visited Scotti when the rehearsal was over and persuaded him to resume his role.

Next day it fell to the theatre's manager, Neil Forsyth, to tell Ruffo that he had been deposed. According to Ruffo's autobiography, which is the origin of the anecdote, Forsyth told him by way of explanation that Melba considered he was "still too young to carry a part like that." One imagines she meant that he was still too immature as a performer to succeed in the role of Rigoletto. However, in the version of the episode usually recounted today, Melba is credited with saying, "I'm not singing with him, he's too young to play my father." This paraphrase sounds more like a jealous comment on his youthful looks than a judgment on his vocal and theatrical immaturity.

Ruffo claimed in his autobiography that he left London the next day, convinced that Melba had deposed him out of jealousy and that there was no future for him in the Covent Garden company. In fact he did not leave the company. As the reviews of the time testify, he sang the lead in The Barber of Seville three weeks later. This makes one wonder what else he failed to remember. Undoubtedly he was upset and resentful, but the exact cause of his resentment is not clear.

The second episode—especially damaging to Melba's long-term reputation—took place four days later, during a performance of La Bohème. Melba was in the wings, watching the ebullient Viennese soprano Fritzi Scheff prepare to take a high B in the last notes of Musetta's waltz. When Fritzi sang her high B, Melba sang it with her and continued to sing with her to the end of phrase. What was going through Melba's head no one knows, but certainly her conduct was unprofessional, even outrageous. Some say she feared the young singer might not reach the high note and was trying to help her. Others say she was consumed by jealousy because Fritzi's Musetta had been praised and she was trying to upstage her. In any event, Fritzi was beside herself with shock and anger.

During the intermission an announcement was made that Miss Scheff was ill, and the last act of the opera would not take place; instead Melba would sing the "mad scene" from *Lucia*, a frequent afterpiece to the opera although on that night it had not been advertised as such. Bemberg, sitting in a box with Percy Colson, assumed that there had been trouble and hurried backstage to investigate. He returned with the news that "Fritzi Scheff had tried to scratch Melba's face and then had hysterics."

Did Melba act simply out of jealousy with Ruffo and Scheff, as some commentators claim? Certainly she liked the lion's share of applause and certainly she was hostile to any singer who seriously threatened her supremacy in the company. But neither Fritzi Scheff nor Titta Ruffo posed a real threat. Fritzi was giving up grand opera and had just signed a contract to sing operetta on Broadway. Ruffo was a beginner whose reviews were encouraging but far from superlative; in any case, he was not a rival soprano.

Melba's attitude to her fellow performers was usually more like that of a tough businesswoman than an overemotional diva. She herself was fond of saying that the "temperamental artist is dead today" and that the best singers exhibited "qualities which would have made them equally successful as managers of big businesses, or generals of great campaigns." While it was true that she spoke her mind and never hesitated to reprove anyone she thought out of line, her common sense told her it was wise to stay on as harmonious terms as possible with those around her. As Colson observed, she was unusual in operatic circles in that she "very seldom indulged in moods and never sulked." If Melba was venting jealousy against singers as unthreatening as Scheff and Ruffo, she was showing an uncharacteristic lapse in judgment.

"I am perfectly aware," Melba wrote near the end of her life, "that ever since I have been Melba, rumours have flown all over the world that I, like so many other artists, have been cruel, jealous, violently antagonistic to anybody who might endeavour to supplant me in the popular affection. I have been referred to in public and in private as 'the hidden hand.'" To this Henry Higgins, chairman of the Covent Garden Syndicate, replied: "You know as well as I that inefficient artists are always ready to put forward every sort of excuse for their failure, and never attribute it to the obvious cause, their own incompetence, and I think that accounts for the rumours you referred to." The incidents with Ruffo and Scheff may well have fallen into this category. They may also have arisen, to some extent, from Melba's temporary sense of insecurity.

That season Melba sang a dozen times at Covent Garden, including a gala performance for the French president on July 7. At the end of September she made her annual migration to New York in some of the wildest weather she had ever known. Recounting the voyage with gusto to her sister Belle, she wrote that there was a "hurricane the whole way, and the consequence was an old lady died from exhaustion after seasickness, another woman committed suicide, and a man was dying when we left the ship." To make matters worse, Haddon Chambers's latest play, *Golden Silence*, had failed on Broadway. Even the stock market was falling. "God knows," she wrote dramatically, "when it will end."

To restore her health and spirits, she spent a few days at a cheery house party on Long Island. Meanwhile Charles Ellis minded her traveling concert party, which consisted of Ada Sassoli, Llewella Davies, a tenor named Ellison van Hoose, and a French baritone called Charles Gillibert who had recently sung with her in London. In the ensuing tour she sang thirty-two times across the United States and Canada. "I am returning again next year," she told Belle by letter, "more hard work—but I like it." She reminded Belle that, like their father, she had to be busy in order to be happy—but Belle hardly needed reminding.

In New York in December, Melba sang twice at Carnegie Hall. After the first concert she received excellent reviews; after the second, the critic from the *New York Times* wrote of "a certain carelessness" in her performance. This fall from musical grace was another sign of the malaise she had been suffering for months, but its mainspring now lay less in Norton's attacks than in her anxiety about George. In October he had turned twenty. Soon he would be legally his own master. She resolved to write him a letter. Anxiously she waited for his reply. The weeks passed, she received no response, and the silence lay heavily on her heart.

In London early in the new year of 1904 Melba quickly prepared for a season in Monte Carlo, where she was to star in a new opera written especially for her by Camille Saint-Saëns. Called *Hélène* and based on the life of Helen of Troy, it pleased her enormously, as did the thought of returning to her beloved Riviera. In Monte Carlo she stayed with the Countess of Wilton, and it was to her villa, Le Nid, that Saint-Saëns came to call. The death of his sons and the failure of his marriage had turned the sixty-eight-year-old composer into almost a recluse, but in Melba's company he lit up like a firework. Although he hated socializing, he happily escorted her about Monaco, and though normally he scarcely spoke, he unleashed in her presence such "a volley of observations on music, opera, and life in general" that those who knew him were astonished. Melba called him "one of the most amazingly youthful old men I have ever met" and she met his ardor with a touching tenderness.

Under Saint-Saëns's instruction, Melba's understanding of the role of Hélène grew apace. After the last rehearsal the old composer exclaimed in French: "She doesn't just play the part. No! She is the living Hélène of my dreams." The opening night on February 18, 1904, was a charity gala, with a crowd as brilliant as any Monte Carlo had seen. The *Journal de Monaco* predicted the opera would be the success of the season, but it received only two performances.

Ten years before this Monte Carlo season, Émile Berliner in the United States had invented a new way of recording sound on a metal master disk, that could then be molded onto a thermoplastic material. Inventing a gramophone to play these disks, Berliner became the originator of the modern record industry. He and his associates formed several companies, among them the Victor Talking Machine Company of America and the Gramophone Company of England. In 1899 Barry Owen, the head of the English company, had the forethought to buy a painting of a dog listening to his master's voice emerging from a gramophone. Eventually this picture would become the trademark of both companies.

At first the Gramophone Company recorded only lesser-known artists requiring a small fee, but by 1902 the gramophone was becoming a significant source of home entertainment, and bigger names were being sought. One of the first to record was the tenor Enrico Caruso, and the success of his records assisted his swift rise to international fame. Landon Ronald was employed to recruit other names, and it was possibly he who suggested Melba. In the end, however, it was handsome Sydney Dixon, a younger member of the company, who was sent to Monte Carlo to gain her agreement. Dixon was skilled in handling difficult prima donnas. When Emma Calvé refused to enter the company's recording studio, declaring that it looked like a den of thieves, it was Dixon who coaxed her through the door.

Sydney Dixon's overtures to Melba fell on fertile ground, because she was already alert to the benefits of recording. Rumor has it that she made a private record of her voice for her father before she visited Australia, and the previous year she had sent her sister Belle a gramophone. Now, in Monte Carlo, she accepted Dixon's offer, not simply to sing for her father—though that was what she later claimed—but because like her father she was eager to embrace new technologies and alert to their commercial potential.

Back in London in March, Dixon arranged for Melba to record her voice, not in the shabby studio, but in her own immaculate home. Cumbersome machines were hauled into her music room at Cumberland Place, and there, standing nervously in front of the recording trumpet, she recorded many of the arias and songs she sang at concerts. Unlike the aging Patti—who on hearing her own voice excitedly exclaimed, "Now I know why I am Patti"—Melba loathed the "scratching, screeching result." She is said to have ordered Dixon to destroy the records. If she did, her wishes were not fully carried out. Eighteen records still exist and were recently transferred to compact disk. The quality of sound is primitive, but the sense of immediacy is thrilling. One can even hear the engineer shout, "Go!" before the music begins; and when Melba's speaking voice calls out, "Now we'll have to do it over again," following a mistake in Handel's "Sweet Bird," one is almost in the music room with her.

The piano accompanist during those sessions was Landon Ronald, and according to his testimony, Melba at first permitted only close friends to hear the result. She needed to be assured of their enthusiastic response before she allowed fourteen records to go on general sale, probably before the end of June. Some were shipped to Australia to be played to crowded audiences at the Melbourne Town Hall. At twenty-one shillings the twelve-inch records, playing for four and a quarter minutes, were highly priced: she is said to have chosen that sum because Caruso's records sold for twenty shillings, and she wanted to go one better. Despite the high price, the first edition sold out in a day and was quickly replaced by another. If advertisements can be believed, by early 1905 her recorded voice was reaching one million people, though it must be said that only a fraction of those listeners had actually purchased a record.

Melba's contemporaries were captivated by her recorded voice. Those whose ears are attuned to the vastly superior recording techniques of the early twenty-first century find it sadly disappointing. Even in the latest remastered versions of those early records, there are screeches and scratches and distortions. It is not possible to hear Melba with any degree of accuracy until she was recorded by the electrical process of the 1920s—and by then she was well past her prime. Nevertheless some of the qualities that made her great can be heard in the early records. The ease Melba brought to her singing is there, especially in the fearsomely difficult trills and runs. So is her evenness of scale and so is her purity of tone. W. J. Henderson wrote that her "tones had a starlike brilliance" and "flamed with a white flame." The flashes of flame are intermittent, but with careful listening they can be heard.

Among the friends who loved to hear Melba sing on the exciting new gramophone was Queen Alexandra. On Sunday, June 6, 1904, Lord and Lady de Grey gave a large dinner party for the king and queen at their house on Kingston Hill. For entertainment they borrowed Melba's records and invited Landon Ronald to play, because it had been discovered that a live accompaniment on the piano drowned out the worst of the scratching.

After dinner Landon started the record of "Caro nome" and then raced to the piano to do his part. "The effect," he would remember, "was electrical," and those present almost believed that it was Melba singing in the room. There was a slight hitch when Queen Alexandra insisted that the needle should not be changed with each record, resulting in the most acute scratching. Tactful Landon managed to change the needle while the royal back was turned, and pretended that it was the queen's injunction to "screw the machine up" that caused the improvement.

Three days later Melba sang at Buckingham Palace to entertain the king's guest, Archduke Frederic of Austria. After the concert Queen

Alexandra pinned on Melba's breast the Order of Science, Art and Music, Melba being, to that time, the order's only female recipient. Soon after Melba gave a dinner at Cumberland Place for Puccini, who was visiting London, and another for Saint-Saëns, who had been inundating her with letters. "Are you still speaking to me, adorable Hélène?" he had written beseechingly. "You who have given me such profound and lofty pleasure, I owe you everything and more. You have in my eyes all the talent, and beauty, and goodness there is."

Melba persuaded Covent Garden to perform *Hélène*, and Saint-Saëns was eager to oversee the rehearsals. But no amount of supervising could save the opera. The critics gave it tepid notices when it went to stage on June 20 and it was performed only once more. Melba herself received tepid notices, for the declamatory music did not suit her voice. Her other roles, however, were praised to the skies. Her Juliette was "more wonderful than ever," gushed the *Times*, and her Mimi was so perfect that "she had a new triumph in the part."

When the season ended late in July, Melba traveled with a party of friends to Henry Russell's villa at Stresa on Italy's Lake Maggiore. Three of her companions were attractive young men: Bernard Rolt, a composer of drawing-room ballads; Robin Grey, the editor of the *Musical News*; and Theodore Byard, a tenor who often sang with Melba at parties. Along with the men came Robin's sister Dolly and Melba's confidante Lady Stracey, and from Venice arrived a gondola that Theo had somehow obtained for excursions across the lake.

In the mornings Melba would practice in the garden of Russell's villa, which stretched down to the water's edge. She took care to restrain her volume, because early in the visit she had been confronted by a neighbor's nursemaid who accused her of waking the baby. One warm night, "when the sky was lit by the August moon and the mountains stood like black ramparts," Melba ignored the nursemaid and sang in the garden, and her voice floated across the waters to the town of Pallanza, some three miles away. Crowds are said to have gathered, "enchanted by the notes so distant and yet so clear."

When the visit ended, Melba, Lady Stracey, and Bernard Rolt continued by train to meet Haddon Chambers in Venice. There Melba was also to meet Puccini in order to study his latest operas with him. She was hoping to sing the role of Tosca at Covent Garden the following season, and possibly that of his newest heroine, Butterfly. Melba claimed to be a godmother of his opera *Madama Butterfly*, believing Puccini had written the role for her after she urged him to see the play upon which the opera was based.

Melba had high hopes of gaining from her lessons with the composer, but they proved turbulent. Lady Stracey, entering the music room, was obliged to duck as a musical score came hurtling through the air. "Damn the thing! I shall never learn it," Melba is said to have shouted. Puccini, still frail from a motoring accident, sat quietly at the keyboard and exclaimed in Italian, "Patience, dear Madame, patience!" Melba had reason to be exasperated, for neither Tosca nor Butterfly suited her voice.

Her mood was still unsettled when she reached Paris. There she was joined by her New Zealand cousins, the Misses Walker, whom she had met while singing in Auckland. She seems to have taken little pleasure in their visit, and even less when, during an afternoon drive, an old man moved into the path of her automobile. The man was killed instantly. The shock was too much for Melba. When she returned to her hotel she retired to her bed and refused to leave it. There she stayed for more than a month in a state of nervous prostration. The accumulated stress of the last few years had finally caught up with her.

The death of the eighty-four-year-old man was no doubt the immediate cause of her collapse, but another cause was George. His twenty-first birthday was fast approaching, after which he would be free from his father's guardianship. Should she write to him again? She must have wondered if she dared, for having received no reply to her previous letter, she feared that Charlie might have turned her boy against her. On the other hand, she was about to leave on her annual tour of America, and it would be foolish not to try to meet him while they were both on the same continent. Fortunately she had an ally in his godmother, Winifred Rawson, who sent George a tactful letter of her own. Then, just to be sure, Melba gathered up her courage and wrote to George herself.

Although George was much on her mind, Melba was obliged to pull herself together and attend a further recording session on October 20, this time at the studio of the Gramophone Company in London's City Road. Bemberg came from Paris to play the accompaniments to three of his own songs, Landon Ronald accompanied four other songs, and Jan Kubelik, the young Czech violinist then galvanizing London, played the violin *obbligato* while Melba sang Gounod's "Ave Maria." An observer named Harold Begbie watched as the artists were guided to their positions around the recording trumpet, which projected from a partition wall of frosted glass. Melba was asked to stand a few inches from the trumpet's mouth, Kubelik, "slight and dusky," was placed beside her, and Landon Ronald was requested to climb up to the piano, which stood about three feet off the floor on a rough wooden stand to the side.

Begbie recalled that Melba poured out her voice "with a passion and a glory, a devotion and an ecstasy, as though she could see posterity glimmering at the end of the trumpet." Afterward at lunch in the office below he asked her how she felt when she stood in readiness before the trumpet. Expecting a serious and even a musicianly answer, he was enchanted when she confessed that she sometimes fancied she "could see a great eye at the narrowing bottom of it, winking at her, as though it would make her laugh!"

When Melba had the large trumpet to herself, she regarded it as her friend, but when she and several singers were jostling for places in front of its open mouth, the trumpet became her enemy. In September of the following year Melba was to record again, this time with a backing of three voices, one of which belonged to the Australian baritone Peter Dawson. At one stage Melba lost her temper. "Stop pushing!" she shouted at Dawson. "You're just one of the bloody chorus!" Her reprimand passed into musical folklore. In Melba's own words, the art of recording "was no rest cure" but she glimpsed that it was the means to a fame far wider than any of her predecessors could possibly have imagined.

Late in October Melba sailed across the Atlantic. In New York she anxiously and eagerly awaited each post, hoping against hope for George's reply. She usually received a huge volume of mail, mostly begging letters which she dealt with briskly, but now she scanned each envelope, hoping to recognize the writing and almost afraid to open it.

Then, miracle of miracles, a letter came from Oregon. "My darling mother," it began, "I received your dear letter today, so overjoyed to hear from you that tears came into my eyes. . . . I have thought of you every day of my life since I left you, and why I have not written is more than I can tell." Now that George was twenty-one and no longer his father's ward, he proposed spending half of each year with her. "To think," he wrote, "that we have not seen one another for eleven long years, but that shall never be again." He added a simple postscript. He was "so overtaken with joy" that he could scarcely hold his pen.

Four days later, on November 10, 1904, George wrote again. By then Charlie had returned to their home in Oregon, and George reported that his father was "delighted to have me come and see you." With a generosity that far exceeded Melba's expectations, Charlie even promised to drive the boy the seventy miles to the railroad so that he could board the train to New York. "Try and be happy till I come," George begged of his mother, for he guessed that she was having difficulty in keeping hold of herself.

George was reunited with Melba at the Manhattan Hotel in New York. His physical appearance must have been a shock, for the chubby child she remembered had grown into a thin and slightly stooped, weather-beaten young man almost six feet tall. To her relief he had kept his English accent and English ways, and she realized with a thankful heart that he was the same loving boy she had always known. Charlie, whatever his faults, had not tried to turn her son against her. Having been brought up among cowboys, George was unused to formal society and was at first somewhat shy even in her presence. But Melba did not care. Like her son, she was "overtaken with joy."

The change in Melba's life was momentous. For the first time in eleven years she could wake in the morning without a sense of loss, confident that within the hour George would be by her side, ready to talk to her, laugh with her, embrace her. She began to make thrilling plans for his future. She would take him to London and introduce him to high society, bestowing on him all the advantages she had striven so long to attain.

While she floated on her cloud of joy, arctic weather descended on the eastern seaboard, and she began to cough. She was far too euphoric to allow herself to worry about incipient bronchitis, and she insisted on appearing on December 10 before the largest audience ever gathered in Boston's Symphony Hall. When the critics pronounced her in excellent voice, she took even less notice of her wheezing chest. Six days later, after more coughing, she gave the first of four scheduled performances at the Metropolitan Opera.

It was more than three years since had she appeared at the Metropolitan and she was nervous. Grau had resigned, and his place had been
taken by a former Viennese actor named Heinrich Conried, who was
said to know "no more about opera than an ordinary chauffeur knows
about aeroplanes." None of this reassured her. Nervousness, along with
her cough, made the appearance an ordeal.

Fortunately American operagoers still loved her, and when she
came on stage as Mimi they applauded warmly. An announcement was
made that she had been unwell, but except for the fact that she sang
with a measure of restraint, little seemed amiss. Indeed, during the duets with Enrico Caruso, the young tenor she had sung with in Monte
Carlo, her voice was said never to have sounded better.

In the following days her cough grew worse, and she began to ago-
nize over her performances. What if she harmed her voice! What if her
next performance was like Brünnhilde all over again! She was to sing
La Traviata on December 19 and Rigoletto on December 21. She could
face neither of them, and insisted on canceling La Traviata on the day
of the performance. Her second La Bohème was not even advertised.
She withdrew entirely from the Metropolitan season, and her old rival
Marcella Sembrich stepped into her shoes.

Melba's doctor diagnosed pneumonia in her right lung, throwing
her into a panic. Even if a patient recovered from pneumonia—which
in those days was often fatal—that patient was likely to be left with
a weakness in the lung. How well would she able to sing with a weak
lung? How long could she continue singing? She was only forty-three
years old: if her career ended, what would she do for the rest of her
life—and how could she support George? These terrifying questions
kept revolving in her mind.

Craving female sympathy, she turned to Isabella Gardner, the cultural leader of Boston society and a woman with whom she had much in
common. Both were devoted to music, both savored high society, and
both had probably had a love affair with the novelist Francis Marion
Crawford. Recalling their conversations, Isabella recorded how Melba's
thoughts centered largely on George's future. "She was the sole support
of her 'boy' as she called her son," wrote Isabella. "She wondered what
would become of him."

To spend her first Christmas in twelve years with George could not fail to cheer her. By New Year her lung had improved, her panic had subsided, and, believing it was better to carry on as normally as possible, she began to contemplate continuing her tour. She also agreed to sing with a charming American protégée named Elizabeth Parkinson, whom Madame had rechristened Parkina. Since graduating from the École Marchesi, Parkina had sung with Melba at Covent Garden and was now, thanks to Melba's influence, waiting to leave on a concert tour of Australia.

On January 5, 1905, the two sopranos appeared at the convention hall in Parkina's hometown of Kansas City. Remembering her own return to Melbourne, Melba was determined to make it a memorable night for her young friend. She played Parkina's accompaniment for the first song, and joined her in a duet. "She was kindness itself," Parkina later told Agnes Murphy.

Two days later Melba sang to 3,500 people at the Chicago Auditorium Theatre. Of the eleven vocal items on the program, she managed to sing three. Her loyal concert party of Gillibert, van Hoose, and Sassoli did the rest. Although her voice was said to be "a degree less crystalline" than usual, the critics agreed that she sounded surprisingly well, and Melba thanked heaven for having made so swift a recovery.

In high spirits she now boarded the Melba train for the continuation of the tour, with George sharing her railcar. Although his presence brought her intense pleasure, she was aware that he often felt lonely and out of place. Seeking to help him, she persuaded young Ada Sassoli to befriend him. Out on the ranch he had guarded the sheep and the cows; now he became the guardian of Ada's harp. As their train arrived and departed from stations across America, Signora Sassoli would shout, "Oh! George, Où est l'harpe?"

Melba and George sailed to England in the *Lucania* in May 1905, and throughout the following summer Melba nursed her lung and worried about George's future. On the night of her forty-fourth birthday she held a grand party at Cumberland Place, filling the house with her fashionable friends and engaging fourteen-year-old Mischa Elman, dressed in a sailor suit, to play his violin. On this carefully staged evening, Melba wished to show off her son, so distinguished in his smart tailcoat, but his shyness was a barrier. He felt happier beside the Thames at Marlow, where Melba had rented a house called Blounts for the summer. Observing his uneasiness and loneliness, Melba wrote to Madame, "I have decided not to work so hard for the future and devote it to my beloved George who is an angel."

This did not come to pass. Melba continued to sing her full share of roles at Covent Garden, and concerts and galas and private recitals. Her Mimi, with Caruso as her Rodolfo, was the sensation of the season. The Italian tenor was fast taking the place of Jean de Reszke in her professional life, even though, as critics noted, Melba was never able to "exactly balance the passionate heat" of Caruso's acting. Even so, his magnificent voice matched hers superbly. "In the third act of *La Bohème*," she told a friend, "I always feel as if our two voices had merged into one."

Caruso could never match Jean de Reszke in her affections, because, even at the age of thirty-two, he remained so unmistakably a child of the Neapolitan slums. His simple warmth amused her, but she deplored his table manners, his addiction to strong-smelling Egyptian cigarettes, his garish clothes, and his crude sense of humor. Like everyone in her social set, she enjoyed a practical joke, but his pranks went too far and seemed designed to bait her: which, since he thought she was conceited, was probably true.

In their first season together at Monte Carlo, he had held a squeaking rubber duck to her ear while she sang Mimi's dying phrases. At Covent Garden he pressed a hot sausage into her palm just as he declaimed the line that her tiny hand was frozen. He tried to sabotage her death scene by bribing a stagehand to place a chamber pot in clear public view under Mimi's bed. On other nights he poured water into a fellow performer's upturned hat so that the unhappy man, putting on the hat, was deluged as he left the stage; and he sewed up another performer's coat sleeves so that his stately exit was ruined. His chum, Tosti, who should have known better, actively encouraged him. One night Tosti sat in the very front row, arranging his white handkerchief like a cavalry mustache and grotesquely waggling it whenever he caught Caruso's eye. "You can imagine what I felt," said Melba, "as I tried to render Puccini's dying heroine."

In the autumn Melba was obliged to leave George to his loneliness and give a lengthy concert tour of the northern British cities. Landon Ronald was her accompanist, and he has left a lively, composite picture of their life on tour. Landon called their tours a mixture of huge crowds, "thunderous applause, lots of polite officials, and hotel servants, hundreds of autograph hunters, heaps of motoring and plenty of fun." Melba always left for the concert hall half an hour before she needed to leave, and an expectant crowd was always waiting for her in the street and even in the hotel foyer. "Oh, ain't she beautiful?" an excited voice would exclaim. "Look at her real *diaminds!*" a voice would call from a vantage point on top of a lamppost. At the theatre door there would be another crowd, and in the artists' room letters and autograph books would be piled up—one maybe from a little girl who had given up sweets for a month to be able to buy a ticket for the concert, or another from a little boy just longing to kiss Madame Melba. About this time Melba would start protesting that she was losing her voice. "This may disconcert the uninitiated until the first solo is over," wrote Landon, "but those who are 'in the know' are prepared for the statement and sympathise with a twinkle in their eye."

At intermission Melba's current concert manager, Percy Harrison, would guard the artists' room against all comers. "But I am a friend of Madame Melba," a voice would demand. "And so am I," Harrison would reply, "and that's why I cannot let you pass." Once the concert was over, fans would rush to the stage door, gazing, while they waited, at Melba's Rolls Royce parked nearby, and at her chauffeur who would resolutely refuse to notice them. Cries of "*bravo*" would greet Melba's appearance, policemen on horses would clear the road, and she would be driven back to the hotel for a quiet supper. On the following day the sequence would begin in another town with "similar scenes of enthusiasm, similar crowds." Remembering those happy tours, Landon wrote, "I have never found a more delightful travelling companion or a kinder, merrier chum."

On November 17 Melba and Landon performed at Windsor Castle in front of their Majesties and Queen Alexandra's brother, the king of Greece. Normally two sopranos were not placed on the same program, but this year the king of England had requested Melba, and the king of Greece had requested a young Scottish-American soprano named Mary Garden; both women had been invited. It proved to be an unwise decision. Four years earlier there had been friction at Covent Garden

between Melba and Garden over the choice of roles, and on this evening there was friction again.

Melba was usually adept at tailoring her manners to the diverse
circles in which she moved, but on this occasion her skill deserted her.
At supper, trying to hide her displeasure under a veneer of jocular-
ity, she piped up, "What a dreadful concert this would have been if
I hadn't come." Probably she intended the remark to pass for humor,
but it appalled Lord Farquhar, the master of household, who tried to
compensate by paying generous compliments to Mary Garden. Eager
to put Farquhar at his ease, Mary replied, "I love Melba's rudeness. It
amuses me."

This may have been a tactful lie, but there is evidence that Mary
Garden—perhaps this time and certainly thereafter—did indeed find
Melba genuinely amusing. "She could be quite funny, Melba, and wherever she went she always had people laughing," Mary mused later; and
added, "When you knew her, you couldn't help liking her. When you
didn't know her, you thought her frightfully rude."

When the time came to leave Windsor, the two women found
themselves sharing the same railway carriage. "Before we reached London," wrote Mary, "Melba and I were fast friends." The young soprano
was well aware that they might not have become fast friends if she had
been Melba's competitor and endowed with her type of voice. Nevertheless the friendship was based on mutual liking and respect.

"I have no hesitation," wrote Mary, "in declaring that Melba had
the most phenomenal effect on me of any singer I have ever heard."
She was speaking particularly of Melba's last high C in the first act of
La Bohème:

> The note came floating over the auditorium of Covent Garden: it left
> Melba's throat, it left Melba's body, it left everything, and came over
> like a star and passed us in our box, and went out into the infinite.
> I have never heard anything like it in my life, not from any other
> singer, ever. It just rolled over the hall of Covent Garden, My God,
> how beautiful it was!

"That note of Melba's," concluded Mary Garden, "was just like a ball
of light."

CHAPTER EIGHTEEN

Hammerstein Swallows the Canary

ON THE EVE of April Fools' Day, 1906, Melba was confronted by a stout man of sixty with a cropped grey beard, a tall silk hat, and a cigar in the corner of his mouth. Melba knew him at once, because for weeks she had been bombarded with letters and cables either from him or concerning him. His name was Oscar Hammerstein, and he was recruiting singers for a new opera house he was building in New York. Regarding Melba as the greatest soprano in the world, he believed it was imperative to put her under contract.

Many years later Melba claimed that through the autumn of 1906 Hammerstein visited or telephoned her apartment in Paris every six days for the space of a month. She remembered that he showed a remarkable persistence, even to the extent of badgering her in her bath. Her memory, however, was somewhat faulty. Newspaper reports make clear that the wooing was in April, and that she capitulated with ease.

The German-born Hammerstein was certainly a commanding personality. When only in his teens he had invented a mold for making cigars, and by means of this and other inventions had accumulated enough wealth to indulge his passion for the theatre. For more than thirty years he bought and sold American theatres, and put on plays, opera, operettas, and vaudeville. His determination to break the Metropolitan's monopoly stemmed from a genuine desire to raise operatic standards and a long-standing hatred of Heinrich Conried, two attitudes with which Melba could sympathize.

According to Hammerstein's version, written a few weeks after the event, he called on Melba at her new apartment at 162 Boulevard Malesherbes at six in the evening while she was entertaining guests. She could grant him only the briefest interview, but it was long enough for them to reach an agreement. Melba was in little doubt that she could dictate the terms, and the thought of singing in New York while at the same time bypassing the tyrannical Metropolitan Opera exhilarated her. "I am Melba," she remembered thinking, and now "I shall sing when and where I like, and I shall sing in my own way." That she was to be the heavy artillery in an opera war did not daunt her; rather, it inspired her. "I felt that I was fighting not only for myself," she wrote, "but for the freedom of the artist."

Anticipating Hammerstein's bid, Conried had already offered Melba two thousand dollars a performance to sing at the Metropolitan. Melba believed this was too small a sum, so she demanded three thousand dollars of Hammerstein, a fee higher than had ever been given to a singer for a season's continuous work. "I come high," she warned Hammerstein, and when he heard the figure he thought: "She certainly did." He begged time to think, but he was scarcely out the door when he decided to accept. Back in her drawing room they sat at her desk and dashed off a simple written agreement. Melba also requested twenty thousand dollars as a guarantee, preferably to be paid into her account at the Credit Lyonnaise. Next day, ignoring the Credit Lyonnaise, he made the dramatic gesture of bringing her the sum in notes. Melba claimed that he flung the notes on the floor at her feet. In Hammerstein's version of the episode, she scooped them up from the top of her desk and swept them into a drawer, not bothering to count a single note.

Melba returned to London on April 26. She had already hired a house for the coming summer from her old friend Lord Charles Beresford, and she and George prepared to move in. Called Coombe Cottage, it was actually a red-brick, gabled mansion with a tower, situated on a hill near the town of Kingston-upon-Thames. Its sixty rooms included six modern bathrooms, a billiard room, a smoking room, and a nursery, and its grounds contained extensive stables, a dairy, and six acres of park and gardens. Extended and remodeled in 1863 for the banker Edward Baring by the noted Victorian architect George Devey, it had for a time been the residence of the Empress Eugénie. By chance it was also close to the boyhood home of the novelist John Galsworthy, whose *Forsyte Saga* Melba later came to love. One of her favorite residences, it survives today as a collection of upscale apartments.

Coombe Cottage provided a mixture of country and city, so it pleased both George and Melba. Socially, too, it was desirable, for it stood down the hill from Lady de Grey's imposing Coombe Court, and it was not uncommon for the king and queen to motor over from Windsor to visit the de Greys. Melba also found it surprisingly convenient for the opera, since it was only forty minutes by automobile to Covent Garden.

Throughout that summer Melba worried about her lung, which continued to remain susceptible to infection. No sooner had she moved in than she developed bronchitis and was barely able to give her opening performance of *La Bohème* on May 17. A relapse sent her back to bed, and she was just recovering when she caught another chill. On the afternoon of June 5 she was about to leave for Covent Garden to sing in *Rigoletto* when her chauffeur was unable to start the car. Fortunately a tradesman's van belonging to the mayor of Kingston was making a local delivery and in desperation Melba clambered onto its open seat and ordered the driver to take her to the station. "I can assure you no one could fancy the trouble I had," she told a reporter from the *Surrey Comet*. The breezy ride in the van brought back her cough. To Madame she wrote a week later, "I am getting better slowly but I have been very ill and intend taking great care of myself."

Melba and Madame were corresponding regularly during these weeks, one topic being Irene Ainsley, a contralto whom Melba had auditioned in New Zealand and sent on to the École Marchesi. Melba had arranged for Irene to sing in London's Bechstein Hall—but what was to be her name? In Madame's stable every new filly needed a glamorous but dignified name, and Madame was all for calling her Irene Zealande. Melba was not impressed: "We must drop Zealande, please," she wrote firmly. "Her name is appearing as "Miss Irene Ainsley, New Zealand, which is very pretty and appropriate I think. I hope you will do as I ask about this."

That summer Melba also smiled on another antipodean singer. She was Amy Castles, a soprano from the gold city of Bendigo, who had left Australia in a burst of publicity that made Melba slightly resentful, remembering her own quieter departure twenty years before. Following in Melba's footsteps, she entered the École Marchesi but failed to prosper. On her subsequent tour of Australia in 1902 neither Melba nor the critics were impressed. Melba told Belle, "She can't phrase, she has no musical intelligence, in fact she is a nonentity, and as such will be known in a few years." Melba's freezing opinion reached Amy, and thereafter the unfortunate girl, searching for an excuse, tended to attribute her lack of success to Melba's malign influence.

Amy's skills improved when she began studying under a London teacher, well known to Melba, named Minna Fischer. Melba was sufficiently impressed to offer to help her. On the evening of July 1, 1906, Gladys de Grey was expecting Queen Alexandra at Coombe Court. Melba was also invited to dine and to sing, but another attack of bronchitis made this impossible. Remembering her offer, Melba invited Amy to take her place, engaging Landon Ronald as her accompanist and mentor. Amy triumphed, and Queen Alexandra was especially delighted. A report of the evening, underlining Melba's generosity, eventually surfaced in the pages of *Melbourne Punch* and must have pleased Melba. It was a poke in the eye for John Norton, because one of his taunts was that Melba never lifted a finger to help Australian singers.

At Coombe Cottage George's boredom and loneliness vanished. Melba was able to report that "George is well and happy and so am I. We revel in the garden here and enjoy ourselves to our hearts' content." It was a relief to be able to write that George was happy, for her efforts to find him new interests had had little success. For a time she tried to gain his admission to Oxford University and hired a tutor to prepare him. But thanks to Charlie's wish to give his son an adventurous upbringing, the boy's schooling after the age of nine had been intermittent at best, and it was impossible to prepare him for the entrance exam. George did better when Melba bought him a commission in the Royal Berkshire Militia. Like Charlie, he enjoyed part-time soldiering, and Melba hoped he might enter the regular army.

George's happiness did not spring solely from his time with the militia. He had fallen in love with Ruby Otway, the only child of rich Lieutenant Colonel Jocelyn Otway of Park Lane, who, though he bore no title, was related to half the peerage. Nineteen-year-old Ruby was barely out of the schoolroom and almost as shy as George, but she had sweet ways and was very pretty and very much in love with George. Melba worried about the couple's obvious immaturity, but George was set on marriage. According to the *New York Times*, Melba gave him an annuity of $7,500 and set about buying him a castle in Ireland as a wedding present. The castle did not materialize, so it was probably a figment of the reporter's imagination.

In October and November Melba sang for the second year running with the San Carlo Opera Company of Naples, which was appearing at Covent Garden for the autumn season. The weather was cold and damp and fog blanketed the London streets. Some days the fog was so thick that it drifted indoors, and at one of Melba's performances, the audience could scarcely see the stage. Melba feared for her weak lung. Nevertheless she sang, wrote one critic, "as if for the sheer delight of hearing the beauty of her own exquisite voice."

On November 3 the king and queen, staying at their country retreat at Sandringham, had the thrill of hearing a live broadcast of Melba performing in *Rigoletto* with the San Carlo Company. By means of a new invention, the electrophone, the sound was relayed over telephone wires the hundred or so miles from Covent Garden. Melba eagerly awaited the time when live broadcasts would be part of everyday life.

The opera season was scarcely over when, on December 18, Melba attended George's wedding at the fashionable St. George's Church in Hanover Square. The church was massed with white flowers and potted palms, and Ruby was followed by nine bridesmaids, one of whom was Ada Sassoli. Among the guests were Prince Francis of Teck and the Dukes and Duchesses of Devonshire, Abercorn, and Sutherland, and also Melba's friend Edward Stuart-Wortley, who lent his Highcliffe Castle for the honeymoon. Melba, with a pang of anxiety, watched George and his bride drive away before transferring her anxiety to Hammerstein's opera season.

Reports from America were not reassuring. Hammerstein, who was the sole financier, designer, and organizer of the enterprise, had perhaps overextended himself. The theatre he was building on West Thirty-fourth Street was behind schedule, and he was in dispute with Ricordi and Company, the Italian publishers of *La Bohème*, which he was determined to stage. Months before he had reached a simple verbal agreement with the publishers over the performance rights, but since then they had granted exclusive rights to the Metropolitan Opera for all of Puccini's operas. An injunction seeking to protect the Metropolitan's claims to *La Bohème* was currently being fought by Hammerstein in the courts. In order to assist the Metropolitan, the wily Ricordis were tracing and numbering all scores of the opera to keep them out of Hammerstein's hands. Meanwhile Hammerstein recruited a cast that undoubtedly dismayed the Metropolitan's management. Among the big names were the conductor Cleofonte Campanini, the tenor Alessandro Bonci, the baritones Mario Ancona and Maurice Renaud, and the soprano Emma Calvé. Of lesser names he had signed so many that he was beginning to cull them.

Melba, who had helped him recruit some of the big names, urged him to take her two most promising Covent Garden protégées, the Canadian soprano Pauline Donalda and the diminutive Italian soprano Emma Trentini. Among the junior sopranos recruited by Hammerstein from Covent Garden, but not recommended by Melba, was a Melbourne girl named Frances Alda. She was the granddaughter of Cecchi's old friend Fanny Simonsen, and had probably disliked Melba from childhood because the Simonsen family disapproved of Melba's treatment of Cecchi. Instruction at the École Marchesi and friendship with Blanche Marchesi had done nothing to lessen her dislike. By the time Alda arrived at Covent Garden in 1906, she seems to have nursed an intense antagonism toward Melba.

Frances Alda was one of those junior singers whom Hammerstein found it necessary to cull. To her dismay she received a cable from New York saying that Hammerstein would not be ratifying her contract. Pouring out her pent-up indignation to Blanche Marchesi in a letter from Brussels, Alda said that she had written to Cleofonte Campanini asking him why she was discarded, and he had written back that the "only thing he could imagine" was that Melba was behind it. She begged Blanche not to tell Madame because that would "spoil the fun." "You can be certain," she wrote, "I am going to pay her back."

Many years later in an autobiography called *Men, Women and Tenors*, Alda would transform the episode into an example of Melba's ruthlessness toward her rivals. Contradicting what she had put down on paper in Brussels in 1906, Alda wrote that she learned her contract had been canceled not by cable but from Campanini in person, and that she remembered him pulling a crumpled cablegram out of his pocket addressed to Hammerstein. It read "Either Alda or myself," and was signed by Melba. This cablegram was clearly a later invention, for it was not mentioned in the earlier letter to Blanche.

The idea of Alda being Melba's rival was nonsense, for that year Alda had received some abysmal notices. A review of her Gilda in the *Times* in June had reported that her voice "has not a very pleasing quality, is frequently affected by a tremolo, and is seldom powerful enough for leading parts." If Melba by chance wished Alda to be sacked, it was not out of a desire to trample on a potential rival—Alda was not a rival. The dubious cablegram, "Either Alda or myself," has passed into operatic history, often quoted to Melba's detriment. Melba, being dead when Alda's book was published, had no opportunity to reply.

The Manhattan Opera House—Hammerstein's palace—finally opened on December 3, the last seats being installed that afternoon, their paint still sticky, as the patrons' clothes soon testified. Otherwise the opening was a huge success, and critics were astounded when six premieres followed in the next ten days, all with excellent casts. Hammerstein kept a sharp eye on detail, sitting on a kitchen chair in the wings during rehearsals and missing nothing. Although the Metropolitan continued to retain the support of New York's powerful families, Conried was worried, especially after his star attraction, Caruso, was arrested in the monkey house at the Central Park Zoo for pinching a woman's bottom. The incident was said to have sparked an acute attack of sciatica in Conried, leading to a brief nervous breakdown.

Hammerstein's first season was not far advanced when Melba arrived in New York on December 30, accompanied by Ada Sassoli. Remembering the publicity that Patti gained when she wore her priceless jewels on stage, Hammerstein begged Melba to bring her costliest tiaras and necklaces and deck herself out like a Christmas tree when she sang in *La Traviata*. Melba's gems were now said to be worth—an exaggeration, no doubt—$2.5 million, and included a five-row pearl collar reputedly made for Marie Antoinette and a huge yellow diamond coveted by the king of Cambodia and given to Melba by Isabella Gardner of Boston. She was relieved when two detectives, hired by Hammerstein, took charge of the jewel boxes even before the *Caronia* docked.

On the wharf the impresario waited to welcome his Queen of Song and show her off to reporters. He was delighted to observe her jocular repartee and glowed with pleasure when she gave him the nickname of "the man who swallowed the canary." She was playing with the familiar metaphor of self satisfaction—"the cat that swallowed the canary"— and she, of course, was the canary! While there was a touch of mockery in her phrase, it was affectionate mockery. A poor immigrant who had done well, Hammerstein reminded her of her father. She presented him with an expensive, wafer-thin gold watch with his initials enameled on the back.

When Melba opened in *La Traviata* on January 2, 1907, the theatre was packed to capacity and crowds were turned away. Later she would remember her intense apprehension and Hammerstein's almost unbearable agitation. But once on stage she swept all before her. To quote her own words: "In thirty seconds—I must say it, though it may sound boastful—I knew that I had won. The rest of the performance was one long triumph." The reviewers agreed. "Her voice," wrote the *New York Times*, "has its old time lusciousness and purity, its exquisite smoothness and fullness. Such a voice is a gift as is vouchsafed but rarely in a generation."

A week later George and Ruby arrived, to be met by a group of reporters. George, a "symphony in grey" with a suit and spats of that color, admitted he preferred London to the Wild West. Ruby, described as a tall, pretty brunette in a fur coat, volunteered that Melba never sang anything she did not like. The young couple then joined Melba at the Barcelona on West Fifty-eighth Street, where she had hired apartments for the family. Originally Hammerstein had reserved a suite for her at the St. Regis, but the bustle and noise and above all the torrid steamy heat had proved insufferable. She dared not expose herself to extremes of temperature for fear of another attack of pneumonia.

For a total of fifteen nights spread over two months Melba sang the roles of Violetta, Lucia, Gilda, Marguerite, and Mimi to full houses and gushing reviews. *Rigoletto* was proclaimed one of the finest productions of the opera ever seen in New York, and even stalwart Metropolitan supporters were to be seen in the boxes. When reporters asked Hammerstein if he would rather make cigars or run an opera company, he smilingly replied, "It's much more fun to make Melba sing than it is to make a cigar."

In February Hammerstein managed to find a score of *La Bohème*, and with the final judgment on the legal injunction still pending, he boldly staged the opera on March 1. Melba appeared in two more *La Bohèmes* and sang the opera at her farewell performance on March 25. That night, amid scenes of the wildest excitement, she took thirty-four curtain calls and a standing ovation that some say lasted forty minutes. Riding on a surge of adrenaline, she shed her ladylike manners and became the uninhibited American Melba. When the audience refused to leave, she shook her fist at them and smilingly shouted, "Won't you go home?" When they cheerfully shouted back, "No," she called for the piano to be wheeled onstage, and sang and played Tosti's "Mattinata." A "pandemonium" followed, and an overexcited fan, while flinging flowers at her feet, flung their cardboard container as well. Melba caught the box and stuck it over her head, whereupon a voice rolled across the theatre, "Ain't she a crackerjack!" The explosion of laughter almost lifted the roof.

Once the theatre was cleared of people, a grand dinner was served onstage. Hammerstein sat between Melba and Emma Calvé and the assembled company consumed *suprème de volaille Hammerstein* and *pêches Melba* while the orchestra played one of Hammerstein's own compositions. At that moment of high excitement and congratulation, anything seemed possible, and together they began to plan the following year's season. Melba incautiously promised to sing in *Aida* and *Otello* and Wagner's *Flying Dutchman*.

Wagner was much on her mind. Although Wagner's widow had forbidden performances of his last opera, *Parsifal*, anywhere but in Bayreuth, the Metropolitan Opera had begun to perform it, and Melba and Ada Sassoli occupied a box at a matinee on February 22. Melba was feeling unusually tired when the curtain rose, which may in part explain her intense response to the music; for something remarkable happened to her that afternoon. "The theatre ceased to exist," she would remember, "I ceased to exist—I was a disembodied spirit, floating in the realms of pure music." When the curtain fell, "I leant back in my chair and sobbed."

Many have insisted that Melba lacked spirituality, and it is true that she only sporadically attended church and seldom spoke of spiritual matters. Her piety was private, though occasionally her hearers had glimpses of it. Once, when singing in St. Paul's Cathedral in Melbourne, she moved many to tears by the emotion in her voice. That same emotion sometimes surfaced when she sang Desdemona's "Ave Maria" in Verdi's *Otello*. She felt deeply about Verdi's "Ave Maria," and in later years when she contemplated leaving the stage, she used to say that it would be "fitting to go out singing the beautiful 'Ave Maria.'"

There seems little doubt that *Parsifal*, with its themes of sin and redemption, moved her powerfully. From childhood she had believed in the immortality of the soul, but sitting in the darkened theatre she felt the force of her faith in an afterlife as never before. It seemed, she said, as though Wagner's music had shone a "light through the open door leading to eternity." She remembered it as "the most wonderful experience of my life."

It was understandable that Melba felt tired and unstrung, for she had much to occupy her. Sandwiched between her operas were concerts with the Boston Symphony Orchestra in Pittsburgh, Chicago, Washington, and Philadelphia, and a long recording session with the Victor Talking Machine Company. Nor was she easy in her mind about George and Ruby. In Texas they had paid a visit to George's old home near Galveston, during which he and Ruby had quarreled bitterly. Whether Melba knew of the quarrel one does not know, but she sensed the undercurrents. For eleven years she had worried about George because she did not know where he was or what he was doing. Now that she did know, it seemed to her that she worried about him more than ever.

She was still feeling the effects of stress when, on the morning of April 2, 1907, she and Ada Sassoli traveled to the dock to board the *Kaiser Wilhelm der Grosse* bound for France. On arrival at the ship's side they saw an intriguing sight. A man wearing a tall silk hat was wandering sadly about the wharf carrying a canary in a gilded cage. Attached to the cage was a poem which ran:

To you, the brilliant songstress fairy,
I give in friendship this canary.

If ever we should part in rage,
I'll swallow the canary and you the cage.

The courier with the cage was Oscar Hammerstein, and the poem and the canary were for Melba. She was so overcome that she seized both his hands and began speaking volubly. Later, as the ship departed, she stood on deck waving her white handkerchief. Her voice could be heard calling to him across the water: "*Au revoir*, Oscar! *Au revoir* until next season."

Nobody Sings Like Melba and Nobody Ever Will

DESPITE MORE PROBLEMS with her weak lung, Melba threw herself into the summer season of 1907, giving a dozen performances of her usual operas at Covent Garden. Nevertheless her thoughts were running to Australia. While feeling raw from Norton's printed assaults she had vowed never to return to her homeland, but changes in her family during the last four years were inclining her toward another visit. Annie and Dora now had husbands and Dora was expecting a baby. Moreover Melba longed to be in Melbourne for her father's eightieth birthday and for the birth of Dora's baby. She profoundly wished to reintroduce George to his grandfather before he died.

She may also have hoped that the warm Australian climate would cure her recurrent bronchitis and that a long holiday would ease her young couple's marital problems. George and Ruby had scarcely returned from America when Ruby developed appendicitis, causing surgeons to extract "the longest appendix they had ever seen." During her convalescence George had taken her to Worthing where he had been at school, and there husband and wife had quarreled again. Perhaps long days whiled away on the Mediterranean and Indian Ocean would improve Ruby's health and restore the pair to wedded harmony.

Melba, George, and Ruby sailed from Marseilles early in August on the mail steamer *Oruba*. Melba had always disliked the route through the Red Sea, and this year her feelings were justified. Near the entrance to the Red Sea she probably learned of Joachim's death; and a few days later she witnessed a serious quarrel between George and Ruby. Memories of herself and Charlie voyaging in the same sea in the same stifling weather must have rushed into her mind. She suppressed her motherly instinct when she intervened. Instead of supporting her son, she took Ruby's side.

In Adelaide, George, Ruby, and Melba left the *Oruba*, heading by train for the gold city of Ballarat. At Ballarat they transferred to Melba's Napier automobile, shipped to Australia in advance along with Eugene, her French chauffeur. With Eugene at the wheel they then drove twenty miles over rough country roads to the house that Melba had rented for the next three months. Called Ercildoune, it was chosen to please George, who was happiest in the country. Its grandeur also pleased Melba, for it looked like a Scottish manor house, with rough-hewn granite walls and a tower, smooth lawns, tall cedars, and garden beds full of geraniums. Beyond the house lay a small lake surrounded by weeping willows, and beyond that a highland glen of ancient trees, luxuriant ferns, and granite crags.

Having suffered during her last tour of Australia from poorly trained servants, Melba had brought her secretary, two French maids, two French cooks, and a German housekeeper. Arrangements were speedily put in place, and Belle and her youngest son wanted for nothing when they came to stay early in September. The little boy is said to have told a friend, "Eh! It's all right there. Scent in your bath, a man to dress you, and a man to undress you—and everything." There were tennis courts, a croquet lawn, and stables well stocked with horses for riding. Ruby's sweet manner soon endeared her to the head stableman, who went out of his way to prepare a spirited thoroughbred for her to ride.

A few days later Melba motored the ninety miles to Melbourne so that she could renew her acquaintance with the celebrated English contralto Clara Butt and her baritone husband Kennerley Rumford, who were then touring Australia. Clara, six feet two inches tall, with a magnificent low voice that sounded like a trombone, was well known to Melba for they had sung together at the Albert Hall and at Windsor Castle. Although Melba had said she wished to remain incognito, she abandoned the wish when she eagerly attended the first of Clara's concerts in the Melbourne Town Hall on September 14. Easily recognized as she sat with white-haired David Mitchell in the fourth row from the front, she was obviously delighted when a wave of applause broke through the audience as she and her father took their seats. The presence of Clara Butt in the same city seemed to fan Melba's fame. "I am treated like a sort of Queen," she wrote with relish to an English friend, "and I have to go along *bowing* and when my motor stops I am mobbed, and have to shake hands with dozens—what fun."

Over the following weeks Melba attended sports meetings, fetes, dinners, a dog show, and a garden party at the Presbyterian Ladies College. So numerous were her social invitations that she decided to rent a substantial villa called Flete in the fashionable Melbourne suburb of Malvern. At first she liked the house, but as the summer advanced she found it was "hot as an oven" and plagued by blowflies. Moreover there was no indoor sewerage, only an outdoor earth closet. "One has to walk into a garden to relieve nature, and oh the blow flies are very lively. . . . I shall be glad," she wrote, "to get back to civilization."

In October she escaped to Gracedale House at the mountain resort of Healesville, taking a merry party with her. Apart from her maids and her French chauffeur, there were George, Ruby, their little grey terrier, and a rich sheep rancher named Sam McCulloch. "Everybody was just sizzling with excitement," wrote a female reporter who happened to be on the spot, but "Melba stood the battery of eyes unflinchingly."

Sam McCulloch, a forty-five-year-old widower with a degree in law and an enthusiasm for horses and music, may originally have been singled out as a companion for George, but being a tall, blue-eyed, fair-haired country man of the type that Melba was attracted to, he soon became her escort. He was with George, Ruby, and herself at a melodrama called *The Midnight Wedding* at the Princess Theatre early in November when the voice of a mezzo-soprano singing offstage took Melba's fancy. Discovering that the singer's name was Evelyn Doyle, Melba urged her to sail back to England with them and to allow herself to be placed in the École Marchesi. "She has everything in her favour to score success," proclaimed Melba, "if only she has the determination and capacity for hard work."

Ruby's visit to the theatre would be her last public appearance for months. The poor girl entered a private hospital with diphtheria, then a potentially fatal disease, on the day before the Melbourne Cup, the high point of the city's social calendar. Melba did not pause in her social stride. Writing to a friend in England she proclaimed, "I went to 12 balls in a fortnight—4 race meetings in a week—not counting dinners, garden parties—*frightful dissipation.*" At the Melbourne Cup she sat in the vice-regal box, wearing a white linen dress and a large white hat decorated with scarlet poppies. Beside her sat Clara Butt dressed in brown chiffon: they were dubbed by the press Her Sopranoship and Her Contraltoship.

The two divas were together again at the Government House ball, both dressed in stunning gowns of silver tissue. When they joined the same set for the dance called the Lancers, Melba tore the hem of her dress. Immediately every gentleman was fumbling in his lapel to supply her with a pin until the lucky governor of Queensland managed to produce one. The pens of the social reporters raced overtime describing the frivolities, but only one magazine spared a thought for poor Ruby. Her life had been saved, but she faced weeks of dreary recovery.

Melba's sympathy for her daughter-in-law was less than it should have been. Announcing the diphtheria to a friend in England, she half-seriously appended the explanation, "*rotten blood,*" then made a joke of it by adding, "Ain't I wicked." Her anxiety over George and his marriage had reached high levels during the voyage to Australia, and there seems little doubt that, without wishing Ruby ill, she now believed that George might be better off with another wife. Maybe he needed a robust Australian girl. One wonders if Evelyn Doyle, the lively young singer whom Melba was trying to persuade to join them on the return journey, did not flash into her mind.

Melba had not intended to sing publicly on this trip, but yielding, as she said, to public pressure, she now agreed to give two concerts in the town halls of Sydney and Melbourne, and two—at cheap prices—in the vast Exhibition Building in Melbourne. Remembering the stern criticism of her prices during her previous trip, she was determined to offer at least two low-priced performances. Once the decision was taken, she hastily mustered a concert party consisting of an Australian pianist named Una Bourne, an English baritone named Andrew Black, a young cellist called Louis Hattenbach, and John Lemmoné, the Ballarat-born flautist who had played for her in London.

Had her voice aged in the four years since she had last sung in Australia? The question was often asked, since most of her audiences had heard her before. The consensus among critics was that her voice had not aged, but some saw a change in her manner. One critic wrote that her "all conquering and somewhat defiant air" had been replaced by "an assumption of dignified repose." Another detected "greater intellectual powers of control and interpretation." When she sang "Vissi d'arte" from *Tosca*, several heard a "genuine abandon" which they had not supposed lay within her capacity.

Her low-priced concerts at the Exhibition Building in December 1907 were moving occasions. Her father had built the gigantic domed edifice, and among the eight thousand present were many who had known her as a child and even known her father as a young artisan. When Melba walked onto the platform, shimmering in her silver gown, a mighty roar rolled through the vast space like a tidal wave, and she was obliged to stand bowing until the echoes died away. There was perfect sympathy between the singer and her audience, wrote one observer, and she sang "divinely." "No matter who comes or goes," wrote another, "Melba is ours, yours and mine."

On the other side of the world, the autumn season at Covent Garden had just concluded. First-class sopranos were becoming rather scarce, and the conductor Campanini had urged the engagement of his sister-in-law, Luisa Tetrazzini, a thirty-six-year-old *bel canto* soprano, well known in Italy and South America but little known elsewhere. At her debut as Violetta on November 2 the sparse audience held few expectations, but once Tetrazzini opened her mouth the atmosphere changed. While her low and middle voices were inferior to Melba's, her high voice was sensational and her personality was exuberant. At the intermission Covent Garden's manager summoned the Fleet Street music critics. Their reviews were superlative. For the rest of the season, the new star's performances were booked out.

Melba no doubt received firsthand accounts of Tetrazzini's triumphs in letters from her London friends. Moreover the Melbourne press was soon agog over Tetrazzini, publishing news items that Melba must have seen. Wisely she refused to comment, exhibiting an indifference that was probably assumed but which might also have reflected her relief at being twelve thousand miles away from her rival. Since she had the powerful de Greys as patrons, she was probably not too much concerned.

At the end of November Melba made a somewhat surprising decision. She canceled her engagement at the Manhattan Opera for the forthcoming January, pleading poor health. Her father "is still ill and she is none too well herself," Hammerstein announced to the press. "She would prefer not to come, but says she will come if I want her to." If she had been hoping to pressure Hammerstein into begging her to come, she was to be disappointed. Her cancellation was accepted because Hammerstein had no need of her. He had just signed a new canary: Tetrazzini.

Meanwhile Melba was confined to a cage of her own making. After braving the summer heat to give concerts in the larger towns north of Melbourne, she was back at Doonside on Sunday, February 16, 1908, for her father's eightieth birthday, appearing with him at the crowded Scots' Church. Her preparations to return to Europe were by now well advanced. "You cannot tell what a glorious time I have had in Australia," she told the *Argus* reporter. "It has been all sunshine and pleasure making." But writing to Sam McCulloch's sister to thank her for kindnesses to "me and mine," she betrayed her true feelings. "I am terribly depressed," she wrote, "and everything seems topsy turvy—however I must be brave for my Father's sake."

During the next days of leave-taking, those topsy-turvy feelings persisted. As she stood beside her train at Melbourne's Spencer Street station, bidding goodbye to her brothers and sisters and Sam McCulloch, she could scarcely keep back her tears. When a women's choir, assembled on the platform to bid her goodbye, swung into "Home Sweet Home," she wept. Her family's last glimpse of her was a tear-streaked face at the train window.

In Adelaide she and her entourage boarded the *Orontes* for Europe, and she immediately jumped into shipboard activities. She was hoping to throw off her depression, but it was not to be. In the adjoining suite George and Ruby quarreled irreconcilably. It must have seemed as though her own marital history was repeating itself in her son and daughter-in-law. On top of all this, her supremacy at Covent Garden seemed to be slipping away, eclipsed by Tetrazzini's astonishing success. If this were not enough, she had just received word that Salvatore Marchesi had died.

Although overwhelmed by care and grief, Melba managed to put on a brave face. Indeed a fellow passenger seems to have been rather taken aback by her jauntiness and her mildly bawdy sense of humor. This was John Grainger, a building colleague of David Mitchell and father of Percy Grainger, a talented young musician whom Melba had helped in London. One mealtime on the ship, John Grainger watched as Melba was offered a plate of unfirm jelly. She is said to have remarked boldly that there were two things she liked firm, and jelly was one of them. Obviously Melba knew of Grainger's addiction to alcohol and barmaids and guessed he would be amused rather than shocked by a little bawdiness. But this is unlikely to have applied to the other diners who, coming from polite society, may well have been profoundly shocked.

Melba certainly had an outspoken, bohemian, and often amusing side to her nature: it was one that theatrical friends like Landon Ronald greatly enjoyed. But normally she tempered her bohemianism with discretion. To risk such an uninhibited remark in a public dining room would seem to suggest that her judgment was slipping.

After disembarking in Naples, Melba made for Paris to comfort Madame, whose loss, after half a century of marriage, was insupportable. Melba's own sense of loss was heavy too, for Papa Salvatore had been her true and loving friend. The visit, however, did allow Melba to mend her relationship with Hammerstein, and she sat with him each day in the Chatelet Theatre, auditioning candidates for the next Manhattan season. She also won an engagement at the Paris Opera, her first for many years. On June 11 she sang *Rigoletto* there with Caruso and Maurice Renaud. "I have had the greatest reception of my life," Caruso told reporters. "So have I," said Melba.

It was fortunate she had such success in Paris, for she needed all her confidence to cope with Covent Garden. Tetrazzini's triumph was even more sweeping than she had feared. By the time Melba entered the season on May 19—her forty-seventh birthday—Tetrazzini had given seven performances of roles that for nearly twenty years had been Melba's own. During the next two months the Italian soprano would sing twenty-two more—Gilda, Rosina, Violetta, Lucia, the queen in *Les Huguenots*—all of them Melba's showpieces. For the rest of the season Melba would be confined almost entirely to Verdi's *Otello* or *La Bohème*—only thirteen performances in all.

It was testimony to Melba's self-discipline that she did not erupt into a fury. Henry Higgins, chairman of the Covent Garden Syndicate, feared that she might. "I have just had a long talk with Melba who is in very good temper and quite reasonable," wrote Higgins to the music director, Percy Pitt. "We shall have no trouble about Tetrazzini as far as she is concerned."

Melba, of course, was accustomed to rivals. Normally she tolerated them, provided she could have first choice of roles and provided that they understood that her word was law. She also insisted on permanent and exclusive use of her own dressing room, lending it to only a very favored few. A notice—"Melba! Silence!"—guarded its door. On those terms, her terms, she had coexisted fairly harmoniously from 1904 to 1907 with a Silesian soprano named Selma Kurz; but the more biddable Kurz was rendered superfluous by the arrival of Tetrazzini.

A pragmatist, Melba quietly accepted the presence of her formidable challenger. Moreover she realized the wisdom of establishing a veneer of courtesy. When on May 26 she and Tetrazzini met at rehearsals for a gala concert in honor of the French president, she smiled, offered her hand, and began a conversation in French about Parisian fashions. "Melba is held to be the much cleverer woman of the world," commented the *New York Times*, and "it is believed she will have the advantage of the joust." The paper also reported that the public was "on tiptoe of excitement" as to which soprano would ultimately win.

When the time came for Melba to invite leading singers to perform at her charity matinee, celebrating her twenty years at Covent Garden, she told everyone that she would invite Tetrazzini. Somehow the invitation was delayed. When finally the letter did arrive, Tetrazzini refused its offer. Her official excuse was that she was singing elsewhere that evening, but she said privately that Melba was patronizing her, and she refused to be treated like a scullery maid.

Not only was the skirmishing providing newspaper copy; it was also fueling gossip. One story maintained that Melba and Tetrazzini were living in adjacent suites at the Savoy Hotel, and that on hearing Melba practice, Tetrazzini had sent for the hotel manager to ask just "how many cats" were housed in Melba's suite. The story was untrue, because Melba was living at Great Cumberland Street, but it captured the spirit of the feud rather cleverly.

Outwardly Melba remained urbane, but in private she fumed. Among her intimates she would refer to Tetrazzini as "the dwarf" and launch into colorful imitations. There were tales of Melba crawling on all fours, pretending to be the horse that carried the fat, squat diva around the stage in *Les Huguenots*. When told that Tetrazzini was being called "the new Melba," Melba snapped, "Many are called but few are chosen."

Gladys de Grey, who had been Melba's devoted protector at Covent Garden, was for once powerless to help. "I am dreadfully sorry," she wrote, "you have had an unhappy season—":

> But you must not be knocked down by the want of appreciation of a few people—when you are "Melba"! We all of us have our troubles, anxieties and disappointments in this sad world. But you have always the great satisfaction, accorded to so very few, of feeling that you are, and have been for many years alone at the head of a great profession—which nothing and nobody can take from you.

Gladys was groping her way toward the truth that, despite the lionization of Tetrazzini, in the public mind Melba was still the queen of Covent Garden. She had sung there every summer for twenty years, and audiences regarded her as an institution. All of fashionable London, including the king and queen, came to her twentieth anniversary matinee on June 24. When she sang the third act of *La Traviata*, the *Times* observed that "all the qualities of tone and phrasing" that had won her "her worldwide reputation were heard to perfection."

The rise of a new rival might just have been tolerable if it had not been for George. He was scarcely back in England when he became emotionally involved with a Mrs. Hoffmann, whose husband was soon suing for divorce and naming George as corespondent. By the day of the anniversary matinee, George was reportedly suffering a breakdown and had been sent by his doctor to the Austrian spa resort of Marienbad. Meanwhile Ruby had begun her own proceedings for divorce.

Although Melba seldom ran away from problems, she had experienced all she could bear. She decided to wash her hands of London for the time being, and went so far as to sell her beloved house. On July 16 she announced to the press that she would miss the following year's season in London and instead would tour Australia and New Zealand.

Vacating her house at Great Cumberland Place, which Lady Randolph Churchill agreed to buy, she tried to take her mind off her troubles by moving to the Ritz Hotel and preparing to make a concert tour of the British Isles. In seven weeks she gave twenty-two concerts, finishing with a grand concert at the Albert Hall, which she found "*very touching.*" "There were 10,000 people present," she told Madame by letter, "and I realise how much the British public adores me." She was touched also by Hammerstein's faith in her, for he offered her a month's engagement at the Manhattan, to be undertaken just before she sailed for Australia. "Nobody sings like Melba and nobody ever will," he told the press, and he backed his words by offering her twice the money he was offering Tetrazzini.

Hammerstein was waiting at the New York docks when she disembarked from the grand ocean liner *Lusitania*. Clad in a dark brown dress and a broad-brimmed hat with a long grey feather, she ran down the gangplank into his arms. He now owned two opera houses, one in Philadelphia and one in New York, and from December 14, 1908, to January 10, 1909, Melba alternated between the two cities, singing *Otello*, *Rigoletto*, *La Traviata*, and *La Bohème*. When it seemed that Hammerstein must shut his Philadelphia house for lack of capital, Melba saw a way of repaying his loyalty. Calling a press conference, she bluntly told the reporters, "Philadelphia must not let this temple be closed." When he managed to negotiate a $400,000 mortgage, she believed that her words may have helped secure the loan.

On January 20, soon after returning to Europe, Melba and George embarked from Marseilles for Australia. Hoping soon to take a first-class opera company to Australia, Melba had persuaded Robert De Sanna, president of the San Carlo Opera in Naples, to seek out suitable singers for her. Deep was her disappointment when she arrived in Naples and found he had fallen ill and done nothing. He seems to have been well enough, however, to take her to the opera, if one can believe Titta Ruffo, the baritone she had refused to sing with at Covent Garden because he seemed too young. Melba is supposed to have watched Ruffo in *Hamlet* and afterward sent a message backstage to ask if he would join her opera company. In his autobiography, he claimed that he sent back the retort: "Tell Melba that she is too old to sing with me." It was a neat reply, but it was probably invented. For one thing, Ruffo did not perform *Hamlet* that month; for another, he would be happy enough to sing *Rigoletto* with her in Philadelphia five years later.

In her present mood Ruffo's words—if really spoken—would have upset her. She was feeling the weight of her forty-seven years. When a fellow passenger implied that she was growing old, she returned a sharp answer. Age was something Melba preferred to forget, for each birthday brought her closer to that time when she would be obliged to stop singing; to someone so addicted to performing as herself, this would be little better than a death sentence. Although usually a realist, it was a prospect she so dreaded that she preferred to banish it from her mind.

CHAPTER TWENTY

So Many Triumphs, So Little Happiness

"THE MORE I KNOW of the world, the more I despise it," Melba had written, "so don't be astonished if I settle in the Australian bush which is so beautiful in its enormous solitude and space." In 1905 this was just a dream. Four years later, having had her fill of England, she decided to make her dream come true. Her first step was to undertake a "sentimental" concert tour of her homeland, and to sing its length and breadth without consideration of profit. All she asked of a town was a public hall with clear acetylene lighting, a comfortable hotel in which to stay the night, and a deposit of one hundred pounds as a guarantee of good faith. As a guarantee of her own good faith, Melba donated one thousand guineas to Australian charities before the start of the tour.

Melba engaged her flautist friend John Lemmoné as her business manager, knowing that the lessons he had learned from managing Paderewski's recent tour of Australia would stand him in good stead. As her social secretary she hired the expatriate Melbourne journalist Agnes Murphy, who had just written a successful biography of Melba, greatly enhancing her in Melba's eyes. Agnes had won more friends with this book than with her previous one, a novel based on Melbourne society which had provoked a libel suit and been withdrawn from sale. To those families involved in the libel suit, Agnes was decidedly unwelcome, and they were vexed with Melba for bringing her back to Melbourne.

Agnes and John Lemmoné were waiting at Melbourne's Spencer Street station when Melba and George alighted from their train in March 1909. The crowd was uncontrollable, and Melba became angry when her hat was knocked askew. A friend standing close by wrote that she suddenly saw a glimpse of "the old Nellie Melba," peering out from under the crooked brim, barely biting back the "blistering things" she longed to shout at the crowd.

Mother and son had reserved adjoining apartments in Fairlea, a mansion converted into apartments in South Yarra, to which Melba had shipped some of her possessions from Great Cumberland Place. Here, among her French gilt chairs and her gold-framed photographs of royalty, she held court and prepared for three town hall concerts. Her concert party was to comprise the Irish baritone Frederick Ranalow, who had recently toured in England with her; the Australian pianist Una Bourne; and versatile John Lemmoné, who was to play her flute *obbligati*. In addition to her long-established program, she was planning to include some simple British songs. She had learned "Believe Me If All Those Endearing Young Charms" and "Ye Banks and Braes o' Bonnie Doon" especially for these concerts. Although serious-minded critics sometimes chided her for singing popular songs and traditional ballads, Melba knew what her fans craved. "Ye Banks and Braes" was certainly what her father enjoyed, and when she appeared onstage to sing it wearing her Cartier tiara, ablaze with South African diamonds and Australian pink tourmalines, his pride knew few bounds.

Her father was also filled with pride in the following week when she sang at the local hall in Lilydale. As he was a local landowner and her brother a home owner, she was accepted as one of Lilydale's own, and so intense was the ovation at the end of "Home Sweet Home" that she left the platform in tears. Her heart confirmed what her head had long believed: that this was the piece of countryside where she and George belonged.

A week later, emboldened, she was ready to sing in the Tasmanian city of Launceston. Remembering the debacle of 1902 when Norton had claimed she was drunk, she had been wary of showing her face in Launceston; but wisely she sent Lemmoné to precede her, and with tact and persistence he more than restored her good name. In both Launceston and Hobart, so eloquent were some of the reviews that they found their way into the *New York Times* as examples of antipodean hyperbole. "The seductive siren voices to which poor Ulysses succumbed were no more entrancing than those which Melba's audience heard" was one sentence that amused American readers.

Melba had decided to include New Zealand in her tour and so, on completion of the Tasmanian concerts, she and her party embarked on the SS *Riverina* for Invercargill. Melba sang in towns and cities across both islands of New Zealand, sometimes in halls so crowded and airless that from time to time she would retreat to her dressing room to fill her lungs from an oxygen balloon. At Wellington 3,800 spectators were packed into a hall that normally held just under 3,000. Fire regulations were defied, with chairs placed in every corner and aisle; even so, it was calculated that a thousand were turned away at the door.

In New Zealand Melba was overtaken by sadness: she learned of the deaths of two of her friends. One was the elderly Earl of Hardwicke, whose wise advice had supported her at the start of her London career; the other was Francis Marion Crawford. Although they seldom met, Crawford's romantic personality had continued to charm her, and she was flattered that three of his novels were inspired partly by her life. Moreover his death from pneumonia, a disease that seemed to dog her own footsteps, roused thoughts of her own mortality. The deeper cause of her sadness was George. He seemed so aimless and depressed, and her efforts seemed powerless to rouse him. To a friend she wrote, "I am very sad too just now. . . . I seem to have nothing to live for."

Her black mood was dissipated by the thermal springs and rural beauty of Rotorua. They provided, she wrote, "one of the most beautiful interludes of my life." The steam vents hissing like a hundred snakes, the turquoise waters, the Maori girls in white dresses who sprinkled her with white blossoms seemed to be "sent as a sort of compensation for the trials and tribulations which had gone before."

Back in Sydney and rehearsing for her forthcoming concert, Melba invited nuns from a nearby convent to form an improvised audience. Among them was her old singing teacher Madame Christian, who was now Sister Paul of the Cross. Theirs was an emotional reunion, for Melba had no difficulty in acknowledging her debt to Madame Christian, whose teaching—since it was confined to Melba's school years—in no way threatened that of Madame Marchesi. The elderly Sister Paul had recently founded the Garcia School of Music, dedicated to perpetuating the *bel canto* technique. It was an initiative of which Melba thoroughly approved. At her first Sydney concert Melba was delighted to see the east gallery of the town hall filled with Sister Paul's students, who applauded knowledgeably whenever she sang.

From Sydney Melba and her concert party set out on tour, traveling in a smaller and humbler version of the Melba train, quickly establishing a routine that would be repeated in town after town. The day before each concert the train would pull into the local station where Melba would be welcomed by a line of schoolchildren, a deputation of local wives, and a sunburned mayor clutching a speech of greeting. Next morning in the simple local hotel she would be awakened by the rumble of carriages and carts and the roar of automobile engines, as outlying families came to town for her concert.

On tours across America even the remotest towns could usually supply an adequate hall and piano, but Melba and her assistants soon discovered that this was not so in Australia. Una Bourne remembered that one of the halls in which they performed was still unfinished. In another, a leaking pipe almost gassed them. Several pianos were so out of tune that Melba's own piano had to be moved from her railcar to the hall.

In some towns the townspeople devised ingenious ways of hearing her concert without paying. At the Theatre Royal in Rockhampton a crowd perched on the theatre's roof and was marooned when the caretaker removed the ladder. Their indignant cries almost drowned out the singers' voices. At a school of arts in Mount Morgan, a building that stood on high wooden piles, about a hundred people crammed into the space beneath the floorboards, and Melba could hear them shoving and bumping while she was singing.

Although Melba sang as far along the tropical coast as Townsville, and gave a concert to an "immense crowd" in the gold town of Charters Towers, she did not sing in Mackay. Perhaps the memories were too painful. Memories, however, did not stop her from singing in Bathurst, where she had failed to gain an audience back in 1886. This time some concertgoers traveled a hundred miles by horse-drawn coach and another three hundred miles by train to hear her: in their own words, no sacrifice was too great to hear the woman they believed to be "the world's first soprano." It was a reception, Melba wrote, "of which even royalty could not have complained."

The tours were strenuous, but Melba found them an antidote to her melancholy. When she returned to Melbourne to sing at the Exhibition Building, friends thought she looked thinner, healthier, and happier than she had for years. "The gallop around Australia has done her good," was one comment. She had regained "the spring of youth."

One reason for her improved mood was George. She had at last found an absorbing interest for him. Knowing his love of horses, she had bought a racehorse, hoping that it might become a focus for his life. Family tradition has it that she sent him to register her membership of the Victorian Racing Club and to nominate the racing colors for her jockeys to wear. It is said that he chose an olive green jacket, mauve sash, and white cap—the colors of the British suffragette movement—to tease and please her. Over the past year she had spoken publicly in England and America in favor of female suffrage, praising Australia and New Zealand for granting women the right to vote. Percy Colson's assertion that she scorned feminism and refused to believe that women were men's equals is surprising, and seemingly without foundation. Melba had few doubts that her own intellect was equal to that of most men, and she admired women who pursued careers. Suggestions that the cultivation of intellect made women less feminine aroused her resentment. "Woman, even when she has the vote, will always be woman," she told reporters. "The greater use of her brain will spiritualize the future woman. Her face will be alight with intelligence."

At Melbourne's Flemington Racecourse on Derby Day, Melba was conspicuous in the governor-general's box, seated beside her old chum Lord Richard Nevill. By then she owned a country property as well as a racehorse. After months of searching through the Yarra Valley, she had come upon a small farm at Coldstream, with magnificent views of those blue mountains and rolling green hills she had so loved as a child. Just twenty-seven miles from Melbourne, it was comfortingly close to her father's vineyard near Lilydale and to her brother Charlie and his family at Cave Hill. Later she bought more land so as to transform the small farm into a large one where George could raise horses and fatten cattle.

Melba also embarked on a new chapter in her own life. Believing, like Madame, that it was one's duty to pass one's vocal skills to succeeding generations, and inspired now perhaps by her old teacher Madame Christian, she set up free *bel canto* classes for Melbourne students. On September 27, 1909, at the Conservatorium of Music at Melbourne University, she selected the girls who would become her pupils. Thereafter each Wednesday afternoon for two hours she conducted an opera class on the same lines as those she had attended at the École Marchesi. Believing, like Madame, that all aspects of her pupils' lives came within her jurisdiction, she instructed them on dress, health, and behavior almost as firmly as she instructed them on singing.

It has often been said in Melba's time and later, that she mixed harmoniously with men but tended to dislike women. In reply Melba told a woman friend, "I wonder why you think I don't like women. Do you know your saying this hurt me dreadfully, for I love women, and I think I have more women friends than most women." On both sides of the Atlantic she had demonstrated her capacity for female friendship with her young protégées, whom she regarded more as daughters than as pupils. Parkina, Ada Sassoli, Donalda, and Trentini were close to her, as was twenty-eight-year-old Lady Susan FitzClarence, the sweet-natured sister of the new Earl of Hardwicke. On the eve of her departure for Australia, Melba had written to Susan, "This is to say goodbye and to tell you to take great care of yourself until I return for I love you very much."

In the singing class at the Conservatorium of Music, Melba found new substitute daughters. One was affectionate and pretty Beryl Fanning, who kept a diary of each lesson and was overjoyed with Melba's candor. When Melba sadly confided to Beryl that the "witches" in the press said that she only wanted to teach contraltos because she feared that a soprano might turn into a rival, Beryl felt like fighting "the narrow minded creatures" who attributed everything to Madame's "selfishness." Those who really knew her, wrote Beryl indignantly, understood how generous and kind she could be. She "never inspires me with fear," wrote Beryl, but with sheer enthusiasm: "I always feel so very eager to do well."

In November Melba rented a house called Craignair in the mountain resort of Macedon, about forty miles from Melbourne, and invited

Beryl and other favored pupils to visit her. The house, wrote one happy visitor, "was always full of guests, girls and boys, who made merry, as well as their more sedate elders." There was "a great deal of talk and a great deal of laughter, some heavenly music, and reading and writing on the veranda, or in some shady nook in the garden." As always, George was central to Melba's plans. She dared to hope that among these carefully selected young people George would make suitable friends and perhaps even find a wife.

On Christmas night Melba's girls and boys sat outdoors under the "great round southern moon," listening to her gramophone play the chimes of London's famous clock, Big Ben. It was "beyond measure strange to hear those familiar notes in such surroundings; and yet it was natural too," wrote an English visitor, "for English life wraps one all round in Australia, and although you are farthest away from England in distance, you are never far away from her in spirit."

Attempting to recreate the atmosphere of her country homes in England, Melba's mind kept returning to that enchanted English summer at Coombe Cottage, the most splendid of the country houses she had rented. It was her dream to transform the simple farmhouse she had bought near Lilydale into a gracious English-style house, not as large as the original Coombe Cottage but with something of its air.

Accordingly she summoned John Grainger, her old companion from the *Orontes*. On the surface he had excellent qualifications, being an architect and builder who had worked with her father, but in reality he was not suited to the task. Grainger was suffering from tertiary syphilis and was described by his son Percy as the "totalest wreck I've ever seen." His pitiable state aroused Melba's compassion: indeed she and her sister Belle would show a continuing concern for him, sending reports of his condition to his wife and son in America. While Melba's compassion for "the funny old man," as she called him, does her credit, her choice of him as architect was less creditable. The farmhouse would suffer ever afterward from his careless supervision.

Melba had booked cabins in the mail steamer *Ophir*, to leave for England on February 9, 1910. Amid the flurry of departure, there arose an obstacle that plunged her back into anxiety. George, ill with "varicose veins in the bladder" suddenly required "a terrible operation." As she watched by his sickbed, almost overcome with worry, she scribbled a letter to her friend Lady Susan FitzClarence in England. "It is so bad Susie," she wrote pathetically, "I have so many triumphs and so little happiness—I am sick to death of it all."

George recovered, but his health remained in jeopardy. His doctors "think he will be delicate for years," Melba reported sadly. As there was no question of his sailing with her, she installed him and his nurse in the unrenovated farmhouse. As she prepared to depart on the long voyage to Europe, she told Beryl Fanning, "My heart is heavy and sad."

CHAPTER TWENTY-ONE

The Greatest Musical Event

SHORTLY BEFORE SAILING on the *Ophir* in February
1910, Melba had conferred with the impresario J. C. Williamson concerning the grand opera tour of Australia that she was hoping to launch in eighteen months' time. She was prepared to make
it a joint venture, sharing the costs, profits, and even the losses with
Williamson. Moved, she said, by patriotism rather than by money, she
believed it would constitute "the greatest musical event" in the history
of her homeland.

Three months later in London, just as plans for the Australian tour
were beginning to gain momentum, Melba received a shock that temporarily pushed opera to the back of her mind. Opening her morning newspaper on May 7, 1910, she could scarcely believe the big black headlines proclaiming that King Edward was dead. His repeated kindnesses
to her over the years had formed a genuine bond between them, and she
mourned him as she would a close friend. On May 20 she and John Lemmoné watched the royal funeral, one of the most memorable pageants of
the twentieth century, from the windows of her suite in the Ritz.

In the following weeks London was plunged into official mourning,
but this did not prevent Melba from returning to her plans. Lemmoné
was sent to Paris to audition singers, and then to Milan, Turin, Bologna, Warsaw, Leipzig, Dresden, and Berlin to search out other possible
recruits. In the course of his journey he called also at Nice, where Jean
de Reszke had become a teacher of singing. "Jean de Reszke is helping
us," Melba wrote excitedly to Beryl Fanning in Melbourne, "so we hope
to get some really good artists."

So engrossed was Melba in her search for talent that Tetrazzini's capture of her traditional roles at Covent Garden seemed almost a minor matter. Nevertheless when Melba sang the only performance of *La Traviata* assigned to her that season, she was pleased by the affectionate reception. "The old airs lose their stiffness and become fresh when she sings them because of the exquisite grace of her phrasing and the ease and spontaneity with which they are given," proclaimed the *Times*. The words reassured her.

Meanwhile she prepared for her usual winter season in North America. Ada Sassoli and John Lemmoné accompanied her across the Atlantic, as did a French-Canadian tenor named Albert Quesnel. On August 30 they left Boston on the Melba train on a tour that encompassed twenty-five towns and cities, beginning in Halifax, Nova Scotia, and ending in New York. When the tour concluded Melba was contracted to appear at Carnegie Hall, to sing concerts in Baltimore and Philadelphia, to perform four operas in New York and four in Chicago, and to endure a five-day recording session for the Victor Talking Machine Company. She was pushing herself beyond her physical and emotional limits, but she refused to listen to reason.

The tour was by no means a failure for, in the words of a reporter, Melba was "unquestionably the singer of greatest renown in the world," and her "mere presence exerted a spell." And there were amusing incidents to cheer her musicians on their way. In Philadelphia the trunk containing Melba's underclothes failed to arrive. Next day a Philadelphia newspaper carried the headline: "Melba Goes to Bed Without a Nightie." In Quebec, where limousines were unknown, the party traveled to the concert in a horse-drawn mourning coach rented from the local undertaker.

Success, nevertheless, was accompanied by fatigue and illness, and a dislike of America that she admitted was ungrateful of her. From Grand Forks in North Dakota, Melba wrote privately, "I wonder if you realise what it is to live in a private rail car for 2 months. Of course it is luxurious and one has an excellent chef and servants; but Oh! the monotony of travelling and singing is sometimes more than I can bear and the noise in the railway stations is sometimes too awful." When the time came for her to appear at the Metropolitan, she was too ill with bronchitis to sing more than twice; likewise her Chicago operas were canceled. On December 10, 1910, in a state of visible weakness, she was helped aboard the *Mauretania*, which went on to make a record-breaking crossing of the Atlantic in four days and twenty hours. Excitement permeated the cabins, but Melba did not feel it. On medical advice she did not leave her bed.

In England George awaited her. Her plan to settle him on the farm at Lilydale seems to have failed, for he longed for the excitement of Europe and she felt easier when she had him under her eye. They shared Christmas together. Whether the all-too-faithful Haddon Chambers was included in the festivities is not known. Melba confided to Susan FitzClarence that she had a mind not to invite him. Since 1904—the year of Haddon's wife's death—Melba's feelings for him had been cooling. Did he want to marry her and did she refuse him? One does not know. Whatever the reason, he was now boring her beyond patience. She told Susan that he always seemed to be hanging around.

Haddon Chambers's eclipse may have been related to the rise of the equally faithful John Lemmoné. Patient and tactful, John had proved himself an indispensable manager and a loyal confidant. His combination of "boyish sweetness with business-like cleverness" was so reassuring. "I know what a dear loyal friend you are and that I can yap to you to my heart's content," she wrote to him one Christmas, "and that no one will ever know what I yap about."

Were they lovers? Some observers assumed they were, but one circumstance seems to point against it. As well as having a wife from whom he seems to have been only partly estranged, Lemmoné possessed an adoring girlfriend, only half Melba's age, named Mabel Batchelor. Melba appears to have been on affectionate terms with Mabel. One doubts if Melba would have tolerated, let alone felt warmly toward, a young and pretty woman who was a sexual rival. More likely she and Lemmoné were comrades, for Melba did well in comradely relationships. Thanks to her frank, tomboyish nature, this type of friendship came easily to her.

In May, Melba was well enough to return to Covent Garden in *La Bohème*, and on May 19, 1911, she celebrated her fiftieth birthday by endowing a scholarship at the Guildhall School of Music. Defying the apprehension she usually felt when she contemplated speaking in public, she decided to announce the award in person. Landon Ronald, the school's newly appointed principal, helped her with her speech, rehearsing it with her twice, but when she stood up to speak her tongue was tied with fear. With a pathetic smile, she turned to her audience and said, "I am awfully sorry but I can't go on." Coming to her aid, Landon took the script from her hand and read it for her. Afterward he was both amused and perturbed to see the headline in an evening paper, "Melba Breaks Down."

By now the coronation of King George V, planned for June 22, was becoming the magnet of London life. Visitors poured into the city, hostesses such as Gladys de Grey gave spectacular parties, and Melba took part in a coronation concert at the Albert Hall. Her co-performers were the brilliant young Leipzig pianist Wilhelm Backhaus and two young men with whom she had been singing at Covent Garden. One was an Irish-Canadian bass named Edmund Burke, and the other an acclaimed Irish tenor named John McCormack. Later she sang with them at a coronation gala, sharing the program with Diaghilev's Ballet Russe, which was electrifying London with its color and drama. Gladys de Grey, who was one-quarter Russian, had been a quiet promoter of the ballet's visit, and entertained the dancers at Coombe Court. Melba attended exciting parties where members of royalty mingled with spectacular dancers like Pavlova and Nijinsky. Rumor had it that Nijinsky and Gladys were lovers.

Less than a month after attending the coronation, Melba assembled her entourage aboard the mail steamship *Osterly*, ready to embark on her grand opera tour of Australia. With her on the voyage went her son, John Lemmoné, a butler, a chauffeur, and five maids. Although the Australian season was to start in Sydney, Melba disembarked in Adelaide and caught the train to Melbourne. Her desire to see her renovated farmhouse was intense, and on the very afternoon of her arrival she was driven out to inspect what the papers were calling her "new palace on the hillside."

Wings had been added to the old farmhouse to make a large one-story villa, and where a year before had stood an asparagus bed there now rose a spacious music room with a magnificent view of the blue ranges. Determined to avoid the tortures she had suffered at Flete during a previous summer, she had ordered wire mesh screens for the doors and windows to protect the house from flies, and arranged for water to be piped from the Yarra River so that the house could be sewered. She also insisted on a machine for generating electricity and a block of stables for the horses and cars. A section of the roof had been laid flat to serve as a roof garden, and outside the irrepressible Signor Catani was laying out acres of lawn, tennis courts, and flower beds. *Melbourne Punch*, permitted to inspect the property, declared it was better equipped than the most up-to-date city hotel.

At the end of August Melba traveled to Sydney to join the fully fledged Melba-Williamson Opera Company, the overseas members of which had just arrived on the steamship *Mooltan*. John Lemmoné and Jean de Reszke had recruited impressively. Offering an extensive repertoire of twelve operas, sung by principal singers drawn from the best opera houses in America and Europe, Melba's season was hailed as the most significant cultural event Australia had ever seen. Notable among its singers were Melba's former partners from Covent Garden, John McCormack and Edmund Burke, and a six-foot-tall American mezzo named Eleanora de Cisneros, who was married to a Cuban count and had sung with Melba at the Manhattan. "For a long time this goal of opera in Australia has been before me," Melba told her public proudly. "All my ambitions, my heart, my brains—if I have any!—have been centred on this project."

Verdi's *La Traviata* opened at Her Majesty's Theatre in Sydney on September 2, and critics and operagoers alike were thrilled to be at last seeing Australia's greatest singer in a full-length opera. Through September houses were sold out; and every day but Sunday, gallerygoers would arrive with camp stools and picnic baskets and wait in line from seven in the morning until two in the afternoon when the box office opened. Then, having bought their tickets and selected their seats, they would settle down to chatter and sing and play the piano and drink cups of tea, for Melba insisted they should have the use of a piano and free tea. Sometimes she herself would sing them a song and they would stand and cheer her. At other times Eleanora de Cisneros would mount the stairs, and when they saw her red head emerging above the staircase, they would shout out, "Hello Cis."

By the third week Melba was showing signs of strain. She was singing three times a week—Mimi, Violetta, Desdemona, Marguerite, Gilda—and was so determined that everything should be perfect that she spent hours at the theatre, superintending the lighting, stage properties, costumes: no detail was too trivial. Although in some ways she was in her element, the pressure began to harm her. By the end of September she was ill with an aching ear and a sore throat. Treated with leeches, she managed to struggle on, but a week or so into October bronchitis set in, and she was ordered to rest in the mountain resort of Medlow Bath. To Beryl Fanning in Melbourne she wrote, "I have been and am so very ill. I don't know what to do." She cautioned Beryl not to tell anyone, "as the public don't know *half* what I am suffering."

To be forced to absent herself from the season she has spent years organizing was a cruel punishment. She missed a string of performances, and attendances fell accordingly. As Norton's allegations, though stale and fanciful, were still to some extent believed, rumors arose that she was drinking again. "Isn't it disgusting?" she wrote to her publicity agent Claude McKay. "The people say I am drunk. What can be done about it?" Deciding that the looming crisis in public confidence called for boldness, McKay sent Melba's letter to the *Sydney Morning Herald* and requested it be published. He almost expected Melba to sack him for acting without her permission, but instead she flung her arms around his neck. To their joint relief, she was cheered as she entered the stage at her next performance.

To Susan FitzClarence she wrote, "The opera is a great success, but Oh! the rows and worries too awful." She was out of temper with John McCormack, who irritated her by arriving late in Sydney and by retaliating when she accidentally lay on his foot during the final tableau in *Roméo et Juliette*. "Stop wriggling, this is a tableau," she is supposed to have snapped at him. "Tableau be damned," he snapped back. "Get off my foot." The story did the rounds, with Melba mischievously imitating his Irish brogue.

McCormack is said to have further annoyed her by taking offense when she refused to share her curtain calls with him. When he barged on stage at her side, uninvited, she is said to have told him, "No one takes curtain calls with Melba." In fact she often did share her curtain calls with selected performers and had been known to drag shy conductors and singers onstage with her like reluctant schoolchildren, but she regarded the sharing as her gift to bestow, not anybody's right.

It was a gift that she did bestow on McCormack at least once during the Sydney season, if one can believe a reporter in the *Sydney Sun*. He described how, following their balcony scene in *Roméo et Juliette*, she pulled McCormack to the footlights to acknowledge the applause. He responded by picking up a laurel wreath that had been thrown on stage and playfully placing it around her neck.

On the last night of the Sydney season, John Lemmoné made a speech on Melba's behalf, thanking the public for attending even on those nights when she was not singing. It was an unfortunate choice of words because it suggested that, of the members of a large and distinguished cast, only Melba was worth coming to hear. On hearing the blunder, the irrepressible McCormack broke into titters of laughter. Melba never forgave him. To Lemmoné she wrote, "John McCormack is a *pig* and a low one *at that*." McCormack retorted by calling Melba a bitch.

On October 28, 1911, Melba and her company arrived by train in Melbourne, to be greeted by a larger crowd than ever at the station. A few hours later they performed *La Traviata* at Her Majesty's Theatre in the most brilliant first night the city had yet seen. For David Mitchell it was a dream come true: he had not before seen his daughter in a fully staged opera. For Melba too it was the fulfillment of a dream. "I have never felt so happy as I do tonight," she told her audience.

Despite these brave words, she was aware of an underlying uneasiness. Melbourne reviewers were mostly Wagner-lovers and tended to despise Italian operas. More important, the opera season coincided with the racing season, and to most Melbournians the horses took precedence over the singers. As November advanced, attendances dwindled. In early December, Melba and Lemmoné decided to cut their losses and return with the company to Sydney. To save face they spread the excuse that Melba wished to compensate Sydney for her two weeks of canceled performances, but few people in Melbourne were fooled.

Just before leaving Melbourne one of the company's minor singers died. He was the twenty-eight-year-old bass Vito Dammacco, who had been hospitalized with lymphoma for most of the Melbourne season. His fellow performers sang at the requiem mass in St. Patrick's Cathedral.

Melba's spirits, originally so high, sank lower and lower. She began to feel that their venture was cursed.

The return season in Sydney was no more than adequate, and thereafter the company disbanded on a dismal note. Melba's inclination was to leave almost at once for Italy, to study the opera *Mefistofele* with its composer Arrigo Boito. She would then open at Covent Garden in May, where she anticipated having complete sway since Tetrazzini had quarreled with her brother-in-law Campanini and was not expected to return. But two considerations were restraining Melba. One was her own exhaustion, the other was her father's health. She postponed her departure to March 1912, then to June, and then to August. To Susan FitzClarence she wrote, "It breaks my heart to miss the London season. I cannot leave, my father is very ill and he clings to me more than any of the others."

She longed also to have time to enjoy her refurbished home, which she had officially named Coombe Cottage. Daily the house seemed to grow dearer to her. She had shipped out many of her European treasures—pictures, furniture, porcelain, silver—and was constantly rearranging them within its rooms. Above the stable roof she had affixed a weathervane and a sign which said, in Scottish dialect, "East, West, Hame's Best." Despite the continuing allure of England and Europe, Coombe Cottage was beginning to feel like her true "Hame."

In early March 1912 Melba organized a dance at the house, and a special train brought sixty guests from Melbourne. The music room became a dance floor, the tennis courts were strung with Japanese lanterns, and tables were placed on the flat roof, which was transformed into a Tuscan courtyard with vines on trellises complete with bunches of grapes. Since Melba viewed the dance as an informal gathering, she dressed informally: just a satin gown with an overdress of embroidered chiffon, a diamond necklet and a rope of pearls, and a bandeau of osprey feathers in her hair caught at the sides with diamond clasps! The guests, who stayed until the special train gathered them at one in the morning, included her sisters Dora and Belle, Beryl Fanning, Lord Richard Nevill, and the governor of Victoria. One object of the dance was to establish George in Melbourne society; another was to interest him in Beryl Fanning.

In June, as if to rub salt into Melba's wounds, another international opera company arrived in Australia. Organized by an Irishman,

Thomas Quinlan, who had once managed a tour of Ireland for Melba, the Quinlan Company had been established for eighteen months and had already toured Britain and South Africa. It offered an impressive repertoire of fifteen operas, four of which had never been performed in Australia. Although none of its singers was in Melba's class, nearly all were competent and pleasing, and some had sung at Covent Garden.

Although Melba had boasted to the press that she had bestowed on Australia a company as talented as any to be found in the capitals of Europe, there was little doubt that many Melbourne critics preferred the Quinlan Company. Eighteen months of performing with its own orchestra and chorus had produced an integrated ensemble, which Melba's underrehearsed company had not. Furthermore the Quinlan operas were sung in English, which pleased the Australian audiences.

Behaving with tact and grace toward her competitor, Melba sent the leading soprano, Melbourne-born Lalla Miranda, a bouquet modestly inscribed: "From a fellow Australian singer." She even attended one of the Quinlan operas. Otherwise she stayed quietly at Coombe Cottage. Late in July, after giving her own series of country concerts, she made a sad farewell to George, who had elected to stay behind, and sailed for England on the *Otranto*.

In England Melba immersed herself in hard work. A concert at the Albert Hall on October 5, 1912, with Wilhelm Backhaus and the celebrated Belgian violinist Eugene Ysaye, was followed immediately by a concert tour of the British Isles. With her went Burke and Backhaus, the cellist Arnold Trowell, the pianist Gabriel Lapierre, and the flautist Philippe Gaubert. Writing privately from Preston in Lancashire, she complained that she had sung thirteen times in three weeks, adding, "*Poor me* I *am* tired." But her tiredness was short-lived for, despite her fifty-one years, she could still draw on surprising reserves of strength. By the end of the tour she had sung in twenty-four cities and claimed she could have sung in more.

Although she knew that Coombe Cottage must now become his home, it still hurt her to leave George behind in Australia. She felt his loneliness almost as though it were her own, and she wished he could find another wife. She had hoped at first he might marry Beryl Fanning, but then she suspected he preferred another of her protégées: pretty, vivacious Evelyn Doyle, whom she had sent four years earlier to study at the École Marchesi. Since leaving Madame's care, Evelyn had joined a touring company and was hoping to make an operatic career; marriage did not enter her plans. Melba nevertheless did her best to promote the match, and in an effort to know the young soprano better, had taken Evelyn with her to America on her final visit to the Manhattan Opera in 1908.

Early in 1913 George arrived in England, greeting his mother with the news that he and Evelyn Doyle were engaged to be married. Melba's pleasure and relief were evident, for it was the outcome she had so long desired. George and Evelyn were married quietly at the Marylebone registry office on February 20, after which Melba sent an urgent letter to Beryl Fanning in Melbourne. "I am writing to tell you," she wrote, "that George was married with my consent last Thursday to Miss Evie Doyle—a lot of ridiculous things have been said, that he had married a chorus girl and that I have disinherited him etc. etc. etc.—I know how fond of me you are, therefore I want you and your dear Father and Mother to be very kind to them, especially as she is *very* sensitive—I am *very* fond of her and I am delighted he has married a really good girl who has a very good influence over him." "You can tell everyone what I have written," she added, for "that will stop *wicked* lying tongues."

George and Evie were still on their honeymoon when George developed appendicitis. His health had been fragile since his bladder surgery three years before, and his recovery from the appendectomy was painfully slow. As soon as he could travel, Evie carried him off to the warmer climate of the Riviera to convalesce. Melba meanwhile journeyed to Paris to decorate an apartment she had taken at 91 Avenue Henri Martin and to give concerts at the newly opened Théâtre des Champs Élysées. She had barely arrived in Paris when news reached her from the south of France that George had contracted double pneumonia, complicated by pus in his lung. His doctors were forced to remove a rib to allow the pus to drain.

"My poor George is still very ill (this is the 7th week)," she wrote to Susan FitzClarence desperately, "and I don't know what to do for him. If only I could take even part of his pain, I should be happy. Oh God, you don't know what I have been through." In the midst of her wretchedness, she was obliged to return briefly to London to sing before twelve thousand people at the Albert Hall. It was testimony to her spirit and determination that she sang exquisitely. As she rushed back to George's bedside she wrote to Beryl Fanning, "It has been dreadful and his suffering is agonizing. He will be delicate for a very long time." She added the heartfelt prayer: "Thank God he is saved."

Melba's spirits revived toward the end of May, for George was recovering and Melba had her own fictitious cause for celebration. According to her own publicity, it was her fiftieth birthday. In fact it was her fifty-second, but she was in the habit of subtracting two years from her age. It was also the twenty-fifth anniversary of her debut at Covent Garden, which meant that she had equaled Adelina Patti's record. Her two anniversaries were announced in the Court Circular as though she were royalty, along with the news that she was spending her Covent Garden anniversary with Alfred Rothschild at Halton. Alfred marked the day by giving her a Japanese pug in a gilt basket tied up with a blue ribbon while the king and the prime minister of Australia sent her telegrams.

Melba celebrated her silver jubilee by singing *La Bohème* with John McCormack. Fans queued all night to buy seats, and three large vans were required to transport her bouquets. At the end of the third act, when she had succeeded in quieting the cheers, she made a touching little speech. "Thanks, thanks," she said "with love from the bottom of my heart." It was a memorable night, but the performance her fans were really anticipating came a month later on June 23 when Caruso and Melba were paired as Rodolfo and Mimi by royal command. It was the first time Caruso had sung Rodolfo in London for six years, and the response to the two stars was overwhelming. Melba relished the success as a reward for her months of anxiety. "After all there *are* compensations in life," she wrote to an Australian friend.

Not only was Melba once more the undisputed queen of Covent Garden, but her pure *bel canto* style—once condemned as outdated— was now hailed as a precious rarity that might all too soon vanish; and her restraint, once deplored as undramatic, was hailed as "her wonderful power of singing well within her limits." One observer, however, remained unimpressed. The writer Osbert Sitwell, an ardent supporter of Tetrazzini, was among the celebrities present at Melba and Caruso's *La Bohème*, and he has left a witty and much-quoted description of the singers. He called them "two fat elderly thrushes, trilling at each other over the hedges of tiaras," adding that Melba's voice "was not invariably true, having about it something of the disproportion of the Australian continent from which she had emerged." Fortunately one need not take Sitwell's recollection of musical matters too seriously, because elsewhere in his memoirs he recalls that Melba once sang *Madama Butterfly*, an opera that was never in her repertoire.

After all her anxieties, Melba's mind and body cried out for rest, but when September came she had again to draw on her reserves of strength to prepare for her usual journey to America. This year her London agent, Lionel Powell, had booked a tour of such importance that she could ill afford to miss it. With her traveled her old associates Edmund Burke and Gabriel Lapierre and the flautist Marcel Moyse. Joined by Jan Kubelik in Montreal, they were due to give more than fifty performances across North America. "A combination of this kind has never been known, even in America," declared the *Times*. The cost of the tour and the financial risk were huge.

Like their English counterparts, the finest American critics now saw Melba as the greatest living exponent of the exquisite but doomed art of *bel canto*, and described her concert at Carnegie Hall as a significant cultural event. By contrast, when she and Kubelik gave the first of two concerts at the New York Hippodrome, their emphasis was on popularity rather than culture. Thousands of rowdy fans packed the vast playhouse, spilling so far onto the stage as to leave only a small oasis for the performers, even cheering and shouting and applauding in the middle of arias. For the *New York Times* the concert was "a typical hurrah evening," but for others it was a "colossal success" and testimony to the extraordinary popular esteem in which Melba was held.

It was scarcely surprising that the rank and file now flocked to hear Melba, for her reputation had permeated all levels of society. She was now probably the most famous singer in the world, partly because she possessed a unique publicity agent: the gramophone. Thanks to her regular recording sessions on both sides of the Atlantic, she had now made more than one hundred records, each of which had gone into multiple pressings. In an era when no woman was prime minister, chief justice, or head of a great church or financial house, and in a time in which the film star was only just emerging, Melba was—apart from a few queens and empresses—perhaps the best-known woman in the world.

As they toured the Midwest, Melba enjoyed more successes and suffered several shocks. On November 19, 1913, she opened a newspaper and almost collapsed. It carried the announcement of Madame Marchesi's death. Melba's grief, which would have been profound in any event, was made deeper by her troubled conscience. The year before, visiting her ninety-one-year-old teacher in Paris, she had found a husk of a woman who looked at her without a glimmer of recognition. "She whom I had known," wrote Melba, "as trim, strict and alert, with a brain as keen as steel, was now only a sad, shrunken figure, almost lost to the world." Soon after Blanche Marchesi had taken her mother to live with her in London, and for a few months it would have been easy for Melba, if she had wished, to visit Madame; but the thought of seeing her Little Mother bereft of her wits was too much. Melba had left for America without saying goodbye. How painfully she now regretted her failure to call on the one person who, she ardently believed, had shaped her fame. Feebly excusing herself to Blanche, she wrote, "I *could not*, it upset me to know the wonderful brain had gone. You understand I know."

Nor was this the only death that shook her. In the new year of 1914 Melba awoke one morning in her railcar to hear the news that Nordica, returning from an unsuccessful tour of Australia, had been shipwrecked on a coral reef in the Torres Strait, far to the north of Mackay. Melba seems to have believed that Nordica was dead, though in fact the poor woman was to linger in tropical hospitals for another three months. Remembering their times together, Melba at once fell into a paroxysm of weeping and remained so distraught that her manager feared that the evening performance would be impaired.

Then in Chattanooga in February 1914—by which time she had traveled more than 25,000 miles and sung nearly 50 performances—she opened a letter telling her that her father's health was failing. Warned by those other deaths, she did not hesitate to make her decision. She cabled Powell to cancel all engagements after the first week in June, telling him that she would then be sailing to Australia. "Something tells me to go," she wrote to Beryl Fanning.

There were many engagements, however, to be fulfilled before June. A month after hearing of her father's frailty, Melba arrived in Boston to sing for her old acquaintance Henry Russell, now director of the

Boston Opera Company. Since their holiday together at Stresa, she and Henry had fallen out, and had just become reconciled through the good offices of Isabella Gardner.

Henry had boldly leased the Théâtre des Champs Élysées in Paris for a season by the Boston Opera the following May. Knowing the prestige Melba would bring to his company, he was delighted to secure her for the Paris season. Meanwhile he persuaded her to sing the role of Mimi at a matinee in Boston on March 7. Great was his dismay when she was too husky on the day of the performance even to attempt it. Ten days later, still ill, she boarded the *Mauretania* and sailed to England.

On June 6 Melba made her final appearance for the season at Covent Garden. Five days later she boarded the *Orsova* in Toulon, thanking heaven that she had already made firm plans to sail. A letter had just informed her that her father required an operation to remove a papiloma from his bladder. It was a serious matter for a man of eighty-five, and she prayed that she might arrive in Melbourne and find him still alive.

To Beryl Fanning she poured out her love and her fear. "I am very sad," she wrote, "because I can't bear to think of my dear old Father suffering and perhaps dying":

> He and I have always been more to each other than ordinary Father and daughter. I have always had a great admiration of him since I was tiny, and he realises it and understands although he is never demonstrative. When I think of what he has done with very little education, it is wonderful, besides that, he has never failed me and he has never said an unkind word to me in his life. So when I think of losing him, it is as though I were losing my life's mate.

CHAPTER TWENTY-TWO

The Queen of Pickpockets

DAVID MITCHELL survived his surgery, and by the time Melba's ship reached the west Australian coast he was making a good recovery. With a serene mind, Melba sang concerts for the miners and their wives on the Kalgoorlie goldfield, then sailed on to Adelaide, and took the train to Melbourne. As she alighted at Melbourne's Spencer Street station on July 26, 1914, she seemed years younger than on her previous visit; and seemed even younger when she found that George and Evie were so healthy and happy.

For a few days she visited her father and basked in the comfort of her own Coombe Cottage, and then the happy spell was broken. German troops invaded Belgium and France, and Britain and Russia declared war on Germany. Australia, as an integral part of the British Empire, followed Britain's lead, and news of Australia's declaration of war reached its citizens on the night of August 4. While Melba had unshakable confidence in the power of the empire, she was nonetheless filled with foreboding. She observed her young Australian friends and relatives enlisting in the army, and the first troopships sailing away, and wondered how many would return.

Although insulated by distance, Melba continued to feel the shock, the more so since France and Belgium were so dear to her. The speed of the German army's advance toward Paris alarmed her, but, knowing it was essential to maintain national morale, she put on a brave face and demanded it of others. When the British defeated the Germans in a naval battle at the Falkland Islands in December, she ordered her chauffeur to drive her around to the larger Melbourne stores and offices. Once inside she demanded to see the manager and, once in his presence, she graciously but firmly instructed him to fly the Australian flag at once from his flagpole. Some businessmen may have privately resented her interference, but they all complied, and the press applauded her action.

There was other patriotic work to be done, raising funds for the Red Cross. In the second month of the war she arranged a concert at the Melbourne Auditorium, and its opening was inspired by one she had sung in at the Albert Hall just before Edward VII's canceled coronation. Then, while she and Clara Butt sang alternate verses of the national anthem, the audience had waved miniature Union Jacks. Now in Melbourne, the Australian contralto Maggie Stirling sang the anthem while Melba and spectators waved their flags and joined in the last verse. They also joined in *Rule Britannia* and the *Old Hundredth*, and listened intently while the distinguished British actress Ellen Terry, who was visiting Coombe Cottage, recited appropriate verses from Rudyard Kipling. Normally uncomfortable making speeches, Melba was discovering that words came easily when she had important sentiments to convey. In no time and without the slightest difficulty or hesitation, she roused the audience to a patriotic fervor.

This new face of Melba amazed the Australian public and press, but its origins were not hard to fathom. In obedience to Madame Marchesi's teaching, Melba had for years suppressed her ebullient nature when she came on stage. When critics complained that she seemed remote and cold, she would reply that a singer had always to watch what she was doing and hold something in reserve. Occasionally in front of American audiences she revealed glimpses of what a friend would describe as her "glorious rowdiness," but those glimpses were relatively few.

One English writer who described this seeming contradiction between Melba onstage and Melba offstage was Clemence Dane. Closely watching Melba and Caruso in *La Bohème*, Dane had defined Melba as a prima donna who impersonated a character solely by means of her voice. She had no alternative but to assume that Melba lacked the instincts of an actress.

A few years later, at a small dinner party at the Savoy, she realized her mistake as she watched the diva make a quietly dramatic entrance that could have upstaged Sarah Bernhardt. Swathed in a dress of scarlet gauze, Melba entered "all in one movement, as if on roller skates."

With a keen glance she surveyed the whole room, beamed at everyone, and from that moment "the party was a party." Throughout the dinner Clemence Dane observed that Melba's theatricality did not flag. When it was revealed that the chef had created a new dish in her honor, she began to clown "shamelessly and endearingly." When a few surrounding diners stared with slight disdain at her conspicuous delight, she flung her napkin over her head and mischievously begged her host to stop them from staring at her. Wrote Clemence Dane admiringly, "I have never seen anyone enjoy herself, nor make others enjoy themselves so much."

Now, in Melbourne, while pleading the cause of starving Belgian citizens and wounded Allied soldiers, Melba behaved as though she was again the focus of all eyes at the Savoy, and the audience loved her. "Patriotism and necessity bring forth many unexpected traits in a person's character as well as talents," commented *Melbourne Punch*, as it described the change in Melba's demeanor.

Melba spread her patriotic activities to other towns and cities. On September 26, 1914, she appeared at the Sydney Town Hall, pursuing a similar formula to the one in Melbourne but introducing one notable novelty. She produced the flags of the Allied nations and proceeded to auction them. Holding aloft a conspicuous Japanese flag, she exclaimed, "Such a lovely little flag," and spontaneously remarked that it matched the colors of her red, white, and blue dress. By a blend of jokes and cajoleries she trotted the price of the flag up to fifty-five guineas. Other flags were sold to enthusiastic bidders who caught the spirit of the evening.

On November 22 in the Adelaide Exhibition Building Melba and John Lemmoné walked among the audience, exchanging farthings— the smallest coin of the realm—for bank notes. She then brought out her flags; and when she flourished what she thought was the French flag—it turned out be the Russian—there was laughter. There was subdued amusement, too, when the flag of Australia initially fetched only fifteen pounds. To raise the price she exclaimed, "But it's where I was born, and is signed by me. Why, Germany would give more for it than that!" She was immediately offered twenty pounds. Her skill at extracting donations was earning her the nickname the "Queen of Pickpockets." She thought nothing of accosting prosperous-looking strangers and saying, "I am Melba, and I want you to promise to give me everything in your pocket-book before you look inside to see how much you have."

Although there were hopes that the war would be short, English and European opera and concert venues were curtailing their seasons or closing down: the theatre at Covent Garden was about to be turned into a government furniture repository. By the start of the new year, most of Melba's engagements for the following twelve months had been canceled. Nevertheless she decided to return to England in March in order to join Gladys de Grey in raising funds for the British Red Cross. She was about to set out when reports of German submarines in the Atlantic changed her mind. "I know I must die some time," she said, "but I don't want to die at the hands of the Germans."

Having decided to stay in Australia, she turned her mind to her singing pupils. So far her allegiance had been to the conservatorium attached to Melbourne University. During past visits she had raised money through concerts for the renewal of its building, and had graciously agreed to give her name to its handsome new concert hall. But old Professor Peterson was now dead, and his successor, Professor Marshall Hall, though her friend and admirer, did not inspire the same confidence, perhaps because he and his staff seemed less biddable. Instead she turned her eyes to Melbourne's second conservatorium, situated in a stone building on Albert Street, East Melbourne, and run by a young Englishman named Fritz Hart. A graduate of the Royal College of Music and friend and librettist of the composer Gustav Holst, Hart had the common sense to see that Melba must receive a free hand. He welcomed her warmly when she conducted her first class on April 15, 1915, and made no attempt to interfere.

Melba's fundraising auctions continued. On April 27 the stage of the Melbourne Town Hall was draped in patriotic colors, and Melba appeared leading an English bulldog, which was one of the mementos to be auctioned. Her first words, once the auctioning began, were cheerful but blunt: "I want a great deal of money from you." When she arrived at the Polish flag, she said, "I had a telegram from Paderewski whom you all know. He asked me to help his countrymen." When the price of the flag reached 160 pounds, Melba intervened. "I can't cable only that to Paderewski," she told them. And so the bidding rose to

200 pounds. Holding up the Belgian flag, she said, "This flag I hold in deepest reverence." When her father, sitting in the audience, led the bidding, she shouted out, "That's my Dad."

In later concerts wounded Australian soldiers who had just returned from Gallipoli or Flanders were among the spectators, and their khaki-clad figures lent an urgency to the proceedings. Melba's pianist also helped: he was Francis de Bourguignon, a former Belgian soldier who had been wounded while defending Antwerp. To Melba he was a god-send, being patient and sweet-natured as well as an excellent pianist. The governor's small daughter, who sometimes watched Melba practic-ing, reported that Melba would shout furiously at another accompanist named Carruthers but would never shout at Mr. de Bourguignon.

The disastrous Allied landing at Gallipoli in Turkey caused terrible casualties, five of Melba's relatives being listed among the dead. She told reporters that of twenty-two male guests at her birthday party in London in 1914, seven were now dead and seven wounded. Fearing that Belle's two sons—aged eighteen and twenty-one—would be killed, she uttered private prayers of thanks that George's poor health precluded him from becoming a soldier; but she dared not say so publicly when so many "brave lads have given their all for freedom." Sometimes her mood was fierce. "Oh, that I were a man," she once said, "and could go to the front and kill some Germans." In other moods she was depressed. To Beryl Fanning she confided: "*It is too horrible.* . . . I am beginning to wonder how any of us can go on living."

Perhaps it was the agony of reading the casualty lists that caused her to consider plans submitted by Charles Ellis for a tour of North America. Certainly she had become restless after almost a year in Aus-tralia, for her normal life was peripatetic and she fretted if she remained too long in one place. But much as she wanted to go, her conscience would not allow her to tour for seven months without helping the war effort. Her old friend Lord Richard Nevill, now chamberlain to the governor-general of Canada, eased her conscience by persuading the Canadian Red Cross to invite her to raise money for its projects. Hast-ily organizing an American concert party, she gathered the baritone Robert Parker, the cellist Beatrice Harrison, and the pianist Frank St. Leger—another wounded soldier—before sailing from Sydney to Ho-nolulu aboard the *Makura* late in July 1915.

After gloomy, wintry Melbourne, the lush tropicality of Honolulu was paradise. Being the first world-renowned artist to sing in the islands, she found herself lionized by local hostesses, and her two concerts at the Honolulu Opera House were sold out. From Honolulu she and her concert party sailed on to San Francisco where the the Panama Pacific Exposition was in full swing. Many of its visitors were admirers of Melba, and they found her new ability to relate to audiences a very pleasant surprise. She strode on stage, wrote one observer, as though she was bringing "a ray of sunshine with her" and in no time the audience was eating out of her hand.

In Pasadena, California, where she stayed in a bungalow on the grounds of the Maryland Hotel and sang in the Trinity Auditorium, the new Melba was hailed with delight. Onstage she was still queenly, but her coldness had given way to a radiating friendliness. Offstage her vivacious manner and energetic body language, especially her way of pirouetting on one heel, suggested a girl of twenty rather than an overweight matron of fifty-five.

Reviewers on the East Coast also noticed that Melba had been revitalized. In Boston a critic at Symphony Hall wrote, "Certainly no concert she has given in recent years has revealed such lovely singing." In Philadelphia at the Academy of Music another critic vowed, "It was Melba at her best and need more be said?" When she appeared with the Chicago Opera Company in *La Bohème* and *La Traviata*, hers was reportedly the youngest and purest voice on the stage.

Signs of age were of course detectable. Her top notes sometimes showed signs of wear, and her florid passages were not always crisp. In compensation her middle voice had acquired a sensuous richness, and her sustained singing was wonderfully controlled. She kept to her same old programs: the "mad scene" from *Hamlet*, "Addio" from *La Bohème*, and a brace of French and English art songs that Landon Ronald had persuaded her to learn, plus several more that he had written for her himself. But significantly she now included in her program two arias from Mozart's *The Marriage of Figaro*—"Voi, che sapete" and "Porgi amor"—which called for sustained singing in her middle range. According to the critics, it was this type of singing that now revealed her voice to best effect.

There were ample signs, too, of an enhanced dramatic sense, springing, one imagines, from her newfound ease with audiences. When the distinguished critic Olin Downes questioned Melba about her transformation, she snapped back: "There is a great deal of fiddle-faddle about dramatic interpretation in song . . . those who imply that the great singers of the past generation knew nothing about dramatic interpretation show how superficial their knowledge is." This did not prevent Downes from asserting that her sense of drama was "more striking today than ever before."

The flaw in this personal idyll was the war. Allied losses on the battlefield and at sea continued to be horrendous, and the neutrality of the United States enraged her. She agonized over the safety of her soldier friends and relatives, and fussed when she opened their letters and found strips cut away by the censor's scissors. She felt uneasiness, too, when she gave concerts with the Boston Symphony Orchestra, whose conductor, Karl Muck, was an old friend but a German citizen. Having heard of Melba's militant patriotism, Muck and his wife must have expected a touch of coldness when she arrived, but her personal loyalty to an old friend prevailed. Melba described their reunion to an Australian correspondent: "Can you imagine what I felt?—we had a long talk—they are very broad minded and said they hoped it would not make any difference to our friendship—*we all wept.*"

It was a relief to reach Canada, for here—as in Australia—the war was the focus of all talk and the arbiter of so many private and public plans. The first of her Red Cross concerts was in Toronto's Massey Hall in October 1915. A fanfare of bagpipes played by kilted Highlanders introduced the national anthem and, as Melba sang it, four thousand flags were vigorously unfurled. The effect, visually and emotionally, was stupendous. Dressed in a cerise silk gown festooned with diamonds, with a miniature ruby and sapphire and diamond Union Jack pinned to her breast, Melba looked like a modern-day Britannia.

Two weeks later the patriotic scene was replicated at the Arena in Montreal, after which Melba briefly crossed into the United States to resume her concert tour. She had parted with her baritone and cellist but was about to be reunited with Ada Sassoli and Edmund Burke, who was now a soldier in the Canadian army. On December 22 she, Ada, and Edmund performed for the Red Cross in Ottawa's Russell Theatre, with a detachment of boy scouts distributing flags.

Melba celebrated Christmas at the governor-general's residence in Ottawa with Ada and Edmund as her fellow guests. Here she received an unexpected Christmas present that sent her patriotic spirits soaring. The British government and the king and queen had heard reports of her spectacular fundraising and had decided to bestow on her the title of Lady of Grace of the Order of the Hospital of St. John of Jerusalem. The governor-general, deputizing for King George V, performed the official ceremony. Later in the United States Melba was amused to be asked if the king of Jerusalem had given her the title in person.

In the new year of 1916 Melba traveled to San Francisco to join George and Evie. They had come from Australia to visit Charlie Armstrong, who had bought a tract of forest fronting beautiful Lake Shawnigan on Vancouver Island, off Canada's west coast. Here in a cottage of cedar shingles that could only be reached by water, Charlie lived an independent life with his horses, cows, and cats. Such was the trust he inspired in his animals that his cats would swim out to greet his boat when he returned home from excursions across the lake. The isolated beauty of his home and the self-sufficiency of his lifestyle brought him deep contentment. It was Evie's first meeting with her father-in-law, and she found him a charming and lovable man.

Melba expressed no desire to see her former husband. At the same time there were signs in both herself and Charlie that the old enmity was fading. With George, who loved both his parents, doing his best to reconcile them, it could scarcely have been otherwise, and Melba, for her boy's sake, allowed past quarrels to rest. Certainly Melba understood George's need to see his father and even encouraged it. When, a few years later, George proposed inviting Charlie to stay at Coombe Cottage during one of Melba's absences, she readily gave her consent.

On March 8, 1916, after more concerts in California, Melba embarked for Honolulu. No sooner was she on shipboard than she was handed a cablegram. Its brief message informed her that David Mitchell again required bladder surgery. For a few agonizing days she waited for more news, fearful that his eighty-seven-year-old body would be unable to survive the ordeal. Her fears proved well founded. A second cablegram reached the ship as it neared Suva. It reported that her father had died on March 25. Melba's grief was insupportable: "My *heart broke*," she wrote, "*I lost my all.*"

Her brother Ernest and her sister Annie met her ship as it berthed in Sydney, and back in Melbourne she tried to offset her grief with work. She started teaching her singing pupils the day after her arrival, and at Coombe Cottage she set about building a swimming pool surrounded by classical columns, which she called her Roman bath. Her energetic fundraising was resumed; and she also campaigned for a "yes" vote in a national referendum aiming to compulsorily enlist men into the Australian army, which had previously contained only volunteers. It was not that she wished to see soldiers going to their deaths; rather she believed that "win we *must.*" For her vigorous political campaigning she received a letter of thanks from the Australian prime minister, Billy Hughes, who later visted her at Coombe Cottage.

What cheered her most in these grief-filled days were two new friends. One was a Melbourne doctor's daughter named Ruby Gray, an aspiring singer who later taught at the Albert Street Conservatorium. The other was Ruby's young cousin, a quiet, bespectacled clerk in the shipping office of the Dalgety pastoral company. Tommy Cochrane adored music, antiques, gossip, and Melba, and was always ready for an amusing outing. Melba found him an ideal companion, and joked with him, bossed him, and confided in him, believing no one would suspect scandal as he was homosexual. Not that she could ever feel entirely safe from scandal, because Norton's libels continued to pursue her. Whenever she was forced to cancel a concert, rumor would claim that she was drunk. How people could continue to believe that a singer so hardworking and self-disciplined was an alcoholic was beyond her understanding.

An attack of influenza in August dragged Melba down, and a holiday at the seaside did not help her. Remembering the restorative warmth of the tropics, she booked a passage on the *Niagara* to Honolulu, but was careful to obtain a return ticket for the following March, for she had just received the thrilling news that Evie was pregnant. If all went well Melba would be a grandmother in March. Overjoyed at the prospect, she was already making plans for the baby's arrival.

At a Nonsense Party to bid farewell to her class at the conservatorium, her high spirits had free rein. She organized silly games, which she joined in as boisterously as any of the students. One involved tossing a gas-filled balloon into a basket, another creating a hat from a pile of odds and ends. At the end of the game, the participants paraded their hats, with Melba in the lead. She wore an inverted wastepaper basket crowned by parsley, with carrots and radishes dangling from the sides. To round off the happy evening, she made a lighthearted speech that hinted at her attitude to setbacks. She told her girls that they must be positive, and when troubles came they should indulge in bits of nonsense to keep their spirits high.

Melba took her young niece, Nellie Patterson, with her to Honolulu, inviting Ruby Gray from Melbourne and Susan FitzClarence from England to join them. She grieved for Susan because her soldier husband had been killed a year earlier, and her baby had died soon afterward. Melba believed it was her maternal duty to cheer the dear girl up, and saw America as just the place for jollity.

In her Hawaiian bungalow beside the beach, Melba's life was idyllic. She bathed in the sea at least once a day in a "rather indecent bathing suit" and went every morning to the market to buy the ingredients for her Chinese cook. "Oh! Tommy, life is so easy here," she wrote to Tommy Cochrane, "it is so wonderful that I am wondering if I shall ever return to Australia."

By January 1917, however, she was less in love with Honolulu and was complaining that the local ladies played bridge as if there were no rules. She was eager now to move on to San Francisco, where she was to meet Susan FitzClarence. By mid-February she, Susan, and Ruby Gray were installed at the luxurious Raymond Hotel in Pasadena, where they found no flies or mosquitoes and everything was perfect. Even the clothes Melba bought off the rack were perfect; Melba told Tommy Cochrane that she wanted to buy them all.

The happy reunion was enlivened when the three women met their film idols, Douglas Fairbanks, Mary Pickford, and Charlie Chaplin. They met Chaplin on March 11 on the studio set where he was creating a picture called *The Cure*. Having expected someone grotesque, Melba was surprised to shake hands with a handsome young man whose voice recalled that of an English public schoolboy and whose teeth were the most beautiful she had ever seen. Just for fun, she played a scene with him in front of the cameras, slapping his face and chasing him round the room. Jokingly he offered her a part in his next film. Seriously he informed her that she was lucky to be an opera singer and not an actor, and to have the chance to play a full gamut of emotions. He added, "I would give my soul to play Hamlet."

That night Chaplin joined Melba and her friends for dinner at the Raymond Hotel. For several hours he was the urbane host, eating *Terrapin à la Maryland* and recounting his experiences in American vaudeville. But when the waiter brought the bill he turned himself instantly into Charlie the comedian. Pretending to have no money, he displayed his empty wallet, then plunged his hands into his seemingly empty pockets. When his hands reappeared they clutched silver dollars, which he scattered across the room.

Melba gave concerts in Los Angeles, San Diego, and Santa Barbara. To the delight of bystanders at the San Diego Exposition, she gave an impromptu performance of Verdi's "Ave Maria," playing her own accompaniment on Dr. Spreckel's "extraordinary outdoor organ." But as the days passed she began to fret because it was almost time for the arrival of Evie's baby. She had long since abandoned her notion of returning to Melbourne for the birth, preferring to return when she could safely hold her grandchild in her arms. As the anniversary of her father's death approached, she hoped the baby would be born that day.

Just over a week later the tide of war began to turn, for the United States entered the war against Germany. Melba celebrated with an enormous concert for the Red Cross in San Francisco. The city had never forgotten her dramatic performance of the "Star-Spangled Banner" when America had declared war on Spain, and ten thousand loyal fans flocked to the auditorium to hear her. Thirty hospital nurses stood behind Melba onstage, waving the Stars and Stripes, and when Melba called for three cheers for the new allies, the crowd "went mad." Toward the end of the concert Melba said she needed more money, and for five minutes coins rained on the stage until she had almost a thousand dollars at her feet. The players in the orchestra had to cover their heads against the shower of dollars, and an enthusiastic old man later told Melba he had seen nothing like it since the California gold rush. What moved Melba most was a voice from the audience shouting out, "What Ho, Lilydale." Melba shouted back, "What Ho, Lilydale," adding for those who could hear her, "where my dear old Daddy used to be."

Her public triumph was followed by tragedy. The long-expected cablegram arrived from Coombe Cottage, but it informed her that her grandchild had died at birth and that Evie herself had been close to death. George met Melba at the wharf in Sydney at the end of April and escorted her back to Melbourne.

Susan FitzClarence, sensitive and affectionate, accompanied Melba home, and her presence cheered the dismal household at Coombe Cottage. A keen rider, Susan went regularly with George to the local hunt club. She also helped Melba with bazaars and knitting parties for the local Red Cross. Most of all she tried to help Evie, because, having lost a baby of her own, she could guess what Evie was suffering.

On July 24 Susan joined one of Melba's fundraising concerts, playing a scene from *The School for Scandal* with the visiting British comedian Cyril Maude, and afterward watching with amusement as Melba replicated the San Francisco concert by calling for a shower of coins on stage. Remembering the danger to her head as the coins rained down in San Francisco, Melba came prepared with an umbrella, and put it up when the money started to fall. Through such concerts in her homeland she raised nearly ninety thousand pounds for war charities. The largeness of the sum did not surprise her friends. For most of her career Melba had been giving generously to charity, either by singing without payment at fundraising performances or by directly donating money. "I will never accept a penny for any work I do on British soil," she told reporters, "as long as this war lasts."

Melba and Susan sailed for North America at the end of September 1917. Melba had agreed to sing eighteen performances of *Faust* and *La Bohème* while touring with the Chicago Opera Company, of which her old colleague Cleofonte Campanini was now director. He had also engaged the fine French tenor Lucien Muratore, and an Italian soprano named Amelita Galli Curci, vivacious, pretty, and twenty years Melba's junior, with an exquisite natural voice and a repertoire like Melba's own. In a few years Galli Curci's poor technique would ruin her career, but for the moment her star was high. Undaunted by Melba's freezing manner, she flaunted around the company train with a self-importance that set Melba's teeth on edge. From time to time Melba would mutter to her companions, "Don't look at that woman."

Melba's performances during the tour remained excellent, but a string of accidents so disturbed her that she began to wonder if German spies were trying to kill her. The first accident occurred while she was singing *Faust* at Fort Worth. During the vision scene, as she sat at Marguerite's spinning wheel, a heavy row of lights crashed down on her. "I was unconscious for 15 minutes," she wrote to Tommy Cochrane, "my left leg lacerated and bruised from thigh to toes, my left wrist broken and bruised—I remember nothing—but, God! how I have suffered since." When she awoke onstage she found Campanini bending over her and shouting, "Madame, please try to sing; you must sing; there is $17,000 in the house." Melba is said to have replied, "Oh, damn the $17,000. I think my back is broken." After medical help and a brief rest, she resumed her performance and did not miss a night thereafter, though she was sometimes in pain and wore heavy bandages beneath her costume.

A few days later in St. Louis, she and Susan FitzClarence were being driven to a dinner party when their car collided with another. Neither Melba nor Susan was physically hurt, but they suffered from shock. In yet another accident just outside Dayton, Ohio, the locomotive of their train ran off the rails and hit a telegraph pole. Melba was uninjured and managed to sing the next day, but she felt far from herself. A reporter noticed that her faithful dresser—known simply as Fastnidge—fussed over her "like an anxious mother hen," brewing her tea in her traveling silver kettle and wrapping a shawl around her shoulders as she left the stage.

In a fourth accident outside Chicago, Melba's personal railcar broke away from the main train and raced down the track. "Anything might have happened then as hundreds of trains were going everyway," she wrote to Tommy Cochran. Luckily the brakeman managed to leap off the train and hold up the red light until help came. To cap her ill luck, a bomb exploded near her box during a performance of *Dinorah* in Chicago. The explosion was slight, causing little damage, but Melba's nerves were blown to pieces. She wrote to George and Evie that her mind was full of presentiments of death. "My Beloveds," she wrote urgently, "Do come to see me as soon as you can. I don't want to die alone—I can't write any more—I am too full of emotion. God bless you both, Mother."

At almost the same time she received news that Gladys de Grey had died. It was half-expected, for Gladys had been wretchedly ill for months and no friend would have wished to prolong her suffering, but it did not mean that Melba did not mourn her. Under the burden of all these shakings and sorrows, she found herself developing a slight impediment in her speech. "The doctors think it will go away in time," she wrote to Tommy. "Promise not to laugh if it continues."

For three difficult weeks in February 1918, Melba sang with the Chicago Opera at New York's Lexington Theatre, keeping her symptoms of anxiety hidden from the public. Meanwhile she began preparations for her concert tour of the Pacific seaboard. She had engaged a concert party to join her from Australia consisting of Frank St. Leger, Francis de Bourguignon, and a newcomer named Stella Power, a former pupil from the Albert Street Conservatorium. Over the years Melba had auditioned numerous aspiring singers, always hoping to find a truly promising voice that she could train in the way that her teachers had trained her. A few protégées had raised her hopes, especially Elizabeth Parkina, but poor Parkina had died of throat cancer and the others were receding into obscurity. Melba's hopes now hinged on pretty, dark-haired Stella, whose voice and vocal mannerisms were so much like Melba's own that she was being called the "little Melba." While Stella's voice held promise, she lacked Melba's drive and suffered from pre-performance nerves. As a critic once remarked, the pupils Melba believed to be swans usually turned out to be geese, and Stella was no exception.

Thanks to the absence of further alarms, Melba had recovered sufficiently by early March to set out in the "Manhattan," the private train that Ellis had hired to convey her and her musicians through Washington, Oregon, and California. They appeared before packed audiences, for Melba's ritual of unfurling the American flag made attendance at her concerts almost a test of patriotism. In Seattle they attracted an audience of three thousand in what one critic called "the greatest musical assemblage in the history of the North West"; and at Camp Lewis, near Tacoma, Washington, they were said to have played to twenty thousand cheering soldiers seated in the open air.

When the train pulled into the mountain town of Walla Walla, Washington, on March 13, the audience was smaller and homelier, but the patriotic spirit burned just as brightly. Nearly all the women had brought their wartime knitting, and as one woman rose for the "Star-Spangled Banner," Melba noticed that the sweater dangling from her needles almost touched the floor. In this rather shabby, rural audience, Melba in her black and gold evening dress and jewels was said to be "as sparkling and exotic as a bird of the tropics" among a flock of homely pigeons.

Two days later, while the train was parked between Walla Walla and Spokane, Susan FitzClarence ran to Melba's side, excitedly flourishing a newspaper. Unknown to herself, Melba had been created a Dame of the British Empire, a new honor instituted by King George V to reward citizens of the empire for outstanding war work. Knowing that it was customary to gain a recipient's consent before publicly bestowing an honor, Melba had momentary doubts whether the announcement was true, but they were quickly dispelled when a cable arrived from the Australian prime minister. For a loyal daughter of the empire such as Melba, there could have been no higher reward, and the surprise only added to the pleasure. She is reputed to have danced around the railway carriage quite naked, singing "I'm a Dame, I'm a Dame."

When the train reached Pasadena in April, Melba's speech impediment was no better and she showed signs of general exhaustion. Her symptoms caused sufficient concern for her secretary Freda Sternberg to book her *incognito* into a private sanatorium. Later she moved to a private house near the sea at Santa Barbara, where fluent speech and physical vigor at last returned to her. But as her strength returned, her restless energy reasserted itself. In no time she had surrounded herself with house guests. As well as Susan, there were Lady Colebrooke, Lord Dunn, and three soldiers recovering from their war wounds, and she was expecting Lord Richard Nevill to arrive for her fifty-seventh birthday. Moreover she was always getting into disputes over the war. One night she was obliged to reprove a man who said that the Germans had virtually won. "*We are not beaten yet,*" she proclaimed emphatically.

At the end of May 1918 Melba sailed for Australia. It was a moving homecoming, for she was now recognized without dispute as the most famous of all Australians and the person who had placed Australia on the cultural map. "Hearty cheers for Dame Melba," proclaimed *Melbourne Punch*. Melba responded more prosaically: "I want a real rest and to sleep in my own house in Lilydale. I want to dig vegetables in my garden, and to have the 'homey' feeling which, after all, is the best thing in the world."

The vegetables had to wait, for she threw herself into her patriotic concerts and her singing classes. She had ordered uniforms for her pupils. These were rather shapeless white gabardine coat-frocks with a badge in the form of a red letter M sewn to the left breast, to be worn with white cotton stockings and white canvas shoes: the girls regarded them as very dowdy. The pupils in their uniforms nevertheless attracted the eye of Lady Stanley, the governor's wife, who, being the granddaughter of an opera singer, understood singing and began attending Melba's classes. Melba was soon a house guest at Government House, even confiding to her hostess the details of what was, almost certainly, her love affair with Philippe. While Lady Stanley was openmouthed to hear these confidences, she became irritated when Melba became flirtatious and "beady-eyed" the moment a handsome man appeared. She committed "the mistake of thinking 'noise' makes a thing go," added Lady Stanley. "However, I forgive her for she sang the whole of Sunday morning" and the "finish and quality of her singing always strikes one anew."

Melba's preoccupation during these months was Evie's second pregnancy, which the doctors warned could be risky. If "anything happened to my beloved Evie," she told George, "I don't know what I should do." Knowing she must do all in her power to help, she was determined to be at Coombe Cottage for the birth, but also knowing her own faults, she promised to repress her urge to be in charge. "I shall not interfere," she reassured her son, "and only try and help you." The weeks dragged by, with Melba and George increasingly anxious, until on September 12, "against all odds" the baby was safely born.

The child was named Pamela Helen Fullerton Armstrong, and an overjoyed Melba set about organizing the christening, which was held in the music room at Coombe Cottage. John Lemmoné played his flute, Melba sang "Oh for the Wings of a Dove," and her singing pupils provided the choir. Lady Stanley and Lady Susan FitzClarence were the godmothers, and the governor-general and Lord Richard Nevill were the godfathers. A few days earlier the war had ended. With her beloved daughter-in-law well, her precious granddaughter safely in her arms, and her own country victorious, Melba had little left to desire.

Soon after the christening, Melba received a summons from King George V to reopen Covent Garden the following May. Eager to be back in her old operatic life, she gave a few hasty farewell concerts and prepared to return to England via America. In Sydney, waiting for the *Niagara* to sail on January 22, 1919, she heard the "alarming and unthinkable" news that her favorite John Lemmoné, on whom she relied so heavily, had had a stroke. Realizing he would need money, Melba gave a benefit concert for him, but remembering his pride she knew he would probably refuse what might be seen as charity. To make the gift more palatable, she placed the check at the bottom of a loving cup, which she filled with plums. On the outside she wrote, "Put in your thumb, and pull out a plum and see what your friends have sent you." To her relief, he showed good signs of recovery, so she sailed across the Pacific with an easier mind.

CHAPTER TWENTY-THREE

Singing to the Ghosts

AFTER AN ABSENCE of almost five years, Melba reached London on St. Patrick's Day in 1919. Her long-anticipated return gave her pain as well as joy. The number of her friends in the lists of the dead was higher than she had feared. Of those twenty-two men who had attended her birthday party in 1914, sixteen were dead, and nearly all of those who died were casualties of war. Fortunately she was deluged with messages and invitations, some from the royal family, all declaring how happy the senders were to have her back. "Oh Beryl," she wrote to Beryl Fanning, "it is *good* to be back, I am so *very* happy."

One old friend whom she longed to meet again was Philippe, Duke of Orléans. As she confessed to Lady Stanley, he was still "the one rock in her life." Although they probably had not met for about a quarter of a century, Melba seems to have had news of him—and maybe messages from him—through her old friend Boni de Castellane and through Philippe's nephew, the exiled King Manuel of Portugal, who now lived in England. She knew that Philippe's marriage had been childless and mostly unhappy and had ended in separation, and that his wife was now dead. With a surprising forthrightness, given their years apart, she telegraphed his house on the outskirts of London: "I am going to stay Hotel Ritz from tomorrow till Friday. Can I see you?"

They met at the Ritz on the evening of March 24. "My dear Nellie," he wrote a few hours after their meeting, "what can I tell you of the tender emotion that I have felt again after so many years?" He was filled with happiness to find her the "*same Nellie*" to whom his "soul and heart" had never ceased to reach out, and the same "constant and faithful friend" who knew and understood him. He was counting the minutes till the following evening when they were to meet again. "I do hope you will give me time to tell you all that I have in my heart," he wrote beseechingly; and he signed himself, "Always your old Tipon." Did they continue to see each other? It seems likely.

Melba's apartment in Paris had been turned into a military hospital during the war, and rather than return to it she decided to rent a home in London. In April she moved into 22 Old Queen Street, a white-stucco and red-brick house in Westminster that she had often visited in prewar years. Its owner and past occupant was the banker Frankie Schuster, homosexual and very rich, whose passion "to create artistic history" by giving generously to the art of music earned him the friend-ship of Elgar and Fauré, and of many celebrated singers. He had long admired Melba, whom he first met through Lady de Grey.

Schuster's house was a showpiece, and Melba exulted in the exqui-site furniture and pictures that he had left behind for her use. The mas-sive front door decorated by a brass lion led to a paved courtyard, which in turn gave entry to a vast music room running almost the length of the ground floor. Upstairs a library and drawing room looked on to St. James's Park, and on the floor above were ample bedrooms for George, Evie, and Pamela, who were to reach England in a few weeks' time.

Melba was to sing Mimi on May 12, 1919, the first performance to be held at Covent Garden since before the war. The theatre was not as she remembered it. The new artistic director was the powerful young conduc-tor Sir Thomas Beecham, who had inherited vast wealth from his father's patent-medicine empire and had formed his own opera company during the war. Beecham and Melba clashed from the start, for she considered him a bumptious tyrant and he dismissed her as an arrogant prima don-na who lacked "spiritual refinement"; although he did admit that when Melba was in the cast, "she made everyone on stage behave well." One of the first disputes between these two autocrats centered on Melba's Covent Garden dressing room, which she had long since come to regard as virtually her private property. When she stormed into Beecham's of-fice objecting to the shade of green it had been painted, she realized she had met her match, though he eventually offered to alter the color. She sensed he was a new broom, determined to sweep away all that she stood for at Covent Garden. It made her furious; it also made her sad.

To her delight, her opening night was graced by many of the old faces, including those of the king and queen. Excitement swept across the house as she came on stage; and when her voice floated into the auditorium as "pure and liquid as of old," a sigh went around the audience, for here at least was something that had barely changed in the swiftly changing world. Melba, however, could scarcely see the stage for her tears. She felt she was singing to ghosts. "Lady de Grey had gone," she wrote, "Alfred de Rothschild had gone, and so many others, all gone; and yet I felt them there, I seemed in my imagination to see their faces again, looking out from the shadows in their boxes, and it was for them rather than this great audience that I sang." Nor was the great audience what it once had been. Among the tailcoats and evening dresses she noted a sprinkling of shabby tweed coats.

One week later, on her fifty-eighth birthday, Melba visited the Guildhall School of Music. Landon Ronald, with vivid memories of her stage fright five years earlier, expected her to make no speech. He was therefore taken aback when she jumped to her feet and spoke fluently with no sign of anxiety. As he observed, "her whole attitude on this point had changed."

The entire summer was studded with other professional engagements, beginning with her concert at the Albert Hall for some eight thousand people. Over June and July Melba contributed her voice, presence, or patronage to a string of fundraising events for children's charities, from the prime minister's house on Downing Street to the People's Palace in the impoverished East End. One notable fundraiser took place at the Children's Salon in the Connaught Rooms where poor children joined rich children for an annual party. Melba radiated pride when she saw Pamela Armstrong, aged eight months, among the rich children.

Her personal diary, too, was crowded with social events, the most arresting—in retrospect—the wedding of Violet Keppel and Denys Trefusis. To the congregation's surprise, Melba appeared from a side chapel and sang "Ave Maria" from *Otello*. Probably the most fashionable wedding of the season, it was one of the least likely to succeed, for the bride was pining for Vita Sackville-West, and the marriage was never consummated.

Melba sang at the wedding as a favor to the Keppels, but her attendance at the lawn tennis championships at Wimbledon was for her own pleasure. Her nephew Gerald Patterson, a winner of the Military Cross in the recent war, was one of the contestants, and to Melba's satisfaction he proved himself a Melba of the courts, defeating all opponents to become tennis champion of England. Melba, usually so conscious of her status, was delighted when the king asked if she were related to Gerald Patterson, rather than the other way round. Indeed she was so proud of him that she financed his return to Wimbledon the following year, when he "played magnificently" but lost.

In the autumn Melba began a demanding concert tour of the Midlands and the North with Frank St. Leger; the celebrated pianist Busoni; and Thomas Burke, a young tenor from Lancashire who had been singing with her at Covent Garden. Melba's warm platform manner was widely praised, as was her choice of songs, for she understood the grief of many of her listeners. "Audiences cry very much more today," she observed to a reporter, adding that her fan mail contained many requests for her to sing "Goodbye." In the course of her twenty concerts, "every hall was filled to suffocation," and she could not help noticing that her old rival Tetrazzini, also making a concert tour, was attracting few people. "Tetrazzini has had to cancel two concerts and the others were bad (*great fun*)," Melba wrote to Evie with glee.

Maintaining a pace that would have done credit to a woman of thirty, Melba's vigor surprised the rising generation. Reporters who interviewed her could scarcely believe her age. In response to their praise, Melba gave the triumphant reply, "Yes, I am rather a wonder," and volunteered the morsel of news that her blood pressure equaled that of a girl of fifteen. She was, however, riding toward a fall. In January 1920 she became seriously ill, first with influenza and then with what she described as "a haemorrhage of the intestines." For a time she feared cancer, but the illness was eventually diagnosed as colitis. Seeking to recover her health in Monte Carlo, she was struck by further mishaps. The young Armstrongs, traveling with her, had scarcely arrived when Melba's gold purse was stolen, along with Evie's money and George's passport.

Then Melba received a letter from the chairman of the Covent Garden Syndicate, Henry Higgins, breaking the news that Thomas Beecham was rejecting her services for the forthcoming season. This would have aroused her anger at any time, but in her frail state of health she was trebly indignant. Writing to Evie who had returned to London, she expressed her wrath at Beecham's conduct: "I don't suppose I shall get a word of thanks for all I have done for 31 years—just the order of the boot. I am most indignant and don't quite know what to do. But I think I shall tell the King."

Having traveled to Paris, Melba retired to bed at the Ritz with a heavy cold and a swollen face. Her once magnificent teeth were failing her, and she was obliged to have several extractions. "I am always in bed," she complained, though she admitted that the doctors prophesied a return to health once her teeth were extracted. To some extent they were correct. She was well enough to perform at the Albert Hall on May 2, 1920, with the rising Chilean pianist Claudio Arrau, and had enough stamina to celebrate her fifty-ninth birthday at Old Queen Street. The green-paneled music room glowed with candles and yellow lilies, royalty was present, and nineteen-year-old Jascha Heifetz played his violin. Two weeks earlier at his London debut, Melba had leaped from her seat in the stalls to present him with a laurel wreath. Now she made him her protégé, finding engagements for him among her rich friends.

Melba realized that her health was declining and that she should rest, but her restless energy dictated otherwise. For the first time since her pneumonia in 1904, her body felt mortal, and—perhaps even more frightening—her voice felt mortal too, for the body is the singer's instrument. A singer needs firm muscles, strong lungs, and abundant energy, but Melba knew her muscles, lungs, and energy could no longer reliably meet the commands of her will. On the edge of that abyss into which all great singers dread falling, she knew she was facing a situation that terrified her. There was a frenetic edge to her activity as she sought to overcome her fears.

Poor health was harming her financially as well as psychologically, for it was doubtful whether she could maintain her current lifestyle without high earnings. Moreover the tax officials seemed more predatory each year, at least in her eyes. "It will probably be my last season in London," she told Evie, "for I shall never be able to afford to live as I have always lived so I intend to have a jolly good one for the last and then exit Melba."

She was as good as her word. A concert at the Albert Hall was followed by numerous charity performances and a cluster of glamorous social engagements, including Susan FitzClarence's marriage to Major

Wyndham Birch. There were also the London launchings of two of her Melbourne students, Dorothy Murdoch and Stella Power. But newly married Stella earned Melba's displeasure by becoming pregnant just before her Albert Hall debut. In Melba's book of unbreakable laws— and there were many—singers did not become pregnant at this stage in their career.

The professional highlight of the season was undoubtedly a radio broadcast from the recently opened Marconi Company offices at Chelmsford. The first radio concert ever held, it was sponsored by the *Daily Mail*, and—thanks to the wave of advance publicity—was heard by a small circle of listeners as far away as Stockholm, Madrid, Warsaw, Paris, Rome, and even on ships in seas as far away as Malta. The signal began at ten minutes past seven on the evening of June 15, 1920, followed by the sound of a voice saying "Hello Hello." Then the famous Melba trill burst upon the airwaves: it was her version, wrote the *Daily Mail*, of calling aloud, "Are you there?"

Promptly at 7:15 p.m., "the words of 'Home Sweet Home' fitted to the familiar melody swam into the receivers." There followed "Addio" from *La Bohème* and two songs by Bemberg, which the composer came from Paris especially to accompany. It was reported that the "songs came mellow and perfect, without scratch or jar," but those listening to this novelty in faraway cities probably heard a dozen scratches and bursts of static. Watching in the bare, stone studio, George and Evie and a handful of guests realized they were witnessing history being made.

In July Melba traveled to Paris with her nephew Gerald Patterson and gave a "divine" lunch, at which her guests were the film stars Mary Pickford and Douglas Fairbanks, the Boston pianist George Copeland, and Wimbledon women's tennis champion Suzanne Lenglen. Suzanne "is in love with Gerald," Melba confided to a friend, but "this is *entre nous*." In Paris, Melba also met the Norwegian ambassador, Baron Wedel Jarlsberg, and decided to accompany him and his wife to Hvalstad, near Christiana, where in their palatial house surrounded by gardens and orchards and sea she regained her peace of mind. "Charming people," she wrote to Evie, and "everything beautifully done." The king of Norway and his English-born queen came to dine and dance, and Melba found herself offering to sing at a charity concert held for the relatives of dead Norwegian seamen. The National Theatre in Christiana was filled to overflowing and the the king and queen of Norway and Prince George of England stood, and clapped and cheered.

Melba, still expending more energy than she could sustain, returned to London with a heavy cold and weariness of mind and body. She had relinquished her house on Old Queen Street, and rather than share the Armstrongs' house at Brompton Square, she took to her bed in the Ladies' Athenaeum Club on Dover Street. Earlier, in one of her buoyant moods, she had contracted to sing a series of concerts through England and Scotland. Now she would have preferred to abandon the concerts. "My nerves," she told her family, "are in a terrible state." Bowing to necessity, she set out in November with a concert party that would include at various times the Australian pianist Una Bourne, the viola player Lionel Tertis, and the distinguished Algerian-born French baritone Dinh Gilly.

The main source of her anxiety was Evie, who was pregnant again and near to her time. Remembering her previous confinements, Melba and George awaited the birth with trepidation. On November 20, 1920, while Melba was singing in Edinburgh, news came that her grandson was born. He weighed nine pounds, two ounces, had fair hair and blue eyes, and was named Frederick. He lived less than twenty-four hours. "God! what a tragedy," she wrote to Tommy Cochrane. "If you could see Evie's heart-broken eyes you would cry like a baby." To another friend she wrote, "I can't cry because I can't console Evie. I don't know what to do for her. . . . Oh God, why should we have to suffer like this?"

In the new year Evie was well enough to accompany Melba to the Riviera and then to Brussels, where Melba was to sing two acts of *Faust* at a charity matinee at the Monnaie. A sentimental pilgrimage, it attracted a surprising number of those operagoers who remembered her Gilda in 1887. Afterward they crowded about her, reminiscing and shaking her hand. "How the whole bright past swam before my dazzled eyes," wrote Melba, remembering with emotion the circumstances of her debut.

Tired by her travels, Melba should have rested for a time in London, but she was now full of plans to visit Australia. On May 8, 1921, she held her *au revoir* matinee concert at the Albert Hall, which was filled to overflowing. The two celebrated Australian aviators Sir Ross and Sir Keith Smith sat in the boxes, as did the Australian cricket team, and the Australian cry of "coo-ee" resounded around the theatre when Melba appeared onstage. Afterward she proudly presented two-year-old Pamela to their Majesties—joking as she made the presentation that it was "not for keeps!" "Melba is a great ambassadress. When she sings we hear the voice of the Empire," pronounced one London paper. In Melba's view, the reviewer could not have paid her a higher compliment.

Before she could leave for Australia, two deaths disturbed her. The first was that of Haddon Chambers. Although he had freed himself from Melba's spell by marrying the actress Pepita Bobadilla, some of his affection possibly remained, for his chosen place of burial was Marlow, close to those houses where he and Melba had spent their summers. The second death was that of forty-eight-year-old Robin Grey, so maimed by war that he was only a shadow of the soldier and musician who had traveled with her to Stresa over a decade before. His death was possibly the more immediately distressing because they had remained close friends. From his hospital bed he had written to her: "Dearest Nell, It's been hell, but I am getting better." The next day he died. At his funeral service in the Guards Chapel, Melba almost broke down. "I cannot realise," she wrote painfully, "that I will never see that beloved face again."

As she completed plans for her departure, much of the detail fell to her secretary, an English girl named Irene Gritten, usually known as Gritty. A naive twenty-two-year-old, Gritty had come to Melba in 1919 from the office of Melba's London manager, the impresario Lionel Powell. She had arrived at Old Queen Street in an ecstasy of hero-worship, but after two years in Melba's employ she knew that working for a diva was no bed of roses. Melba, like many of her English friends, regarded servants as almost her personal slaves, especially when, like Gritty, they were too young and unsure to withstand her demands. When upset by troubles of her own, Melba was not above venting her feelings on her servants, especially on those too timid to answer back. The conductor Adrian Boult recalled an incident in which Melba castigated her maid in a Paris railway station with a flow of colorful language that would have pleased her father's workmen. The maid was presumably Melba's faithful lady's-maid, Blow, on whom she depended so utterly that Blow was said to rule Melba with "a rod of iron." If the indispensable Miss

Blow could receive such treatment, then someone as shy and inexperienced as Gritty stood not a chance. On the other hand, Melba was capable of impulsive kindness, and her generous presents helped Gritty forget the lean days.

In 1921 Gritty's duties were so undefined that Melba had many chances to put upon her. In addition to dealing with her usual chores, the hard-pressed girl now found herself arranging shipping tickets and engaging a good-tempered butler to travel with Melba to Australia: the butler must be *"not too pompous,"* Melba warned her, and he must be prepared to work with women. Moreover since Melba did not want the expense of engaging a nurse for the voyage, Gritty was obliged to learn the abdominal massage that had been prescribed for Melba's colitis. The thought of pounding Melba's large stomach filled the girl with embarrassment, but Melba brushed such scruples aside.

Clutching a bunch of roses given her by her singing pupil Princess Mary, and farewelled by the "coo-ees" of Australian cricketers, Melba boarded the train for Liverpool on June 4. There she joined the *Megantic* bound for Canada, along with George, Evie, Pamela, and Susan FitzClarence's brother, Bernard Yorke. Gritty sailed too as part of Melba's entourage, and was thrilled to be taking an ocean voyage.

According to entries in Gritty's diary, she enjoyed the journey by ship and train as far as Vancouver, but after boarding the *Niagara* for the long voyage to Australia, her enthusiasm began to falter. Melba now seemed to be full of complaints. Objecting to the deck games because they prevented her from walking freely along the deck, she was in no way mollified when the captain advised her to walk instead around the funnel. She resented the loud dance music after dinner. Above all she objected to Gritty fraternizing freely with the other passengers. The mystique of a diva called for measured aloofness, which, in Melba's view, applied to her employees as well.

At times Gritty dared to defy her employer. In Honolulu she went ashore with a Mr. Charles Sperling and spent the day enjoying the sights. As they crossed the equator, the captain held a celebratory dance, and while Melba retired early to bed "to escape the music," Gritty and Mr. Sperling danced on deck in the moonlight. In Auckland she went ashore again with Mr. Sperling, and on the following day he proposed marriage. With her head in a whirl, Gritty refused him, largely because he was more than twenty years her senior. The next day, though the ship was rocking in a gale, he proposed again, and yet again the day after. When the ship steamed into Sydney Harbour on August 3, Mr. Sperling was still proposing, and a harassed Gritty was still refusing.

On the wharf in Sydney waited John Lemmoné, Fritz Hart, George Allan, Ernest Mitchell, and a crowd of photographers and reporters. Dodging journalists and organizing the luggage were such tricky occupations that Gritty temporarily forgot all else. There were also new diversions and attractions. Gritty soon adored John Lemmoné. He went out of his way to help her, and she confided to her diary that he was "the dearest thing in the world." How he managed Melba's tours single-handedly was beyond her. In London it required the attention of all Lionel Powell's staff to manage the printing, advertising, hotels, artists' programs, rehearsals, and finances; yet in Australia John Lemmoné did it all, and played the flute at Melba's concerts as well.

On August 6, 1921, Melba held her first concert at the Sydney Town Hall. Two governors were present, the hall was packed, and Melba was splendid in a rose-pink gown over which she appeared to have sprinkled "a quart or two of diamonds." After a second concert Gritty shared a sleeping berth with Nellie Patterson in the train that carried Melba and her followers away from Sydney. She was astonished at the welcome that awaited them in Melbourne. Gerald Patterson and Tommy Cochrane were on the platform, along with most of the conservatorium students and so many photographers, reporters, and spectators that Melba's party could scarcely reach their waiting cars.

At Coombe Cottage there was trouble in the servants' hall, for the house was too isolated to please servants, and Melba's demands were too exacting. With the kitchen maid, cook-housekeeper, and footman all either departing or on the point of departing, the family and guests had no alternative but to help with the housework. Melba set the example by seizing a broom and sweeping down the veranda. She even turned her zeal to the birdcages. "Madame has asked me to help her clean the parrot and canary cages and feed them everyday," wrote Gritty. "Blow refuses to tackle the job!" Blow, the rocklike servant, had the measure of Melba and stood firm when other servants quailed or resigned.

From then on Gritty hardly knew if she was on her head or on her heels. At eight each morning she massaged Melba's stomach and received a long list of orders, many of which were altered during the day. After breakfast she made beds and cleaned the birdcages; later she sorted and catalogued Melba's possessions, answered letters, and helped Bernard Yorke paint the inside of the swimming pool. She also looked after Pamela, but that was no chore because she loved the little girl. Pamela called her Miss Gritten-Pitten and used to say, "Oh do dance funnily." Together they would do their "kangaroo dance," amusing all who watched.

Journalists reported that Melba appeared more vigorous than ever— as any diminution of energy seemed to bring her closer to the dreaded day of retirement, she was determined to prove the journalists right. Her social schedule filled her family and servants with dismay. Refusing to concede that incessant entertaining was impossible when servants were scarce, she kept on inviting people to meals, and then worrying whether the kitchen could supply enough food. George, Evie, Gritty, and even Bernard Yorke were forbidden to take more than the tiniest portion of any communal dish. She was also repeatedly asking friends to stay, then realizing there were not enough bedrooms. On those occasions Gritty would be told to sleep at the house of distant Mitchell cousins, which entailed a half-mile walk through dark fields at night.

Several of those whom Melba invited to stay were Australian artists, in whom she took a keen interest. John Longstaff, who was planning to paint her portrait, was one, and Hans Heysen, whom Melba called the Australian Turner, was another. Heysen arrived wearing knickerbockers and a jersey and carrying his painting gear, for he was to paint scenes at Coombe Cottage. Gritty thought he looked artistic. Other visitors were Melba's brothers and sisters, of whom Gritty wrote patronizingly that they were all "rather ordinary middle-class people" with Australian accents. She believed they stood in awe of Melba and that Melba looked down on them, which showed how little she understood the unpredictable and individualistic Mitchell family. Gritty was especially censorious of Melba's "taboo" brother Charlie, of whom it must be admitted that Melba also sometimes disapproved. Charlie, a practical joker, once shot out the lights beside Melba's front gate. He also pretended to sell pies outside the Melbourne Town Hall on the night of one of her concerts. Fearing there might be a row when he visited Coombe Cottage, Melba prudently sent the servants away.

Throughout the next three months new servants came and went, leaving only the butler and the faithful Blow in permanent residence. Meanwhile a galaxy of English guests descended on the cottage. The first was the newspaper magnate Lord Northcliffe, whose body was swollen with heart disease, but who proved an easy guest because he spent most of his time playing with Pamela in the nursery.

Next came Clara Butt and her husband Kennerley Rumford, who arrived with Gritty's former employer Lionel Powell, who promptly saw Gritty's plight and did his best to support her. George and Evie also tried to help her, consoling her with stories of her long-suffering predecessors. Gritty felt special concern for Evie, on whom fell the brunt of coping with both Melba and the departing servants. She had little doubt that Evie would have preferred a home of her own.

After singing in a series of homecoming concerts in Melbourne, Sydney, and Adelaide and in many provincial centers, Melba developed bleeding from the uterus. Although she felt afraid, her doctors do not seem to have been unduly alarmed, and in mid-October she entered St. Ives private hospital for minor surgery. While there she heard that her brother Frank had died from pneumonia at Doonside. The first of her adult siblings to die, his death was a shock, the more so since she herself was feeling physically frail. At the burial on October 21 at the Lilydale cemetery, Melba carried a wreath of white roses made by Dunsford, the Coombe Cottage gardener.

Charles Sperling, Gritty's shipboard lover, now arrived in Lilydale to continue his courting. He came with a diamond engagement ring, and this time she accepted him. Afraid to tell Melba, she finally plucked up the courage, and the response was as loud as she had feared. Melba accused Gritty of breaking her contract and censured Sperling for staying nearby night after night. "The village will talk," she kept saying. Eventually she relented and offered to pay Gritty's passage home.

Melba replaced Gritty with a more docile Miss Ballantyne, and concentrated on her forthcoming season of popular concerts in Melbourne and Sydney, at which all seats were to be sold for five shillings. Assisted by Una Bourne and John Lemmoné and the conductor Alberto Zelman, Melba decided to hold sixteen concerts through December and January, with a special concert for country fans who were allowed to book by letter. The railways provided special return trains from country towns so that the journey could be completed in a day.

At these concerts the American-style Melba was much in evidence. She joked with the spectators and humorously shouted "Cut that out" when they kept on calling for encores. She threw her flowers into the audience and plucked two little girls from the organ seats to give them kisses. The audiences responded to her mood, roaring forth "For She's a Jolly Good Fellow" when a concert was ending. A few were critical of her lack of dignity, but mostly her audiences loved her.

At the final concert Melba presented Alberto Zelman, the conductor, with one of the special tiepins that she now awarded to those who faithfully served her. His was made of gold, with the letter M worked in enamel and a diamond set in the center. There were other versions of the tiepin for the more and less worthy. John Lemmoné received a platinum pin with the M composed of diamonds, the less exalted received pins with a gold M decorated with ruby chips. To Miss Carrington, who was in charge of Allan's box office, Melba gave a diamond brooch, in recognition of her cool head on the morning the bookings opened. Eleven thousand seats had been sold in two hours, during which twenty people fainted, several had hysterics, and one ticket seller was in danger of having his clothes ripped off.

The popular concerts had scarcely ended when Melba began a farewell concert tour which took her as far afield as Brisbane, where she sang with great success to two thousand in the crowded Exhibition Hall. There were also charity concerts in Melbourne, including a memorable children's matinee in which she was supported by Corporal J. Phillips, who performed unique vocal imitations of an automobile horn, a gramophone, and a canary. While Melba rejoiced in her own success, the children had no doubt that the masterpiece of the afternoon was the corporal's canary.

Between concerts, Melba's morning classes at the Albert Street Conservatorium continued to absorb her. One morning, at promptly at nine o'clock, she began auditioning the first of about two hundred girls seeking entry to her singing classes. Wearing grey suede Russian boots, Melba used her feet to indicate tempo and dynamics and to show her approval and disapproval. When she approved of an aspiring student, the toes of her boots pointed up, and when she disapproved they pointed down. Onlookers were impressed by the infinite pains she took over every detail, often leaping onstage to sing a phrase herself or to correct a pupil's posture or way of breathing. They also observed the kindness she showed to fearful girls, especially those applying for scholarships. "Don't be nervous, I am not at all terrible," she would tell them soothingly.

Years before, when Melba began teaching her vocal classes, she had embarked on a crusade to save the endangered art of *bel canto* singing by passing on her skills to a succession of students. She now stepped up her campaign by explaining the art to reporters and by carefully writing articles for leading newspapers. Through March and April 1922, in Melbourne and Sydney newspapers and later in the London *Daily Mail*, she explained in clear prose the details of her vocal method, having enlisted Fritz Hart and his senior singing teacher Mary Campbell for help in clarifying and assembling her thoughts. While staying in Sydney at the house of her brother Ernest, she told one interviewer about the crisis in her career nearly thirty years earlier, when her thoughtlessness had accidentally produced the first nodule on her vocal cord.

Early in September she told reporters, "Every time I leave Australia, the wrench is bigger." She went on to add a patriotic affirmation: "When you are born and brought up in a country and come to love it and its people there is no other land as good!" She had now been thirteen consecutive months in Australia, a longer stay than any except in her youth, and she felt more comfortable in her homeland than ever before. One reason for her contentment was Pamela, whom she adored. "I would visit her in the early morning, when only we were awake," Pamela would remember lovingly. "She would be brightly awake, shiny and clean in her pretty boudoir cap and ready for any surprise I cared to spring on her."

Pamela was paramount in Melba's mind as she planned her farewell garden party at Coombe Cottage. She recruited a fortune-teller and a brass band to amuse the adults, but for Pamela and a group of children that included Prime Minister Billy Hughes's small daughter, she ordered a puppet show. A few days later Pamela sat in a box at Her Majesty's Theatre and watched Melba at her farewell matinee. When Granny came onstage the "animated little figure" responded by wriggling and waving and throwing kisses to her grandmother without a trace of self-consciousness. Later, introducing her granddaughter to reporters, Melba announced, "She's all mine."

Just before Pamela's fifth birthday, Melba caught the train to Perth on the first leg of her journey to Europe. Pamela cried painfully when Melba kissed her goodbye and begged, "Granny don't go." From the ship Melba sent her a poignant note: "Do write to me often as I am so lonely and miss you more and more each day. Bless you darling. I love you. Granny."

Bernard Yorke accompanied Melba in the *Naldera* as far as Bombay, where she was met by emissaries of the viceroy. She saw the sights, including the towers of silence "with the birds ready to gobble the dead—ugh!—I hated it." In stifling heat she spent two days and two nights on the long train journey to the viceroy's summer palace in the mountains at Simla. As Lord Reading's personal guest, Melba witnessed the splendor of vice-regal life in India. At dinner a bowing servant in red livery stood behind every chair, and in the open air no guest walked even the slightest distance: a journey of fifty yards in the palace grounds was taken in a rickshaw pulled by five men. Melba conceded this mode of transport had its advantages, for she felt very short of breath in the high altitude. "I shall become very *sybaritical* if I stay here," she informed Tommy Cochrane.

Ten days later at Lord Reading's birthday party, she sang the "Jewel Song" from *Faust* and "Addio" from *La Bohème*. She also presented him with her *Gift Book*, an anthology of Australian writings and drawings that she had sponsored in 1915 to raise money for war charities. His response was to offer her his vice-regal railcar for her trip to Delhi and Agra, where she was to stay with the maharaja. At the Taj Mahal, the beauty of which transfixed her, she sang a long trill and was rewarded with an echo that possibly represented the truest replica of her voice that she had heard up to that time. The experience made a deep impression. "The moonlight, the warm scented darkness, the soft radiance of the marble and then—my voice echoing out in a trill which never seemed to stop," she wrote excitedly, was "in some ways the most uncanny sensation I have ever experienced." It was an anticlimax to resume her journey to England aboard the crowded *Macedonia*.

By mid-October, installed at the Ladies Athenaeum Club, she celebrated her return to London by appearing at a matinee with Wilhelm

Backhaus at the Albert Hall, where the autumn fog almost obscured the stage from the ten thousand who had flocked to see and hear her. Then she set off on a long concert tour of England, Scotland, and Wales with Backhaus and a young Australian accompanist, Lindley Evans, who remembered how "frightfully pernickety" she was over his playing and his dress: he had to appear for her inspection before every performance. He also remembered her kindness and her ready offer of money when she suspected that he needed it.

Lindley Evans appeared with Melba at a London concert in December 1922 in aid of the League of Mercy, at which a cello solo was played by another young Australian named Laurie Kennedy. The queens of Italy, Norway, and Britain were present and Evans was astounded by the familiarity with which the queens and Melba greeted one another. Melba presented her Australian protégés to the royal ladies and did her best to further the young men's prospects. Kennedy recalled that Queen Mary said to him, "I suppose you have a wonderful instrument." At this Melba "positively nudged her in the ribs" and replied cheekily, "He'll have a better one Ma'am, when he can afford it."

Australia was on Melba's mind a few weeks later when she shared a box at Covent Garden with Clara Butt to hear Florence Austral sing the role of Aida for the British National Opera. One ventures to suggest that of all Australian sopranos of the next generation, the Melbourne-born Austral was possibly the one most worthy to inherit Melba's crown. Afterward Melba happily stepped backstage to congratulate the young singer, inside the very dressing room that she had once claimed as her own.

Melba admired the struggling but plucky British National Opera, formed by the remnants of the bankrupt Beecham Company. It provided her with a way of wiping out the hurt of Beecham's rejection and of reclaiming Covent Garden as her own. Shrewdly she offered her services to the company without a fee, and on January 17, 1923, amid a blaze of publicity, she sang the role of Mimi, following it three days later with the last two acts of *La Bohème* on the final night of the season. Both performances were broadcast over the radio, being the second and third performances of opera ever to go on air. Newspapers estimated that forty thousand heard the broadcast from as far away as

Madrid and Stockholm and the success of the concert led to a surge in sales of the early radio receivers known as crystal sets.

Melba was about to leave the Ladies' Athenaeum Club in January 1923 when she was confronted by a twenty-four-year-old journalist named Beverley Nichols. Charming, boyishly good-looking, an Oxford graduate, and a talented pianist, Nichols had much to commend him and Melba was quickly captivated. He was homosexual, which may also have suited her, since she did not wish to be seen too frequently with a man who might be viewed as her lover. Nonetheless there are raconteurs who, in Australia today, maintain that Melba and Beverley Nichols had a torrid affair, so pervasive is the legend of Melba's nymphomania.

Nichols had been commissioned by his editor to obtain Melba's views on the notorious Edith Thompson, currently standing trial for murdering her husband. The resulting article, cleverly written as though by Melba herself, so pleased her that she adopted Nichols as a protégé, showing him off to her friends and basking in his admiration of her trill. "Please do a trill for me," Nichols would say coaxingly to Melba, and he was seldom refused. Once she trilled for him all the way up London's Regent Street, and passersby stared "as though they had heard the voice of a truant angel." Eventually Nichols persuaded her to trill into a special machine known as an audiometer. The device produced line drawings in response to sound. Melba's result was perfect. Whereas other sopranos' trills meandered across the page, Melba's trill, wrote Nichols, was "uniform and parallel and flawless."

Nichols also helped with the refurbishment of Melba's new house on Mansfield Street in Cavendish Square. An eighteenth-century gem with four magnificent reception rooms—one with a ceiling designed by Robert Adam—it required careful and sympathetic restoration. Melba again sought the services of Boni de Castellane, who, cast off without a penny by Anna Gould, now eked out a livelihood selling antiques on commission. Delighted to have so generous a client, Boni summoned French craftsmen to decorate the bathroom with lapis lazuli, and found Adam furniture for her drawing room and dining room. Melba spent happy days selecting fabrics and arranging furniture and paintings, this being one of her favorite occupations. She once said that if she had not been a singer, she would have become an interior decorator.

Even more of her energy that spring and summer went into the creation of a second Melba-Williamson Opera Company, with which she was planning to tour Australia the following year. As assistants, she had Henry Russell and quiet and capable Nevin Tait, the London representative of J. C. Williamson. Melba and Tait traveled to Nice to consult Jean de Reszke and then on to Rome and Naples, where Henry Russell was auditioning singers. In Naples, Melba became "terribly ill," the cause seemingly her teeth. Feeling desperately weak, she struggled aboard the *Orsova* and returned by sea to London, where she had two infected teeth removed. Writing to Tommy Cochrane from Claridges Hotel at Easter, she admitted that she seemed to be "cracking up." "I don't care much if I do go," she told him gloomily. "I don't feel I have much to live for." She was depressed by the death of Sarah Bernhardt. In Paris a few weeks earlier Sarah had clung to her and murmured, "You have always your golden voice and me, I must die." The words had left a deep impression. *"What a tragedy life is,"* she told Tommy.

Although her weakness undoubtedly stemmed in part from her teeth, a greater cause lay in the "irrigations," as she termed them, issuing from her uterus. This malady, which had hospitalized her in Melbourne in 1921 and troubled her intermittently in London a year earlier, now reappeared in acute form. Fearing cancer, her doctors dispatched her to a Mayfair hospital where she underwent an immediate hysterectomy. To Evie she wrote, "Don't be frightened, darling, but I am dreadfully ill" and went on to explain that she had a small growth in the uterus. "I am terrified but can't go on suffering like this," she wrote, "and prefer to die if I can't be cured."

It says much for Melba's remarkable vitality that after a few weeks' convalescence in the seaside town of Hove, she was back in London and ready to sing three performances of *La Bohème* and *Faust* for the British National Opera. A reporter was amazed at her high spirits and energy when he interviewed her in the gold-walled music room at Mansfield Street. Nearby sat her pet African grey parrot, Greybird, who had cheered her convalescence by imitating her way of singing. "A bar or two is always on his beak," she told her interviewer proudly, adding that, unlike herself, Greybird could sing while upside down! There had been rumors of Melba's standing for the House of Commons, and she half endorsed them. "After all," she told the reporter, "I can speak well, and have a few brains, you know." She had gained a taste for electioneering when she supported the conservative candidate Lord Apsley at a rowdy meeting at the Southampton docks. When a voice in the crowd had called, "Give us a song, Nellie," she had happily obliged, thus ensuring the success of the meeting. Behind her interest in politics was a concern for the growing number of unemployed. She detected a cynicism and "soul-weariness" in British society that she believed must be remedied.

Melba's recovery may have seemed miraculous, but her energy was quickly spent. In July 1923, on medical advice, she took a cure at the spa town of Evian les Bains, across Lake Geneva from Ouchy, where she had stayed so long ago with Philippe. Passing her days bathing in or drinking the mineralized waters, she devoted her evenings to gambling at the casino. "I cannot get my strength back," she wrote to Henry Russell, "and I don't know what to do." Part of her exhaustion came from worrying about the Australian opera tour. "*We cannot possibly* give 20 operas in 8 weeks," she informed Henry.

Exhausted she may have been, but her unquenchable spirit again prevailed. A friend once said of her that she was "full of wild enthusiasm and vitality and as impetuous and uncontrolled as a child," and in September she gave ample proof of this. Refusing to yield to age and ill health, she set out to tour the major Canadian cities, crossing the border from time to time to sing in America, before ending in Vancouver, from where she sailed to Australia. The distances traveled and the performances given would have tired someone in perfect health and half her age. Inevitably the wild flurry of activity drained her. As she sailed toward Australia, the question of her future could no longer be ignored.

Most of Melba's biographers have believed that Melba had close to perfect health almost until her death. John Hetherington wrote that she was "a remarkably robust woman" who "for many years before her last illness never suffered any ailment worse than a feverish cold or an ache or a pain lasting a few hours." In fact, since her pneumonia in 1904, she had had many attacks of illness, and in the last few years they had grown more serious and more frequent.

Melba's head now relayed that message to her heart. It told her that she was old and often ill and that it was time to retire. Normally she obeyed her head, but as a lifelong performer she knew that appearing before an audience was like a drug of addiction. To give it up seemed akin to suicide. To her accompanist Lindley Evans she confided, "I must sing or I will die."

On the other hand, she had watched aging prima donnas struggle to sing for years longer than their voices permitted, until ultimately they became objects of mockery or pity. She could not bear the prospect of being laughed at or pitied. As she tried to come to terms with her conflicting emotions, she did her best to derive comfort from an optimistic maxim: "Don't linger on the first act of life," it ran. "All acts are beautiful, including the final roll of the drum."

She spent Christmas 1923 at Coombe Cottage, making plans for the forthcoming opera tour, and in January she traveled to Tasmania to give concerts in Launceston and Hobart. At the end of the Launceston concert she took her first painful step toward retirement. "The time is coming," she warned her audience, "when I must say Goodbye to you." She must "make way for younger people." Back at Coombe Cottage, with an uncertain year ahead of her, she filled the house with guests, among them Tommy Cochrane, who noted that she surrounded herself with people to keep depression at bay. She required and demanded and found "amusing people," he observed, "interesting people, people who would animate her, and keep her animated. Sympathetic friends warmed her, and destroyed that feeling of loneliness which she appeared to dread." Nor were her animators necessarily rich and famous. While she still delighted in the high life, her friends these days were drawn from many walks of life.

Among the guests at Coombe Cottage was Beverley Nichols, whom Melba had impetuously summoned from London to be her secretary. She continued to find him amusing, but those around her were not so amused. One friend described Nichols as "a silent young man" whose "mission in life seemed to be holding her crocodile handbag" while Melba darted about like an eager child, poking her nose into everything. There were suspicions that he stayed with Melba only for what he could get out of her. Someone composed a telling rhyme:

Melba had a Nichols lamb
Its name was Beverley,

And everywhere Dame Nellie went
The lamb went cleverly.

Although Nichols ostensibly behaved like a surrogate son, even calling
Melba "Madre," as did George and Evie, his private attitude was often
contemptuous. He had a troubled relationship with his own parents,
especially his father, whom later in life he would boast in print of twice
trying to murder. These attempts at murder seem to have been figments
of his imagination, but there was nothing imaginary about his capacity for holding grudges and seeking revenge. Melba, usually so shrewd,
seems to have been blind to his true character. She went on bossing
him, ignoring his sulks, and increasingly taking him into her confidence, little realizing the trouble she was courting.

Henry Russell and his wife, also visiting Coombe Cottage, irritated Melba's friends almost as much as Nichols. At first Melba seems
to have had boundless faith in Henry, describing him as the "greatest
teacher of singing in the world." Within weeks her opinion dropped
as Russell, usurping her authority, styled himself the artistic director
of her opera company and made decisions that only she and Tait were
entitled to make. A friend remembered her slamming down the telephone after speaking to Henry "as though she were dashing something
loathsome from her," and shouting, "That man Russell!" The last straw
came when she announced she would be singing Marguerite as well as
Mimi and Desdemona. Russell is said to have shouted, "No, you shall
not sing Marguerite! I forbid it." No one forbade Melba, as she soon
made plain.

Relations were no smoother with Russell's wife Donna, who wrote
novels under the pen name of Serene Gray. On February 27, 1924,
Melba held a dance at Coombe Cottage. Since both she and Mrs. Russell patronized the Parisian couturier Poiret, they both wore Poiret
gowns, and on this special evening they turned out to be almost identical. In the words of an observer, "When the two ladies confronted one
another, Dame Nellie's eyes flashed." At that moment, Serene lost her
serenity.

Melba wanted her dance to be the "greatest party ever held in Australia," and she supervised it with the same care with which she ran her
opera companies. A young jazz player named Leslie Ross, one of five

hired to provide the dance music, has left a charming picture of Melba, the party-giver. He and his fellow bandsmen arrived early to find Melba in an apron and headscarf, organizing Japanese lanterns in the garden and barking orders like a general commanding an army. Temporarily abandoning her barking, she took the shy young jazz players on a tour of the house and, anxious to put them at their ease, issued a cheeky invitation as they came to her bedroom. "This is the holy of holies," she exclaimed. "Everyone wants to say they've lain on Melba's bed. Go on, lie on it!"

That night the festivities lasted till three in the morning, at which hour the guests were discreetly herded into the darkened ballroom. There, by the light of a single candle, Melba sang "Home Sweet Home," and Ross, who normally liked only jazz, thought it the most exquisite music he had ever heard. Half an hour later, when the guests had gone, Melba rolled up the sleeves of her Poiret gown and made for the kitchen to cook her young bandsmen bacon and eggs.

A week or so later Melba welcomed the nearly sixty overseas performers who were to make up her opera company. Two of the leading singers were glamorous figures. One was the dashing White Russian bass Prince Alexis Oblensky, whom she had brought with her from England as her protégé, and whose family Melba knew through Gladys de Grey. The other was Miss Toti dal Monte, a small plump Italian with baby eyes and a beautiful *bel canto* soprano voice. Arriving only five days before the opening, she was in a fractious mood because she was forbidden by quarantine laws to bring her dog into Australia. Melba and Nevin Tait had the bright idea of spending twelve guineas to buy her an Australian silky terrier, which she dressed up in a green bow for the press photographers.

Rumor had it that Toti and Melba were bitter rivals, though there is no evidence to support the allegation. Indeed Toti, deservedly, was a drawcard, to Melba's gain. Beverley Nichols would nonetheless cultivate the rumor in *Evensong*, a novel he published soon after Melba's death. Its main character, an aging and cantankerous diva, was widely accepted as a vindictive pen-portrait of Melba.

From its opening night on March 29, 1924, the ambitious Melbourne season proved a success. Sixteen different operas were staged over two and a half months, and Melba felt well satisfied. As usual she devoted immense energy to every aspect of the tour. "Her business acumen," wrote her publicity manager, Claude Kingston, "would have done credit to an international banker." On the train to Sydney for the next phase of the tour, she told Kingston to tear up the publicity statement he had prepared for the press because she had a superior idea.

Two years earlier, while traveling on the Sydney Express, she had been forced to complain about the fleas; and she now decided to enlist those fleas in her publicity campaign. "Bother the opera," she said when reporters came aboard to interview her about the coming season. "What I want to talk to you about are the fleas on this beastly express." She even offered to lift her skirts to show where she had been bitten. Every newspaper featured the story, and people not normally interested in the arts knew that the opera had come to town.

Her expenditure of energy had the usual consequences. She had scarcely arrived in Sydney when she developed bronchitis and was unable to sing. For four weeks she coughed in her apartment at 52 Macleay Street, tended by Evie and George and Beverley Nichols, and even after her return to Melbourne she suffered recurrences of the cough. In Adelaide early in October she was sufficiently well to appear twice, but the message was nevertheless clear. To sing in opera put too great a strain on her health. She should retire from the operatic stage.

With the painful decision finally taken, Melba tried to offset her distress by planning a grand farewell. She chose *La Bohème* for her final operatic performance, and announced she would donate its receipts to disabled Australian soldiers. Remembering her radio broadcasts in England, she arranged for the performance to be the inaugural broadcast of Melbourne's first radio station. She even cabled Signor Marconi, the inventor of radio transmission, in the hope that the broadcast could be relayed to England. He cabled back regretfully that technically this was not yet possible.

On the eve of the public announcement of her retirement, the enterprising editor of the *Melbourne Herald* elicited comments from prominent citizens of Great Britain, America, and Australia about the significance of the event. On the afternoon of October 13, 1924, his front page was devoted to their contributions, the tone being one of mourning, and many of the comments reading almost like obituaries.

To her Australian public, just as much as to herself, Melba's retirement seemed like a form of death.

In contrast, her farewell performance at Her Majesty's Theatre in Melbourne that evening was a gala event. After the singers had taken their final bows, the curtain rose on a backdrop of flowers in which electric lights spelled out the triumphant message: "Australia's Greatest Daughter Our Melba." But there was a touch of bereavement about it, too. As she stood in the foreground, knee deep in bouquets, listening to a speech by the prime minister, an observer wrote that Melba looked as if she was standing "in a vast bier."

CHAPTER TWENTY-FOUR

Australia's Greatest Daughter

MELBA RETURNED to England in January 1925 feeling old and somewhat jaded, but she rose above her mood in order to give Beverley Nichols the fruits of her memory. After much urging in Melbourne, she had agreed to let him preside over the writing of her memoirs. As she paced up and down her music room, first at Coombe Cottage and then at Mansfield Street, she poured out her life history. "Madre has been wonderful about it," Nichols gushed to Evie, "the most wonderful stories about her career." But what emerged was not necessarily what Melba wished to see in print. She fought back and argued and excised. To Nichols's chagrin, whole sections of the manuscript were scoured by her pen. She wanted, wrote Nichols bitingly, "to appear as an angel of sweetness and light" and "all the guts and humour had to be taken out of it." Since the sensational chapters would sell the book, he saw his half-share of the profits melting away with each deletion. To make the most of what survived in the manuscript, he began some of his own varnishing. A biographer must use *Melodies and Memories*—as the book came to be called—with caution. Between Melba's faulty memory and Nichols's journalistic license, many episodes in the book have little or no basis in reality.

One episode devoid of sweetness and light concerned poor Pietro Cecchi; and though it very likely owes something to Nichols's embellishments, the reader senses that the underlying sentiment was Melba's. Certainly she was happy enough to put her name to it. For more than forty years Melba had refused to acknowledge Cecchi's role in training her, and, in Agnes Murphy's 1909 biography of her, she had tried to

330

offer an explanation. Writing, presumably, on Melba's advice, Agnes explained that pupil and teacher had fallen out just before Melba left Melbourne for London for the first time. On the eve of her departure, Cecchi had demanded payment for those singing lessons he had given without charge during the preceding two years, and this breach of friendship had caused her "sorrow and disappointment." While "she has been resolutely silent as to his share in her early vocal training," wrote Agnes, "her lips have also been as resolute in the still more characteristic silence that refused to link his name with one word of blame."

In *Melodies and Memories* Melba broke her silence. In a scene alive with drama, she recounted how she would never forget Cecchi's "small, dark, swarthy figure and the bright avaricious eyes that examined me coldly as he remarked, 'You owe me eighty guineas. That money must be paid before you leave.'" "I was in despair," she continued, and "did not dare to ask my Daddy." Borrowing the money, she flung it on Cecchi's table and proudly declaimed, "If I ever do have success, I shall never mention your name as having been a teacher of mine." By way of commentary, she added that her studies in Paris soon taught her that he "was not a good teacher, for all that he taught me I had to unlearn when I was privileged to study under Madame Mathilde Marchesi."

She could not have foreseen that her story would be disproved when the affectionate letters she wrote to Cecchi from London surfaced many years later. Nor could she have imagined that such experts on singing as George Bernard Shaw would continue to insist that her technique could have come only from years of skilled training long before she reached Europe. Even if she had foreseen these disproofs, it would probably have made little difference. Her loyalty to Madame was little short of fanatical.

Nichols claimed to have ghosted a second book for Melba that year. This was *The Melba Method*, a manual for singers. Since he was no vocal expert, one assumes that his contribution was more in matters of expression. Melba's acknowledged co-authors were Fritz Hart and Mary Campbell, who shared with her the profits of the book. *The Melba Method* is still in print and still used by students of singing.

By February 1925, Melba was so unwell that her doctor placed her in a hospital. "I have been terribly ill again and in a nursing home for 5 weeks and now I am having *insulin* twice a day. Need I say more?" she wrote to John Lemmoné. "Fancy me having the dread disease *diabetes* and *badly too.*" She finished her letter with a sentence of overwhelming sadness: "Goodbye dear friend tell *no one* but think of me and pray for me, *I don't want to go yet.*" Ill as she was, she resolved to travel to Paris to consult an eye specialist, for a film was spreading across one eye. To her relief she learned it was not a cataract, but a less serious condition amenable to treatment. Paris was covered in heavy snow, but the warmth of old friends made her feel secure. Returning to London in time for her sixty-fourth birthday, she held a dinner at Mansfield Street and sang two Mozart arias at a benefit performance for Madame Albani.

In August, somewhat recovered, Melba went on vacation. Traveling now was rather a bore, because she needed a nurse to inject her with insulin twice a day; but Susan FitzClarence Birch came with her and eased some of the burden. After staying at Evian les Bains, which Melba had come to love, their next stop was the Lido at Venice. Although Melba had come for the sea-bathing and sunbathing, she did not think much of the Lido. "The people here are dreadful and I hate them," she wrote. "They go about *naked* and lunch the same way." Her mood improved when she was joined by Bemberg and the pianist George Copeland and Beverley Nichols. It would seem to have been during an evening with Bemberg that Melba decided to give a concert from a gondola on the Grand Canal, in the style of the one she had given with Tosti years earlier.

There followed a rehearsal in a palazzo on the Grand Canal that has become a classic Melba anecdote. How truthful the story is one cannot know, but Beverley Nichols certainly turned it into a dramatic story. Somehow, during that rehearsal, Melba conjured up the matchless voice of her youth, managing the trills and roulades of the "mad scene" from *Lucia*, a piece she had not attempted for years. Outside the palazzo, a floating audience hung on every note and called for encores. But there could be no encore, wrote Nichols dramatically: Melba would never sing like that again.

It so happens there survives a letter written by Melba to Tommy Cochrane when she was in Venice on September 2. She told Tommy that she and Bemberg had rehearsed the previous day. As they left the rehearsal room, she was accosted by two little Italian girls who wished to know if she was the singer and if Bemberg was her husband. When Bemberg said "yes" and gave Melba a kiss, they cried out *"brava"* and ran off. "How enthusiastic these children are," she commented. "It made me quite happy." She made no mention of the "mad scene"; if she had actually sung it, she would almost certainly have informed Tommy. It would seem that Nichols and his varnishing brush had been at work again.

After returning to London, Melba abandoned Mansfield Street, selling the house and most of its contents and moving to an apartment at 161 Avenue Victor Hugo in Paris. Here she quietly contemplated a question she could put off no longer. While being realistic enough to accept that in a year or two she must permanently leave the concert platform, she was determined to do so in her own time and her own way. As a first step she engaged the agents Ibbs and Tillett to arrange her farewell concert tour of the British Isles, commencing in Glasgow in January 1926. The tenor Hackett Granville and the violist Lionel Tertis were to assist her, and she planned to end the tour in Brighton in mid-March. She agreed as well to a few concerts in London, including one for the inmates of Wormwood Scrubs Prison, at which she was to sing with a cousin of Susan FitzClarence, a schoolboy tenor named Alwyn Best. Writing of the concert years later, Alwyn recalled that Melba fortified them both with a jolly lunch at the Ritz before setting out for the prison. Prudently, she left behind most of her jewels.

The arrival in London of George and Evie and little Pamela lifted Melba's spirits. Although she had longed for them during her illness, she had dared not summon them because George was ill. Influenza followed by a lung infection had left him acutely depressed, and Australian friends had feared for him. Melba was relieved to see how fit and cheerful he now seemed. She was delighted, too, at the prospect of seven-year-old Pamela giving her first party—for twenty children and twelve nannies—at the Armstrongs' new home in Edwardes Square. "Pamela is too wonderful," she wrote to Beryl Fanning. "I adore her—I am her slave—she pulls my leg but I enjoy it and nothing matters as long as she is well and happy."

Melba was cheered in these months by the company of a sympathetic American soprano named Helen Daniels, known onstage as Elena Danielli. Like Madame before her, Melba was intent on superintending

the lives of her protégées, and when Helen recorded songs at the Gramophone Company's studio, Melba insisted on going with her. When she
saw the boyish and seemingly inexperienced accompanist, she barked at
the company's manager, "Can't you find somebody who can get tone out
of the piano?" The remark was misguided, to say the least, for the "boy"
at the piano was Gerald Moore, soon to become one of England's finest
accompanists. Thereafter Moore would to refer to her as "the terrible
Melba."

Helen and Melba were together in Melba's Paris apartment at the
end of March when they heard on the radio that the Duke of Orléans
had died in Palermo. Helen recalled how Melba, on hearing the news,
paused at the door of the room to whisper the poignant words, "Ah,
Philippe." The lover to whom she had clung in her heart for so long
had gone the way of so many of her old and dear friends.

Her mind was now set on her retirement from Covent Garden, advertised for June 12, 1926. Intending to go out in a blaze of glory and
patriotism, she was determined to have her protégé John Brownlee in
the cast. He was a promising young baritone from the Australian port
city of Geelong, whom she had sent to study with Dinh Gilly; and he
was also "*Scotch*," she told Tommy Cochrane approvingly, "with a very
level head on his shoulders." He would be perfect as Marcello in the
third and fourth acts of *La Bohème*, which she included along with
the second act of *Roméo et Juliette* and the opening of the last act of
Otello. In a flow of patriotism, she chose the Australian bass baritone
Frederic Collier to play Schaunard and the Australian tenor Browning
Mummery to play Rodolfo. It was no wonder that Lord Stanley, in his
gracious speech after the final curtain, spoke of Melba's devotion to the
land of her birth. So moved was Melba by his speech that she could
scarcely find her voice to reply. Once she did regain her composure, she
spoke slowly, making a charming play on the word "farewell." The word
was part of a prayer, she told her audience, and it "means fare *thee* well,
which I wish you all and I feel sure that you wish me the same." The
cheers that followed, and the deluge of flowers on stage made it a scene
"unequalled in British opera."

The singing and the speeches can still be heard, recorded by the
Gramophone Company using its much-improved electrical method,
and transferred in our own time to compact disk. For a soprano of sixty-

five, Melba sounds surprisingly well. The *Daily Telegraph* was not simply being nostalgically generous when it proclaimed that here was "a glorious exhibition of the noble art of singing as singing should be."

Melba was excited by the quality of the electrical recording. "For the first time I hear something of what I think my voice really sounds like," she exclaimed to John Brownlee. "Why wasn't this thing invented before?" It was Melba's misfortune to reach her prime well before the era of electrical recording. While, thanks to this method, there are good quality reproductions of the voices of her younger rivals, like Galli Curci and Tetrazzini, the recordings of Melba's voice when at its best are primitive and distorted.

The farewell over, Melba intended to give herself up to pleasure. Renting a country house called Camfield Place near Hatfield, she entertained grandly; when not at Camfield she was at the Stanleys' house on the Welsh coast, or at Evian les Bains taking a spa cure, or in Switzerland visiting Paderewski, or in Warsaw calling on Jean de Reszke's sister. Australia, too, was beckoning again: she was booked to sail on the *Naldera* in December, and was even packing her trunks when an invitation suddenly made her jettison her vow never to sing in opera again. On December 5 she appeared with a largely Australian cast at the Old Vic Theatre, repeating those selections from *Otello* and *La Bohème* she had sung at her Covent Garden farewell. Confronted by gentle accusations that she had promised not to appear again, Melba said she was not backsliding; she was merely fulfilling her long-standing promise made on the eve of war to appear at the Old Vic. The truth was that, already missing the excitement of singing in opera, she was eager to snatch any excuse to perform. Sixty years earlier the great Giulia Grisi had dispersed her farewells over ten years, and more recently the great Adelina Patti had done the same. Melba was following that same leisurely proceeding. Not that anyone seriously minded, except a few contrarians. It was what divas did, and most of their fans rather expected it.

Melba, in her permanent state of near retirement, arrived in Australia at the end of January 1927. She was in high spirits, which was as well, for George, Evie, and Pamela had remained in London, and Melba had to cope single-handedly with a hole in the roof of Coombe Cottage, cracks in the walls, and the usual comings and goings of servants.

Needing advice, she applied to two young artistic friends, Daryl and Joan Lindsay, who brought an architect out to see her. They arrived to find her "on the lawn in a brilliant Chinese coat, looking almost as exotic as a pair of macaws she was feeding." She was still very much at the center of every stage, and quickly exclaimed, when she heard that the architect's surname was Cheetham, "Young man, change your name. It is a very bad one for an architect." On seeing his embarrassment, she apologized in words and spirit. Melba "was courteous and truly kind to people she liked," wrote Joan Lindsay, though she also rather "enjoyed being rude to people she didn't like when she felt they deserved it."

As the garden at Coombe Cottage was hopelessly overgrown, Melba approached a well-known landscapist named Edna Walling, who engaged three women gardeners to tame the weeds and drew up an ornate plan for a water garden to replace one of the tennis courts. Melba promptly balked at the expense of the water garden. To Edna's mind this was rather a relief, for she privately feared that, once employed, she might never be paid. Her fear had arisen mistakenly one day when she watched Melba quickly sorting her mail into two piles, one pile being letters and the other being what Edna thought were bills. Edna was alarmed to see Melba throw the bills into the fire and, presuming she had no secretary, imagined that this was her normal way of dealing with them. The likely explanation is that these were begging letters, for Melba always paid her bills promptly. Tommy Cochrane and Claude Kingston testified that each day Melba dealt with a large sheaf of begging letters, expertly separating the real from the bogus, and either throwing the letters away or writing a check immediately.

Putting her house in order always pleased Melba, but her thoughts were turning to her farewell concert tour of Australia, which John Lemmoné had been organizing for months. As her assistant artist, she had brought a young bass with her from England named Stuart Robertson, whom she had discovered at a village concert near Camfield Place. Lindley Evans was summoned to accompany the two singers, and John Lemmoné was ready with his flute. The first concert was held at the Melbourne Auditorium early in March 1927, followed by a ten-day tour of Tasmania. After tackling the country towns north and west of Melbourne, the company performed in Sydney, Brisbane, and provincial towns as far north as Rockhampton. In November Melba sang two concerts in Adelaide. "Her witchery was as supreme as ever," wrote one admiring critic. Only the *Truth*, her old enemy, struck a sour note. Although Norton had died long ago, the newspaper complained that she acted with the unbecoming "coquetry of a girl in her teens" and that her "farewell concert should have been given many moons ago."

Between concerts there were happy engagements. When the king's second son, the Duke of York, arrived in Australia, Melba was part of the welcoming festivities. She sang at a private dinner at Government House in Melbourne, "as easy and informal as an old fashioned musical evening at a friend's home," according to Lindley Evans who accompanied her. The capital of Australia was about to be transferred from Melbourne to Canberra, and Melba agreed to stand on the steps of the newly built Parliament House on May 9 and sing "God Save the King" as the Duke of York—later King George VI—arrived to open the building. The ceremony in the open air did not go strictly to plan. Melba opened her mouth just as noisy ceremonial aircraft flew overhead, and she was in no mood for the parliamentary lunch that followed. Her neighbor at the lunch, a minor politician, after attempting a few conversational sallies, turned away, but a few minutes later was surprised to feel a tiny pinch on his leg. "I'm sorry," said Melba, and began to talk to him charmingly. In recognition of her many services to her country, Melba's name appeared on the honors list at the king's next birthday. She was now a Dame Grand Cross of the Order of the British Empire, the highest order of damehood.

Shortly before Melba sang outside Parliament House, Pamela had undergone an appendectomy in London. Two months later, just as the young Armstrongs were entering Canada on their way to Australia, Charlie Armstrong was operated on for a perforated duodenal ulcer. Since he lived alone at Lake Shawnigan, George, Evie, and Pamela elected to remain with him through most of his convalescence. Meanwhile, at Coombe Cottage, Melba fretted at the alarms and delays, worrying inordinately over Pamela, and more than a little over her former husband. When her beloved family finally returned to her in August 1927, Melba asked with real concern, "How was Charlie?"

She now had a fresh stage for her energies. Nevin Tait, on behalf of J. C. Williamson, was proposing to assemble the largest company of singers with the largest repertoire of opera yet to be seen in Australia, and to tour the Australian capitals through the middle months of the following year. Melba, longing to be part of the scheme, eagerly lent her name to it, and with a fanfare of publicity she and Tait announced the formation of a third company under the auspices of J. C. Williamson and Nellie Melba.

In May 1928, thirty-three overseas singers converged on Melbourne, a third of them from Melba's former company and thus known personally to her. One was Toti dal Monte, who arrived with twelve suitcases, eleven trunks, and a tiny dog whose quarantine had been waived by the Australian authorities. She was the undoubted star, and brought welcome publicity when, three months after the tour commenced, she decided to marry her tenor, Enzo de Muro Lomanto. The ceremony in Sydney's St. Mary's Cathedral attracted a vast crowd.

Melba was supposed to be a silent partner in the opera tour, but she poked her nose into everything. Anything slovenly aroused her anger, and her inability to appear on stage probably sharpened her zeal for faultfinding. Indeed, as the season progressed, the strain of not singing in public became unbearable. "I am not very happy unless I am singing to you," she told her public, and their letters urging her to return to opera magnified her unhappiness. In Sydney the longing became too much: she decided to abandon retirement and prepare for yet another Australian farewell. Partly repeating the program of her Covent Garden farewell, she gave her fans the last three acts of *La Bohème* and the opening of the last act of *Otello*. In September and October she sang similar performances in Melbourne and Adelaide.

One critic confessed that he attended her performance with misgivings but found himself applauding. "The diva knows the singing business from A–Z," he wrote. "She has skill enough to miss a high note now and again without making it noticeable, and in the death scene she made an asset of the weakened voice." Lindley Evans also found the performances a personal triumph: "She *was* the young girl Mimi and she *was* the terrified Desdemona. I can still hear in my mind the scream of terror when she beseeched her maid not to leave her."

Melba's numerous returns to the stage after her formal retirement puzzled or amused Australians and has continued to fascinate them. The phrases "more farewells than Melba" and "doing a Melba" have passed into the Australian language and are still current. Another is "sing 'em muck." Melba is reputed to have used it when talking to Clara Butt before the contralto's first tour of Australia in 1907. "What are you going to sing?" Melba is supposed to have inquired before offering her own emphatic answer, "All I can say is—sing 'em muck! It's all they can understand." The conversation was published in August 1928 in Winifred Ponder's new biography of Dame Clara, and at once many Australians were up in arms.

While Melba denied making such a statement, the word "muck" has a blunt Melba ring to it. She was referring of course to sentimental ballads like Tosti's "Goodbye" and "Three Green Bonnets" and "Home Sweet Home," pleasing in themselves—indeed, loved by her own father—but boring to a singer who had to trot them out continually. On the other hand, these songs were what her fans, and even some of the critics, wanted to hear. A reviewer in the *Sydney Morning Herald* once wrote of "Three Green Bonnets" that Melba would "be gratefully remembered by it when some of her more brilliant efforts have fallen into oblivion." It was the same in England and North America, where she was deluged with mail begging her to sing those sentimental songs. "I try Debussy, I try Duparc, Ravel; I try anything and everything which strikes me as beautiful and fresh," she wrote, "and always I am treated by the same response, enthusiastic it is true, but tame compared with the positive uproar I receive when I sing the old favourites."

After the anecdote was published, Clara Butt was in a panic and sent Melba a long and apologetic cablegram, calling it a "silly story." The offending passage was deleted at some expense from the 11,850 copies of Ponder's book as yet unsold in Australia, the publisher presumably fearing that if Melba chose to sue, she might win. Nevertheless the hurt remained. Even today Australian music lovers recall the episode with some unease. "Melba laughed at us," they say. "She sang us 'muck' because she believed that was all we could understand."

The last of Melba's tours ended in Perth in October 1928. A month later she and Helen Daniels returned to a freezing London winter and an influenza epidemic. Melba rented a house in Cadogan Square but said it was like living in Siberia. She was glad to retreat in the spring to Paris, where she set about renting an apartment from Princess Radziwill at 8 Boulevard de Latour-Maubourg. In May 1929, against doctors' orders, she returned to London, staying at Claridges Hotel for the opening of an opera season in which, again, she had no part. Sitting in Gladys de Grey's old box—which often brought a lump to her throat—she entertained friends, including the young Prince of Wales, and felt her spirits reviving.

It was in London that she met Rosa Ponselle, the American dramatic soprano who was about to make her debut at Covent Garden in *Norma*. A worshipper of Melba from girlhood, Rosa had even tried to take the name of Melba at her Catholic confirmation. To meet her idol should have been a rare experience, but it proved to be a disappointment. Rosa was intensely nervous when she entered Claridges Hotel, and Melba did not try to put her at ease. Maybe Melba felt resentful, for Norma was one of the great *bel canto* roles she never sang, and that she must have coveted. That a dramatic soprano outside the *bel canto* tradition was invited to sing it at Covent Garden could have roused her resentment. According to Rosa's recollection, Melba remained stony-faced and brusque throughout their meeting.

In June, Melba traveled to Evian les Bains for her annual cure, accompanied by her sister Belle's youngest boy, Tommy. To be escorted by a personable young man in his twenties pleased her immensely, and after the cure they set out on a motoring tour of Switzerland and Germany, with Tommy driving her big black Cadillac. The days passed pleasantly, but she was often tired, and she longed to be able to settle into her flat in Paris, which the workmen were still redecorating. October brought financial worries. Her last few years had been plagued by tax officials, who sought to make her liable for British income tax on the mistaken grounds that Coombe Cottage in Australia was not her primary home. "Does the cottage have a bathroom?" one suspicious British official asked, trying to suggest that the house was just a bush cabin. "Eight!" Melba barked back in a fury. Amidst such financial concerns, at least her American investments seemed secure, but the share market on Wall Street began to crash in October. After her anxious cables to Charles Ellis went unanswered, she flew into a panic.

In the midst of her anxiety, Tommy Cochrane arrived in Paris. Now middle-aged and balding, he had quit his job to become a roving gossip columnist for the Australian press, and as usual he understood Melba's mood. Sensing she needed distraction, he set about organizing a motor tour, with himself and Herman Bemberg and Boni de Castellane as her companions. First stopping at the fashionable Atlantic resort of Biarritz, where the proprietor of their hotel persuaded Melba to plant an Australian eucalyptus tree, they drove south to Pau in the lower Pyrenees, renowned as a winter health resort. At every stop Melba added souvenirs to the already crowded car: a gilt fender, baccarat glass, Basque linen, overripe cheeses, a jar of conserve, and a dish of *pâté* when they reached Chartres. There they attended an evening service in the great cathedral, the windows glowing brightly in the setting sun. As they listened to the choir boys, Melba whispered to Tommy Cochrane, "I hate these boys. At thirteen they are doing what it took me years and years to do. And I don't know that they're not doing it better."

Aboard the *Naldera* in January 1930 Melba sailed to the fashionable destination of Egypt to escape the European winter. "It will be good to get some desert sun on my body," she told Evie. "I feel the cold much more than I did." Bemberg went with her, and while Melba joined an English house party at Aswan he stayed at a nearby hotel. When the house party proved too dull, she took refuge in his company. "He is always merry and bright but, oh! so changed and frail," she wrote to Evie sadly. She feared he soon might die.

From Aswan she wrote anxiously to Tommy Cochrane. "I am really very delicate (*entre nous*) now and must not be worried." She hoped that he would accompany her aboard ship to Australia at the end of September and protect her from problems. Tommy did not accept; but he did attend small dinner parties at her apartment when she returned to Paris in April, and contentedly accompanied her around the antique shops, applauding when she detected a fake and rejoicing when she found a bargain. He also seems to have gone with her to the Monnaie, where she stood for the last time on the stage and sang a phrase from "Caro nome" to the empty opera house. In London in June, stylishly dressed in blue with a chinchilla wrap and a long diamond necklace, she sang at a charity concert in the Park Lane Hotel. At such times she lit up like a candle—but on most days she felt decidedly redundant.

At the end of July she was at the Wagner Festival at Bayreuth and feeling more content. "Why are you not here to revel in the music?" she wrote to Fritz Hart, "—the whole place is Wagner, you feel him, you almost see him." By August 12 she was at the Salzburg Festival and thoroughly enchanted. There was an Old World beauty about the city, she wrote to Evie, that she had not felt before; and the perfection of the performances was beyond description. She had heard the most beautiful *Don Juan* and was anticipating a superb *Der Rosenkavalier*. The enactment of *Everyman* in the great square had reduced her to tears. She felt "blessed to be there."

Her next stop in Munich was also intoxicating. She arrived knowing no one but she was treated like a queen, being presented with tickets for performances of *Tristan*, *Lohengrin*, *Parsifal*, and *Die Meistersingers*. She lunched with Richard Strauss, who presented her with an autographed copy of his *Rosenkavalier*. Strauss also arranged for her to play on Mozart's spinet. "I felt inspired," she wrote excitedly. "Oh, Evie, I am so happy to be here."

Melba told Evie that she planned to drive to the German spa town of Baden Baden, then to Strasbourg, and back to Paris. And here one comes to a puzzle. Rumors persist that while in Egypt, Melba met a German surgeon who invited her to visit his clinic in Baden Baden, and that there she underwent a facelift. For many years the rumor of the facelift has persisted, even though it has been denied by Melba's family. Today it is widely accepted as a fact.

The evidence of facial surgery comes primarily from the statement of a nun, a Sister of Charity, who nursed Melba at St. Vincent's Private Hospital in Sydney the following year. "While in Europe," wrote the nun, "Dame Nellie Melba had a face-lift, possibly in Switzerland." She went on to say that the surgery had left Melba with "incisions on each side of her face," and that, having become seriously ill on the voyage to Australia, she was taken from the ship "directly to St. Vincent's." It should be pointed out that the nun's statement, written some thirty years after Melba's death, was somewhat astray in its account of the sequence of events, for Melba was not taken straight from the ship to St. Vincent's. In fact she had been in Australia for more than two months before she entered the Sydney hospital. Whether other details were misremembered, one cannot know. The nun's evidence, while valuable, is not entirely persuasive.

Although a social stigma surrounded cosmetic surgery in the 1930s, there is some evidence that Melba generally approved of facelifts. As a woman of the theatre, her appearance was of prime importance to her, and she had used discreet cosmetics for years, buying them from a

Mrs. Watson at an expensive shop on Conduit Street. She was equally concerned about the appearance of her protégées. Of one pupil she wrote, "If she would only realise how important it is to *look well*. Her voice is very beautiful but that is *not enough*." Even more to the point, she is said to have advised an aspiring singer named Norah Long to undergo cosmetic surgery. Nor can there be any doubt that Melba was distressed by her own aging looks. She disliked her portrait by John Longstaff because it made her seem "solid and elderly"; and in the final years of her life she tried to elude news photographers, preferring to be photographed by sympathetic professionals who knew how to touch up her drooping jowls and double chin.

A facelift was less straightforward medically. Melba was sixty-nine years old, in poor general health, and, most serious of all, was suffering from diabetes, which even today poses a risk in surgery. Before the advent of antibiotics, the risk of infection was high, and to someone with her medical history the risk could have been grave. Would a responsible doctor have performed surgery on a patient presenting so much risk? And would Melba have subjected herself to such a danger? And if she did decide to undergo the surgery, would she not have planned the timing of it with more care and caution? She could not have reached Baden Baden earlier than the last week in August, and she knew she had to be in Paris on September 20 to act as godmother to John Brownlee's baby. Surely Melba, the efficient organizer, would have allowed herself more than three and a half weeks for recovery.

When Melba stood on the steps of Notre Dame d'Auteuil Church beside the tiny Brownlee daughter, she relaxed her vigilance and submitted to a photograph by one of the guests. He was a former member of Melba's own troop of boy scouts in Melbourne, and was wearing his scout's badge in his buttonhole. When Melba saw it, she called out to him, "Take your photo, Boy Scout." The photo survives, and is another link in the puzzling chain of evidence. Admittedly her manner of dressing could have hidden any telltale incisions at the side of her face, for her cloche hat is pulled down around her forehead and ears, and the collar of her fur coat nestles about her neck and chin. On the other hand, there is no sign of bruising on her face or of general physical weakness. She looks in radiant health, as Melba herself recognized as soon as she saw the photograph. So delighted was she with it that she instructed the boy scout to have large prints made at her expense, and to dispatch them to the leading Australian newspapers for publication.

On October 8 Melba boarded the *Cathay* in Marseilles to sail to Australia. She was depressed, worrying about the disastrous fall in American stocks of which she owned so many. To John Lemmoné she wrote, "The bottom seems to have gone out of *everything* . . . the doctors say if I am worried it will kill me: but *I don't* care: I think I have lived too long and shall be *glad to go*." As she sailed through the heat of the Red Sea, a stage of the voyage she always hated, her face became inflamed. The inflammtion was later described as "a pimply rash" and attributed to staphylococcus bacteria, but this might well have been a euphemism for an infected incision resulting from the facelift. Of the exact mix of causes of her physical decline, we may never be certain.

At the first Australian ports of call, Melba was too ill to go ashore or see the waiting reporters, and when the *Cathay* docked in Melbourne on November 10, Evie and George met her with an ambulance and escorted her to Mount St. Evin's Hospital. Here she partly recovered, and by Christmas was home at Coombe Cottage with nurses in attendance. She was weak, Pamela remembered, but "still restless, hating her helplessness." One morning she decided she wanted to go on a picnic. George drove her to a favorite spot, and Evie and Pamela helped her sit against a tree. But she had no appetite for the chops George grilled, and was soon ready to go home. Pamela recalled that she relied increasingly on Evie, and that her voice could be heard crying plaintively through the house, "Evie, Evie."

Melba tried nonetheless to retain some semblance of normal life. She sent out Christmas cards, kept up her correspondence, and had herself driven into Melbourne, where she called at her favorite bookshop; for contrary to what Percy Colson and Beverley Nichols wrote of her, she liked good books and at that time delighted in Surtees and E. F. Benson. Some say her face was veiled during her visits to Melbourne, but she wore no veil when she visited the Hill of Content Bookshop, and asked the proprietor's wife, "How do you think I am looking?" "Much better," came the reply. "Your eyes are now clear and bright."

After Christmas, Evie had the good sense to invite her brother, Dr. William Doyle of Sydney, to visit Coombe Cottage. It was he who suggested that Melba was suffering from paratyphoid. The diagnosis cheered Melba because it seemed to explain her weakness and to offer hope of recovery. William Doyle's work, however, summoned him back to Sydney, and after his departure Melba plunged into depression. On January 13 she wrote to John Lemmoné, "I am *very ill* and very thin so don't get a shock when you see me—and don't let me see what you are feeling—the doctors are doing nothing here and I am losing ground every day." Almost as soon as Melba sent the letter, she set out with Evie on the train for Sydney, where Doyle arranged for her to enter St. Vincent's Hospital. A very special patient, she was placed under the care of Drs. Doyle and Utz and Sir Alexander McCormick. The hospital released a bulletin to the newspapers on January 26, 1931, saying that she was improving but that her condition was serious because of a general decline in her health.

For three weeks she rallied. According to the hospital's bulletins, "the skin infection from which she originally suffered had completely disappeared." She was well enough to see visitors and began to make tentative plans for the year ahead. But on February 16, to the doctors' dismay, a "fresh infection had made its appearance." The following day her condition worsened; the battle was lost. She knew that she was dying. She said to John Lemmoné, "John, why must I be subjected to a lingering death?" At times she was frightened, at others tranquil. She had not forgotten the glimpse of eternity that she believed had been given to her during the performance of *Parsifal* in New York almost exactly twenty-four years before. The memory had returned to her many times since, and never more so than now.

On February 22 the doctors diagnosed septicemia, and from then on she was only intermittently conscious. In one of her lucid intervals she sang a few bars of "Ave Maria," and in another she called for a clergyman. By evening she had drifted into a coma which lasted until her death the following afternoon.

Melba had left her affairs in order. Along with most of her estate, she bequeathed Coombe Cottage to George, who she had previously requested to keep the house up "as though I were there; because I have put my heart's blood in this beloved little spot." Happily George, and after him Pamela (Lady Vestey) have respected her wishes, and Coombe Cottage and its gardens look almost as though Melba had just stepped out of it.

Melba bequeathed most of her jewelry to Pamela, to whom she also left her cherished traveling silver tea kettle. A few personal treasures and legacies ranging from one hundred to one thousand pounds went to other relatives, friends, servants, and charities. To John Lemmoné, Beryl Fanning, Tommy Patterson, and Dora's husband Charles Lempriere, she bequeathed life annuities. She also left instructions about her burial, but they were less straightforward. At the time she wrote her will in 1928, she had wanted to lie on a hill within sight of Coombe Cottage; but in the last days of her life she elected to be buried beside her father at Lilydale cemetery.

As befitted her fame, the funeral was stupendous. Her embalmed body was carried to Melbourne by train in a carriage fitted with a plate-glass window so that the public could see the flag-draped coffin. At major railway stations the train halted, speeches were read, wreaths were laid, and brass bands played "Abide with Me" and other appropriate music. At little bush sidings, crowds gathered in silence and said a private farewell as the train passed by.

That night and next morning she lay in Scots' Church in Melbourne, where five thousand people filed past her coffin. The following afternoon, February 26, 1931, after a service conducted by the chief minister of the Presbyterian church, the funeral procession set out for Lilydale: first the flower-covered hearse and five open vans carrying wreaths, then a long cavalcade of cars and a mounted police escort. Through hushed crowds, the cortege moved up Collins Street, turned onto Spring Street, and passed Parliament House, where the flag flew at half-mast, and paused on Albert Street outside the conservatorium. Here Melba's pupils came forward to place flowers on the hearse; many of them were sobbing. A few yards further on, the cortege paused again, this time outside her own Presbyterian Ladies' College. Here uniformed schoolgirls stood in ranks along the footpath and more wreaths were laid on the coffin. Then the long line of cars passed onto Victoria Street, which was thronged with mourners, and paused at the Yarra River Bridge near the site of Doonside. Here all Richmond seemed to have turned out to honor the woman who was once little Nellie Mitchell.

And so her funeral procession moved slowly toward rural Lilydale. People sat in their cars and buggies, or stood bareheaded beside the road and watched the funeral pass: few stretches of the country road were without their spectators. The procession was so long, and so often obliged to slow down, that the summer sun was close to setting before it reached Lilydale. There the coffin was hoisted onto a gun carriage to be pulled to the hilltop cemetery by soldiers, and by the pack of Dame Nellie Melba's own boy scouts.

"I know," wrote Melba a few years before her death, "that the best of me will live, and the worst will die. There may be fires to pass, tempests to face, but there is something that fire cannot burn nor storm quench. Call it soul, ego, astral body—what you will. I call it the true eternal me."

Acknowledgments

MELBA'S LONG CAREER, centered on three continents, raises obstacles for any researcher. I was surprised to find that many of the great European and North American opera houses have no accurate records of when or what Melba sang. To piece together Melba's appearances in the United States alone was a considerable task, and I discovered tours not mentioned in any book.

By good fortune I have had access to new resources. At the Lilydale Museum I was the first biographer to study Melba's own collection of news clippings, a valuable resource though marred by gaps. At the Australian National Library I was able to read a recently acquired series of letters from Belle Patterson to her sister Melba. In the State Library of Victoria I was able to examine the private diary of one of Melba's secretaries, which had just been purchased. By yet another slice of good fortune, I gained access to the London records—not previously released—of Charles Armstrong's divorce action and Melba's petition for separation.

My task would have been impossible but for the kind assistance of the staff of those and other libraries. I thank particularly the archivists of the National Library of Australia in Canberra, the Museum of Lilydale, the Mitchell Library in Sydney, the Performing Arts Collection at the Melbourne Arts Centre, the National Archives of Great Britain, the State Library of Victoria, and the archives of the Melba Conservatorium and the Presbyterian Ladies College in Melbourne. The archivists of the Royal Opera House, Covent Garden, and the Museo Teatrale alla Scala have also given me useful information.

I also thank my editors Christopher Feik and Denise O'Dea, and my translators, Thomas Berstad, Annette Dolderer, Denise Formica, Danielle Kemp, and Jozef Rynik. My editors have made many helpful suggestions while working on my manuscript, and my translators have spent many hours rendering the Scandinavian, German, Italian, French, and Russian reviews of Melba's performances into clear English.

I am deeply grateful for the practical help of a number of my friends. Richard Hagen has solved my computer problems; Sam McCulloch has given me access to his family papers; Berenice Wright has uncovered extensive material in Mackay in Queensland, where Melba spent a crucial year of her life; Martin Price has unearthed obscure facts in British sources; John Day has corrected errors and inconsistencies; and Alastair Jackson and Elizabeth van Rompaey have generously shared their knowledge of singing and discography. Of Renn Wortley I make special mention. His enthusiasm in pursuing research clues, especially overseas, and his alertness in reading my typescript have earned my best thanks.

Lastly I express my gratitude to my daughter, Anna Blainey, and husband, Geoffrey Blainey. They have been obliged to live with Melba for a long time, and their support has never flagged.

Notes and Sources

ABBREVIATIONS

Divorce Papers: Armstrong against Armstrong and Duc d'Orléans and the Petition of Helen Porter Armstrong for a Judicial Separation, in the High Court of Justice, Probate, Divorce and Admiralty Division (Divorce) J 77/ 478, J77/480, National Archives, United Kingdom of Great Britain.

Divorce Papers George: Armstrong against Armstrong in the High Court of Justice, Probate, Divorce and Admiralty Division (Divorce), J77/ 943 #8638, National Archives, United Kingdom of Great Britain.

M: Nellie Melba

Marchesi: Madame Mathilde Marchesi

Belle: Melba's sister Isabella Mitchell, later Isabella Patterson, sometimes addressed as "Tib."

Dora: Melba's sister Dora Mitchell, later Dora Lempriere

NLA: Manuscript Collection, National Library of Australia, Canberra, Australia

LM: Museum of Lilydale, Victoria, Australia

ML: Manuscript Collection, the Mitchell Library, State Library of New South Wales, Sydney, Australia

M and M: Nellie Melba, *Melodies and Memories* (New York, 1926)

Moran: *Nellie Melba: A Contemporary Review*, compiled by William R. Moran (Westport, 1985)

Murphy: Agnes Murphy, *Melba: A Biography* (New York, 1909)

Scrap: Melba's scrapbooks, containing newspaper cuttings concerning her career, held in the Museum of Lilydale, Victoria, Australia

SLV: La Trobe Manuscript Collection, State Library of Victoria, Melbourne, Australia

Vestey: Pamela Vestey, *Melba: A Family Memoir* (Melbourne, 2000)

Chapter 1: The Incomparable Miss Mitchell

M's childhood concerts: *The Richmond Australian*, 16 Oct. 1869, and 11 Dec. 1869; M, "Singing round the world," Scrap H, 61, LM. **M's childhood:** P. Vestey, *David Mitchell: A Forfar Man* (Coldstream, 1992) 4–19; Vestey, 5–16; Murphy, 1–12; M and M, 3–21; Freda Barrymore, "Melba," The *Australasian*, 12 May 1945, 14; R. V. Billis and A. S. Kenyon, *Pastoral Pioneers of Victoria* (Melbourne, 1974), 280; *Glasgow News*, May 25, n.y. Scrap F, 93, LM, for love of Dickens's books. **M's schooldays:** John Moody, *Melba's Richmond; Some Recollections of an Era* (Richmond, 1981) *passim*; M, *The Musical Age*, 25 Aug. 1898, quoted in Moran, 32–35; K. Fitzpatrick, *PLC: The First Century* (Melbourne, 1975) 52–86; M. O. Reid, *The Ladies Came to Stay* (Melbourne, 1960) 90–91; Enrollment Book for Presbyterian Ladies College; "Melba and Her Schoolmates by an Old PLC Girl," Melbourne *Table Talk*, 25 Sept. 1902; M, "How I Began My Singing Career," *Every Lady's Journal*, 6 Dec. 1914, 714; M, *Vancouver Daily Province*, 9 July 1921, Scrap H, 26, LM, for rating correct breathing above beauty of voice; *Patchwork* (Presbyterian Ladies College Student Magazine) 1898, Dec. 1913 and May 1925; The Melbourne *Argus*, 19 Feb. 1910. **Famine relief concert:** The Melbourne *Age*, 12 Nov. 1877 and the Melbourne *Argus*, 10 Nov. 1877.

Chapter 2: The Coming of Kangaroo Charlie

M's appearance and manner: "A Woman's Letter," Sydney *Bulletin*, 27 Sept. 1902; F. Barrymore, the *Australasian*, 12 May 1945, 14; Fitzpatrick, *PLC: The First Century* 144–145. **Belief in success:** Cutting from *Weekly Dispatch*, 1919, in Scrap G, 203, LM. **Studies with Cecchi:** Melbourne *Table Talk*, 6 Dec. 1889, 16 Sept. 1898; Melbourne *Argus*, 5 March 1897; Sydney *Truth*, 15 June 1901; Thorold Waters, *Much Besides Music* (Melbourne, 1951), 119; P. Game, *The Music Sellers* (Melbourne, 1976), 72–76. Cecchi would have taught M how to "place" her voice correctly, notwithstanding the fact that, later in life, M claimed she had already learned to do this naturally through humming. **Piano studies:** M's piano teacher Alice Charbonnet was the mother of the future aquatic star Annette Kellerman; M, "The Gift of Song," *Century Magazine*, June 1907; *Australasian*, 2 April 1881 for review of Charbonnet concert; Melbourne *Herald*, 13 Oct. 1924. **Mother's illness and death:** Winty Calder, *Golden Dreams and Geordie Nous* (Mt. Martha, 1991), 50; Isabella Mitchell's death certificate; Melbourne *Argus*, 22 Oct. 1881. **Vere's death:** M and M, 20; Vere Mitchell's death certificate. **Voyage to Mackay:** Passenger list for *Ly-ce-moon* in Melbourne *Argus*, 14 Aug. 1882 and *Sydney Morning Herald*, 15 Aug. 1882; passenger list for *Alexandra* in *Brisbane Courier*, 21 Aug. 1882 and *Mackay Mercury*, 23 Aug. 1882. **M in Mackay:** *Mackay Mercury*, 16, 20 and 27 Sept., 14 and 28 Oct., 1 and 15 Nov. 1882; Berenice Wright, "Melba Enchanted Mackay," Mackay *Daily Mercury*, 3 Jan. 1995; Mackay *Daily Mercury*, 2 Nov. 2002; M. D. "Melba: A Reminiscence," Mackay *Daily Mercury*, 24 April 1931; *Mackay Mercury*, 24 April 1931; Waters, *Much Besides Music*, 110–111. **Charles Armstrong:** *Melbourne Punch*, 23 Dec. 1897, for Kangaroo Charlie as a nickname; Julian Stuart, *Part of the Glory* (Sydney, 1967), 67, for Charlie's horsemanship; Vestey 17–19. **Voyage to Brisbane:** *Brisbane Courier*, 22 Dec. 1882,4. **M's wedding:** M. Ogg, "Saw Melba Married,"

Mackay *Daily Mercury*, 11 Nov. 1948; John Hetherington, *Melba: A Biography* (Melbourne, 1967), 31; Vestey, 20–21; *Australian Etiquette, or the Rules and Usages of the Best Society in the Australasian Colonies* (Melbourne, 1885), 360–363; *Brisbane Courier*, 18. Dec. 1882, for shipping lists for Annie's arrival and the Armstrongs' departure. **M's quarrels with Charlie:** Divorce Papers. **M rejoins Charlie in Mackay:** T. Waters, *Much Besides Music* 112–115; *Mackay Mercury*, 12 March, 4 and 7 July 1883, and 31 Jan., 2 and 3 Feb. 1884; Vestey, 222; M and M, 21–22; Murphy, 13 for yachting accident, also Scrap A, newspaper cutting, n.d., LM; George Armstrong's birth certificate; Mackay *Daily Mercury*, 22 Oct. 1931; Divorce Papers for quarrel. **M's date of leaving Mackay:** *Mackay Mercury*, 13 Feb. 1884, see shipping list. Previous biographies have her leaving in January.

Chapter 3: A Voice in Ten Thousand

Melbourne in 1884: P. Game, *The Music Sellers*, 80–81. **Charlie follows M to Melbourne:** *Mackay Mercury*, 27 Feb. 1884. **M determines to be a singer:** M, "Gift of Song," *Century Magazine*, June 1906. **Elsasser concert:** M and M, 24–25; Melbourne *Argus*, 19 May 1884; *Australasian*, 24 May 1884; *Federal Australian*, Scrap A, 4, LM. **M resumes lessons with Cecchi:** Melbourne *Table Talk*, 16 Sept 1898; Sydney *Truth*, 15 June 1901; Waters, *Much Besides Music*, 118. **M returns briefly to Mackay:** *Mackay Mercury*, 10 Sept., 18 and 22 Oct. 1884. **Sorrento concert:** Reviews in Melbourne *Herald* and *Bulletin*, Scrap A, 62, LM; Program of concert held in Melba Conservatorium, Melbourne; *Geelong Advertiser*, 10 Sept. 1921. **Ballarat concert:** Article by R.M., n.s, n.d, Scrap B, 69, LM; *Ballarat Courier*, 14 Feb. 1885. **Leidertafel concerts:** Reviews from *Argus*, *Daily Telegraph*, *World*, *Australasian*, Ballarat *Evening Post*, and *Ballarat Courier*, Scrap A, 12–15, LM. **Concerts with Kruse:** Melbourne *Table Talk*, 3 July 1885; Melbourne *Age*, 1 Aug. 1885; Sydney *Daily Telegraph*, 6 July 1885; Sydney *Morning Herald*, 7, 9, 15 July 1885; Sydney *Bulletin*, 18 July 1885; Waters, *Much Besides Music*, 115–116; M to Arthur Hilliger, n.d. and 31 Aug. and 6 Sept. 1885, ML, AM82/2; Waters, *Much Besides Music*, 115; Reviews in Scrap A, 36–38, LM. **Jack Moore:** "Melba: An Impression of the Eighties by JM," *Sydney Morning Herald*, 16 Oct. 1926. **M planning to go to Europe and not Mackay:** M to Maggie Emblad, 16 Aug. 1885, ML, AM82/11; M to A. Hilliger, 20 Aug. 1885, ML. **Hilliger correspondence:** M to A. Hilliger, 31 Aug., 10 and 21 Sept., 31 Oct., Dec. 1885, ML; Annie Mitchell to A. Hilliger, 31 July, 6 Sept., 1 Oct., 10 Nov., 12 Dec. 1885, 29 March 1886 AM82/2, ML. **Concert reviews:** Melbourne *Argus*, 5 and 20 Oct. 1885; Melbourne *Age*, 10 Oct. 1885; *Federal Australian*, 10 Oct. 1885; *Australasian*, 19 and 20 Oct. 1885; Sydney *Daily Telegraph*, 24 Dec. 1885; *Bathurst Free Press*, 2 Feb. 1886; *Bathurst Daily Times*, 1 Feb. 1886; *Clarence and Richmond Examiner*, 2, 4, and 5 Jan. 1886. **M awarded medal:** *Melbourne Punch*, 4 March 1886; Waters, *Much Besides Music*, 16. The medal was a gold star with a lyre at its center, attached to a blue ribbon on which was embroidered the letter A, for Armstrong. It was inscribed "Honour to Mrs Armstrong from friends and admirers, 22 January 1886." **Preparations for departure:** News clippings, Scrap B, 103, LM; *Mackay Mercury*, 10 Feb. 1886 for ship's passenger list showing date of Charlie's departure from Mackay; Melbourne *Argus*, 4, 8, and 11 March 1886; *Australian Musical News*, 1 March 1933; Sydney *Bulletin*, 11 and 18 March 1886; *Melbourne Punch*, 4 March 1886; Murphy, 20.

Chapter 4: My First Great Moment

Voyage: Divorce papers for quarrels. **London, Rustington, Exhibition opening and M's first concerts:** M and M, 29–32; London *Times*, 5 May 1886; M to Rudolph Himmer, 13 May 1886, NLA, MS1496; Waters, *Much Besides Music*, 116–117; W. Ganz, *Memories of a Musician* (London, 1913), 316–319; London *Times*, 1 and 19 June 1886 (advertisements); *Musical World*, 5 June 1886 and *Daily News*, 3 June 1886; Cole Lesley, *The Life of Noel Coward* (London, 1976), 2; David Mitchell was received at a royal levee: see London *Times*, 1 June 1886. **Adelina Patti:** John Dizikes, *Opera in America: A Cultural History* (New Haven, 1993), 178–183. **Madame Marchesi:** Murphy, 24; Typescript by Leopold Podhragy, "Melba, Garcia and Marchesi," and also photographs of the École Marchesi. Podhragy Collection, NLA, MS2647; M, "You Sing: Memories of Marchesi," news clipping, n.d., n.s., ML, QA927.84; M and M, 33–36. **Quarrels with Charlie:** Divorce Papers.

Chapter 5: I Am Melba

Training at the École Marchesi: Blanche Marchesi, *A Singer's Pilgrimage* (London, 1923), 22–57; Emma Eames, *Some Memoirs and Reflections* (New York, 1937), 51–60; newsclipping of interview with M, Spokane, 13 March, n.y., Scrap G, 38, LM; Vestey, 30–31 and 35 for M calling Marchesi "mother"; M and M, 36–43; Mathilde Marchesi, *Marchesi and Music: Passages from the Life of a Famous Singing Teacher* (London 1898), 252–259; M to A. Hilliger, 29 March and 24 Aug. 1887, ML, MS82-2; M, "Gift of Song," *Century Magazine*, June 1906; news clipping, *Vancouver Daily Province*, 9 July 1921, Scrap H, 26, LM; Murphy, 24–27. **M becomes Melba:** Murphy, 24; Melbourne *Argus*, 5 Feb. 1910; M and M, 62. **Strakosch:** M and M, 44–48; Murphy, 26; Marchesi, *Marchesi and Music*, 253, states that Lapissida and Dupont heard M on 21 March. They must surely have known of M's previous contract, as references had appeared in newspapers. **Audition at Paris Opéra:** M and M, 27. **Taffanel *cadenza*:** M and M, 177. **Concerts:** Marchesi, *Marchesi and Music*, 252, also assorted newpaper cuttings—NLA, MS2647. **Charlie buckjumps with Buffalo Bill:** *Mackay Mercury*, 1 March 1892. **M's trill:** M, "How I Began My Singing Career," *Every Lady's Journal*, 6 Dec. 1914, 714. **M's house in Brussels:** Divorce papers give M's address as Rue de Bailli or Bailly, as does *Evenement*, 20 Oct. 1887. However, M called the street Rue de Bac in M and M, which would seem to be a mistake. **Quarrel with Charlie:** Divorce Papers. **Debut in Brussells:** M and M, 48–51; Murphy, 27–30; Vestey, 34–36; M, *Every Lady's Journal*, 6 Dec. 1914.

Chapter 6: At Last a Star

Reviews of debut: *Gallignani's Messenger*, 18 Oct. 1887; *La Chronique*, 18 Oct. 1887; *La Réforme*, 15 Oct. 1887; *Le Figaro*, 19 Oct. 1887; *L'Étiole Belge, Journal de Bruxelles* and *La Gazette*, 15 Oct. 1887; *Le Sport*, 19 Oct. 1887; *Il Mondo Artistico*, 27 Oct. 1887, NLA, MS2647; *Every Lady's Journal*, 6 Dec. 1914; *Mackay Mercury*, 18 Oct. 1887; London *Times*, 15 Oct. 1887; Murphy, 27–29. **Marchesi's reaction:** Vestey, 36–37. **M's undramatic style of singing**: News clipping, *Vancouver Daily Province*, July 1921, Scrap H, 26, LM; Eames, *Some Memories and Reflections*, 53, for Marchesi insisting on no gesturing while singing; Murphy, 148, for too much emotion ruining sound. **Marchesi's letters:** Vestey, 38–41. **Quarrels with Charlie:** Divorce Papers; Percy Colson, *Melba: An Unconventional Biography* (London, 1932), 31; *Melbourne Punch*, 24 Dec. 1891, for Charlie at Salle Dupont. **Charlie at Sarina:** *Jane Bardeley's Outback Letterbook: Across the Years (1896–1936)*, ed. John Atherton Young (Sydney, 1987), 143, 145; Patricia C. Phillips, *Sarina Shire in Retropsect* (1988, self-published), 170; *Mackay Mercury*, 14 Oct. 1882; Survey map of Sarina, vol. 6, folio 390 (C124135). In the 1890s, Sarina was called Plane Beach. Part of the area is now called Armstrong's Beach. **The Paris Opéra or Covent Garden?:** Vestey, 42, 47. **Covent Garden debut:** M and M, 57–60; Murphy, 33–38; London *Times*, 1, 25 and 29 May and 18 June 1888; *Illustrated London News*, 23 June 1888. **Lessons with Gounod:** M and M, 41–42; Marchesi, *A Singer's Pilgrimage*, 48–49; Eames, *Some Memories and Reflections*, 64. **De Reszke and Patti:** M and M, 52–53; J. de Reszke to M, n.s. n.d., LM. **Joachim:** Colson, *Melba*, 32; Vestey, 47; J. Joachim to M, 27 Dec. 1888, LM. **Marchesi and Paris Opéra:** Vestey, 47, 48. **Charlie returns to Australia:** *Mackay Mercury*, 8 Sept. and 2 Oct. 1888. **Marchesi critical of M's Violetta:** Marchesi to M, 24 Feb. 1889, LM. The tenor Pierre Emile Engel was the "bellower." **Lady de Grey:** M and M, 60–61. **Fear of Charlie:** M to Marchesi, n.d. NLA, MS2647. **M leaves Brussels:** Murphy, 39–40; Marchesi to M, n.d., LM.

Chapter 7: It Is Applause I Live For

Debut in Paris: Vestey, 54–58; Murphy, 41–46; M and M, 61–65. French newspaper cuttings of reviews, n.s., n.d, and an interview for *Pall Mall Gazette*, n.d., Scrap B, 9, LM. Vestey, 54–58; London *Times*, 10 May 1889. **Reaction of M's sisters:** Melbourne *Herald*, 13 Oct. 1924. **Upstaging Emma Eames:** News clipping, n.s., n.d., Scrap B, 7, LM. **Cossira loses voice:** M and M, 64–65. Melba placed this incident in the open-ing performance, but it may have occurred later; news clipping, n.s., n.d., Scrap B, LM. **Lady de Grey and her circle:** M and M, 74–78; E. F. Benson, *As We Were* (Lon-don, 1930), 158–166; E. F. Benson, *Mother* (London, 1925), 138; Augusta Fane, *Chit Chat* (London, 1926), 95–99; Laura Beatty, *Lillie Langtry* (London, 1999), 56, 74–75, 155–156, 167–169; Margot Asquith, *The Autobiography of Margot Asquith* (London, 1920), 164. Beverley Nichols, *All I Could Never Be* (Sydney, 1949), 66; Vestey, 59–63; Virginia Cowles, *Edward VII and His Circle* (London, 1956), 70. **London Opera sea-son:** London *Times*, 19 and 29 June 1889; London *Punch*, 29 June 1889; news clipping, "Chat with a Nightingale." n.s. Scrap B, 9, LM. **George:** Vestey, 62; news clipping, n.s., n.d., Scrap B, 13, LM, for interview with George. **Quarrels with Charlie and holiday at Ouchy:** Divorce Papers. **Reviews of Hamlet:** Scrap B, LM. **Sarah Bernhardt:** M and M, 66–67. **Faust performance:** The *British Australian*, 11 April 1918; news clip-ping, Scrap B, 44, LM. **Monte Carlo:** T. J. Walsh, *Monte Carlo Opera* (London, 1975), 50–53; A. Edwards, *The Grimaldis of Monaco* (London, 1992), 130–132, 161–168. In-terview with M by Blanche Roosevelt, news clipping, Scrap B, 5, LM.

Chapter 8: Melba's Duke

M's operas for 1890: Murphy, 53–54; P. G. Hurst, *The Age of Jean de Reszke* (London, 1958), 121–124. **Reviews:** Assorted news clippings, Scrap B, 43, 44, 46, LM. **Philippe:**

Cornelius Otis Skinner, *Elegant Wits and French Horizontals* (Boston, 1962), 12–13; *Annual Register* for 1890, 8–9, 29, 280; London *Times*, 6, 7, 10, 11, and 13 June 1890, 27 June for Zoe Caryll's concert; James Pope–Hennessy, *Queen Mary* (London, 1959), 196–197. Scrap B, 11, LM for newspaper cutting marked by M; *Melbourne Punch*, 30 April 1891 for Philippe's likeness to Charlie; B. Marchesi, *A Singer's Pilgrimage*, 63, for Philippe's knowledge of singing. **Concert at Windsor Castle:** London *Times*, 5 July 1890; "The Queen and the Prima Donna," news clipping, Scrap B, 11, LM; M and M, 82–85. Melba included Tosti among the performers, but newspaper accounts do not mention him. **Music at Marlborough House and at Lady de Grey's:** Vestey, 71; London *Times*, 26 July 1890; Benson, *As We Were*, 60–61; M and M, 82, 87. **Nodule:** Melbourne *Herald*, 13 May 1922; Michael Scott, *The Record of Singing to 1914* (New York, 1977), 20; W. J. Henderson, "The Art of Melba" in Moran, 244. **Philippe in Marienbad and America:** London *Times*, 27 June 1890, *Annual Register* for 1890, 57. **Les Avants:** Melbourne *Herald*, 13 May 1922. The reporter called the town Les Abants, but Switzerland has no such town so I am assuming it is a misspelling of Les Avants. Interestingly, Les Avants is the present home of the Australian soprano Joan Sutherland. **M and Philippe at Ouchy:** Divorce Papers; Maie Casey, "Melba Revisited" in Moran, 361. **M in Paris:** M and M, 78–79, 86–87; news clipping, Scrap B, 49, LM for Kate Moore's concert; Cowles, *Edward VII and His Circle*, 329, and M and M, 154–155 for Worth; *Home News*, n.d. Scrap B, 37, LM and *Standard*, 6 July 1891, Scrap B, 24, LM for Micaela's dress. **M's Operas in Paris:** Scrap B, 11, LM for reviews; Melbourne *Argus*, 7 March 1891; M and M, 90–91. **Journey to Russia:** Lady Lytton to M, 23 Dec. n.y., LM; M and M, 105–106; *The Lady*, July 1891, Scrap B, 24, LM, for Elsa's cloak. The cloak is now in the Performing Arts Collection, Melbourne Arts Centre. **St. Petersburg:** M and M, 107–111; Murphy, 60–63; Reviews of operas, *Do, re mi, Theatre and Music, Courier of the Theatre, Russian Opera*, Scrap B, 17, 20–21, LM; London *Times*, 2 and 24 Jan. 1891 for Philippe's journey to Russia. **Quarrel with Charlie:** Divorce Papers.

Chapter 9: What Say They? Let Them Say

M in Vienna: Divorce Papers; Colson, *Melba*, 64–66. **Charlie mistaken for Philippe:** *Mackay Mercury*, 19 May 1891; *Melbourne Punch*, 30 April 1891. **Charlie returns to Australia:** Charlie left England in *Massilia* on 20 March and arrived in Melbourne on 1 May 1891; see London *Times*, 20 March and 4 May 1891; *Mackay Mercury*, 19 May 1891; Stuart, *Part of the Glory*, 67; K. H. Kennedy, *Mackay Revisited* (Mackay, 2002), 107–110 for strike; Divorce Papers. **M in a fire:** *Melbourne Punch*, 7 May 1891 and 20 Nov. 1902. **George at school:** Vestey, 96; Newspaper interview with M, n.s., n.d., Scrap B, 60, LM; Divorce Papers. **M at Paris Opéra:** *Le Sport*, 11 March 1891. **M at Ashley Gardens:** Divorce Papers; Colson, *Melba*, 30; London *Times*, 23 May 1891; Valery Kingman, *Ashley Gardens: Backward Glances* (London, 1990). Melba rented her apartment from a Mr. William Graham. **M at Covent Garden:** Newspaper reviews, Scrap B, 34, 35, 37, 46, 108, LM; *Melbourne Punch*, 16 July 1891; news clippings, Scrap B, 32 and 34 for Juliette's dress. **Gala for kaiser and concerts:** London *Observer*, 12 July 1891, Scrap B, 29, LM; *The Queen*, 4 July 1891, and *Daily Standard*, 26 June 1891, Scrap B, 25, 37, LM; Murphy, 65–66, for M's lost curls. **Ward of Chancery:** Armstrong versus de Grey, see Index of Pleadings at the Court of Chancery, Public Record Office of Great Britain. The papers relating to the action were lodged 5 Sept. 1891, and a motion was granted by a judge on 30 Jan. 1892; *Melbourne Punch*, 15 Oct. 1891. **M applies for a legal separation and Charlie applies for a divorce:** Divorce Papers. **Reactions to divorce action:** *Melbourne Punch*, 24 Dec. 1891 for Charlie wanting to duel; *Mackay Mercury*, 7 and 10 Nov. 1891 for ladies' deputation; London *Times*, 5 and 6 Nov. 1891 for the serving of the divorce papers and comte's anger. *The Reminiscences of Lady Randolph Churchill* (London, 1908), 218, for Baron Hirsch's castle. **M's Paris apartment:** Scrap B, 60, LM. **George as schoolboy:** Vestey, 63 (photo); John Hetherington's typescript of *Nellie Melba*, 129, quoting a letter from Isabella Mitchell, 27 Nov. 1952, SLV, MS9740. **M's reception at Paris Opéra:** *Melbourne Punch*, 17 Dec. 1891. **Verdi refuses to teach M:** Charles Osborne, *The Complete Operas of Verdi* (London, 1969), 81. **Braga:** Murphy, 73; M and M, 112. **The effect of a cold audience:** M, "The Gift of Song," *Century Magazine*, June 1907. **Success in Palermo:** Reviews in Scrap B, 43, 82, LM. **Success on Riviera:** News clippings, Scrap B, 42, LM; Murphy, 66. **Failure in Rome:** *Panufula, Il Popolo Romano, La Tribuna, Messaggero*, 6 March 1892, Scrap B, 42 and 43, LM.

Chapter 10: Fear Nothing, Melba

A woman's emotional safeguard: Mrs. Patrick Campbell, *My Life and Some Letters* (London, n.d.), 85. **Progress of the divorce case:** Divorce Papers; London *Times*, 17 and 20 Feb., 14 and 24 March 1892; *Melbourne Punch*, 24 March 1892. **M refuses Harris:** *Melbourne Punch*, 5 May and 23 June 1892. **Bemberg and Elaine:** *London Punch*, 16 July 1892; M and M, 87–94; news clippings, Scrap B, 69, LM; London *Times*, 6 July 1892; sheet music inscribed by Bemberg to *"ma petite soeur d'adoption"* from *"ton vieux frére"* at Melba Conservatorium, Melbourne; news clippings, Scrap B, 45, LM, for *Elaine* and for Goring Thomas concert. **G. B. Shaw on *Elaine*:** "Words from Bernard Shaw," in Moran, 67–68. **Concerts and expression of sympathy by royalty:** *Melbourne Punch*, 16 June 1892; London *Times*, 2 July 1892; news clipping, Scrap B, 64, LM. **Philippe returns and relatives give jewelry:** London *Times*, 5 and 19 Sept. 1892 (court circular) and news clipping, Scrap B, 13, LM. **Aix-les-Bains:** News clippings, Scrap B, 69, LM; M to Marchesi, Aix-les-Bains, n.d. NLA, MS2647. **Fire at Metropolitan Opera**: M and M, 112–113. M places the fire and her interview with Abbey and Grau in February 1892 after leaving Sicily. The fire occurred on 27 August, 1892. **Aida:** Vestey, 75–76; P. Tosti to M, 27 August, n.y. LM; news clippings, Scrap B, 50, 53, 54, 57, LM; Mabel Wagnalls, "Melba: The Australian Nightingale" in Moran, 165–168. Wagnalls's article assumes M was little known in 1892, which is not so; W. J. Henderson, "The Art of Melba" in Moran, 244, for "clarion quality" of M's voice; *New York Times*, 13 Nov. 1892, for incident with flowers; M and M, 234–235. **Otello:** News clippings, Scrap B, 53, 54, 64 and 103, LM; Vestey, 76. **Louie Bennett:** *Melbourne Punch*, 11 July 1895, 2 Aug. 1896; news clippings, Scrap F, 99 and Scrap B, 71, LM. **London's Savoy Hotel:** Stanley Jackson, *The Savoy* (New York, 1964), 18–24; Kingsley Amis, ed., *The Savoy Food and Drink Book* (London, n.d.), 11–16; Vestey, 82; *Melbourne Punch*, 8 Dec. 1892, for party with Cheiro; M and M, 232–235. **Elaine in Paris:** Marchesi, *Marchesi and Music*, 284. **To sing *Lucia* at Scala:** News clippings, Scrap B, 57, 64, LM; Vestey, 80; newsclippings, Scrap B, 57, LM. **M's Paris apartment:** News clippings, Scrap B, 56, 60, 71, LM. **Tour of British Isles:** Vestey, 78–79; reviews, Scrap B, 56–87, LM; *Melbourne Punch*, 5 July 1894 and Scrap B, 103, for M preferring opera to concerts;

J. B. Priestley, *The Edwardians* (London, 1970), 108, for serious concert audiences; *Manchester Guardian*, 11 Aug. 1921, for M confessing that her first tour of the British Isles was a failure. **La Scala:** News clippings, Scrap B, 82, 85, LM; M to Marchesi, 16 March 1893, Performing Arts Collection, Melbourne Arts Centre; Vestey, 80; Murphy, 73–81; M and M, 114–117; news clippings, Scrap B, 59, LM, for "no standing still for us." **In Milan, Florence, Genoa, Lyon, and Marseilles:** News clippings, Scrap B, 70, 77, 79–90, LM. Quotation concerning M's "magic" is from *Express de Lyon*, Scrap B, 89, LM. The archives at the Teatro della Scala seem to indicate that M sang only in *Lucia* in 1893. Reviews, however, suggest that early in April she sang one performance of *Rigoletto*, taking over from the German soprano Sophie Stehle. M also sang one act of *La Traviata* at a charity performance at Scala. On leaving Milan, M sang *Lucia* in Florence and Genoa, and *Hamlet* in Lyons at the Grand Theatre.

Chapter 11: Across the Atlantic

Pagliacci: News clippings, Scrap B, 56–57, LM; London *Times*, 20 May 1893; Vestey, 84. **I Rantzau and Mascagni:** David Stivender, ed., *Mascagni: An Autobiography* (New York, 1988), 106–110; reviews, Scrap B, 56,63, LM; London *Times*, 10 July 1893. **State performance for Prince George's marriage:** News clippings, Scrap B, 59, LM. **M's continuing devotion to Philippe:** Adelaide Lubbock, *People in Glass Houses* (Melbourne, 1977), 106. Lubbock wonders to whom M is referring, but the context makes clear it is Philippe. **Charlie at Lingfield:** *Mackay Mercury*, 11 March 1892. Lingfield Park is now the site of a well-known racecourse. **Charlie and George:** Vestey, 65, 86. **M Joins Mascagni in Italy:** M to Flo, n.d. ML. Flo may be Mrs. Hwfa Williams, a leading hostess and friend of Gladys de Grey; news clippings, Scrap B, 103, LM. **M's look of sadness:** Murphy, 90. **Scandinavia:** News clippings, Scrap B, 93–101, LM; M and M, 81, 121–124. **Arrival in America:** M and M, 125–127: M is incorrect in saying she stayed at the Waldorf Hotel—she was at the Savoy. **Rival sopranos:** Ira Glackens, *Yankee Diva* (New York, 1963), 225; Murphy, 89; Rupert Christiansen, *Prima Donna* (London, 1984), 175. M to Blanche Marchesi, 23 May 1914, NLA MS2647; Calvé was a past pupil of the École Marchesi, where she did not flourish; but she remained on good terms with Marchesi. Calvé and M are said to have upstaged Eames by taking a box together for the U.S. premiere of *Werther* and ostentatiously following the score whenever Eames sang. The audience soon watched them and not Eames—see Moran, 159. **Metropolitan season 1893–1894:** G. Fitzgerald, ed., *Annals of the Metropolitan Opera: The Complete Chronicle of Performances and Artists* (Boston, 1989), 47–54. I have used this excellent book for all Met seasons; Murphy, 88–99; news clippings, Scrap B, 72–76, 103–105, LM, *Melbourne Punch*, May 3, 1894; Vestey, 92; Murphy, 144–145 for incident with newsboy—Murphy places the incident later but it would seem to be on M's first visit. **Boni de Castellane and Francis Marion Crawford:** M and M, 159–161 and 130–131; C. Otis Skinner, *Elegant Wits and Grand Horizontals*, 84–88; L. H. Tharp, *Mrs. Jack: A Biography of Isabella Stewart Gardner* (Boston, 2003), 69–71, 172–174; Murphy, 116; M is said by Murphy to have met de Castellane during the 1894–1895 season, and Crawford during the 1895–1896 season. However, de Castellane was courting Gould during the winter of 1893–1894, and Crawford was in New York in the winter of 1893–1894 and in Constantinople in 1895–1896; see *New York Times*, 26 Dec. 1895. **Final Lucia:** Murphy, 98.

Chapter 12: I Won't Sing "Home Sweet Home"

La Scala and Verdi: M to Marchesi, n.d., NLA, MS2647; Mary Jane Phillips to Matz, *Verdi: A Biography* (Oxford, 1993), 719, 726–727; Charles Osborne, *The Complete Operas of Verdi* (London, 1969), 81; Charles Osborne, *Verdi* (London, 1987), 301; M and M, 119–120; Vestey, 81, for photograph of Verdi; Cast list from La Scala archives, Museo Teatrale alla Scala. **Tosti and Venice:** M and M, 98–99. **Covent Garden Season 1894:** London *Times*, 11 and 16 June and 9 July 1894; Moran, 69, for Shaw. **Pêches Melba and Melba Toast:** M and M, 235–236; Jackson, *The Savoy*, 25; *Savoy Food and Drink Book*, 14–18; The painter Rupert Bunny claimed he was one of Melba's twelve guests who first sampled Pêches Melba: see Colette Reddin, *Rupert Bunny Himself: His Final Years in Melbourne* (Melbourne, 1987), 122–123. Some say Philippe was present, but according to the London *Times*, 26 July 1894, he did not arrive in England until 25 July. **Ada Crossley:** M to Marchesi, n.d., NLA, MS2647; *Melbourne Punch*, 29 March, 13 and 20 Sept. 1894. **Lemmoné:** Moran, 171; Donald Westlake, *Dearest John: The Story of John Lemmoné* (Bowerbird Press, 1997), 41–42. **Australian tour:** *Melbourne Punch*, 19 July, 20 Sept., 11 Oct. 1894; *Melbourne Argus*, 5 Feb. 1910 for vow to earn individual fame and associate it with Australia. **Metropolitan season 1894–1895:** *Annals of the Metropolitan Opera*, 55–62; Reviews in *New York Times*, 28 Oct., 14 and 20 Nov. 1894; Irving Kolodin, *The Metropolitan Opera* (New York, 1967), 118; Moran, 245; Walter Damrosch, *My Musical Life* (New York, 1923), 130–131; Jean de Reske to M, n.d., LM; Murphy, 217 for de Reske; M to Marchesi, n.d., NLA, MS2647; M and M, 139–141 for Tamagno. **Bemberg:** Michael Scott, *The Record of Singing to 1914*, 84. **M with Boston Symphony:** Tharp, *Mrs. Jack*, 186. **Melba's popularity:** M to Madame, NLA, MS2647; Murphy, 110. **American opera houses:** Dizikes, *Opera in America*, chapter 25. **Ellis and starring fever:** *New York Times*, 14 and 18 April 1895; M and M, 142–144; Damrosch, *My Musical Life*, 128–129. **Final Metropolitan concert:** Murphy, 110. Murphy gives an incorrect date for the concert. **Fire during Faust:** London *Times*, 10 June 1895. Murphy places this incident incorrectly in 1889; see Murphy, 49. **Fernley:** M and M, 99–100, 156–157; J. B. Atkins, *Incidents and Reflections* (London, 1947), 155, contains an account of M singing on the river at Henley in the early 1900s—it may be a confusion with this; London *Times*, 3 June 1895; *Melbourne Punch*, 11 July 1895. **Covent Garden season and concerts 1895:** London *Times*, 17 June 1895; *Melbourne Punch*, 1 and 22 Aug. 1895; Moran, 69, for Shaw's comment, M to Marchesi, n.d., NLA, MS2647; M and M, 152–153. **Philippe at the Savoy:** Jackson, *The Savoy*, 28–29. **Landon Ronald:** M and M, 101–103; Landon Ronald, *Variations on a Personal Theme* (London, 1922), 101–103. **Massenet:** M and M, 154; Murphy, 113; Vestey, 88. **Melba Operatic Concert Company:** *New York Times*, 22 Sept. 1895. *Montreal Herald*, 5 Oct. 1895. The tour started in Montreal on 4 Oct.; Ronald, *Variations on a Personal Theme*, 54, 61, 67–69; Landon Ronald, *Myself and Others* (London, n.d.), 168–169; Murphy, 118–119, 105–106. Murphy gives an incorrect year for the robbery in Chicago—it occurs while Ronald is with her; Dizikes, *Opera in America*, 252–254 for Auditorium; M to Marchesi, 23 Nov. 1895, NLA, MS2647; *Melbourne Punch*, 13 Jan. and 2 April 1896. **In New York:** Murphy, 113–114; M and M, 162; Vestey, 94; M to Mr. Morris, n.d., Performing Arts Collection, Arts Centre, Melbourne; Moran, 161 for madman on stage. **Last night of season:** *New York Times*, 3 May 1896; Ronald, *Myself and Others*, 166.

Chapter 13: Brünnhilde

Death of Madame's granddaughter: M to Blanche, Boston, 16 Feb. 1896 (postmark), NLA, MS2647. **Grau:** Damrosch, *My Musical Life*, 105. **Covent Garden season 1896:** *Melbourne Punch*, 6 Aug. 1896; Ronald, *Myself and Others*, 18–19; M and M, 103–104. **Haddon Chambers:** Moran, 174–176 for Henry Russell's dinner party; Morris Miller, *Australian Literature*, vol. 1 (Sydney, 1973), 360–362; Hesketh Pearson, *Beerbohm Tree* (London, 1956), 52–54. **Brünnhilde:** *Philadelphia Inquirer*, 11 and 12 Nov., 24 Dec. 1896; *New York Times*, 13, 17, 22, 24, 26, 27, 28, 29 Nov. and 2, 3, 4, 6, 12, 17, 19, 22, 27, 31 Dec. 1896; and 10, 18, 19, 20, 24, 31 Jan. 1897; Christiansen, *Prima Donna*, 177, 129; Kolodin, *The Metropolitan Opera*, 125; Murphy, 124–126; M and M, 163–164; Joseph Wechsberg, *Red Plush and Black Velvet* (Boston, 1961), 254, for quote from Bispham. Bispham had sung a small role earlier in *Siegfried* and was now watching from a box; M and M, 163–164; Glackens, *Yankee Diva*, 187–190; Murphy, 139, claims that M sang the Forest Bird in *Siegfried* in a private performance before the queen, but gives no place or date.

Chapter 14: With the Americans Heart and Soul

The Voice: M to Marchesi, n.d. n.s. (written in the U.S. some time in 1896, from internal evidence), NLA, MS2647; Felix Semon, *The Autobiography of Felix Semon* (London, 1926), 217. **M, Nordica, and de Reske:** Glackens, *Yankee Diva*, 194, 198–200. **M, Ernest, and Annie:** Murphy, 123; *Melbourne Punch*, 25 Nov. 1897; Vestey, 11. **M's London season:** London *Times*, 10 June 1897; Elizabeth Longford, *Queen Victoria* (London, 1964), 688–689; Harold Rosenthal, *Two Centuries of Opera at Covent Garden* (London, 1958), 284; *Melbourne Punch*, 15 April, 19 June, 22 July 1897; M and M, 51; Morris Miller, *Australian Literature*, vol. 1, 361 for Haddon Chambers quote; *New York Times*, 29 Nov. 1896 for Henderson on M's Juliette. **Dora:** Dora to Belle (addressed by the pet name "Tib"), 25 Aug. n.y. Rue de Prony, and Dora to Belle (Tib), n.d., Paris, NLA, MS9561. **Bergamo:** Murphy, 130–131, 267; M and M, 157; M to Jeannie Armstrong, n.s., n.d., ML. **M misses her family:** Dora to Belle (Tib), n.d., n.s., fragment of letter, NLA, MS9561. *Melbourne Punch*, 25 Nov. 1897; Melbourne *Table Talk*, 10 Nov. 1897; M, Dora and Joachim seem to have visited Ernest in Berlin in 1897. **Provincial tour:** Melbourne *Table Talk*, 31 Dec. 1897; M to Marchesi, Savoy Hotel, n.d., NLA, MS2647. **Damrosch tour:** M to Belle (Tib), 25 Nov. (postmark), n.y. NLA, MS9561; M to Marchesi, 30 Dec. 1897, NLA, MS2647; Damrosch, *My Musical Life*, 123–127; Glackens, *Yankee Diva*, 200–203. In Philadelphia with the Damrosch Company, M sang Rosina on 10 Jan. 1898 and Nordica sang Brünnhilde in *Gotterdammerung* on 11 Jan. 1898; *Philadelphia Inquirer*, 5 and 28 Dec. 1897, 2, 9, 14 Jan. 1898; *New York Times*, 18, 23, 25, 29 Jan., 6, 16, 17, 18, 26 Feb., 8 Aug. 1898; *Melbourne Punch*, 3 March 1898. M's failure in *Aida* in New York and not in Philadelphia could have been influenced by the size of the opera houses: the Academy of Music held 2,900, while the Metropolitan Opera House held 3,600. *Chicago Tribune*, 15, 20, 26 March 1898; *Boston Post*, 20 Feb. and 12 March 1898; Murphy, 132–136; M to Marchesi, 1 April 1898, Denver, NLA, MS2647. **California:** M and M, 164–171; Murphy 135–136; *San Francisco Chronicle*, 20 and 22 April 1898; *San Francisco Bulletin*, 1 May 1898; *Los Angeles Times*, 26 April 1898, and also Moran, 160, for an account of the fire by William Armstrong. Contrary to M's account in M and M, 170–171,the theatre was not badly damaged nor did M make a speech. **M and the candy-seller:** Murphy, 134. *La Bohème:* Kolodin, *The Metropolitan Opera,* 131; *New York Times,* 17 May 1898; for M and Miss Bennett at Manhattan Hotel see *New York Times,* 18 May 1898. M also might have seen *La Bohème* the previous October in London. **London season 1898:** Murphy, 137; London *Times,* 28 June 1898. **Joachim:** Ronald, *Variations on a Personal Theme,* 61–63; the manuscript of the *cadenza* for "L'Amero," with a letter from Joachim on its back page, was discovered by the present author in a pile of unsorted music at the Melba Conservatorium, Melbourne; London *Times,* 28 June 1898; Arthur Rubinstein, *My Young Years* (London, 1973), 46, for Joachim's infatuation with M provoking malicious gossip. **Dora and Ernest return home:** Melbourne *Table Talk,* 16 Sept. 1898. **M disappointed that Ernest had abandoned his studies:** M to Belle (Tib), Halton, NLA, MS9561. **Haddon Chambers:** Melbourne *Table Talk,* 30 Dec. 1898, 31 March and 21 April 1899; Colson, *Melba,* 210. **Puccini:** M and M, 118 119, 249; Murphy, 142–143; M to Marchesi, Florence, 9 Sept. 1898, NLA, MS2647; Howard Greenfield, *Puccini* (New York, 1980), 114–115.

Chapter 15: There Is No Melba But Melba

Melba's Metropolitan salary: Rupert Christiansen, *The Grand Obsession: An Anthology of Opera* (London, 1988), 141–142. M had the second-highest salary at the Metropolitan, receiving $1,650 per performance. De Reske received $2,101, Sembrich $800. **M at the English language *La Bohème*:** *New York Times,* 29 Nov. 1898. **M on tour:** Murphy, 142–145; *Philadelphia Inquirer,* 18, 27, 31 Dec. 1898, 10 Jan. 1899; M to Belle (Tib), 1 Jan. 1899, NLA, MS9561; *San Francisco Chronicle,* 12, 14, 16, 19, 21, 22, 24, 26 March 1899; On tour M sang *La Bohème, Faust, Les Huguenots, Roméo et Juliette, The Barber of Seville,* and *Lucia.* **England 1899:** Murphy, 149–152; *London Punch,* 12 July 1899; M to Belle (Tib), Hinchinbrooke and M to Belle (Tib), Halton, NLA, MS9561; Arthur Sullivan to M, 16 May 1899; M and M, 77; Frederic Morton, *The Rothschilds* (London, 1961), 161–162; London *Times,* 6 Nov. 1899, LM. **Dutch tour:** Murphy, 153. **German and Austrian tour:** M to Belle (Tib), New Year's Eve, 1899, and M to Belle, 2 Jan. (postmark) 1900, Vienna, NLA, MS9561; M to Marchesi, n.d., Vienna, NLA, MS2647; M to Marchesi, 20 Jan. 1900, Performing Arts Collection, Arts Centre, Melbourne; M to Fritz Muller, 14 Jan. 1899 (postmark) and 2 Feb. 1900 (postmark), SLV, MSB500; Murphy, 153–161; M and M, 172–181; *New York Times,* 4 Feb. 1900, for review of Berlin concert; Henry de la Grange, *Gustav Mahler: The Years of Challenge* (Oxford, 1995), 219–220 for Mahler's comments. **Divorce and speculation on M's remarriage:** *New York Times,* 17 Feb. and 11 April 1900; *Mackay Mercury,* 5 June 1900; Roger Neill, "Haddon Chambers and the Long Arm of Neglect," *Quadrant,* July 2008, 77–86; M to Belle (Tib), 21 April 1900, NLA, MS9561. **Monte Carlo:** M to Marchesi, Metropole Hotel, n.d., NLA, MS2647; M to Belle (Tib), 17 Feb. 1900, NLA, MS9561; Walsh, *Monte Carlo Opera,* 269–273; M sang two Violettas and two Rosinas, with her final performance being 13 March. **Return to Germany:** M to Belle (Tib), Hotel Bristol, n.d., NLA, MS9561. **M and the Dreyfus case:** Pierre Dreyfus (ed. and translated by D. C. McKay), *The Dreyfus Case* (New Haven, 1937), 269–272; E. R. Tannenbaum, *The Action Française: Die Hard Reactionaries in Twentieth-Century France* (New York, 1962), 333–334; De Castellane was a prominent supporter of Philippe and consequently anti–Dreyfus, but M nevertheless used his help in furnishing her house. **Great Cumberland Place:** London *Times*, 14 Dec. 1907 for sale advertisement of the house; *Melbourne Leader*, 9 Aug. 1902; Moran, 158. **Thames–side house:** Thérèse Radic, *Melba: The Voice of Australia* (Melbourne, 1986) for photograph of Bemberg and M's guests, opposite 55; Colson, *Melba*, 70; M and M, 89. **London Season 1900:** London *Times*, 13 June 1900; *London Punch*, 30 May, 13 June, and 20 June 1900; M sang one Mimi, two Lucias, three Marguerites, one Rosina and five Juliettes. **Ireland:** Murphy, 162–163. **Galveston hurricane:** Vestey, 95. **American tour:** Murphy, 164–165; *Los Angeles Daily Times*, 10 Nov. 1900; *San Francisco Chronicle*, 13, 16, 17, 18, 20, 23 Nov. 1900. Performances were at the Grand Opera House; *New York Times*, 12 and 17 Jan. 1901; *Boston Post*, 31 March and 7 April 1901. M was ill for part of the Boston season. *Chicago Tribune*, 21 and 23 April 1901. **London season 1901:** Rosenthal, *Two Centuries of Opera at Covent Garden*, 293; London *Times*, 7 June and 13 July 1901. **Quarrywood Cottage:** Vestey, 104 and 106 for photograph. **Plans to tour Australia:** M to Belle (Tib), 28 Sept. n.y., Baron's Court, and 19 Oct. n.y., Great Cumberland Street, NLA, MS9561; M to J. C. Williamson, Barons Court, n.d., NLA. **Ireland:** Murphy, 167; M to Jeannie Armstrong, Holyhead, n.d., and M to Jeannie Armstrong, Baron's Court, 15 Oct. 1901, ML, MSS3500. **M and Eton boy:** M to Eton Boy, n.d., NLA, MSB73; M to Jeannie Armstrong, Isle of Mull, n.d., and Haddon Chambers to Jeannie Armstrong, Isle of Mull, n.d., ML, MSS3500. **Discusses Australian tour and difficulties with her family with Belle:** M to Belle (Tib), two undated letters from the Ritz Hotel, Paris, NLA, MS9561. **Monte Carlo:** Murphy, 168–169; Walsh, *Monte Carlo Opera*, 154–157, 270–271; M and M, 190–193; three undated letters from Monte Carlo, M to Belle (Tib), two of them postmarked 17 Feb. and 6 March 1902, NLA, MS9561; three undated letters from Monte Carlo, M to Jeannie Armstrong, two from Hotel L'Ermitage, one from Le Nid, ML, MSS3500. **Paris:** M to Jeannie Armstrong, Elysée Hotel, n.d., ML, MSS3500; Glackens, *Yankee Diva*, 212; Patricia Fullerton, *Hugh Ramsay: His Life and Work* (Melbourne, 1988), chapter 9, especially 92–93; M to Marchesi, n.d., for *Tristan*, NLA, MS2647. **Germany:** M to Marchesi, n.d., for golden wedding and Madame being M's only teacher, NLA, MS2647. **Cecchi:** *Melbourne Punch*, 11 March 1897; "A Geebong Goddess," *Sydney Truth*, 15 June 1901; Waters, *Much Besides Music*, 119; *Table Talk*, 16 Sept. 1898. **London season 1902:** Murphy, 169–172; London *Times*, 26 May and 11, 17, and 25 June, 1902; M to Belle (Tib), Great Cumberland Place, n.d., NLA, MS9561; Fullerton, *Hugh Ramsay*, 96–98; Colson, *Melba*, 96; *Melbourne Leader*, 9 Aug. 1902; Shaw Desmond, *The Edwardian Story* (London, 1949), 228; M to Belle, 31 May 1902, for jewels, quoted on 174 of John Hetherington's manuscript, SLV, MS9740; M to Belle (Tib), Great Cumberland Street, 25 June 1902 for canceled coronation, NLA, MS9561. **Departure for Australia:** *Australasian*, 9 Aug. and 13 Sept. 1902; *Table Talk*, 11 Dec. 1902 for May Donaldson.

Chapter 16: My Native Land

M's arrival in Brisbane and Sydney: Melbourne *Age*, 19 Sept. 1902; *Sydney Morning Herald*, 18, 19, 20 Sept. 1902; Murphy, 183–187. **Reporters question M:** Hetherington, *Melba*, 115. **M meets her father:** The *Bulletin*, 23 Sept. 1902 and M and M, 200–202. **Arrival in Melbourne:** M and M, 203; Murphy, 187–191; *Melbourne Punch*, 2 Oct. 1902; Melbourne *Argus*, 22 Sept. 1902; The *Bulletin*, 27 Sept. 1902. **Settling into Myoora:** M and M, 204–206; *Table Talk*, 16 Oct. 1902 and 12 Feb. 1903; Melbourne *Argus*, 7 and 8

Oct. 1902. Melba was an early giver of telephone interviews while at Myoora. **Melba's jewels:** Melbourne *Argus*, 7 and 8 Oct. 1902; *Table Talk*, 9 Oct. 1902; *Melbourne Punch*, 16 Nov. 1902. In New Zealand M was accompanied by an ex–Scotland Yard detective; see Christchurch *Press*, 21 Feb. 1903. **Social life in Melbourne:** Melbourne *Age*, 23 and 24 Sept. 1902; Melbourne *Argus*, 19, 20, 23, and 24 Sept. 1902; *Table Talk*, 25 Sept. and 16 Oct. 1902; The *Bulletin*, 4 Oct. 1902. **Melbourne and Sydney concerts:** The *Bulletin*, 4 Oct. 1902; *Melbourne Punch*, 2, 16 and 23 Oct. 1902; *Table Talk*, 2 Oct. 1902; Melbourne *Argus*, 29 and 30 Sept., 1 and 3 Oct. 1902; *Sydney Morning Herald*, 13 and 24 Oct. 1902; *Sydney Daily Telegraph*, 13 and 24 Oct. 1902; Melbourne *Herald*, 24 Feb. 1902, for smashing of attendant's thumb; Moran, 310, for David Mitchell approaching Musgrove. **Brisbane concert:** *Mackay Standard*, 3 Nov. 1902; *Mackay Mercury*, 4 Nov. 1902; *Sydney Morning Herald*, 28 and 30 Oct. 1902; "Three Green Bonnets" was composed by M's friend Madame Guy d'Hardelot, and was a favorite of audiences around Australia; see *Bendigo Advertiser*, 20 Dec. 1902; Melba also gave four concerts in Adelaide in Nov. 1902 and Jan. 1903; see *Sydney Morning Herald*, 14 and 17 Nov. 1902. **Opera concerts in Melbourne and Sydney:** *Melbourne Punch*, 20 and 27 Nov. and 11 Dec. 1902. **Parties at Myoora:** *Melbourne Punch*, 25 Dec. 1902, 12 Feb. 1903. **M visits Yarra Valley:** Murphy, 200–201; Sue Thompson, *A Diva's Day Out* (Melbourne, 2002), 3–26; Melbourne *Age*, 10 Nov. 1902. **Lord Richard Nevill:** ed. Alexandra Hasluck, *Audrey Tennyson's Vice Regal Days* (Canberra, 1978), 13, 38, 243–245, 256, 262, 284, 305. **Reaction to Melbamania and mishaps:** Murphy, 198–200. Marshall Hall's speech, reproduced in Murphy, was among those considered fulsome by some Melburnians; see *Melbourne Punch*, 27 Nov. 1902; *Melbourne Punch*, 8 and 22 Jan. 1903; *Table Talk*, 11 and 25 Dec. 1902; Waters, *Much Besides Music*, 118. **Drought relief:** Melbourne *Argus*, 3 and 4 Nov. 1902; London *Times*, 3 and 5 Nov. 1902. **Perth concerts:** The *West Australian*, 13, 16 and 20 Jan. 1903. **Tasmania:** *Melbourne Punch*, 12 March 1903; *Launceston Examiner*, 12 and 13 Feb. 1903; *Hobart Mercury*, 14 Feb. 1903; Hetherington, *Melba*, 22 for Kirby anecdote. **New Zealand:** *Lyttleton Times*, 18, 20 and 21 Feb. 1903; Christchurch *Press*, 20 and 21 Feb. 1903; Robert Gibbings, *Till I End My Song* (London, 1957), 21, for supposed verbal thrashing of editor, quoted by Hetherington, *Melba*, 73; *New Zealand Herald*, 2, 3 and 4 March 1903; M and M, 216–222. M is incorrect in saying that she went to New Zealand in Oct. 1902, accompanied by "John"—presumably John Lemmoné; Murphy, 206. **John Norton:** Melbourne *Truth*, 28 Feb., 28 March, 18 April, 10 and 24 Oct., 28 Nov. 1903; Cyril Pearl, *Wild Men of Sydney* (Melbourne, 1965), 214–216. **M about to leave Australia:** *Melbourne Punch*, 2 April 1903; *Sydney Morning Herald*, 16 and 18 March, 14 and 15 April 1903; Melbourne *Argus*, 14 and 15 April 1903; Melbourne *Herald*, 14 April 1903. Violet Clarke studied with Marchesi, adopted the stage name of Violette Londa, and died of meningitis in Bombay in 1907.

Chapter 17: Patience, Dear Madame, Patience

To hear lies: M, "If I Had My Life Over Again," *Brisbane Daily Mail*, 25 Feb. 1931. **Tita Ruffo and Fritzi Scheff:** *The Autobiography of Titta Ruffo* (Dallas, 1995), 193–195; Michael Scott, *The Record of Singing to 1914* (New York, 1977), 117; London *Times*, 12, 16, and 27 June, 1903; *New York Times*, 1 July 1903; Rosenthal, *Two Centuries of Opera at Covent Garden*, 299; Colson, *Melba*, 226. **M rumored to be cruel:** M and M, 326–328; *Sydney Daily Telegraph*, 21 June 1924 for M declaring that the temperamental artist is dead today. **Rough crossing of Atlantic:** M to Belle (Tib), Douglas House, n.d., NLA, MS9561. **American tour 1903–1904:** *Boston Post,* 3 and 28 Dec. 1903; *New York Times,* 11 and 19 Dec. 1903; M to Belle (Tib), Hotel Touraine, Boston, n.d., NLA. **Monte Carlo season:** Walsh, *Monte Carlo Opera,* 179–182; Prince Albert of Monte Carlo to M, 24 March 1904, LM; Saint-Saëns to M, 11 and 24 May and 24 June 1904, LM; M and M, 197–198; Murphy, 211–213; Brian Rees, *Camille Saint-Saëns* (London, 1999) 354–358. **M and recording:** Ronald, *Variations on a Personal Theme,* 95–104; *Encyclopaedia Britannica* under "Phonograph"; M to Belle (Tib), 2 Dec. n.y., but 1904 from text of letter, for gift of gramophone, NLA, MS9561; Walsh, *Monte Carlo Opera,* 181–182; M and M, 250–252; Murphy, 218, 225–226; Melbourne *Argus,* 17 and 19 Sept. 1904 for playing M's records at concerts in Melbourne; London *Times,* 20 Jan. 1904 for list of fourteen records of M on sale. **De Greys' party:** London *Times,* 6 June 1904 for party announcement in court circular; Lord De Grey to M, 4 June 1904, LM, and Vestey, 115; Ronald, *Myself and Others,* 114–119. **Covent Garden season 1904:** London *Times,* 21 June 1904 for *Hélène* review, 30 May 1904 for *La Bohème* review, 11 May 1904 for *Roméo et Juliette* review; Saint-Saëns to M, 4 July 1904, LM; Vestey, 116; *New York Times,* 11 June 1904 for arts and sciences medal; Murphy, 217–218. **M at Stresa:** Moran, 176. This is a difficult visit to date, but it is known to have preceded the trip to Venice. **Venice:** Colson, *Melba,* 102. Another visit that is difficult to date. From mid-1903 onward, M was hoping to sing *Tosca* at Covent Garden—see Moran, 290—and hoping to study *Tosca* and *Madama Butterfly* with Puccini. *Madama Butterfly* was not completed until December 1903 and M was in America and England for the spring and summer of 1904, so the autumn of 1904 is the likeliest date; Murphy, 212, for the role of *Madama Butterfly* written for M. **Accident in Paris:** *New York Times,* 12 Sept. 1904; Murphy, 218. **Second recording session:** London *Times,* 20 Jan. 1905. Begbie is describing the recording session on 20 Oct. 1904—see notes accompanying "Nellie Melba, The 1904 London Recordings," Naxos Historical Recordings, 8.110737 and 8.110738. **M's letter to George and George's reply:** Vestey, 118–119; *New York Times,* 13 Nov. 1904 for an announcement that M was staying at the Manhattan Hotel. **M's illness:** *New York Times,* 29 Nov. 1904 for canceled concert in Pittsburgh, and 11 Dec. 1904 for Boston concert; Stanley Jackson, *Caruso* (London, 1972), 106, for quote about Conreid; Tharp, *Mrs. Jack,* 254. **M tours:** *Chicago Tribune,* 9 Jan. 1905, for Auditorium concert; Vestey, 119, for George on tour. **Parkina:** Murphy, 217, 221; *New York Times,* 29 April 1906; M to Marchesi, Great Cumberland Place, n.d., NLA, MS2647; *Melbourne Punch,* 8 Dec. 1904 and 12 Jan. 1905 for Parkina's Australian tour; *New York Times,* 29 April 1906. **Covent Garden season 1905:** Jackson, *Caruso,* 115–116 for Caruso's jokes; also M and M, 189–190. **George's shyness:** M to Marchesi, Blounts, n.d., NLA, MS2647; Murphy, 223–224 for M's birthday party. **M's concert tour of Britain:** Ronald, *Variations on a Personal Theme,* 53–59 and 63–64. **M at Windsor Castle:** Mary Garden and Louis Biancolli, *The Mary Garden Story* (New York, 1951), 91–94; Lionel Cust, *King Edward and His Court* (London, 1930), 213–215; Murphy, 230; *New York Times,* 1 Aug. 1907 for friction over roles between Garden and M.

Chapter 18: Hammerstein Swallows the Canary

Hammerstein: Moran, 101–105; M and M, 240–243; *New York Times,* 3 April and 6 May 1906; Vestey, 123; Freddie Stockdale, *Emperors of Song* (London, 1998), 91–116.

Coombe Cottage in England: London *Times*, 27 April 1906 for M back in London; London *Times*, 24 July 1886, for advertisement for Coombe Cottage; M. Girouard, *The Victorian Country House* (London, 1971), 178, 197; *Surrey Comet*, 2 Sept. 1988. **M's health:** *Surrey Comet*, 9 June 1906; M to Mrs. Robertson-Grant, 15 May 1906, SLV, MSB185; M to Marchesi, Great Cumberland Place, n.d. NLA, MS2647—also for Irene Ainsley; London *Times*, 11 July 1906 for review of Ainsley concert (Bechstein Hall is later Wigmore Hall). Murphy, 241–243, also for Ainsley. **Amy Castles:** M to Belle (Tib), 31 May 1902, Hetherington Papers, SLV, MS9740; Waters, *Much Besides Music*, 121–126; *The British Australasian*, 19 Oct., 23 Nov. and 28 Dec. 1905, 25 Jan. and 5 July 1906. After leaving Marchesi, Castles is usually said to have repaired her voice by studying with Jacques Bouhy, but in 1905–1906 she was successfully studying with M's friend, Australian-born Minna Fischer; see *Melbourne Punch*, 24 Oct. 1907. The news of Amy Castle's Coombe Court concert was supplied to *Punch* by the Duchess of Westminster; Murphy, 244; *Melbourne Truth*, 15 June 1901 for Melba supposedly not helping other singers. **George's marriage:** Vestey, 122, 126; *Musical Standard*, 29 Dec. 1906; *New York Times*, 9 Sept. and 19 Dec. 1906; London *Times*, 18 Dec. 1906. **San Carlo Opera and electrophone relay:** London *Times*, 6 Oct. and 5 Nov. 1906. **Hammerstein's preparations and Alda's accusations:** Frances Alda to Blanche Marchesi, 26 Oct. 1906, Performing Arts Collection, Arts Centre, Melbourne; Frances Alda, *Men, Women, and Tenors* (Boston, 1971), 72; Murphy, 262, for Trentini and Donalda being M's protégées; London *Times*, 14 June 1906 for review of Alda's poor singing; *New York Times*, 26 Aug. 1906 for copyright row over *La Bohème*. **M at Manhattan Opera:** *New York Times*, 6 May 1906; Stockdale, *Emperors of Song*, 116–125; Murphy, 251–266. During the preceding year, performances of *La Traviata* at Covent Garden had been dressed in mid-nineteenth-century style, instead of the customary seventeenth-century style. At Melba's insistence, Hammerstein's *La Traviata* was also set in the mid-nineteenth century—see *New York Times*, 3 Jan. 1907; *New York Times*, 31 Dec. 1906, 1, 3, 4 , 6, 8, 9, 12, 14, 24, and 31 Jan., 9, 11, 20, and 24 Feb., 1, 2, 10, 12, 13, 16, 17, 20, 21, 24, and 26 March, 2 and 3 April 1907; Tharp, *Mrs. Jack*, 95, 254, for the yellow diamond; M and M, 244–249. **George and Ruby quarrel:** Divorce Papers George; London *Times*, 14 Nov. 1908 for report of divorce; M to Belle (Tib), n.d., 165 West 58th Street, LM. **Parsifal:** Murphy, 266–267; *Weekly Dispatch*, 1 June 1919; M and M, 249–250; Also *Table Talk*, 24 Aug. 1922, and Alison Gyger, *Opera for the Antipodes* (Sydney, 1990), 278, for M's singing of religious music. At St. Paul's she sang "Magdalen at Michael's Gate" by her friend Liza Lehmann and the American spiritual "Swing Low, Sweet Chariot." Her interpretations deeply moved her audience; Hetherington, *Melba*, 274 for M's supposed lack of spirituality. **M's departure from New York:** Murphy, 272–274; *New York Times*, 3 April 1907.

Chapter 19: Nobody Sings Like Melba and Nobody Ever Will

M's illnesss: London *Times*, 25 May 1907. **Ruby's appendicitis and quarrel:** M to Marchesi, n.d., ML, AM82; Divorce Papers George; London *Times*, 14 Nov. 1908. **Voyage to Australia:** Though some have thought otherwise, George and Ruby did in fact travel with M on the *Oruba*, and M witnessed their quarrel—see London *Times*, 14 Nov. 1908 and Divorce Papers George. **Ercildoune:** J. A. Froude, *Oceana* (Sydney, 1985), 46–48; *Melbourne Punch*, 31 Oct. 1907. **M in Melbourne with Clara Butt:** *Melbourne Punch*,

19 and 26 Sept. 1907; two undated letters, M to Susan FitzClarence, Ercildoune and Flete, NLA, MS9331. **Gracedale House:** *Melbourne Punch,* 10 Oct. 1907—Mr. and Mrs. Robert Power were also in Melba's party. **Evelyn Doyle:** *Melbourne Punch,* 7 Nov. 1907; *Table Talk,* 9 Jan. 1908. **Ruby's diptheria:** M to Susan FitzClarence, n.d., Flete, NLA; *Melbourne Punch,* 7, 14, and 28 Nov. 1907—see also for Melbourne Cup. **Government House ball:** *Melbourne Punch,* 2 Jan. 1908. **M's concerts:** *Melbourne Punch,* 28 Nov. 1907; Melbourne *Argus,* 2 Dec. 1907, *Sydney Morning Herald,* 11 and 16 Dec. 1907; Melbourne *Herald,* 2, 3, and 27 Dec. 1907; Murphy, 286–287. **Tetrazzini:** Christiansen, *Prima Donna,* 294–295; Rosenthal, *Two Centuries of Opera at Covent Garden,* 324–325; London *Times,* 16 Nov. 1907 for review of *Lucia*; *Melbourne Punch,* 23 Jan. 1908 for news items concerning Tetrazzini intended for the "eye of a certain diva"; *New York Times,* 1 Dec. 1907 for M canceling Manhattan Opera contract. **M's departure:** *Table Talk,* 6 Feb. 1909 for country concerts; Melbourne *Argus,* 2 March 1908 for "sunshine and pleasure"; M to Kate McCulloch, n.d., Flete, by courtesy of the McCulloch family; *Melbourne Punch,* 27 Feb. 1908, for M's farewell at station. Murphy, 290–291. **Voyage on *Orontes*:** Murphy 291–292; Divorce Papers George; London *Times,* 14 Nov. 1908; Radic, *Melba: The Voice of Australia,* 128, for quote concerning jelly; John Bird, *Percy Grainger* (Melbourne, 1977), 65, for M thinking John Grainger "a funny old man"; Ronald, *Myself and Others,* for M's bohemian manner. **M in Paris:** Murphy, 292–293, and London *Times* and *New York Times,* 12 June 1908, for Paris Opera performance, also Greenfield, *Caruso,* 139. Caruso was under great stress during the performance, having just heard that his father had died and his wife had left him. *New York Times,* 17 May 1908 for Hammerstein at Chatelet Theatre. **Covent Garden season 1908 and rivalry with Tetrazzini:** Moran, 290, for Higgins's letter to Pitt; *New York Times,* 12, 17, 20, and 27 May, 21 June, 18 and 19 July, and 9 Aug. 1908 for skirmishing and confrontation between the divas; news clipping, Melba Conservatorium, Melbourne, for "many are called"; Charles Nelson Gattey, *Luisa Tetrazzini* (Portland, 1995), 103–104, for Tetrazzini's enmity toward M; Jackson, *The Savoy,* 98, for Tetrazzini and M both supposedly at the Savoy. **Lady de Grey's letter and M's anniversary matinee:** Gladys de Grey to M, n.d., Ritz Hotel, LM; Vestey, 131–132; London *Times,* 25 June 1908. The matinée raised nearly $10,000 for the London Hospital. **Breakdown of George's marriage:** London *Times,* 26 July and 14 Nov. 1908; Murphy, 311, for George in Marienbad. **M's projected tour of Australia**: London *Times,* 16 July 1908. **M leaves Great Cumberland Place:** London *Times,* 16 Jan. 1909. Mrs. George Cornwallis West is named as the new owner of the house, but she was better known as Lady Randolph Churchill; London *Times,* 4 Nov. 1908, for M moving to the Ritz. **M's second season with Hammerstein:** *New York Times,* 8, 12, 15, and 16 Dec. 1908, 3, 6, 10, and 12 Jan. 1909; *Melbourne Punch,* 28 Jan. 1909. Stockdale, *Emperors of Song,* 132–136. **M in Naples:** *Melbourne Punch,* 18 Jan. 18, 1909; M to Susan FitzClarence, n.d., at sea, NLA, MS9331; *The Autobiography of Titta Ruffo,* 195, 424 and n154. Ruffo was a friend of Tetrazzini, which may account for some of his animosity to M.

Chapter 20: So Many Triumphs, So Little Happiness

M to live in Australian bush: M to Louise, n.d., Coombe Cottage, Kingston, copy of letter in Hetherington Papers, SLV, MS9740. **Sentimental tour:** *Melbourne Punch,* 11 Feb. and 4 March 1909; *New York Times,* 8 Nov. 1909; *Table Talk,* 5 March 1903 for Agnes Murphy's novel. **Arrival in Melbourne:** *Melbourne Punch*, 4 and 11 March 1909. **Melbourne concerts:** *Melbourne Punch*, 21 March and 1 April 1909. **Tasmanian concerts:** *Tasmanian Mail*, 10 and 17 April 1909; *Hobart Mercury*, 8 April 1909; *New York Times*, 26 Dec. 1909 for laughing at the hyperbolic Tasmanian review. **New Zealand concert:** London *Times*, 25 May 1909; Westlake, *Dearest John*, 65; M to Susan FitzClarence, 28 April 1909, Wellington, NLA, MS9331; M and M, 218–222; M dates this tour with Lemmoné as 1902, but it should be 1909. **Sydney concerts:** *Melbourne Punch*, 3, 10, 18 June 1909. **Queensland concerts:** *North Queensland Register*, 19 July 1909; Westlake, *Dearest John*, 64–65. **Outback concerts:** Una Bourne, "A Few Unusual Notes of Pianists Life" (a pamphlet published in Melbourne and lodged at the Melba Conservatorium, Melbourne), passim; M and M, 255–264. **Melbourne Exhibition Building concert:** *Melbourne Punch*, 21 Oct. 1909. **M's racehorse:** *Melbourne Punch*, 9, 16, and 23 Sept. 1909; London *Times*, 24 Sept. 1909. **M as suffragette:** *New York Times*, 8 Nov. 1908 and 2 Jan. 1909; Colson, *Melba*, 201. **M buys a farm:** *Melbourne Punch*, 4 Nov. 1909 and 30 Nov. 1911. **M and female friendship:** M to Louise, n.d., Coombe Cottage, Kingston, Hetherington Papers, SLV, MS9740; M to Susan FitzClarence, 5 Aug. 1907, NLA, MS9331. Lady Susan FitzClarence, born Lady Susan Yorke, changed her name by marriage to FitzClarence in 1910 and to Birch by marriage in 1920. For convenience I refer to her throughout as Susan FitzClarence. **M's singing classes:** Prof. Peterson to Beryl Fanning, 10 and 24 Sept. 1909—also entries from Fanning's diary for 27 and 29 Sept. 3, 4, 11, 18, and 28 Oct. and 1, 9, and 16 Nov. in "Scrapbook and diary belonging to Beryl Fanning," SLV, MS9902. Beryl Fanning changed her name by marriage to Kingsley-Newell in 1917, but for convenience I refer to her throughout as Beryl Fanning. **Craignair:** Archibald Marshall, *Sunny Australia* (London, 1911), 84–86. **Farmhouse which became Coombe Cottage:** Vestey, 133, 136; Bird, *Percy Grainger*, 86; Eileen Dorum, *Percy Grainger, The Man Behind the Music* (Melbourne, 1986), 97–107, for John Grainger's syphilis and M and Belle's continuing concern for him. M and Belle did not understand the nature of his illness until Mrs. Grainger informed them of it shortly before his death. **George's operation:** M to Beryl Fanning, 3 Feb. 1910, SLV, MS9902; M to Susan FitzClarence, n.d., off Colombo, NLA, MS9331.

Chapter 21: The Greatest Musical Event

Projected opera tour: Gyger, *Opera in the Antipodes*, 149. Westlake, *Dearest John*, 66–67, 105; two undated letters from M to Beryl Fanning, Boulevard Malesherbes, and one undated letter from M to Beryl Fanning, Belvoir Castle, SLV, MS9902; in May, M visited Monte Carlo and Paris and saw Bernhardt and the de Reskes. **M in London:** London *Times*, 27 July 1910. **M's American tour:** Westlake, *Dearest John*, 69–72, 113; *The Toledo Blade*, 5 Nov. 1910; M to Beryl Fanning, 18 Oct. n.y., Grand Forks, SLV, MS9902; *New York Times*, 25 and 30 Nov. 1910 for M's Metropolitan performances, all of which had excellent reviews; *New York Times*, 7 and 10 Dec. 1910 for M becoming ill. **M leaves America:** M to Susan FitzClarence, 18 Aug. 1910, NLA, MS9331 for Christmas plans and the cooling of her relationship with Haddon Chambers; See also Roger Neill, "Haddon Chambers and the Long Arm of Neglect," *Quadrant*, July 2008, 83; *New York Times*, 19 and 23 Dec. 1910, for *Mauretania* crossing. **John Lemmoné:** Westlake, *Dearest John*, 91–96, for Lemmoné's relationship with his wife and Mabel, and 106 for M's attitude to Mabel and for M regarding Lemmoné as her confidant; *Diary* kept by Irene

Gritten, 23, SLV, PA96/168 for Lemmoné's sweetness and cleverness. **M at Guildhall School:** London *Times*, 20 May 1911; *New York Times*, 4 June 1911; Landon Ronald, *Myself and Others*, 167–168. **Concerts and Covent Garden gala:** London *Times*, 23 May, 27 June 1911. **M's arrival in Melbourne and Coombe Cottage:** *Melbourne Punch*, 17 Aug., 30 Nov., 7 Dec. 1911. **Sydney season:** Alison Gyger, *Opera for the Antipodes*, 149–163; *Sydney Morning Herald*, 4 Sept. 1911; *Sydney Daily Telegraph*, 4 Sept., 24 Oct. 1911, for M and gallery goers; Melbourne *Herald*, 8 Dec. 1911 for M's attention to detail; *Melbourne Punch*, 31 Aug. 7, 14, and 28 Sept., 5, 12, and 26 Oct., and 2 Nov. 1911; M to Beryl Fanning, Macleay Street, n.d., SLV, MS9902 for M's illness; Moran, 311, for M and Claude McKay. **M and John McCormack:** Lily McCormack, *I Hear You Calling Me* (Milwaukee, 1949), 71, for M and McCormack in tableau; L. A. G. Strong, *John McCormack: The Story of a Singer* (London, 1941), 165–169, and also *Melbourne Punch*, 2 Nov. 1911, for Lemmoné's speech on M's behalf; M to Susan FitzClarence, n.d., NLA, MS9331 for M's dissatisfaction with McCormack; Westlake, *Dearest John*, 106, for McCormack being a pig; Alison Gyger, *Opera for the Antipodes*, 162, for M sharing a curtain call with McCormack. **M's opera season in Melbourne:** *Melbourne Punch*, 9, 16, 23, 30 Nov. and 7 Dec. 1911; Melbourne *Herald*, 8 Dec. 1911, for interview with M; Melbourne *Argus*, 11 Nov. 1911 for death of Dammarco; Gyger, *Opera for the Antipodes*, 163–168. **Final night of tour:** *Sydney Daily Telegraph*, 23 Dec. 1911. **M stays in Melbourne and gives ball at Coombe Cottage:** *Table Talk*, 7 March 1912; M to Susan FitzClarence, 1 May 1912, NLA, MS9331. **Quinlan Opera Company:** Gyger, *Opera for the Antipodes*, chapter 15; *Melbourne Punch*, 23 May and 1 Aug. 1912. **M worries about George:** Vestey, 137. **M's provincial tour:** M to Beryl Fanning, Preston, 31 Oct. 1912, SLV, MS9902. **George's marriage:** Marriage certificate for 20 Feb. 1913; M to Beryl Fanning, 24 Feb. 1913, SLV, MS9902; Vestey, 137–142. **George's illness:** M to Susan FitzClarence, Avenue Henri Martin, n.d., NLA, MS9331; M to Beryl Fanning, Ritz Hotel, n.d; SLV, MS9902. **M sings in Paris:** *New York Times*, 24 April 1913. **Concerts and galas:** Two undated letters: M to Beryl Fanning, Highcliffe Castle, and Avenue Henri Martin, SLV, MS9902; London *Times*, 5, 23, and 25 May, 21 and 24 June 1913; *New York Times*, 23 May 1913; Rupert Christiansen, *The Great Obsession*, 252, for Sitwell quote; Osbert Sitwell, *Tales My Father Taught Me* (London, 1962), 15, for claim that M sang *Madama Butterfly*. **M in America:** London *Times*, 13 Sept. 1913, for Kubelik tour; *New York Times*, 22 Oct. and 3 Nov. 1913 for Carnegie Hall and Hippodrome concerts; M to Beryl Fanning, Buffalo, 14 Oct. n.y., SLV, MS9902. **Marchesi's death:** *New York Times*, 19 Nov. 1913; M to Blanch Marchesi, 26 Nov. 1913, Performing Arts Collection, Arts Centre, Melbourne; M and M, 40. **Nordica's supposed death:** Glackens, *Yankee Diva*, 271. Nordica in fact died 10 May 1914. **Tour:** M to Blanche Marchesi, Chicago, 26 Jan. 1914 (postmark), NLA, MS2647. **M's father's health failing:** M to Beryl Fanning, 12 Jan. 1914 and 10 Feb. 1914, SLV, MS9902. **Henry Russell:** Moran, 176–177; *New York Times*, 8 March and 14 June 1914. **M at Covent Garden:** London *Times*, 21 April and 8 June 1914. **M's father's illness:** M to Beryl Fanning, 15 April 1914, SLV, MS9902; obituary of David Mitchell, *Yarra Glen Guardian*, 11 April 1916.

Chapter 22: The Queen of Pickpockets

M arrives in Melbourne 1914: *Melbourne Punch*, 30 July 1914. **Falklands victory:** *Melbourne Punch*, 9 March 1916. **Patriotic concerts:** Murphy, 174, for Albert Hall

Coronation Concert on which M's Australian patriotic concerts were based; *Melbourne Punch*, 10 and 17 Sept. and 8 Oct. 1914; Melbourne *Argus*, 11 Sept. 1914; *Sydney Sun*, 27 Sept. 1914; *Lilydale Express*, 18 Sept. 1914 for Evie and Beryl Fanning singing at M's patriotic concert in Lilydale. **M's unexpected ease in public speaking:** *Melbourne Punch*, 2 Nov. 1916; Clemence Dane, *London Has a Garden* (London, 1964), 118–119. **Cancellation of M's return to Europe and Boston Opera tour of Australia:** *Melbourne Punch*, 5 Nov. 1914, 11 Feb. and 6 May 1915. **M as Queen of Pickpockets:** M and M, 292–293; *Melbourne Punch*, 15 and 29 April 1915, 19 July and 2 Aug. 1917; Melbourne *Argus*, 28 April 1915; Adelaide *Daily Herald*, 22 Nov. 1914. **M at Albert Street Conservatorium:** Vestey, 145; news clipping describing her first opera class, Melba Conservatorium, Melbourne. M did not charge for her classes. **Francis de Bourguignon:** Vestey, 56; *Melbourne Punch*, 10 May 1915; Adelaide Lubbock, *People in Glass Houses* (Melbourne, 1977), 64, 153. **M's reaction to Gallipoli:** *Sydney Sunday Times*, 20 June 1915; *Sydney Daily Telegraph*, 26 May 1915; M to Beryl Fanning, 16 May 1915, SLV, MS9902. **Hawaii 1915:** *Melbourne Punch*, 5 Aug. 1915; *Honolulu Sunday Advertiser*, 22 Aug. 1915; *Honolulu Star Bulletin*, 23 Aug. 1915. **M on American west coast:** News clippings, n.s., Scrap E, 40, LM; *San Francisco Chronicle*, 29 Aug. 1915; *Los Angeles Examiner* and *Los Angeles Times*, 18 Sept. 1915. **M in America's east:** *Philadelphia Press*, 4 Oct. 1915; *Chicago Examiner*, 20 Nov. 1915; *New York Times*, 1 Nov. 1915; *Boston Post*, 15 Oct. 1915, and 17 Oct. 1915, for interview with Olin Downes. **M and Karl Muck:** M and M, 173; M to Beryl Fanning, New Haven, 21 Oct. 1915 (postmark), SLV, MS9902. **Concerts in Canada:** *Toronto Star*, 1 Oct. 1915; *Montreal Herald*, 14 Oct. 1915; news clippings, n.s., Scrap E, 42, 47–49, 58, LM for concerts in other Canadian cities; Eileen Dorum, *Percy Grainger*, 96–97, for concerts in America with Percy Grainger. **M in California with George and Evie:** Vestey, 149–153. **David Mitchell's death:** Death certificate of David Mitchell; fragment of letter, M to Fritz Hart, for "my heart broke," n.d., SLV, MS9528; Vestey, 154. **M arrives in Melbourne 1916:** *Melbourne Punch*, 13 April 1916; Leoncavallo writes to M from Italy proposing a joint tour of Australia, see Leoncavallo to M, 11 Aug. 1916, LM. **Conscription campaign:** *Lilydale Express*, 27 Oct. 1916; Billy Hughes to M, 10 Nov. 1916, LM. **Nonsense party and departure for America:** *Melbourne Punch*, 12 Oct. and 23 and 30 Nov. 1916. **Hawaii 1916:** Two letters: M to Tom Cochrane, Honolulu, n.d., and Christmas Day, n.y., SLV, MSB447; M to Beryl Fanning, Honolulu, Christmas Eve, 1916, SLV, MS9902. **Chaplin:** M and M, 296–300. **San Francisco concert:** Melbourne *Age*, 11 May 1917. **M returns to Australia 1917:** *Melbourne Punch*, 29 March and 10 May 1917. **M and Susan FitzClarence at Coombe Cottage:** *Melbourne Punch*, 31 May and 5 July 1917. *School for Scandal*: *Melbourne Punch*, 26 July 1917. **Money raised by M for war charities:** *Melbourne Punch*, 2 Aug. 1917; news clippings, n.s., Scrap G, 17, LM. **Chicago opera tour and accidents:** Vestey, 160–161; M to Tom Cochrane, 15 Nov., n.y., Chicago, SLV, MSB447; M to Beryl Fanning, Copley Plaza, Boston, 2 Dec., n.y., SLV, MS9902; news clippings, n.s., Scrap G, 15–28, 40, 56, LM; two letters: M to Fritz Hart, 1 Nov., n.y., and 25 Nov. 1917, SLV, MS9528. **M's female protégées:** Moran, 306–307, for Parkina, and for M's swans being really geese; *Glasgow Herald*, 24 Nov. 1919 for Stella Power's style of singing. **M's rail tour 1918:** *Melbourne Punch*, 25 April 1918; news clippings, n.s., Scrap G, 37, 38, 44, 48, 51, LM. **M's damehood:** News clipping, Scrap G, 51, LM; Hetherington, *Melba*, 190. Hetherington says M was pretending when she claimed not to know of the dameship in advance, but in fact she spoke the truth; see Vestey, 162. **M in sanatorium:** Vestey, 163; M to Beryl Fanning, 9 May 1918 (postmark), SLV, MS9902; newsclipping, Scrap G, 49, LM. **M's return to Melbourne as Dame:** *Melbourne Punch*, 20 June 1918. **M's singing classes and Lady Stanley:** Adelaide Lubbock, *People in Glass Houses*, 105–106, 152–153; *Melbourne Punch*, 8 Aug. 1918 for pupils' uniforms. **Pamela's birth:** Vestey, 162, 165. **Christening:** *Melbourne Punch*, 21 Nov. 1918. **Lemmoné's stroke:** Westlake, *Dearest John*, 104, for loving cup; M to Beryl Fanning, n.d., SLV, MS9902.

Chapter 23: Singing to the Ghosts

Arrival in London: Vestey, 168–169; M to Beryl Fanning, 22 April 1919 (postmark), SLV, MS9902. **Death of M's friends:** M and M, 303; news clipping, Scrap F, 99, LM. **Philippe:** Lubbock, *People in Glass Houses*, 106; Moran, 361; telegram in Irene Gritten's papers, SLV, PA96/168. **Old Queen Street:** News clippings, Scrap G, 109, 153, 184–185, 187, LM; the *Spectator*, 3 Feb. 2007 for description and history of the house, which now houses the *Spectator* offices; *New York Times*, 22 Nov. 1915 for M's Paris apartment used as a wartime hospital. **Covent Garden reopening:** M and M, 306–307; Vestey, 170; news clipping, n.s., Scrap G, 87–101, 117, 143, LM; Thomas Beecham, *A Mingled Chime* (London, 1944), 246. **Guildhall School of Music:** Ronald, *Myself and Others*, 166–167; London *Times*, 20 May 1919; news clippings, n.s., Scrap G, 117, 123, LM. **Albert Hall concert:** News clippings, Scrap G, 117, LM. M gave two Albert Hall concerts. At the concert on 8 Oct. 1919 she included a tribute to Patti, who had died on 27 Sept 1919. **Children's charities:** News clippings, Scrap G, 137, 141, 155, 173, 176, LM. **Trefusis's wedding:** News clippings, Scrap G, 171, LM. **Gerald Patterson at Wimbledon:** News clippings, Scrap G, 171, LM; M to Belle (Tib), Ladies Athenaeum Club, n.d., LM. **Concert tour:** Una Bourne, "A Few Unusual Notes of a Pianist's Life," 7; Vestey, 175; M to Beryl Fanning (who was now Mrs. Kingley Newell), 27 Oct., n.y., SLV, MS9902; news clippings, Scrap G, 219, LM. **M's health:** Vestey, 174, 177–179; news clippings, Scrap G, 184–185, LM, for interview with M; M to Beryl Fanning, Hotel Hermitage, n.d., SLV. **Birthday party:** Vestey, 179–180; London *Daily Telegraph*, 20 May 1920; three undated letters: M to Jascha Heifetz, Old Queen Street, NLA, MS1356. **Debut of M's protégées:** London *Times*, 24 Nov. 1919; London *Daily Mail*, 6 Nov. 1919. **FitzClarence wedding:** *Pall Mall Gazette*, 23 June 1920. **Marconi broadcast:** London *Times*, 16 June 1920. **M in Paris:** M to Beryl Fanning, Old Queen Sreet, n.y., SLV, MS9902. **M in Norway** M and M, 310–313; Vestey, 182–183; news clippings, Scrap G, n.s., n.d., 246, 250, LM. **Death of M's grandchild:** News clippings, Scrap H, 13, LM; M to Tom Cochrane, Ladies Athenaeum Club, n.d., and M to Beryl Fanning, Ladies Athenaeum Club, n.d., SLV, MS9902; London *Daily Telegraph*, 22 and 23 Nov. 1920 for birth and death notices for the baby. **M at Monte Carlo and Brussels:** Vestey, 184; *Sydney Morning Herald*, 4 July 1921; news clippings, Scrap H, 22, LM. **Farewell concert at Albert Hall:** News clippings, Scrap H, 16–18, 40, LM; London *Times*, 9 May 1921. **Death of Robin Grey:** News clippings, Scrap H, 21, LM; Robin Grey to M, n.d., LM; Marjorie Brooke to M, 20 May 1921, LM; M and M, 303–304. **Death of Haddon Chambers:** London *Times*, 29 March 1921. **Irene Gritten and voyage to Australia:** Diary, SLV, PA96/168 for voyage; news clippings, Scrap H, 27, LM, for concerts and ports; Adrian Boult, *My Own Trumpet* (London, 1974), 73–74, for M's attitude to servants; London *Times*, 6 June 1921 for M sailing from Liverpool. **Concerts in Sydney:**

Sydney Sunday Times, 7 Aug. 1921. **Arrival in Melbourne:** Melbourne Herald, 11 Aug. 1921. **Life at Coombe Cottage:** Irene Gritten, "Diary," passim, SLV, PA96/168; Hans Heysen to M, 21 March, n.y., LM. **Australian popular concerts:** Vestey, 189–191; Melbourne Argus, 9 and 14 Dec. 1921, 23 Jan. 1922; Westlake, Dearest John, 57, 99; P. Game, The Music Sellers, 106–107; Brisbane Courier, 15 May 1922; Patchwork, Aug. 1922; news clippings, Scrap I, part 2, 117, LM. **Auditions:** News clippings, Scrap I, part 2, 9, LM; Vestey, 189; Melbourne Herald and Argus, 5 July 1922. **Vocal advice:** Sydney Morning Herald, 8 April 1922. **A wrench to leave Australia:** Melbourne Herald, 5 Sept. 1922; Vestey, 192, for M's love for Pamela; Table Talk, 31 Aug. and 7 Sept. 1922 for M's farewell party and concert. **M in India:** Lord Reading to M, 11 Oct. 1922, LM; M and M, 313–316; M to Tom Cochrane, 1 Oct. 1922, Simla, SLV, MSB447. Vestey, 193. **Albert Hall and League of Mercy concerts and provincial tour:** Vestey, 193–196; Lindley Evans, Hello, Mr. Melody Man (Sydney, 1983), 48–53; Moran, 347–348; M also organized other concerts in England with Australian performers at the Peoples' Palace and at Tunbridge Wells and Australia House—see London Times, 25 Jan. 1923; news clippings, Scrap 1, part 2, 48, and Vestey, 198, 200. **British National Opera:** Daily News, 22 Dec. 1922. It must be remembered that Florence Austral was a dramatic soprano with a different type of voice from that of M; London Times, 4, 15, 17, 18, and 22 Jan. and 22 June 1923. **Beverley Nichols:** Moran, 209–213; Beverley Nichols, The Sweet and Twenties (London, 1958), 112–115 and photo opposite 64 for the regularity of M's trill. **Mansfield Street:** Daily Sketch, 16 June 1923; Leeds Mercury, 22 May 1923; Western Times, 22 Jan. 1923. **M auditions European singers and becomes ill:** Australian Musical News, 1 May 1924; M to Tom Cochrane, Easter Sunday, n.y., Claridges Hotel, SLV, MSB447; Vestey, 200; M and M, 317–318; London Times, 2 June 1923. **M considers standing for Parliament:** Daily Mail, 21 June 1923; Daily Mirror, 31 May 1923; Launceston Examiner, 17 Jan. 1924 for what M believed was wrong with England; Yorkshire Telegraph, 15 Nov. 1922 for M singing at an election meeting; Vestey, 202; M to Beryl Fanning, Highcliffe Castle, n.d., SLV, MS9902. **M at Evian les Bains:** M to Henry Russell, n.d., NLA, MS1354. **North American tour:** George Miquelle to J. Hetherington, 28 March 1972, Hetherington Papers, SLV, MS9740; Lubbock, People in Glass Houses, 97 for M's impetuous enthusiasm. **M's health:** Hetherington, Melba, 273. **M faces retirement:** Sydney Daily Telegraph, 21 June 1924; Melbourne Herald, 13 Oct. 1924; Evans, Hello, Mr. Melody Man, 55, for M believing she must sing or die; Sydney Evening Sun, 2 Aug. 1924. **Tasmanian tour:** Vestey, 204; Launceston Examiner, 16 and 17 Jan. 1924. **Beverley Nichols at Coombe Cottage:** Joan Lindsay, Time Without Clocks (Melbourne, 1962), 32; P. Game, The Music Sellers, 108–110; Bryan Connon, Beverley Nichols: A Life (London, 1991), 116–118. **Henry and Mrs. Russell:** Moran, 174, 179–182; Waters, Much Besides Music, 224–225; Westlake, Dearest John, 109, for M to Lemmoné, 1 March 1925, in which M claimed that her illness originated in Henry Russell's bullying. **Coombe Cottage dance:** Vestey, 205; Hetherington, Melba, 233–235. **Opera season:** Gyger, Opera for the Antipodes, chapter 19 for detailed account. **Prince Alexis Oblensky:** Serge Oblensky, One Man in His Time (London, 1960), 207; Sunday Chronicle, 10 June 1923; Morning Post, 16 June 1923. **Toti dal Monte:** Gyger, Opera for the Antipodes, 232. **M's business acumen:** Melbourne Argus, 3 Feb. 1922 for the original flea story and Claude Kingston, It Don't Seem a Day Too Much (Melbourne, 1971), 114–119, for the later flea story; also see Kingston, 117, for discussion of Nichols's novel Evensong. **M's illness:** Sydney Morning Herald, 2 Sept.

1924. **Impossibility of radio transmission to Europe:** Marconi to M, 10 June 1924, LM. **M's farewell:** Melbourne *Herald*, 13 Oct. 1924; Melbourne *Argus*, 18 June 1924; *Melbourne Punch*, 11 and 18 Sept. and 16 Oct. 1924; M and M, 324.

Chapter 24: Australia's Greatest Daughter

Nichols writes *Melodies and Memories*: Vestey, 210–212; Moran, 215–216; Beverley Nichols to John Hetherington, 8 Aug. 1964, SLV, MS9740. **Cecchi episode:** Murphy, 19; M and M, 22–24. **Melba method:** M to Fritz Hart, 13 Jan. 1926, SLV, MS9528. M had already published six articles on the theory of singing in the *Sydney Morning Herald* and Melbourne *Herald* through March, April, and May 1922 and in the London *Daily Mail* in Nov. and Dec. 1922. **M diagnosed with diabetes:** Vestey, 210–212; Westlake, *Dearest John*, 109. **M in London:** London *Times*, 20 and 26 May and 16 June 1925. **M in Venice:** Moran, 219–221; M to Tom Cochrane, Excelsior Palace, 2 Sept. 1925. SLV. **M in Paris:** M to Tom Cochrane, New Year's Eve, Avenue Victor Hugo, SLV, MSB447; M to Beryl Fanning, Avenue Victor Hugo, n.d., 1925, SLV, MS9902. **M's concerts in London and British Isles**: Evans, *Hello! Mr. Melody Man*, 48–49; Vestey, 212; Moran, 281–285; M to Tom Cochrane, Government House, Hillsborough, n.d., SLV, MSB4475; M to Beryl Fanning, Le Touquet, n.d., SLV, MS9902. **Helen Daniels**: Gerald Moore, *Am I Too Loud?* (London, 1966), 55; Vestey, 212. **John Brownlee and Melba's farewell and subsequent recordings**: Moran, 441–443; M to Tom Cochrane, New Year's Eve, n.y., SLV, MSB447. **Farewell at Covent Garden:** London *Times*, 9 June 1926; M to Fritz Hart, n.d., Penrhos, SLV, MS9528. **Old Vic:** London *Times*, 1 and 6 Dec. 1926. **Camfield Place:** The *Home*, 2 Aug. 1926, 70, and 1 March 1927, 15; M to Beryl Fanning, Le Touquet, n.d., SLV, MS9902; Vestey, 214–216. **At Coombe Cottage:** Daryl Lindsay, *The Leafy Tree* (Melbourne, 1965), 133–134; Joan Lindsay, *Time Without Clocks*, 31; Vestey, 217, 220; Sara Hardy, *The Unusual Life of Edna Walling* (Sydney, 2005), 110–113; Claude Kingston, *It Don't Seem a Day Too Much*, 116–117, for begging letters; Melbourne *Herald*, 24 Jan. 1927. **Australian concert tour:** Evans, *Hello! Mr. Melody Man*, 61–71; Melbourne *Argus*, 3 March 1927; *Hobart Mercury*, 15 March 1927; *Launceston Examiner*, 11 March 1927. **Opening of Parliament House, Canberra:** Gavin Souter, *Acts of Parliament* (Melbourne, 1988), 222; *Table Talk*, 12 May 1927; Evans, *Hello! Mr. Melody Man*, 63, for dinner at Government House; Vestey, 220. **Illnesses of Pamela and Charlie:** Vestey, 217, 222–225. **Opera tour of 1928:** Gyger, *Opera for the Antipodes*, chapter 21, esp. 278; Evans, *Hello! Mr. Melody Man*, 79. **Sing them muck:** Winifred Ponder, *Clara Butt: Her Life Story* (London, 1928), 138; Hetherington, *Melba*, 269–272, for an account of the books being withdrawn from sale; M and M, 329, for the public's taste in songs; Vestey, 227–228. **M returns to Europe in 1928:** Vestey, 231–236; James A. Drake, *Rosa Ponselle: A Centenary Biography* (Portland, 1997), 227–228, for M's meeting with Rosa Ponselle. **Trouble over income tax:** Evans, *Hello! Mr. Melody Man*, 78. **Car tour of Europe:** Hetherington, *Melba*, 281–282; *Courrier Biarritz*, 28 Feb. 1931 in Scrap K, 89, LM. **Egypt:** The *Home*, 1 May 1929; Vestey, 233, 236–238; M to Tom Cochrane, Kashabanarti, n.d., SLV, MSB447. **Tour of Germany and Austria:** *Australian*, 11 April 1971; Vestey, 240–242. **M's possible face-lift and last illness:** Waters, *Much Besides Music*, 306, and M to Marchesi, Great Cumberland Street, ML, AM82, for M's emphasis on appearance; *Melbourne Punch*, 27 Feb. 1908 for M's use of cosmetics; Mabel Brookes, *Crowded Galleries* (Melbourne, 1956), 178, for M's distrust of photographers; A. H. Spencer, *The Hill of Content* (Sydney, 1959), 12, 15, for M's reading habits and M's last visit to a bookshop; Melbourne *Herald*, 9 April 1931, for Nichols's assertion that M had no literary taste; "Death of Dame Nellie Melba at St. Vincent's Private Hospital," unsigned but written on paper headed "The Sisters of Charity, St. Vincent's Hospital" for mention of M's face-lift; death certificate of Helen Porter Armstrong, known as Nellie Melba; R. N. Carrington, "The Last Days of Nellie Melba," ML, AM82; Melbourne *Age*, 23 Feb. 1931; Westlake, *Dearest John*, 83, for M's last letter to Lemmoné; Melbourne *Herald*, 25 Feb. 1931; the London *Times*, 27 and 29 Jan. and 3, 17, 18, 19, 21, 23, and 24 Feb. 1931 for bulletins concerning M's illness; Vestey, 243–244; Hetherington, *Melba*, 284–286. Hetherington puts M at Baden-Baden in the spring of 1930, but M's letters in Vestey, 241, make clear that she could not have reached Baden-Baden until late August 1930. **Will:** M to Fladgate, n.d., Royal Opera House Archives, Covent Garden; copy of will of Helen Porter Armstrong. **Funeral:** London *Times*, 26 Feb. 1931; Melbourne *Argus*, 25 and 27 Feb. 1931; Melbourne *Herald*, 2 Feb. 1931. **Belief in afterlife:** Moran, 234.

Index

A NOTE ON THE AUTHOR

Ann Blainey, who lives in Melbourne, Australia, has also written *Fanny and Adelaide*, a biography of the Kemble sisters, as well as *The Farthing Poet* and *Immortal Boy*, two literary biographies. She was educated at Warwick and Korowa Girls' Schools and the University of Melbourne. She is a member of the National Council of Opera Australia, the nation's chief opera company, and an elected member of the governing council of the University of Melbourne.